BLACKS

IN APPALACHIA

BLACKS

IN APPALACHIA

Edited by
William H. Turner and **Edward J. Cabbell**

Foreword by Nell Irvin Painter

THE UNIVERSITY PRESS OF KENTUCKY

Copyright © 1985 by The University Press of Kentucky

Scholarly publisher for the Commonwealth,
serving Bellarmine College, Berea College, Centre
College of Kentucky, Eastern Kentucky University,
The Filson Club, Georgetown College, Kentucky
Historical Society, Kentucky State University,
Morehead State University, Murray State University,
Northern Kentucky University, Transylvania University,
University of Kentucky, University of Louisville,
and Western Kentucky University.

Editorial and Sales Offices: Lexington, Kentucky 40506-0024

Library of Congress Cataloging in Publication Data

Main entry under title:

Blacks in Appalachia.

  Bibliography: p.
  Includes index.
    1. Afro-Americans—Appalachian Region—History—
Addresses, essays, lectures.   2. Appalachian Region—
History—Addresses, essays, lectures.   3. Applachian
Region—Race relations—Addresses, essays, lectures.
I. Turner, Willaim Hobart.   II. Cabbell, Edward J.,
1946-   .
E185.912.B53 1985   974′.00496073   84-27130
ISBN 0-8131-1518-3
ISBN 0-8131-0162-X (pbk.)

To William Earl Turner and "Punkin" Turner
and Uncle Homer Walker

Contents

Part Five. Black Coal Miners

Part Six. Blacks and Local Politics

Part Seven. Personal Anecdotal Accounts of Black Life

Part Eight. Selected Demographic Aspects

Tables

Foreword

NELL IRVIN PAINTER

The plural nature of American society makes its study endlessly fascinating, yet scholars and policymakers sometimes disregard the nuances of our complicated culture. Black Appalachians, whose experiences have not conformed to stereotypes of black life, are, for that reason, an invisible people. Southern and Afro-American studies, the two fields of inquiry that ought to have noticed black Appalachians, have traditionally described a generalized black-belt plantation South and have divided Southerners into two categories: planters and their descendants (the powerful, the oppressors) and slaves and their progeny (the powerless, the oppressed). Wilbur Cash's classic *Mind of the South* (1941) is one of the few influential works on the region that keeps ordinary people in view, but Cash envisioned blacks as shadowy figures, aliens in their native South. Southern blacks have yet to find a Wilbur Cash of their own, but this collection makes a start by paying attention to southern blacks outside the plantation economy who were able to forge their own destinies and to pay their own way. This book begins to define some of the nuances of southern life by concentrating on a people who appeared in several capacities and migrated out, who worked in the mines and lived among whites of modest means.

For several reasons, the present volume will prove valuable to its readers, whether they are humanists, social scientists, or shapers of policy. The varied essays on history, communities, race relations, labor, politics, and personal experience are the work of scholars with intimate and extensive knowledge in the fields of Appalachian and Afro-American studies. For me, however, two sections of this volume are especially attractive, those on historical perspectives and on black miners.

Just as southern history is only beginning to take Appalachia into account, so American history has only recently considered blacks worthy of notice. Afro-American history was acknowledged as a legitimate field of study only after decades of research and writing by hundreds of historians who gradually unearthed the black past. Among these investigators, one man, Carter G. Woodson, has come to be known as the father of black history. He is represented in this book by an early essay published in the *Journal of Negro History,* which Woodson founded and which more than any other publication made Negro history into a respected field. That Carter G. Woodson contributes here is fitting; as a black Appalachian, he now presides over an important addition to black Appalachian studies.

Labor history, like black history, is just now coming into its own. Having written about working people, I am pleased that black workers occupy a central place in this collection. It is also gratifying to see that another giant of Afro-American studies, W. E. B. Du Bois, opens the section on black coal miners. His essay and the others on black industrial workers extend our understanding of the ways in which workers succeeded (and failed) as they sought to forge enduring biracial labor organizations at a time when unions were not yet protected by federal legislation. Taken together, the selections in this volume describe the activities of blacks in unions and begin the task of explaining the multiracial unions as pioneering precursors of the industrial unions that became dominant in the twentieth century. This crucial black labor history supplements our knowledge of working people in the United States as a whole.

Preface

This volume evolved from the editors' reaction to some common assumptions about the black population of America in general and about that of Appalachia in particular. These assumptions, which enjoy almost axiomatic status, include the belief that "American minorities (especially blacks) desire assimilation into mainstream America" and that "they have shared the majority commitment to the American creed, and the rate of their assimilation is directly proportional to their access to the socializing agencies of the dominant culture."[1] The liberal-assimilationist view of American race relations focuses on the need to provide adequate opportunities for black individuals to move from racial isolation into mainstream culture. "Opportunity," as the word is used by the liberal sociologists, means "the opportunity to discard one's ethnicity and to partake fully in the American way of life."[2]

In spite of the "movement for self-knowledge on the part of members of the third and fourth generation of Southern and Eastern European immigrants in the United States,"[3] American students of ethnicity attribute the existence of black society (they identify dual social structures) to the "dynamics of anti-black prejudice and discrimination rather than . . . [to] the ideological commitment [self-consciousness] of the minority itself."[4] Glazer and Moynihan succinctly wrote, "It is not possible for Negroes to view themselves as other ethnic groups viewed themselves . . . , because the Negro is only an American and nothing else. He has no culture to guard and protect."[5] Such views, which incidentally interpret the black experience in terms of "natural social processes" (processes that advance as racism and racist institutions "wither away" in the modern postindustrial state), encourage blacks to pursue an open society—a nonexistent reality that is the premise of racial integration.[6] Cruse notes regarding the crisis that "the three main power groups—Protestants, Catholics, and Jews—neither want nor need to become integrated with each other."[7] For him and for other proponents of democratic cultural pluralism, there is no great homogenized, interassimilated (white) America but rather an America in which individual primary social participation remains limited, at least in part, by ethnic boundaries. This view of the United States can be described as "structurally pluralistic along ethnic, racial, and political lines."[8] In preparing this volume the editors have hoped first and foremost that it would prompt reexamination of the idea that the absorption of blacks into the mainstream of middle America is evident or inevitable. Such absorption is possibly not even desirable from the standpoint of the requirements of a democratic society. Accordingly, in selecting articles for inclusion, we have been guided by the idea that a unified and coherent black community with a sense of peoplehood is no more un-American than is the idea of a community of some other American minority. Black Appalachians are depicted in this book as such a community.

Our second assumption stems from the view of mainstream social science that we outlined above. As professionals in the field of Appalachian studies, we believe our colleagues tend to conclude that "the number of Negroes in the [Appalachian] Region . . . is such a small proportion of the total population [that] . . . the social consequences [of their presence and migration] are not of any great [significance]."[9] In what is perhaps the primer in Appalachian studies, John C. Campbell noted that Appalachia may be said to show "white purity" when the statement refers to selected counties; in those with "few large valleys, few mining and industrial developments, or few cities . . . , there are few Negroes."[10] But we challenge students of Appalachia to chart the research course suggested in James Branscome's thesis of ethnogenesis:

One group of Appalachians who are consistently overlooked and underserved by the institutions of the region is the blacks. While the percentage of blacks in the region as a whole is low, about eight percent, they make up the entire population of many isolated small hollows and ghost coal towns abandoned by the corporations and welfare and poverty agencies. Because the backbreaking jobs that brought black imports into the region are gone and because of the discrimination and competition with the majority of poor white people for jobs and welfare funds, their existence is a poor one indeed. As yet no agency or journalist has documented the presence and needs of these people, let alone described the culture of a minority group in the midst of another cultural minority.[11]

Taken together, the readings in this book offer a broad view of Appalachia that will, we hope, provide some direction and impetus to new research into, and policymaking for, blacks in Appalachia and their migrant brothers and sisters. This anthology is, alas, a note on the experience of an "invisible" people.

The present book would not have developed had it not been for the sustained concern and encouragement of a number of individuals and institutions. John Stephenson introduced the editors to one another. He and Loyal Jones of the Berea College Appalachian Center helped to sustain us in our work, offering advice at critical periods of the research and writing. John and Loyal have become lasting friends, counselors, and front-line supporters of studies of the Black Appalachian experience. They both attempted to make Black Appalachian studies a central part of the research and community service of Kentucky and Berea, respectively, long before a line of this book was written.

We are grateful to David Walls and Ramona Lumpkin of the James Still Faculty Development Project at the University of Kentucky for their excellent editorial assistance and for their flexibility in coping with our needs. Our thanks also to Beverly Martin, Pam Gunn, Caryn Zelasko, Ann Campbell, and Daveena Sexton for their assistance in typing and in library searches.

Our colleagues at the University of Kentucky and at Appalachian State University encouraged us by creating courses focusing on Black Appalachians that were firsts at the two institutions, and we thank the many students who tested our framework and judged the usefulness of the readings.

Finally, we would be remiss if we did not acknowledge the strength and stamina that derive from our Appalachian roots. This book came into being thanks to sacrifices made by many families. The Supreme Being gave us the first and final measure of inspiration to undertake this worthy struggle and all others.

1. L. Paul Metger's "American Sociology and Black Assimilation: Conflicting Perspectives" embodies the most useful summary of the theoretical perspectives through which most American sociologists view race relations in the United States. See *American Journal of Sociology*, 76 (Jan. 1971), 627.

2. John Pease, William Form, and Joan Rytina, "Ideological Currents in American Stratification Literature," *American Sociologist*, 5 (May 1970), 65.

3. Michael Novak, "The New Ethnicity," *Center Magazine*, 7, no. 4 (July-Aug. 1974), 58.

4. Milton M. Gordon, *Assimilation in American Life* (New York, 1964), p. 205.

5. Nathan Glazer and Daniel Patrick Moynihan, *Beyond the Melting Pot* (Cambridge, Mass., 1963), p. 101.

6. William J. Wilson, "The Declining Significance of Race," *Society Magazine*, Jan.-Feb. 1978, p. 45.

7. Harold Cruse, *The Crisis of the Negro Intellectual* (New York, 1967), p. 88.

8. Gordon, *Assimilation in American Life*, p. 25.

9. John C. Belcher, "Population Growth and Characteristics," in *The Southern Appalachian Region: A Survey*, Thomas R. Ford (Lexington, Ky., 1967), p. 152.

10. John C. Campbell, *The Southern Highlander and His Homeland* (Lexington, Ky., 1921), p. 201.

11. James G. Branscome, "Annihilating the Hillbilly: The Appalachian's Struggle with American Institutions," *Journal of the Committee of Southern Churchmen*, Winter 1971, 40.

"No person, regardless of importance, must consider himself above the People. Before reaching out for international prestige he must look within his own land, direct himself to restoring the dignity of all citizens, filling their minds and feasting their eyes on human things."

FRANTZ FANON
The Wretched of the Earth

Introduction

WILLIAM H. TURNER

During the past quarter century, there has been a profound and marked interest in Afro-American and Appalachian studies. This book combines the perspectives of both fields to examine some social themes about Appalachia as a geopolitical and social region of the American South and to trace the history and development of Appalachia's black people as well as the culture and the quality of life they have drawn from the region.

The essays selected for inclusion demonstrate that blacks in the Appalachian region are neither aberrations nor epiphenomena, neither invisible nor insignificant. The project that led to this book began as part of the participant-observation research of Edward J. Cabbell, a civil rights worker who coordinated black heritage activities in central Appalachia. During a decade of travel and work in the region, he was shocked by the paucity of information about blacks. They were ignored in the media and were virtually "invisible" to a public that associated inscrutability and endemic (white) poverty with Appalachia. Cabbell's effort was linked to the work of Carter G. Woodson, who wrote of Black Appalachians in 1916 in one of the earliest issues of the *Journal of Negro History*.[1] There has been little published scholarship about Black Appalachians in either Afro-American or Appalachian studies. In editing the present volume, Cabbell and I have attempted to consider all mentions of blacks in the regional literature and in Afro-American studies. Although the Black Appalachian experience has been discussed in the major works on Appalachia and in the general Afro-American research on the region, no manuscript or compendium has treated it fully.

The essays in part 1 seek on philosophical and practical grounds to establish the legitimacy of studying blacks in Appalachia in order to advance our knowledge of the histories, cultures, and experiences of different groups in American society. In the past quarter century, Appalachia, with its variant of southern culture, its amalgam of ethnic influences, and its distinctive sociopolitical character, has attracted the attention of scholars, researchers, journalists, and makers of public policy. Cabbell examines the ways in which Appalachian blacks, a minority within a minority, are rendered invisible, while my own essay explores historical evidence regarding the Black Appalachian. While the whites of the region may be ethnically mixed, bearing the trace of Germans, Scots, Irish, and English, so that they are collectively distinct in only a geographical sense, most blacks of Appalachia are southern migrants with a common background and common relationship to the various economic forces that brought them to America. Blacks (as a group) have been excluded from the history of Appalachia and continue to suffer the worse economic conditions of any subgroup in the region.

The reader will find in part 2 evidence that blacks were in the Appalachian region long before the major migrations of white settlers took place. Black Appalachians, analyzed as a subgroup of African rebels, slaves, and freedmen, "explored" and, together with the Spaniards and the French, fought against the Appalachee and Cherokee native subgroups in the 1500s. In the context of a specific geographical setting, the first readings establish time-specific histor-ical and material conditions which demonstrate that Black Appalachians were some of America's *first* blacks—appearing almost a century before the landing at Jamestown.

The contact between the Black Africans and the native Americans of the Appalachee and Cherokee nations began, according to Theda Perdue, as early as 1526—including the cohabitation of the Cherokee Lady of Cofitachequi and the Spaniard's black slave. Perdue concludes:

Indians probably regarded Africans simply as other human beings who were either traversing or invading their territory. Since the concept of race did not exist among Indians and since the Cherokees nearly always encountered Africans in the company of Europeans, we may suppose that at first Cherokees equated the two and failed to distinguish sharply between the races. Soon after their first contact with Africans, however, the Cherokees no doubt realized that Europeans regarded blacks as inferiors and that they themselves were in danger of being so regarded.[2]

As black slavery became entrenched in the rest of the South, with the complicity of the Cherokees, most blacks in Appalachia were removed to the plantation region. Some remained with white mountain masters, and a few remained as the captives of the last remaining Cherokee planters. In 1838, when the Cherokees were removed from their homelands in the Great Smoky Mountains of the Carolinas, Tennessee, and Georgia, nearly a thousand black slaves accom-panied them on the infamous Trail of Tears. This group comprised Oklahoma's slave population even before statehood. The blacks who originally inhabited northwest South Carolina (Spartanburg County) and the central and northeast corridors between Birmingham and Chattanooga that extend north to the Cumberland Gap of Tennessee, Virginia, and Kentucky were also slaves before these states came into being. Blacks in the Appalachian region thus predated the arrival of black slaves in the Cotton South, who had arrived en masse by the time of the first census in 1790.

In the two centuries between the arrival of blacks in this region and the Civil War, the Appalachian region was conquered by the combined forces of Germans and Scotch-Irish, with a sprinkling of Huguenots, Quakers, and poor whites who had served their time as indentured servants in Virginia and the Carolinas. Among the chief characteristics of the white settlers in Appalachia was a set of beliefs that differed from that of the aristocrats and the planter class east of the Shenandoah Valley and south of the Cumberland Gap.[3] The region's west rampart, Ohio, and the northern tip, Pennsylvania, were of course already free states. Although slavery in Appalachia did not fit the southern model, the black people in Appalachia were caught in a pinch between the proslavery and antislavery movements of the upper South. In *The Mind of the South*, Cash observed that the mountaineer "had acquired a hatred and contempt for the Negro even more violent than that of the common white of the lowlands, a dislike so rabid that it was a black man's life to venture into many mountain sections."[4] In the absence of a plantation economy that made blacks both prisoner and jailer, whites' treatment of blacks (as evidenced by the culture of prejudice and segregation that was rigidly maintained in the Cotton Belt) created a different sort of social contact between the races in Appalachia. As Loyal Jones notes, and as the remembrances of Booker T. Washington and the observations of James Klotter suggest, "Appalachians have not been saddled with the same prejudices about black people that people of the deep South have."[5]

Parts 1 and 2 establish the parameters of Black Appalachian social history: (1) Blacks had been in the Appalachian region for nearly two centuries when the major influx of white immigrants arrived.[6] Some few blacks accompanied the French and Spanish explorers. As slaves aboard European ships, or as slave guides with frontiersmen such as Daniel Boone a century and a half later, blacks were one of Appalachia's first non-Indian populations. (2) Blacks' disenfranchisement following the Civil War was exemplified in two notable incidents, biracial education in Kentucky and biracial unionism in Alabama. (3) During Reconstruction, Appalachia emerged as a culturally distinct region where the stereotyped black slave reappeared as the white Appalachian. (4) Blacks' status in Appalachia was peculiar: they suffered both intellectually and socially from poverty and from special regional constraints and problems different from those of 99 percent of the blacks in America. The rural isolation of the region explains part of the blacks' distinctiveness as well as the fact that they were few in number compared with blacks elsewhere in the South. Black Appalachians were, and are, a racial minority within a cultural minority.

Parts 3, 4, and 5 offer microanalytical glimpses of five generations and networks of the blacks in central and southern Appalachia. The first and smallest group, most probably the ancestors of black explorers and runaway slaves, was also the most assimilated: the rural blacks of Appalachia who were landowners at the time of Emancipation. Second, there were the blacks who came from the lowlands of the South to be laborers in the salt mines and workers on the rail lines that traversed Appalachia by the turn of the nineteenth century. The largest number of blacks in the region migrated between 1900 and 1930, most notably from Alabama, to southeastern Kentucky, West Virginia, and southeastern Virginia. Another generation of blacks was born in the region after 1925, the time of the precipitous decline of the black population in the coal-mining sections, and a fifth generation of Black Appalachians was born after World War II.

In a sense, the readings in parts 3, 4, and 5 suggest that for blacks, as for many other American ethnic groups, the melting pot did not work. A case study and the general experience of the original "rural Negroes" of Appalachia are described in the last pages of part 2, while the essays in part 3 trace the origins and adaptation of the people who formed highly visible black enclaves in the industrial towns that came to dominate the region between World War I and the Great Depression. The work of Laing, Parker, and Corbin illustrates the major social changes which resulted from the twentieth-century industrialization of Appalachia. The arrival of blacks in large numbers undermined the traditional social order (there were very few blacks in the region at the turn of the century), throwing southern blacks, the remaining native Indians, the European immigrants, and white settlers with roots going back two centuries into new social contacts and interactions. As a result a social order emerged in central and southern Appalachia that was in keeping with the intrinsic and general features of industrialism. Beyond the small and isolated company-dominated towns sprang up moderate urban regional cities (Knoxville, Chattanooga, Asheville, Winston-Salem, Spartanburg, Lexington, Roanoke) and, of course, major manufacturing and transportation centers such as Birmingham and Pittsburgh.[7]

Black Appalachians' experiences, again, like those of other southern blacks, showed a historical progression. At one time they were struggling for life amid native Indians and white settlers. The cultural frames of survival also shifted with the transformation of the region in the generation after the Civil War from a simple agricultural economy to a "cacophony of voices and industrial sounds."[8] Just as blacks had been the axis of the agrarian wheel, in Appalachia they became (between 1870 and 1930) the vanguard of a working class with industrial experience in logging, in steel, and in coal and salt mining. Blacks in the Deep South were by and large still bound to the land-peonage system when the Great Depression realigned the booming economy of industrial Appalachia. The region, at the turn of the century, seemed no different to southern blacks seeking refuge from the ravages of post-Reconstruction agricultural methods (economic opportunity) and the doubly oppressive racial etiquette of the lower South. As part 3 makes plain, while Appalachia did not confront blacks with a culture of segregation that was distinctive by comparison with the Cotton Belt South, it was no Eden free from racial prejudice and economic discrimination. The situation led blacks in Appalachia to assimilate aspects of (white) culture and society as they accommodated themselves to the prevailing ethic of racial subordination. There subsequently emerged a subsociety of Black America far more visible than it was fluid and as integrated as it was disruptive. It showed a peculiar mixture of southern black folkways, a distinctive and unique cultural heritage both with rural dimensions and with the social features of industrialism.[9] Black Appalachians have thus acquired a quality of distinctive ethnicity (eth-class) that mediated their transformation as they (and their white counterparts) moved from rural tradition-bound countryside to a region that was tied to, yet peripheral to, the dominant modern industrial society.

The diversity of white ethnic groups who came to Appalachia made the region virtually an experiment in race and class dynamics. Parts 4 and 5 contain essays that consider in microcosm conditions that, according to Nkrumah, pertain worldwide, wherever "the nature of the development of productive forces has resulted in a racist class structure."[10] These essays offer the class analyst a unique opportunity to understand the extent to which blacks, European immigrants, and native white settlers did not develop common class consciousness in spite of the obvious class oppression shared to a great extent by the first two.[11] The company-dominated towns to which the masses of Black Appalachians migrated were quite unlike the centers to which most blacks migrated just before the first World War. Stanfield's analysis of urban Appalachia highlights the similarities and differences in political economy between the Appalachian regions and areas beyond Appalachia. During the first quarter of the twentieth century, blacks leaving the Cotton Belt moved chiefly from rural areas to urban ones (northern industrial cities). Migrating Black Appalachians, however, moved by and large from one rural area to another that was industrial.[12] Robert Blauner wrote that the conditions of American capitalist interests in the prosperous late 1890s "pressured [mobile] Southern blacks into the coalfields."[13] Du Bois argued that "all black workers, bent at the bottom of a growing empire of commerce and industry . . . became the cause of new political demands and alignments, of new dreams of power and visions of empire."[14] In the essays of Northrup, Lewis, and Straw, we consider the important role of blacks in the union movement of Appalachia. Laing, Bailey, and Corbin all focus on West Virginia (where Black Appalachians migrated in greatest numbers and concentrated in areas given over to coal mining where the United Mine Workers of America were active). Of all the commercial contributors to the industrialization of America, the bituminous coal industry was singular both for its historically central role as an economic activity and for being one of the earliest and major employers of blacks.[15] Consequently, the black in Appalachian mining became the initial focus of union organizing efforts. The essays in part 5 return us to a theme articulated earlier, the process by which blacks in Appalachia, and indeed throughout America to a greater or lesser degree, became viewed as malefactors. The region was memorably described by Caudill as "an area haunted by the pathetic and disturbing story of forgotten backcountry people—a tragic tale of the abuse and mismanagement of resources, and the human erosion of shortsighted exploitation . . . , a bleak and demoralizing poverty almost without parallel on this continent."[16]

Parts 6 and 7 document the ways in which Black Appalachians reacted significantly to an environment in which race-based political solidarity could not flourish (in other regions there were greater numbers of blacks). Furthermore, blacks were largely excluded from the recent efforts to alleviate the depressed conditions of the region. The work of William and Guillebaux lends support to the thesis that blacks' proclivity for political agitation manifests itself in actual civil rights activity when they are in metropolitan areas or constitute a significant proportion of the population. Of course, while the two conditions are often both true, visible black political action did not take place in rural Appalachia—the coal towns—because of their absence. Blacks were few in the population of the region, having migrated from it at increasing rates with the advent of the national civil rights movement of the mid-1950s. By the end of the 1960s, fully 60 percent of the black population found in West Virginia half a century before had left the state entirely.[17] It is noteworthy that the ratio of black students at Bluefield and West Virginia state colleges, two traditionally black institutions, was completely reversed between 1950 and 1970.[18]

The accounts of Millner, Cornett, and Dobbie Sanders return us to the original focus of the book: the derived customs, manners, world view, and black perception of Appalachia's *nature* and its meaning for black people. These essays give us vivid portraits of the private, customary, communal, and affective ties that enabled blacks to develop and sustain their communities. At the same time, personal anecdotes show the bonds—functional and contractual relationships—that blacks had to form with the white public, as Appalachia modernized. Finally, the oral histories help us comprehend yet another variant on the Afro-American experience that suggests a challenge to the nature and meaning of pluralism in American society.[19]

Part 8 brings together demographic and other pertinent information about the black population of Appalachia in a form that is easy to read and easy to use. The bibliography, like Cabbell's manuscript,[20] offers much accurate and objective data. The user will find assembled here for the first time listings of organizations in the social, political, educational, and cultural affairs of black Appalachians.

As we readied these essays for publication, we as editors hoped to verify and complete the documentation for most, if not all, chapters. The notes to the original texts, however, were in some cases so incomplete that we were often unable to find the necessary information even with the aid of major libraries. We regret the omissions in notes to the present volume, but we nevertheless believe that the texts themselves will provide a firm foundation for ongoing scholarship.

This book begins with a "call" for social policy and scholarship that will address the Black Appalachians. There follow historical narratives, descriptive community studies, and essays that examine the social and political dynamics of Appalachia in terms of black people. The volume concludes with some directions for further research. It is intended to satisfy the needs of both policymakers and individuals in the combined enterprises of Afro-American and Appalachian research, providing a basis for the formulation of policies to ameliorate the condition of Black Appalachians as well as enhancing their visibility as a community deserving research and study.

1. "Black Appalachians" is capitalized as a proper noun designating for blacks in the region a status like that of other identifiable ethnic groups in the region (the Scotch-Irish, the Germans, and so forth).

2. See chapter 3, this book.

3. See chapter 4, this book.

4. W. J. Cash, *The Mind of the South* (New York, 1941), p. 219.

5. Loyal Jones, "Appalachian Values," in *Voices from the Hills: Selected Readings of Southern Appalachia*, ed. Robert J. Higgs (New York, 1975), p. 512.

6. French and Spanish priests and explorers of the Mississippi River Valley were accompanied by blacks who fled to live among the Chickasaw and Cherokee Indians in the early 1500s. Therefore, it is plausible to assume that many blacks were on the western ramparts of Appalachia (as well as its southern tip) long before the trans-Allegheny movements and a full century before the height of the slave trade and the plantation economy of the Cotton Belt. Daniel Boone's initial expedition through the Cumberland Gap was recorded officially by a black man. See Felix Walker, "Daisy," *DeBow's Review of 1884*, quoted in Thomas D. Clark, *Bluegrass Calvacade* (Lexington, Ky., 1956), p. 7.

7. See Carter G. Woodson, "The Redistribution of the Negro Population of the United States, 1910-1960," in *Journal of Negro History,* 51 (July 1966); Carter G. Woodson, *The Rural Negro* (Washington, D.C., 1930); and E. Franklin Frazier, *The Negro in the United States* (New York, 1957), pp. 197-228.

8. Ronald D. Eller, *Miners, Millhands, and Mountaineers: Industrialization of the Appalachian South, 1880-1930* (Knoxville, Tenn., 1982), p. 140.

9. Thad Radzialowski, "The Future of Ethnic Studies," *Forum,* 3, no. 5 (Mar. 1981). Radzialowski combines Appalachian studies, including a central focus on the black experience, with Scandinavian, Chicano, Irish-American, and American Indian studies. He argues that Appalachians form, as do these other groups, a complex modern identity (ethnicity) organized around a discernible pattern of roles, value patterns, and regional loyalties.

10. Kwame Nkrumah, *Class Struggle in Africa* (New York, 1975), p. 207.

11. David S. Walls, "Central Appalachia: A Peripheral Region within Advanced Capitalist Society," in *Journal of Sociology and Social Welfare,* 4 (1976).

12. Douglas Glascow looks at the Cotton Belt origins of blacks migrating to the industrial eastern and north-central states in *The Black Underclass* (San Francisco, 1980).

13. Marxist-Leninist thought includes but a few penetrating analyses of blacks in Appalachian company-dominated towns, even though the setting reflects material examples of the classical Marxian model. At the general level of the black experience considered in terms of political economy, Robert Blauner is credited with initiating debate in sociological circles by his widely circulated paper "Colonized and Immigrant Minorities," which appeared in his *Racial Oppression in America* (New York, 1972).

14. Du Bois's thought centered on his perception of blacks as they figured in America's industrial development, on their racial and economic exploitation as the dark proletariat. Black mill and mine workers are central to the Marxian view of racism as a link between social structure and arrangements relating to material economic organization and power in society. This view is also central to the dispute of the notion that race in human society (in Appalachia, as elsewhere) is ultimately irrational, insignificant, unimportant, and nonrational.

15. Donald T. Barnum, *The Negro in the Bituminous Coal Mining Industry* (Philadelphia, 1970).

16. Harry M. Caudill, *Night Comes to the Cumberlands* (Boston, 1963).

17. See *Black Culture in the Mountain State,* special issue of *Goldenseal,* 5, no. 4 (Oct.-Dec. 1979).

18. William H. Turner, *Traditionally Black Institutions of Higher Education: A Profile and an Institutional Directory* NCES 79-361 (Washington, D.C., 1979).

19. Although blacks in Appalachia and other "small" groups (such as the Sea Island Gullahs of the Carolinas) do not receive attention from scholars and public policymakers that is accorded Delta and urbanized regional subgroups within the panorama of the Afro-American experience, there is a growing interest in the study of such enclaves. See, for example, *Promiseland: A Century of Life in a Negro Community* by Elizabeth R. Bethel (Philadelphia, 1981).

20. Edward J. Cabbell, "Like a Weaving: A Bibliography of Black Appalachia" (master's thesis, Appalachian State University, 1982).

Abbreviations

ACOA	Alabama Coal Operators Association
AEF	American Expeditionary Force
AFL	American Federation of Labor
ALCOA	Aluminum Corporation of America
AMA	American Missionary Association
ARC	Appalachian Regional Commission
BAC	Black Appalachian Commission
CAMP	Creativity in Appalachian Minorities Program
CAP	Community Action Program
CIO	Congress of International Organizations
CSM	Council of Southern Mountains
FRB	Federal Reserve Board
ILD	International Labor Defense
NAACP	National Association for the Advancement of Colored People
NIRA	National Industrial Recovery Act
NRA	National Recovery Administration
NYA	National Youth Administration
SMSA	Standard Metropolitan Statistical Area
SWOC	Steel Workers Organizing Committee
TVA	Tennessee Valley Authority
UMWA	United Mine Workers of America
UMWJ	*United Mine Workers Journal*
USWA	United Steel Workers of America
WPA	Works Progress Administration

PART ONE

Basic Approaches

The two essays in part 1 inquire into, and review key studies relating to, the existence of blacks in Appalachia.

Edward J. Cabbell asserts that institutional racism and overt forms of individual discrimination combine to suppress the human and work-related energies of blacks in the region. William H. Turner calls upon the academies, foundations, and research institutes to note Appalachia's unique setting, which provides the opportunity for studies of race and class dynamics. The Berea and Birmingham stories explain how historical relations influenced the current status of blacks in the region.

Both of the analyses come under the influence of black studies—as noted in connection with the need to combine theory and social action. It is important to recall that Cabbell was America's first student to earn a graduate-level degree in this field; he specialized in black Appalachian studies at Appalachian State University in Boone, North Carolina. He is also director of the John Henry Memorial Foundation—a regional collective which attempts to foster the institutionalized study and development of black Appalachian cultural activities. While Turner was completing the work on this anthology, he was awarded a Ford Foundation postdoctoral fellowship in Afro-American social history. During the 1983-1984 academic year, he was affiliated with the Duke University History Department. His senior-level fellowship, administered by the National Research Council, gave him a year's leave from the University of Kentucky to write his manuscript "Black Harlan: On the Origins, Adaptation, Migration, and Evolution of Black Enclaves in Appalachian Kentucky."

1

Black Invisibility and Racism in Appalachia: An Informal Survey

EDWARD J. CABBELL

Ever since the formative years of the John Henry Memorial Foundation, Inc., in 1969, I have traveled extensively throughout the ARC-defined Central Appalachian Region seeking to understand the attitudes and values and heritage of fellow black Appalachians. From 1975 to 1978 I traveled full-time as the coordinator of the Foundation's Creativity in Appalachian Minorities Program (CAMP). I talked with black and white Appalachians identified as community leaders or potential community leaders who were responsive to social justice programs and activities in the mountains. My observations are concluded in this informal survey.

Black people in Appalachia are a neglected minority within a neglected minority. There are few studies on their existence and plight in the hills and valleys of Appalachia; it is, therefore, a most difficult task to analyze their situation. Even the most basic kinds of information about blacks in the region are difficult to obtain. Statistical data and published materials are scarce, and the media frequently ignore their experiences.[1] When black people in Appalachia are recognized, their experiences are often so "artfully clouded in myth and reality" that they remain virtually "invisible."[2] This creates a very serious dilemma for black Appalachians.

   Black invisibility provides strong support to the myth that the number of black people in the mountains is inconsequential.[3] In reality, one out of every fourteen Appalachians is black,[4] and many of these black Appalachians have played important roles in working with whites for improved conditions in the mountains for everyone. Black invisibility also supports the myth that Appalachia is a land of "poor white hillbillies,"[5] beset solely with "white problems" and not the "color problems" that plague the rest of America.[6] In reality, the 1.3 million blacks in Appalachia suffer worse economic status than white Appalachians, and their problems are compounded by racism and discrimination.[7]

   As a result of myths based on black invisibility in the mountains, scholars and analysts of the region have failed to focus on the existence and plight of black Appalachians. As a consequence, "Blacks in Appalachia live in some of the worst colonial-type racism and exploitation in the country," according to Fayetta Allen, a black journalist who came into the region to meet with, talk to, and study the existence and plight of black Appalachians.[8] Ms. Allen was shocked by the number of blacks in Appalachia who appeared to be unaware of the lack of control they had over their lives. She was also amazed by the number of blacks who had not even reached the point of organizing in order to provide "visibility" to their problems in the mountains. As a result of the numerous accounts of racism, joblessness, and poverty she heard in her travel in the region, she concluded that the black Appalachian situation was "unreal" and that the Civil Rights Movement of the 60's had not even reached the mountains.

To Leon F. Williams, a professor of social work at West Virginia University, the problems made known to Ms. Allen were very real. Calling on his own experiences as a black Appalachian, Williams discovered that black Appalachians are as invisible to themselves as they are to white Appalachians. He further stated that racial and class exploitation came with modern industrial development into the mountains and was increasingly pushing blacks out of the region. As a possible solution to this situation he called on white Appalachians who were not passive towards racism to help insure active black participation in the struggle for social justice and to reaffirm the place of blacks in Appalachian history.[9]

Unfortunately, with the exception of a few non-status quo organizations such as the Highlander Research and Education Center and the Council of the Southern Mountains, white Appalachians do not appear willing to work with blacks in their programs and activities. Even though Highlander and the Council are generally considered liberal (or even radical), they lack significant black input in the decision-making processes of their organizations.

Moreover, in many cases, white Appalachian scholars appear to be unaware of the existence and plight of blacks in Appalachia. A case in point is the recent detailed look by some well-known Appalachian scholars at the "colonial" aspects of Appalachian life and culture.[10] In an attempt to define class, status, and power in Appalachia, these scholars totally omitted black Appalachians, although Robert Blauner's model of the process of internal colonization of black Americans was one of the main components used in their study.

Very few other studies in or about the mountains have ever paid any significant attention to black Appalachians.[11] Indeed, very few Black Studies or Afro-American Studies scholars have ever included black Appalachian experiences in their courses and research either. No Black Studies scholar has even approached the black Appalachian theme in a serious manner since Carter G. Woodson's early attempts in the initial stages of the *Journal of Negro History* in 1916.[12] This lack of inclusion by black and white academics further points out the severity of black "invisibility" in Appalachia.

The effects of racism in the mountains can be easily observed if one takes a close look at the segregated housing, unequal employment opportunities, under-representation on juries and in government, lack of government services, lack of health care services, denial of meaningful educational opportunities, and other impediments that have pushed racism, joblessness, and poverty to extreme levels in the black communities scattered throughout the hills and valleys of Appalachia. Since 1969, I have traveled extensively throughout the area defined by the Appalachian Regional Commission as Central Appalachia (southern West Virginia, eastern Tennessee, eastern Kentucky, and southwestern Virginia) and to a lesser extent through other areas in the Appalachian region. During my travels I often met both black and white Appalachians who strongly felt that "everything is okay between the whites and the coloreds" in their community. Yet at the same time I observed, or was told of, blacks living in dilapidated houses in the segregated or "colored" sections of the villages and towns. Usually these sections lacked adequate roads, streets, facilities (fire hydrants, sewers, street lights), and services (trash removal). I rarely met blacks in the mountains with really good, reasonable jobs. The few blacks with token white collar jobs usually appeared to be quite proud of being the "only one" in this or that position in their community.

Affirmative Action programs, which usually existed on paper in local and county offices to meet the guidelines for federal funds, were almost totally ignored in the mountains. Labor unions were often silent on race issues, and adequate legal services, for both blacks and whites, were non-existent or ineffective in many mountain communities. Black union representatives were often "good old boys" who were relatively silent on racism and discrimination issues, and black lawyers were extremely rare.

Few blacks, especially "outspoken" blacks, have ever been called for jury duty by local magistrates or county courts. The same held true for blacks in town- and county-level government participation. Few blacks were even seen in clerical positions in municipal or county court houses in the mountains. It was extremely rare to find blacks in the mountains involved in local, county, or state government positions, appointive or elective. However, through talking with fellow black Appalachians, I found that quite a few were very much aware of vital problems in their communities and had possible solutions for some of these problems. Many were more than qualified for elective positions but were not involved in politics because, by custom and tradition, blacks had never run for elective positions. This was a most unfortunate situation, for we have far too many "Carter Country" and "Dukes of Hazzard" style government and law officials in Appalachia today,[13] which has helped create a severe lack of adequate government services in the Appalachian region for both blacks and whites.

There are also far too many people, regardless of race or color, suffering from all kinds of inadequate health care services. There is a critical shortage of black health care workers above the nurse aide, orderly, and clerical levels in the hospitals and clinics of the region. Moreover, silt-filled streams, polluted air, burning slag heaps, acid water, and dried-up wells make for continuing health problems in Appalachia. Many of these problems are involved with political, economic, social, and environmental concerns that require activism, but activism, in turn, requires community education to lift the level of community consciousness to create positive actions for possible solutions to these increasingly complex concerns.

Appalachians, in general, have tended not to confront their problems through their local governments. They have traditionally taken care of their individual problems themselves. They are now unable to handle their increasingly complex problems with the family-based social structure that usually called on violent, individualistic approaches to problem-solving. Collective, community problem-solving is new to the mountains. Community activism and education are not fully developed in the region. Thus, there is a serious problem-solving dilemma in Appalachia. So far no agency or organization has been created within the region that can seriously help the people of Appalachia with their problem-solving needs.

Education, often seen as the "panacea" of most problems in America, is perhaps the one area where meaningful and significant opportunities are blatantly denied blacks and poor whites in the Appalachian region. Accompanying the "integration" movement of the 50's and 60's has been, ironically, a sharp decline in black administrators, teachers, and coaches in the public schools and state-supported colleges and universities in the mountains. As a result of this decline, it is possible to attend all levels of school in Appalachia without seeing a single black administrator, teacher, or coach.[14] Also, due to the lack of research and courses on black Appalachian life and culture, it is possible to complete all levels of education in the mountains and never learn about the heritage and life history of blacks in the region. This is a dilemma which must be corrected by Appalachian scholars as soon as possible.

Added to these regional problems, the federal government has failed or refused to recognize the plight of black Appalachians in its "War on Poverty" agencies and programs of the 60's. The brainchild of the War on Poverty, the Appalachian Regional Commission (ARC), has continued to ignore black Appalachians although blacks have problems at least as severe as those "discovered" in white Appalachia in the 60's.[15] The hastily created programs and agencies of the War on Poverty, especially ARC, have always been quite controversial, and the real purposes, goals, and constituencies of these basically regional "economic development" programs have remained confused.[16]

In reaction to the failure of the Appalachian Regional Commission to focus or respond to the problems of black Appalachians, the Black Appalachian Commission (BAC) was established in 1969 as one of the new commissions of the Council of the Southern Mountains. BAC became an independent black regional organization in 1971. However, plagued by external and internal problems and pressures, BAC ceased to function in 1975.[17]

During its functional years, BAC managed to focus a great deal of attention on the problems of black invisibility in the Appalachian region. The Commission also located, identified, and mobilized black Appalachian community leaders at the grass roots level; among them were Mattye Knight, Wylda Dean Harbin, Viola Cleveland, Attorney Donald L. Pitts, Bill Worthington, Helen Powell, and the late Anise Floyd, to name but a few.[18] BAC was also extremely successful in monitoring federal programs and agencies in Appalachia and revealing the institutional racism in these programs and agencies as well as the organizations which they funded in the mountains.

Having learned their skills and techniques from such non-status quo organizations as the Highlander Research and Education Center and the Council of the Southern Mountains and, to a degree, from the Southern Conference Educational Fund (SCEF), BAC was becoming a black powerhouse in the mountains. It was establishing itself as a technical assistance and information resource center for blacks in Appalachia. Unfortunately, it was dissolved before it could make a truly significant impact on the life and culture of blacks in Appalachia.

During the initial formation of BAC, I was director of the Upward Bound and Special Services for Disadvantaged Students projects at Concord College (Athens, West Virginia), and I was advisor to the Black Student Union. Through several black cultural programs I coordinated at the college, I had already begun to lay the groundwork for the formation of the John Henry Memorial Foundation, Inc., chartered in 1973.[19] Encouraged by BAC's communications and research coordinator, Clarence "Butch" Wright, to pursue a cultural-intellectual program for dealing with the problems of black Appalachian invisibility, I began to advocate a communications network between black Appalachians and other concerned and interested people. I also became instrumental in establishing the annual John Henry Folk Festival in 1973, and later *Black Diamonds* magazine and John Henry Records in 1976, as a means of publicizing black Appalachian life and culture. These projects and activities are still functioning, although in a low-key and sporadic manner due to inadequate funding. However, success has been realized in providing some awareness of blacks in Appalachia.

With the support of BAC, other grassroots groups and leaders in Appalachia also developed in the early 1970's. Perhaps the most successful of these groups and leaders has been Mattye Knight's Greater Cumberland Corporation in Cumberland, Kentucky.[20]

On December 15, 1972, the 44 families of the long neglected Sanctified Hill community in Cumberland, Kentucky, were ordered by a city police dispatcher to evacuate their homes. The Hill was threatened by a gigantic mud slide. The houses of this predominantly black neighborhood shortly began to break open in sections and slowly move down the dirt roads and paths toward the streets of the white neighborhood below. For years the members of the black community had complained to the city officials about the possibility of such a mud slide to no avail. Insurance companies immediately began to call the Sanctified Hill mud slide "an act of God," thereby relieving themselves of any legal responsibilities to possible claimants. Federal, state, and local agencies considered the situation too small for declaring "national disaster" assistance. The life's work and investment of this community of widows and retired miners had just slipped away.

Wylda Dean Harbin informed BAC of the plight of the blacks in Cumberland, and BAC's Board chairman, Carl Johnson of Asheville, North Carolina, held a meeting with the local blacks at the local black Baptist church and helped them to form the Sanctified Hill Disaster Committee. Mattye Knight, a local black school teacher, was named the Committee spokesperson. It was decided that the goals of the Committee would be to go to Washington, D.C., to publicize the plight of the community, to seek financial and technical assistance in relocating and rebuilding the community, to determine the cause and future of the slide, and to seek legal assistance.

Receiving national media coverage at the Capitol, the Committee stirred a great deal of controversy among several agencies that perhaps should have already been doing something to help them. After much discussion, buckpassing, criticism, and questioning, the agencies and some congressmen decided to go to Cumberland and survey the slide and try to find a solution to the problem. The result of this visit, after much hard work by Mattye Knight and the Committee, was the formation of the Greater Cumberland Corporation, a nonprofit housing development corporation, organized to purchase land and to sponsor housing for the relocated Sanctified Hill families. Families that already owned their homes on Sanctified Hill would receive new homes in the relocated area at no costs to them. Homes that were mortgaged on the Hill would be mortgaged at the same rates in the new area. Homes that were rented would also be rented in the new location at the same rate as on the Hill prior to the disaster. The relocated families were to be provided a model community, Pride Terrace. The area to be developed was a seventeen-acre site formerly deeded to the University of Kentucky. Presently, twenty-six homeowners are living in the Pride Terrace planned community development, and sixteen rental units are under construction.

Less successful than the efforts of Mattye Knight has been the struggle of Wylda Dean Harbin of Harlan, Kentucky, to have the predominantly black Georgetown community raised above the flood level of Harlan. She also wanted improved housing and facilities and services for the 40 black families on ten acres of the most potentially valuable land in Harlan. Some estimates value this land at $60,000 per acre according to Ms. Harbin. The city wants the black community to move out and make room for a shopping center and a highway. The city has challenged assessments of $7,500 an acre as too high for property in Georgetown. Moreover, no realistic relocation plans have been offered the Georgetown residents by city or county officials. Ms. Harbin formed the Save Our Georgetown Committee and continues to fight removal of the Georgetown residents without adequate relocation plans.[21]

Despite obstacles and discouragements, the efforts of Wylda Dean Harbin place her in the ranks of such black Appalachian activists as Viola Cleveland of Middlesboro, Kentucky, who continues to call for equal justice for blacks and women in Appalachia, and Attorney Donald L. Pitts of Beckley, West Virginia, who constantly works for increased black political involvement in Appalachia.[22]

Some black Appalachians have chosen to join predominantly white organizations in the mountains and provide a black voice in the decision-making processes of these organizations vital to the region. Included in this group is Bill Worthington of Coxton, Kentucky, who has continuously provided a black input into the black lung struggles of the miners in the Appalachian coalfields. The late Anise Floyd of Charleston, West Virginia, was also influential in the black lung struggle from the perspective of the wives and widows of Appalachian coalminers. Helen Powell of Glen Jean, West Virginia, has also been an extremely effective voice in the health care programs of the Appalachian region.[23]

Other black Appalachian community leaders, unknown to me, are scattered throughout the 397 counties of the Appalachian region, fighting various struggles on a local level. Unfortunately, since the demise of the Black Appalachian Commission, no other black Appalachian organization has been strong enough to gather the various leaders and potential leaders in black Appalachia together for a major conference whereby a true regional black voice could be heard.[24] In the meantime, black Appalachian invisibility continues to support myths and their resulting racism. This is a most unfortunate dilemma.

Appalachia can no longer afford to sit back and do nothing about the fact that the civil rights movement of the 50's and 60's by-passed the mountains. It is time that Appalachia confront rampant forms of institutional racism brought on by industrialization in the mountains as well as covert racism rooted in the traditions and customs of the mountains. Appalachia must seriously examine the nature of the black Appalachian experience. The leadership and energies of black Appalachians are a resource for all Appalachians, a resource badly needed.

1. The fall 1975 and fall 1978 issues of *Appalachian Issues and Resources,* a catalog published by the Southern Appalachian Ministry for Higher Education (Knoxville, Tenn.), offered the editors little information on blacks in Appalachia.

2. See Clarence Wright, "Black Appalachian Invisibility—Myth or Reality?" *Black Appalachian Viewpoints,* 1 (Aug. 6, 1973), 3. The greatest problem confronting black people in Appalachia is their invisibility, according to Wright ("The Black Appalachian Movement: People, Power, and Change," *Black Appalachian Viewpoints,* 1 [Aug. 22, 1973]). Described as a "temporary" publication of the Black Appalachian Commission, only two issues of *Black Appalachian Viewpoints* are known to have been released.

3. Most Appalachian resource materials mention and treat the number of blacks in Appalachia in this manner. See, for example, Samuel Tyndale Wilson, *The Southern Mountaineers* (New York, 1914), p. 204.

4. This is one of the "Appalachian and Black Facts" offered in a brochure released by the Black Appalachian Commission in 1973.

5. Appalachia is very commonly and controversially portrayed as a land of "poor white hillbillies." According to Cratis D. Williams, "The Southern Mountaineer in Fact and Fiction" (Ph.D. diss., New York University, 1961), the hillbilly image began to emerge as a distinct fictional type in pioneer and southern literature in the 1880s and became increasingly popular in humorous presentations of mountain people. Henry D. Shapiro, *Appalachia on Our Mind: The Southern Mountains and Mountaineers in American Consciousness, 1870-1920* (Chapel Hill, N.C., 1978), also presents interesting insights on the "creation" of Appalachia.

6. Wilson's *The Southern Mountaineers* openly dismisses the "color problems" of Appalachia because of the small number of blacks in the mountains.

7. See chapter 17, this book.

8. Fayetta Allen, "Blacks in Appalachia," *Black Scholar,* 5 (June 1974), 47.

9. See chapter 16, this book.

10. Helen Matthews Lewis, Linda Johnson, and Donald Askins, ed., *Colonialism in Modern America: The Appalachian Case* (Boone, N.C., 1978).

11. A few Appalachian scholars, teachers, and writers call attention to the lack of ethnic and minority groups in their study and research. The special issue of the *Appalachian Journal* (vol. 5 [Autumn 1977]), *A Guide to Appalachian Studies,* cites the need for ethnic and minority studies in the mountains; see especially Ronald D. Eller, "Toward a New History of the Appalachian South," and David S. Walls and Dwight B. Billings, "The Sociology of Southern Appalachia," p. 131.

12. Carter G. Woodson's "Freedom and Slavery in Appalachian America" appears as chapter 4, this book.

13. "Carter Country" and "The Dukes of Hazzard" are controversial portrayals of Southerners and/or Appalachians on commercial television. These programs, along with "Hee Haw," have created much discussion about these groups' influential role as an image of the life and culture of the southern mountains.

14. See chapter 16, this book.

15. See chapter 17, this book.

16. Several black people I talked with during my travels in the black communities of Appalachia felt that the War on Poverty programs were hastily created to divert attention from the civil rights movement, which was embarrassing the American government around the world.

17. Information on BAC was taken from the files of Attorney Donald L. Pitts of Beckley, W. Va. A limited number of letters, memoranda, proposals, etc., were in the files of this former member of the BAC Board of Directors.

18. I personally visited and talked with the listed community leaders about their roles as activists in Appalachia.

19. For historical information on the John Henry Memorial Foundation and its projects and activities, read available issues of *Black Diamonds* magazine, released by the Foundation beginning in 1978. Also see newspapers, magazines, and other publications that emphasize Appalachian life and culture and you will find comments about the projects and activities of the Foundation, especially its annual John Henry Folk Festival.

20. The following account is taken from "The Sanctified Hill Story," written by Mattye Knight and given to me while I visited her in Cumberland during the summer of 1977 for CAMP.

21. Wylda Dean Harbin told me the story of the plight of Georgetown while I was visiting her to seek information on the status of the Save Our Georgetown Committee. My visit with Ms. Harbin was during the summer of 1977 and was supported by a grant from The Youth Project (Washington, D.C.).

22. CAMP allowed me to visit many black Appalachians like Cleveland and Pitts between 1975 and 1978 in an attempt to locate and identify creative projects and activities among blacks in Appalachia. A great deal of support for this project was from funds from the National Endowment for the Arts (Washington, D.C.), the West Virginia Arts and Humanities Commission (Charleston, W. Va.), and the We Shall Overcome Fund (New Market, Tenn.). The Benedum Foundation also offered some support.

23. I found that the blacks who chose to work in predominantly white organizations were very well known among whites in the mountains as well as among blacks.

24. In its heyday BAC was able to gather more than 200 black Appalachians for conferences and meetings. Many national and regional organizations supported the efforts of BAC.

2

Between Berea (1904) and Birmingham (1908): The Rock and Hard Place for Blacks in Appalachia

WILLIAM H. TURNER

Students of the population(s) and culture of Appalachia, as well as scholars of the "general" black experience, have consistently overlooked blacks in the region. The presence of black people in the Appalachian Mountains (especially the central highlands), the labor of blacks in the industrialization of the region, their needs, and the culture that they have developed in the area have yet to be systematically analyzed. This essay offers some historical evidence and sociological interpretation of the experience of black Appalachians. It reviews the blacks' arrival in the region, the general character of their social and cultural development, and two specific instances which bear on the present status of blacks in the Central Appalachians.

HISTORICAL PERSPECTIVE

Ironically, the paucity of scholarship on black Appalachians may reflect the fact that white settlers in the region (unlike their neighbors to the south) "were loath to follow the pro-slavery element."[1] Although actual abolition movements were not "popular," the immigrants into the uplands and mountains of the Carolinas, Tennessee, Kentucky, and West Virginia arrived in the region hoping to find political liberty and religious freedom. The German, Scotch-Irish, Huguenot, and Quaker newcomers and assorted "poor white indentured serfs" had fled Europe during the seventeenth and eighteenth centuries. The Lutheran and heavily Calvinist ethic of these people, though they varied in ethnic stock, emphasized equality, freedom of conscience, practical religion, homely virtues, and democratic institutions. Thus, aside from the fact that the land west of the Shenandoah offered little physical space in which slaves could work, there was little room for slavery in the ideological framework of the solidly independent yeomen. Woodson, a premier black historian, considered the original settlers in the region as holding "differing opinions as to the extent, character, and foundations of local self-government, . . . differing ideas of the magnitude of governmental power over the individual, and differing theories of relations between church and State."[2]

Indeed, the original white settlers were among the avante-garde fighting against the British in the Revolutionary War; and not surprisingly, when they demanded liberty and justice for the colonists, they spoke also of the slaves.[3] Of course, the record shows clearly that even *after* the overthrow of Great Britain's colonial rule, manhood suffrage was still tied to skin color, religious orientation, payment of taxes, and wealth (that is, land ownership and possession of slaves). This legacy of English tradition pitted southern aristocrats against the progressive westerners in the Alleghenies. To the frustrated and embattled people, individual freedom, the divine right of secular power, and personal responsibility (as contrasted with the aristocrats' idea of the liberty of kings, lords, and commoners) were fundamentally threatened by slavery. The immigrants had left Europe to avoid such threats, and they hated the slave *as such,* not as a man! It must be noted, however, that this spirit of equality and freedom of all men to live together did not extend to the Indians in the Appalachians—specifically, not to the Cherokee nation.[4]

In each of the central Appalachian states, a bitter struggle evolved between the white mountaineers and their planter class enemies. The enmity diminished with the invention of the cotton gin and the expansion of slavery, which culminated finally in a "community of interest" between planters and mountain pioneers, both of whom were able to profit from the industrial revolution engendered by the rise of the plantation system. Before the uneasy agreement emerged, however, mountaineers fought slavery with relative vigor.[5] For non-slaveholders, competition for jobs was made worse, since slaves were (by law) free laborers. Slavery constricted the development of public schools because slaveowners would not pay the needed taxes, and the peculiar institution and free society could not exist and prosper simultaneously. As early as 1783, organized antislavery efforts existed in East Tennessee and in Davie, Davidson, Granville, and Guilford counties in western North Carolina, and of course practically all of western Virginia showed an ardent antipathy to slavery. This arm of the antislavery movement was well entrenched at the start of the nineteenth century. In 1815 the Manumission Society of Tennessee was second only to the Kentucky's "Friends of Humanity" (circa 1807). Factionalism resulted from the organizational weaknesses of these groups. One element formed the American Colonization Society.

On the radical side, there were people like William Lloyd Garrison, who helped to organize the Underground Railroad. The upper chamber of slavery's heart (Chattanooga and the lower ranges of the Cumberland Mountains, through Tennessee and North Carolina up through the highlands of West Virginia and Kentucky) became the most common way to freedom for fugitives. This "South Pass of the Alleghenies" had served as the gateway for thousands upon thousands of emigrants from Virginia and North Carolina en route to the virgin lands of the West. Cumberland Gap became a major focal point in the development and evolution of highland abolition movements. Of note is one famous mountain abolitionist, John E. Rankin, later president of Howard University and reader of Frederick Douglass's funeral sermon in 1895. The white Baptists and Methodists emphasized the education of blacks as equivalent to an evolutionary manumission; and developments related to Berea College were a milestone in the story of their efforts.

BEREA COLLEGE, KENTUCKY:
BLACK EDUCATION REFORMED

As the throes of Reconstruction continued the uneasy alliance between the Union and the recalcitrant South, the Appalachian region "emerged" as a haven of old-stock morality, a virgin refuge from new-wave immigration in the East, and a haven inhabited by "the purest of Anglo-Saxon stock in the United States."[6] The characterization of the white natives in the region as lazy, shiftless men and hard-working women, the worst housed, worst fed, most ignorant, and most immoral religious people, who believed in spells and witchcraft and who had speech patterns difficult to understand and so forth—this description might lead a person to think that blacks were being described. Indeed, as Klotter[7] discerned, such qualities, as attributed to whites, enabled the tired and frustrated coterie of abolitionists and missionaries to turn their backs on the black populace. The "white Negro" in the mountains resembled Sambo.[8] The blacks' social development had been retarded by isolation and the history of indenture. To white reformers, faced with an ever-stabilizing Jim Crow system, the highlands of Appalachia symbolized humanitarian needs that seemed politically unachievable for blacks. The race factor that was basic to blacks' needs appeared inexorable, ineluctable, inextricable; and as Klotter gauged the mood, "Perhaps the Southerners had been right about them [blacks] after all."[9] If we return to the exact point at which reformers abandoned the cause of the freedmen and left them to their own resources in ensuring their rights of enfranchisement, we shall find ourselves in the Appalachian Mountains. Here in Appalachia, far from the plantations of the Mississippi Delta, far removed from the major battlegrounds of the Civil War, and in the remote serenity where relatively few blacks lived, "Appalachian Anglo-Saxons began to replace blacks in the national awareness."[10] The very physical space traversed by the Underground Railroad, in which rugged mountaineers "forfeited life for the furtherance of the ends of justice, and mingled blood . . . with the blood of millions of slaves,"[11] became the intersection at which the missionary efforts for the cause of the freedmen literally made a right turn. The diminution of the liberals' efforts on behalf of blacks was exemplified most dramatically by the head of the Freedmen's Bureau—General O. O. Howard—for whom Howard University is named! Hailing "these our brothers" now as "our people," Howard led the American Missionary Association (then the preeminent organization fighting and financing black empowerment) in redirecting funds and support *from* black people *to* the cause of Appalachian whites. Klotter noted words that Howard had written in 1902 that were not unlike those he used in gaining support for Hampton and Tuskegee institutes.[12] General Howard also argued persuasively that the mountain whites evidenced a need for concerted efforts, as these Christians were as needy as any blacks. General Howard had been decorated for his military exploits against Indians. In his capacity as chairman of the board of Lincoln Memorial University, which was located in the heart of the Cumberland Gap, he wrote, "These people were not entirely like blacks but rather have our best blood in their veins, and yet . . . have been overlooked and left behind in all our educational privileges."[13]

That the Appalachian Mountains were the quiet battleground on which blacks lost their most dependable source of support is further confirmed by the defeat of interracial efforts at Kentucky's Berea College. Between its founding in 1855 and 1870, fully 60 percent of the Berea student body was black. John Fee and Cassius Clay, cofounders of the school, were staunch abolitionists. For nearly four decades, blacks and whites interacted at Berea College with mutual respect and without making rigid racial distinctions until Carl Day, a state representative from Breathitt County in Appalachia, expressed shock at "this stench in the nostrils of all true Kentuckians."[14] Day's Law, as it came to be called, forbade the continuance of any institution which admitted both black and white students; furthermore, teachers providing instruction in such settings—as well as students—were to be fined. Fee's successor at Berea, President William Frost, faced adverse publicity and found the school less attractive than it had been to Appalachian whites. He changed the school and eliminated the stigma of integration. Until 1904, Berea's stated mission paralleled those of the AMA and other well-known philanthropies in their support of a number of colleges for the newly freed slaves: Howard (Washington, D.C.); Fisk (Tennessee); Lincoln (Pennsylvania); Hampton (Virginia); Tougaloo (Mississippi); and to a lesser extent many other colleges established for blacks between 1865 and 1880. Reluctantly, given Berea's historic opposition to slaveholding and to a caste system, the trustees abided by Day's Law. President Frost was given some flexibility to continue working for both white mountaineers and black freedmen. Subsequently, the Berea board helped blacks go elsewhere by establishing Lincoln Institute outside Shelbyville, Kentucky (near Louisville). After a bitter battle waged by townspeople who were convinced that a Negro school would ruin their homes and lower the value of their land, Lincoln Institute was finally built. Relieved of the Negro problem, Berea "combined the theme of the modernization of a retarded people with talk of the preservation of their more noble qualities" to become a world-renowned college "In Lincoln's State—For Lincoln's People."[15]

Berea's new focus on searching out "the great army of the disadvantaged and unreached people who are our kin" conformed to the national mood of retrenchment and retreat from black enfranchisement. Concern for southern blacks was abandoned with a clear conscience, and events at Berea in Appalachia came to mark part of the unfolding of acts both deliberate and unintentional which eventuated in the era of legal segregation and the containment of black Americans.[16]

KING COAL IN BIRMINGHAM:
THE RACIALIZATION OF LABOR

We must link education (the Berea story) with black labor force participation in Appalachia at the beginning of this century, since "Negro education" was by then equated with "industrial and normal education." Blacks were, after all, more important as workers and laborers in American commercial and industrial enterprise than were educational pursuits. The reasons related to blacks' material significance, to their prominence and visibility, and to capitalistic interests.

In fact, blacks as workers were a large though manipulated segment of modern mountain industries from the 1880s until the mid-1950s.

The first wave of blacks reached the coal fields (and, earlier, the salt mines) of central and southern Appalachia long after blacks had begun work as miners. Barnum notes that blacks worked the mines of eastern Virginia as far back as 1750.[17] Slightly fewer than 200,000 blacks lived in present-day Appalachian Kentucky, Tennessee, North and South Carolina, Georgia, Alabama, and Virginia (later West Virginia) at the time of the 1860 census. U.S. Census data from 1840 through 1860 indicate that the greater number of blacks lived in the Appalachian slaveholding states. In Madison County (Huntsville), Alabama, there were 14,490 blacks in 1850, of whom only 164 were free. By contrast, Jackson County, Kentucky, listed 21 free blacks and 7 slaves in 1860. The pattern in Jackson County was typical for the Appalachian Mountains—blacks were few in number, and the majority were slaves.[18] Most had come to the region as slaves with white families in the Transylvania movement to help in the clearing of forests for the westward expansion associated with Daniel Boone.[19] These "native hillbillies," some of whom had mixed with Indians and with the Scotch-Irish, eked out a meager livelihood from hillside farms and from timbering and worked the salt deposits.[20]

Upon Emancipation, blacks left these mountain areas for the growing towns of Appalachia—Chattanooga, Knoxville, Birmingham, Asheville, and Roanoke. Between Emancipation and the opening of the coal fields, some of the blacks in the mountains became freeholders of land and established black enclaves which awaited the influx of other blacks after 1890.[21] The only general thing to be said about Appalachian blacks during this period (1863-1890) is that they "were isolated socially and culturally. . . . Whites feuded internally over the splits caused by the Civil War and the question of slavery,"[22] and whites "were not bothered by the same prejudices about black people that [white] people from the Deep South had."[23]

Whites in Appalachia, while never crusading for their racial prejudices prior to the opening of the coal fields, found much cause to do so beginning in the mid-1880s. The legendary John Henry entered the mountain picture[24] (as Sambo had two and a half centuries earlier entered the lowland plantations) to build the railroads. Similarly, an army of blacks had already taken half of Alabama's coal-mining jobs only three years before Emancipation.[25] Alabama coal mining, with its virulent racism, set the tone and tenor for the black experience in the southern and central coal fields. Just as the breakup of the Berea experiment hindered the development of an effective interracial educational experience in Appalachia, black miners came to be considered the traducers in white Appalachia's relations with the coal barons who replaced the planters. In view of the sprawled geopolitical and cultural boundaries of the region, it is understandable that these events took place in the southern section of Appalachia—Alabama.

Significantly, Virginia has the distinction of being the first state in which blacks were employed as coal miners. Near Jamestown, where black slaves first appeared, some 500 blacks worked the mines in 1796. Slaves living in the few valley farms of the Shenandoah in the northwest sector of Virginia, those along the southern line from Spartanburg, South Carolina, west to Chattanooga and Birmingham and up to the Cumberland Plateau, left to form black settlements in the middle of the triangle—in central Appalachia. This move from cotton and other agricultural pursuits followed the discovery and exploitation of vast coal deposits in the region. By 1890, 46 percent of all Alabama miners were black. By 1890, in the Appalachian regions of Alabama, Tennessee, Kentucky, Virginia, and West Virginia, blacks ranged from 46 percent (Alabama) of the miners to 15 percent in Kentucky. They were to yield to the same forces that had abolished the racial equality promised by the Berea experiment.

As far as black workers were concerned, the extractive industries of Appalachia (timbering and mining) proposed in economic terms the same conditions as the institution of education. For white Appalachians, though, the matter of free labor in pre-Civil War days was easily argued from afar. After 1877, when the possibilities of Radical Reconstruction had dwindled, the industrial development of Appalachia highlighted the question of race. If the educators at Berea had acted to guarantee the racial purity of Appalachia, the coal barons shattered it, recruiting blacks vigorously from the agricultural sections. As the blacks saw their first promise of cash wages and a better life, they became unwitting pawns in the chess game played by emergent (white) unionists and the northern economic empires that began to replace the planter class. The white workers were advancing and exercising a fundamental right as laborers that was unknown to men who had been slaves and sharecroppers—the right to strike.[26]

In some cases industry had to recruit workers from other sectors, and many a black miner began his sojourn in the coal fields of Appalachia, helping form an industrial labor reserve.[27] Together with a coterie of European immigrants, blacks replaced striking native white laborers. "Most, if not all blacks, probably agreed with [Booker T.] Washington's assertion that the true friends of black workers were the capitalists who supplied them with jobs, rather than the unions which excluded them."[28] In addition, blacks were played off against a multinational labor force that included Germans, Serbs, Poles, Greeks, Italians, Russians, Mexicans, and other peoples. The struggle of such disparate, mainly uneducated workers fostered disunity, disrupted labor solidarity, and forestalled efforts to unionize.[29] In only ten years, during which time the number of southern Appalachians employed as miners doubled, the in-migration of blacks to the coal fields almost tripled. Race and class dynamics, combined with political isolation from mainstream American culture, transformed the black mine worker into a malefactor not too unlike other blacks who migrated to Chicago, Philadelphia, New York, and other northern manufacturing centers. The first series of major miners' strikes (between 1894 and 1908 in Alabama) occurred at a time when white miners drew some of the country's lowest wages, laboring for the shortest working hours for the worst type of work.

The progressive supporters of the Berea experiment (pre-1904) found their counterparts within the United Mine Workers when the organization entered Alabama's rich fields in 1893. At that time, nearly half of the coal miners in the state were black. The UMW, unlike most other labor unions, erected no restrictive covenants against blacks because it was well aware that "the Negro question" had been employed to use as strikebreakers blacks who were standing ready as a reserve labor force. When the UMW had recruited the majority of black miners in Alabama, the operators drew on southern racial prejudice to crush the 1908 strike by employing large numbers of armed black deputies and by playing up "the great differences of opinion among blacks about the value of labor unions" and the tenuous racially based solidarity in the black community.[30] The ensuing violence pitted black scabs, black guards, and black deputies against black and white union loyalists.

The economy of Birmingham in August 1908 was stagnant much as it would become a half century later when it suffered from boycotts and was under siege by the civil rights movement. Governor Braxton Bragg Comer, like "Bull" Conner, sided with the business sector of the city, believing that UMW organizers, while ostensibly pursuing the equal-wage-for-equal-work canon, were really attempting to establish social equality between black and white miners.[31] The Alabama Coal Operators Association even invoked the spirit of Booker T. Washington's famous Five-Fingers Speech, delivered at the 1895 Atlanta Cotton Exposition. Perhaps the ACOA took him to mean that "in all things social [the intermingling and brotherhood portended in unions] we can be as separate as the fingers, yet one as the hand in all things [producing coal] essential to mutual progress." The UMW obviously intending its position to play down the notion that the union's biracial organizing efforts were a threat to the area's racial etiquette, declared that its work pertained to the job and nothing more. Straw found in a 1908 issue of the *Labor Advocate* a UMW-sanctioned disclaimer: "We [the UMW] acknowledge that there is not at present and never was and can never be social equality between the whites and blacks in this state."[32]

The cumulative effect of such hesitancy on the union's part resulted in reduced worker solidarity and deepened the strain in relations between white and black workers. The emphasis of the strike shifted as the UMW was charged with attempting to foster social equality; biracial unionism was equated with the abolition of norms and values held "near and dear" in the South. Subsequently, UMW strength fell precipitously in the South, creating the conditions for "nigger work" throughout the industry. The racial antipathy generated by this event brought a total setback for black Appalachian miners. Only the collapse of the industry could have reduced them further, and they could not rise without threatening white miners' efforts to guard against the possibility of "nigger domination."

The events in Berea in 1904 and in Birmingham in 1908 combined to solidify the opposition to biracial education and biracial unionism. Following the Berea decision, blacks seeking a liberal arts education were obliged to leave Kentucky; the defeat of the UMW in Alabama eliminated the possibility that blacks and whites would succeed there in overcoming the artificial antagonisms of the race problem. Certainly both seemingly isolated events checked the growth of libertarianism and unionism in the region. Thousands of blacks who played a part in the 1908 strike joined the "Great Exodus" to more tolerable points north, and the blacks who took their mining skills to the virgin fields of eastern Kentucky and West Virginia did not leave their memories behind.

Higher wages and the promise of better working and living conditions lured many blacks to the new fields where, once again, they were used as strike-breakers and thus became the albatross of Appalachia.

Such stress on the events in Berea, Kentucky, in 1904 and in Birmingham, Alabama, in 1908 as keystones in understanding the present status of blacks in the Appalachian highlands is open to challenge. It is doubtless possible to charge that the analysis exemplifies the fallacy of reification—Whitehead's "fallacy of misplaced concreteness."[33] Most contemporary students of the black Appalachian experience agree, however, that we must start somewhere in making our studies concrete and in formulating useful conceptual models of this "neglected minority within a neglected minority."[34] Additional historical and sociocultural analyses are needed to define the diverse sociocultural patterns among blacks in Appalachia's subregions. Scholars are now obliged to exaggerate certain "events and aspects" of the southern, central, and highlands regions. In fact, it becomes necessary to magnify the black Appalachian experience in order (1) to establish blacks' presence historically and (2) to evaluate their socioeconomic and cultural patterns relative to those of whites in the region and those of blacks nationally.

The present status of blacks in Appalachia reflects these, and certainly other, events in the social history of the region. Collectively blacks offer a classic illustration of socioeconomic deprivation and racial discrimination—as these terms are generally applied to poor blacks in ghettos surrounded by affluent whites—and a singular example of *black* poverty in the context of considerable *white* poverty.[35] The failures of biracial unionism in Birmingham eventually meant that economic conditions for both races became constant throughout Appalachia, and the racial aspect of events at Berea suggests that "whiteness" in the mountains may, after all, be regarded as only a set of symbols used to appeal to white people for the purpose of "organizing" them to further the capture and exploitation of their resources by coal barons and the propagation of internal colonialism by outside interests. Certainly the study of the region's forgotten blacks offers rich new insights into the history and culture of a racial minority in the midst of a cultural minority.

1. See chapter 4, this book.

2. Ibid.

3. The famous Battle on King's Mountain in 1780 and the Battle of Yorktown are noteworthy.

4. See chapter 3 for Theda Perdue's illuminating thesis regarding the complicity of some Appalachian Cherokees in the capture and trade of black slaves.

5. James W. Taylor, *Alleghenia: A Geographic and Statistical Memoir* (St. Paul, Minn., 1862).

6. D. H. Davis, "The Changing Role of the Kentucky Mountains and the Passing of the Kentucky Mountaineer," *Journal of Geography,* 24 (Feb. 1925), 41.

7. See chapter 6, this book.

8. Stanley Elkins, *Slavery: Problems in Institutional Life in America* (New York, 1964).

9. See chapter 6, this book.

10. Ibid.

11. This statement is attributed to John Brown, made before he was sentenced by the court

following his conviction in connection with the raid on the military arsenal at Harpers Ferry, W. Va., in Oct. 1859. See Suzanne Crowell, *Appalachian Peoples' History Book* (Atlanta, Ga., 1973), p. 63.

12. Booker T. Washington, General Howard's main spokesman, grew up in West Virginia and became the recognized architect of blacks' accommodation to the reduced efforts of reformers. It is noteworthy too that the conferences which culminated in the widespread adoption of industrial education for blacks convened in Appalachia at Capon Springs, W. Va. In addition, Carter G. Woodson, quoted above, is himself a graduate of Berea College.

13. Oliver Otis Howard, "The Folk of Cumberland Gap," *Munsey's Magazine,* 27 (Nov. 5, 1903), quoted in chapter 6, this volume.

14. George C. Wright, "The Founding of Lincoln Institute," in *Filson Club Historical Quarterly,* 49, no. 2 (Fall 1975), 54.

15. Passages quoted appear in chapter 6, this book.

16. Henry A. Bullock, *A History of Negro Education in the South: From 1619 to the Present* (Cambridge, Mass., 1967), p. 214.

17. Donald T. Barnum, *The Negro in the Bituminous Coal Mining Industry,* Racial Policies of American Industry (Philadelphia, 1970).

18. Richard Drake, "Black Appalachian Shifts, 1850–1970," *Appalachian Notes,* 3 (1st quarter, 1973).

19. John C. Campbell, *The Southern Highlander and His Homeland,* (Lexington, Ky., 1921).

20. Mabel Green Condon, *A History of Harlan County* (Nashville, Tenn., 1962).

21. Luther P. Jackson, *Free Negro Labor and Property Holding in Virginia, 1850–1866* (New York, 1942).

22. William Lynwood Montell, *The Saga of Coe Ridge: A Study in Oral History* (Knoxville, Tenn., 1970), p. 107.

23. Loyal Jones, "Appalachian Values," in *Appalachia: Social Context and Present,* ed. Bruce Ergood and Bruce E. Kuhre (Dubuque, Ia., 1976), p. 214.

24. The black legendary hero John Henry was supposed to have worked at the Big Bend Tunnel on the C&O Railroad during its construction in 1870-72.

25. Robert Ward and William Rodgers, *Labor Revolt in Alabama: The Great Strike of 1894* (Tuscaloosa, Ala., 1965).

26. See chapter 12, this book.

27. Sterling D. Spero and Abram L. Harris, *The Black Worker, 1915-1930* (1931; reprint ed., New York, 1974).

28. See chapter 14, this book.

29. Herbert Northrup, *Organized Labor and the Negro* (New York, 1944).

30. See chapter 15, this book.

31. Ibid.

32. Ibid.

33. Alfred North Whitehead, *Science and the Modern World* (New York, 1925), p. 65.

34. See chapter 1, this book.

35. David Bellows, "Blacks in Appalachia: A Demographic Analysis" (master's thesis, Rutgers University, 1974).

PART TWO

Historical Perspectives

In part 2 of this volume we present some knowledgeable accounts of historical particularities that have shaped the current status of blacks in Appalachia. Theda Perdue offers information about the different kinds of blacks in Appalachia (those who arrived with white pioneers in the region as contrasted with those who migrated after 1880) and documents events between colonists, native Americans (Cherokees), and blacks. Hers is a unique analysis of the hostility and fear generated between Indians and blacks (slaves) as the colonists sought to keep Africans and native Americans separate and to make them regard each other with misconceptions and an awareness of difference.

Carter G. Woodson, once a student at Berea College and the founder of the Association for the Study of Negro Life and History, focuses on Virginia's problem of reconciling freedom (in the mountains) with slavery (in the Tidewater) as different types of whites entered the New World and settled the state, bringing divergent ideals with regard to the development of castes (generated by slavery and by capitalism in general).

Booker T. Washington, surely one of the best-known Appalachians, traces his poverty in the salt mines of Malden, West Virginia, the beginnings of education for blacks in the region, and his introduction to coal mining at about the time that the region opened up to the industry. His essay ends on a strong note, reflecting the author's race pride—grounded in his belief in individualism and supported by his reflections on the notion of superior races. James Klotter's article, the last in part 2, defines the form and substance of racism in the mountains of Kentucky. Klotter stresses the redirection of liberal reformist efforts away from black freedmen to poor whites, who were, after all, he concludes, "black people in white skins."

3

Red and Black in the Southern Appalachians

THEDA PERDUE

The first black Appalachians did not live under the control of white planters, railroad builders, lumber companies, or mine operators; instead, they lived within the domain of the Cherokee Indians. The Cherokee Nation extended from its spiritual center at Kituwah, near present-day Bryson City, North Carolina, into what has become the states of South Carolina, Georgia, Alabama, Tennessee, Kentucky, West Virginia, and Virginia as well as North Carolina. Much of this vast territory was hunting ground, but Cherokee villages lined the riverbanks of western North Carolina, eastern Tennessee, northern Georgia, and northwestern South Carolina. The Cherokees were agriculturalists long before the arrival of whites and blacks, but they practiced only subsistence farming. Restrained by a belief system which condemned producing more than was necessary for survival, these Cherokees made no attempt to farm on a commercial scale which might have demanded slave labor. Cherokee society was relatively egalitarian compared with European society and with some African societies; the only distinctions derived from superior knowledge or skill. European contact dramatically changed Cherokee society—its economy, its political structure, and its attitudes—and the transformation of Cherokee society profoundly affected black Appalachians.

The Cherokees encountered Africans at least as early as they did Europeans and may have seen blacks even before Spanish conquistadors visited their towns. When the black slaves in Lucas Vázquez de Ayllón's ill-fated colony on the Pedee River revolted in 1526, some of the rebels fled to the Indians, and it is at least possible that the Cherokees saw these Africans or their offspring. Black slaves later accompanied the Spanish expeditions of Fernando de Soto in 1540 and Juan Pardo in 1566. When de Soto's prize Indian prisoner, the Lady of Cofitachequi, escaped from the Spaniards, a black slave belonging to one of his officers accompanied her to Xuala, perhaps a Cherokee town, where they "lived together as man and wife." Although the initial reaction of Cherokees to Africans with their black skins is unknown, the cohabitation of the Lady of Cofitachequi and the Spaniard's black slave indicates that the Indians probably regarded Africans simply as other human beings who were either traversing or invading their territory. Since the concept of race did not exist among Indians and since the Cherokees nearly always encountered Africans in the company of Europeans, we may suppose that at first Cherokees equated the two and failed to distinguish sharply between the races.[1] Soon after their first contact with Africans, however, the Cherokees no doubt realized that Europeans regarded blacks as inferiors and that they themselves were in danger of being so regarded.

In the years following their initial meeting, the enslavement of Indians and their employment alongside African slaves produced extensive contact between the two peoples. The English colonists purchased their first cargo of Africans at about the same time that they began enslaving Indians, but blacks proved to be more desirable slaves than Indians.[2] Consequently, the Indian slave trade in the South reached its peak in the Yamassee war of 1715-1717 and declined steadily thereafter until United States policy in the postrevolutionary era formally ended the trade. Although early historians attributed the dwindling market for Indian captives and termination of the Indian slave trade to the racial and cultural unsuitability of Indians for forced labor,[3] contemporary accounts portrayed the Indian as a good worker. Brickell, for example, reported in his natural history that "some that are Slaves prove very industrious and laborious."[4] The demise of Indian bondage can probably be attributed to the fact that the African wrenched from his homeland with no opportunity to escape and return represented a better investment. Certainly the higher prices commanded by Africans reflect the planters' preference for them. Between 1722 and 1730, for example, an African slave brought as much as 333 pounds at the Charleston market, while no Indian sold for more than 250 pounds.[5]

While Indian slavery and the resultant warfare existed, Cherokees became acquainted with blacks not only through the experience of common bondage but also as warriors capturing black bondsmen. Antoine Bonnefoy, a Frenchman taken prisoner, reported the existence of black captives among the Cherokees. "We found also a negro and a negress who formerly belonged to the widow Saussier, and having been sold in 1739 to a Canadian deserted on the Quabache on their way to Canada, and were captured by a group of Cheraquis who brought them to the same village where I found them." Another account of the capture of blacks by Cherokees is that of David Menzies, whom the Cherokees seized along with the gang of slaves he was supervising, and in a similar episode Chief Bowl attacked a boat on the Tennessee River in 1794 and took twenty black slaves captive after having killed the thirteen whites on board.[6]

The Cherokees discovered that the capture of black slaves was particularly profitable, and by the American Revolution most Cherokees traded almost exclusively in black slaves. The Indians stole slaves from settlers in one location and sold them to planters living on another part of the frontier, rarely keeping black servants for their own use. Whether Cherokees abducted slaves or lured them away with the promise of freedom, the capture of Africans quickly replaced the capture of other Indians when the market for Indian slaves disappeared.

The most notorious Cherokee kidnapper of slaves was Chief Benge, one of the Chickamaugan warriors who refused to make peace with the Americans until 1794. On his last raid into southwest Virginia, Benge captured Susanna and Elizabeth Livingston and three black slaves and attempted to transport them back to northwest Alabama where the Chickamaugans resided. While on the trail Benge queried Elizabeth about the slaveholders who lived on the North

Holston River, particularly a General Shelby, and told the white women that he would "pay him a visit during the ensuing summer and take away all of his Negroes." On the third day after the raid, the Virginia militia attacked the abductors and killed Benge and most of his comrades. Colonel Arthur Campbell, the military officer of the area, wrote Governor Henry Lee of Virginia: "I send the scalp of Captain Benge, that noted murderer . . . to your excellency . . . as proof that he is no more." The death of Benge marked the end of such brash slave raids.[7]

Some Africans who came into the possession of the Indians were not captured but had instead sought refuge among the Cherokees, whose mountainous territory discouraged all except the most avid slave catchers. The treaty signed between the British and Cherokees in London in 1730 contained a provision for the return of these fugitives. "If any negroes shall run away into the woods from their English masters, the Cherokees shall endeavor to apprehend them and bring them to the plantation from which they ran away, or to the Governor, and for every slave so apprehended and brought back, the Indian that brings him shall receive a gun and a matchcoat."[8] In 1763 whites agreed to pay Indians one musket and three blankets, the equivalent of thirty-five deerskins, for each black slave captured and returned.[9]

The fear that runaways might establish maroon communities in the relative safety of the Cherokees' mountains motivated slaveholders to offer such lavish rewards for the recovery of their slaves. In 1725 a prominent South Carolina planter expressed concern that some slaves had become well acquainted with the language, the customs, and the hill country of the Cherokees. The possibility that slaves and Indians might join forces against the whites made the colonists shudder. In 1712, Alexander Spotswood of Virginia wrote the Board of Trade that he feared "the insurrection of our own Negroes and the Invasions of the Indians." The dread of such an alliance continued throughout the colonial period and gave rise to "law and order" political parties. John Stuart's North Carolina rivals, for example, successfully capitalized on this anxiety because, as Stuart pointed out in 1775, "nothing can be more alarming to the Carolinas than the idea of an attack from Indians and Negroes."[10] The fear of raids by maroons also partly shaped colonial Indian policy:

In our Quarrels with the *Indians,* however proper and necessary it may be to give them Correction, it can never be our interest to extirpate them, or to force them from their Lands: their Grounds would be soon taken up by runaway *Negroes* from our Settlements, whose Numbers would daily increase and quickly become more formidable Enemies than *Indians* can ever be, as they speak our Language and would never be at a Loss for Intelligence.[11]

This fear was not wholly unfounded, as the following deposition given in 1751 by Richard Smith, the white trader at Keewee, demonstrates:

Three runaway Negroes of Mr. Gray's told the Indians as they said that the white people were coming up to destroy them all, and that they had got some Creek Indians to assist them so to do. Which obtained belief and the more for that the old Warriors of Kewee said

some Negroes had applied to him, and told him that there was in all Plantations many Negroes more than white people, and that for the Sake of Liberty, they would join him.[12]

The colonists went to great lengths to prevent conspiracies of Indians and slaves. They soon discovered that the most effective way to accomplish their goals was to create suspicion, hatred, and hostility between the two peoples. The colonists not only employed Indians to find escaped slaves but also used blacks in military campaigns against Indians. In 1715 during the Yamassee war a company of black militiamen participated in the invasion of the Cherokee Nation and remained after other troops departed to assist the Cherokees in an attack against the Creeks. After the Yamassee war the colonists ceased using black soldiers, although the South Carolina General Assembly during the Cherokee war of 1760 defeated by only one vote a bill to arm 500 blacks. Nevertheless, slaves continued to contribute to the war effort in other ways, and more than 200 blacks served as wagoners and scouts for Colonel James Grant's expedition against the Cherokees in 1761.[13]

In another move to prevent the development of congenial relationships between Africans and Indians, the southern colonies enjoined whites from taking their slaves into Cherokee territory. Trade regulations imposed by both Georgia and South Carolina under various administrations almost always made it illegal for the traders to employ blacks in their dealings with the Indians.[14]

Stringent efforts to keep Africans and native Americans separate and hostile sometimes failed. When red and black men successfully resisted or overcame the misconception fostered by whites, they probably recognized certain cultural affinities between themselves. Both emphasized living harmoniously with nature and maintaining ritual purity; both attached great importance to kinship in their social organization; and both were accustomed to an economy based on subsistence agriculture.

African and Cherokee relationships to their environments reflected similar attitudes toward the physical world. The spiritual merged with the environmental. Common everyday activities, such as getting up in the morning, hunting, embarking on a journey, and particularly curing illness, assumed for both races a religious significance, and even topographical features were invested with religious meaning. Africans associated mountains and hills as well as caves and holes with spirits and divinities, while Cherokees viewed streams and rivers as roads to the underworld and "keep pools in the river and about lonely passes in the high mountains" as the haunts of the *Uktena,* a great serpent with supernatural powers.[15]

Just as in Cherokee society, kinship rather than economics ruled the lives of most Africans. Kinship groups governed marital customs and relationships between individuals, settled most disputes, and enabled individuals to exercise their personal rights. Kinship was also a major factor in shaping the nature of both indigenous West African slavery and aboriginal Cherokee bondage. A slave generally lacked kinship ties, and he therefore lacked the personal rights and claim to humanity which stemmed from kinship.[16]

Cherokees acted upon their assumptions about blacks, and when they founded their republic in 1827, the Cherokees excluded blacks from participa-

tion in the government. The founding fathers granted all adult males access to the ballot box except "negroes, and descendants of white and Indian men by negro women who may have been set free." The Constitution restricted officeholding to people untainted by African ancestry: "No person who is of negro or mulatto parentage, either by the father or mother side, shall be eligible to hold any office or trust under this Government." The Cherokees also sought to discourage free blacks from moving into the Nation and enacted a statute warning "that all free negroes coming into the Cherokee Nation under any pretence whatsoever, shall be viewed and treated, in every respect as intruders, and shall not be allowed to reside in the Cherokee Nation without a permit."[17]

By the time the Cherokees had established their republic, the use of black slaves on plantations had become a feature of their society. In part, the United States government was responsible for the introduction of plantation slavery. Following the Revolution, American Indian policy focused on the pacification and "civilization" of southern tribes. In compliance with the "civilization" program, Cherokees adopted the white man's implements and farming techniques, and individuals who had substantial capital to invest soon came to need extra hands. Because of the government's pacification policy, Cherokee planters could not satisfy their demand for labor by capturing members of their tribes, and few Cherokees worked for wages because the tribe's common ownership of land enabled every Indian to farm for himself. Therefore, the Cherokee upper class followed the example of its white mentors and began using African bondsmen. While most Cherokee masters owned fewer than ten slaves, and on the eve of removal, 92 percent of the Cherokees held no slaves at all, a few Cherokees developed extensive plantations in the broad valleys of eastern Tennessee, northeastern Alabama, and north Georgia. The most famous, Joseph Vann, lived in a magnificent red brick, white-columned mansion which still stands near Chatsworth, Georgia. He owned 110 slaves in 1835, cultivated 300 acres, and operated a ferry, steamboat, mill, and tavern.[18]

In the late 1830s, the United States government forced the Cherokees to relinquish the fertile valleys of their homeland and move west of the Mississippi River to what is today the state of Oklahoma. Many slaves accompanied their masters on this sorrowful migration, which has become known as the Trail of Tears. The only Cherokees who remained in the Southern Appalachians were those who lived along the Oconaluftee River high in the Smoky Mountains. And among those Cherokees lived at least one black slave. In the 1840s, Charles Lanman visited the North Carolina Cherokees and spoke with Cudjo, who had belonged to Chief Yonaguska, or "Drowning Bear," before his death. Cudjo told Lanman that Yonaguska "never allowed himself to be called master, for he said Cudjo was his brother, and not his slave."[19] Perhaps Yonaguska treated Cudjo as his brother because the mountainous region gave him no opportunity to exploit his slave.

Since removal, interaction between blacks and Indians in the southern Appalachians has been limited, but their experiences in some ways have been similar. Until recently, legal discrimination made both groups second-class citizens. For example, only in the 1950s did North Carolina repeal legislation prohibiting marriage between blacks or Indians and whites. Educational and

social discrimination affirmed this second-class status. Generally offered only
menial jobs at wages below those paid whites, blacks and Indians have also been
victims of economic discrimination. Indians, of course, had a land base, which
blacks lacked, but frequently the land served as an invitation or provocation to
further exploitation. Nevertheless, the Cherokees have continued to view themselves as radically different from blacks and their situation as significantly better
than that of blacks. Such an attitude is the legacy of three centuries of hostility
and fear. Perhaps if an atmosphere of cooperation and trust pervades the next
three centuries, a new legacy will come into being.

1. R. R. Wright, "Negro Companions of the Spanish Explorers," *American Anthropologist*,
4 (1902), 217-28; Edward Gaylord Bourne, ed., *Narratives of the Career of Hernando de Soto*, 2
vols. (New York, 1922), vol. 1, p. 72; Herbert Aptheker, *American Negro Slave Revolts* (New York,
1943), p. 163; Woodbury Lowery, *The Spanish Settlements within the Present Limits of the United
States, 1513-1561* (New York, 1911), pp. 165-67; Michael Roethler, "Negro Slavery among the
Cherokee Indians, 1540-1866" (Ph.D. diss., Fordham University, 1964), p. 16; Nancy O. Lurie,
"Indian Cultural Adjustment to European Civilization," in *Seventeenth-Century American: Essays
in Colonial History*, ed. James M. Smith (Chapel Hill, N.C., 1959), p. 16.
2. Almon W. Lauber, *Indian Slavery in Colonial Times within the Present Limits of the United
States* (New York, 1913), p. 118; Kenneth M. Stampp, *The Peculiar Institution: Slavery in the Ante-
Bellum South* (New York, 1956), p. 18.
3. Sanford Winston, "Indian Slavery in the Carolina Region," *Journal of Negro History*, 19
(Fall 1934), 437-38.
4. John Brickell, *The Natural History of North Carolina* (Dublin, 1737), p. 282.
5. Winston, "Indian Slavery," pp. 435-36; William R. Snell, "Indian Slavery in Colonial
South Carolina" (Ph.D. diss., University of Alabama, 1972), p. 144.
6. Samuel Cole Williams, *Early Travels in the Tennessee Country, 1540-1800* (Johnson City,
Tenn., 1928), p. 154; David Menzies, "A True Relation of the Unheard of Sufferings of David
Menzies, Surgeon, among the Cherokees, and of His Surprising Deliverance," *Royal Magazine*,
July 1761, p. 27; John Haywood, *The Civil and Political History of the State of Tennessee* (1823;
reprint ed., Knoxville, Tenn., 1969), pp. 321-22.
7. Luther F. Addington, "Chief Benge's Last Raid," *Historical Society of Southwest Virginia*,
2 (1966), 126.
8. Ibid., p. 190; Alexander Hewatt, *An Historical Account of the Rise and Progress of the
Colonies of South Carolina and Georgia, 1779*, 2 vols. (London, 1779), vol. 2, p. 8.
9. William S. Willis, Jr., "Divide and Rule: Red, White, and Black in the Southeast," in *Red,
White, and Black: Symposium on Indians in the Old South*, ed. Charles M. Hudson (Athens, Ga.,
1971).
10. William L. Saunders, ed., *The Colonial Records of North Carolina*, 10 vols. (Raleigh,
N.C., 1886-90), vol. 1, p. 886, vol. 10, p. 118; Gary B. Nash, *Red, White, and Black: The Peoples of
Early America* (Englewood Cliffs, N.J., 1974), p. 295.
11. George Milligan-Johnston, "A Short Description of the Province of South Carolina," in
Colonial South Carolina: Two Contemporary Descriptions, ed. Chapman J. Milling (Columbia,
S.C., 1951), p. 136.
12. William L. McDowell, *Documents, 1750-1754* (New York, 1958), p. 103; Nash, *Red,
White, and Black*, pp. 291-92.
13. Kenneth W. Porter, "Negroes on the Southern Frontier, 1670-1763," *Journal of Negro
History*, 33 (Spring 1948), 56-58; Willis, "Divide and Rule," p. 106.
14. McDowell, *Documents, 1750-1754*, pp. 88, 136, 199; John Richard Alden, *John Stuart
and the Southern Colonial Frontier, 1754-1775* (New York, 1944), pp. 19, 210; Mary U. Rothrock,
"Carolina Traders among the Overhill Traders, 1690-1760," *East Tennessee Historical Society
Publications*, 1 (1929), 3-18.

15. Charles Hudson, *The Southeastern Indians* (Knoxville, Tenn., 1976); James Mooney, *Myths of the Cherokee and Sacred Formulas of the Cherokees*, Seventh and Nineteenth Annual Reports of the Bureau of American Ethnology (reprint ed., Nashville, Tenn., 1972), pp. 240-51, 264, 270; John S. Mbiti, *African Religions and Philosophy* (New York, 1970), pp. 72, 80.

16. Mbiti, *African Religions*, pp. 135-38; John Grace, *Domestic Slavery in West Africa* (New York, 1975), p. 7.

17. *Cherokee Phoenix and Indians' Advocate*, Feb. 21, 1828, Apr. 13, 1828.

18. Theda Perdue, "Cherokee Planters: The Development of Plantation Slavery before Removal," in *The Cherokee Indian Nation: A Troubled History*, ed. Duane H. King (Knoxville, Tenn., 1979), pp. 110-28.

19. Charles Lanman, *Adventures in the Wilds of the United States and British American Provinces* (Philadelphia, 1856), p. 418.

4

Freedom and Slavery
in Appalachian America

CARTER G. WOODSON

To understand the problem of harmonizing freedom and slavery in Appalachian America we must keep in mind two different stocks coming in some cases from the same mother country and subject here to the same government. Why they differed so widely was due to their peculiar ideals formed prior to their emigration from Europe and to their environment in the New World. To the Tidewater came a class whose character and purposes, although not altogether alike, easily enabled them to develop into an aristocratic class. All of them were trying to lighten the burdens of life. In this section favored with fertile soil, mild climate, navigable streams and good harbors facilitating direct trade with Europe, the conservative, easy-going, wealth-seeking, exploiting adventurers finally fell back on the institution of slavery which furnished the basis for a large plantation system of seeming principalities. In the course of time too there arose in the few towns of the coast a number of prosperous business men whose bearing was equally as aristocratic as that of the masters of plantations.[1] These elements constituted the rustic nobility which lorded it over the unfortunate settlers whom the plantation system forced to go into the interior to take up land. Eliminating thus an enterprising middle class, the colonists tended to become more aristocratic near the shore.

In this congenial atmosphere the eastern people were content to dwell. The East had the West in mind and said much about its inexhaustible resources, but with the exception of obtaining there grants of land nothing definite toward the conquest of this section was done because of the handicap of slavery which precluded the possibility of a rapid expansion of the plantation group in the slave States. Separated by high ranges of mountains which prevented the unification of the interests of the sections, the West was left for conquest by a hardy race of European dissenters who were capable of a more rapid growth.[2] These were the Germans and Scotch-Irish with a sprinkling of Huguenots, Quakers and poor whites who had served their time as indentured servants in the East.[3] The unsettled condition of Europe during its devastating wars of the seventeenth and eighteenth centuries caused many of foreign stocks to seek homes in America where they hoped to realize political liberty and religious freedom. Many of these Germans first settled in the mountainous districts of Pennsylvania and Maryland and then migrated later to the lower part of the Shenandoah Valley, while the Scotch-Irish took possession of the upper part of that section.

Thereafter the Shenandoah Valley became a thoroughfare for a continuous movement of these immigrants toward the South into the uplands and mountains of the Carolinas, Georgia, Kentucky, and Tennessee.[4]

Among the Germans were Mennonites, Lutherans, and Moravians, all of whom believed in individual freedom, the divine right of secular power, and personal responsibility.[5] The strongest stocks among these immigrants, however, were the Scotch Irish, "a God-fearing, Sabbath-keeping, covenant-adhering, liberty-loving, and tyrant-hating race,"[6] which had formed its ideals under the influence of philosophy of John Calvin, John Knox, Andrew Melville, and George Buchanan. By these thinkers they had been taught to emphasize equality, freedom of conscience, and political liberty. These stocks differed somewhat from each other, but they were equally attached to practical religion, homely virtues, and democratic institutions.[7] Being a kind and beneficent class with a tenacity for the habits and customs of their fathers, they proved to be a valuable contribution to the American stock. As they had no riches every man was to be just what he could make himself. Equality and brotherly love became their dominant traits. Common feeling and similarity of ideals made them one people whose chief characteristic was individualism.[8] Differing thus so widely from the easterners they were regarded by the aristocrats as "Men of new blood" and "Wild Irish," who formed a barrier over which "none ventured to leap and would venture to settle among."[9] No aristocrat figuring conspicuously in the society of the East, where slavery made men socially unequal, could feel comfortable on the frontier, where freedom from competition with such labor prevented the development of caste.

The natural endowment of the West was so different from that of the East that the former did not attract the people who settled in the Tidewater. The mountaineers were in the midst of natural meadows, steep hills, narrow valleys of hilly soil, and inexhaustible forests. In the East tobacco and corn were the staple commodities. Cattle and hog raising became profitable west of the mountains, while various other employments which did not require so much vacant land were more popular near the sea. Besides, when the dwellers near the coast sought the cheap labor which the slave furnished, the mountaineers encouraged the influx of freemen. It is not strange then that we have no record of an early flourishing slave plantation beyond the mountains. Kercheval gives an account of a settlement by slaves and overseers on the large Carter grant situated on the west side of the Shenandoah, but it seems that the settlement did not prosper as such, for it soon passed into the hands of the Burwells and the Pages.[10]

The rise of slavery in the Tidewater section, however, established the going of those settlers in the direction of government for the people. The East began with indentured servants but soon found the system of slavery more profitable. It was not long before the blacks constituted the masses of the laboring population,[11] while on the expiration of their term of service the indentured servants went West and helped to democratize the frontier. Caste too was secured by the peculiar land tenure of the East. The king and the proprietors granted land for small sums on feudal terms. The grantees in their turn settled these holdings in fee tail on the oldest son in accordance with the law of primogeniture. This produced a class described by Jefferson, who said: "There were then aristocrats, half-breeds, pretenders, a solid independent yeomanry, looking askance at those above, yet not venturing to jostle them, and last and lowest, a seculum of beings called overseers, the most abject, degraded and unprincipled race, always cap in hand to the Dons who employed them for furnishing material for the exercise of their price."[12]

In the course of colonial development the people of the mountains were usually referred to as frontiersmen dwelling in the West. This "West" was for a number of years known as the region beyond the Blue Ridge Mountains and later beyond the Alleghanies. A more satisfactory dividing line, however, is the historical line of demarcation between the East and West which moved toward the mountains in the proportion that the western section became connected with the East and indoctrinated by its proslavery propagandists. In none of these parts, however, not even far south, were the eastern people able to bring the frontiersmen altogether around to their way of thinking. Their ideals and environment caused them to have differing opinions as to the extent, character, and foundations of local self-government, differing conceptions of the meaning of representative institutions, differing ideas of the magnitude of governmental power over the individual, and differing theories of the relations of church and State. The East having accepted caste as the basis of its society naturally adopted the policy of government by a favorite minority, the West inclined more and more toward democracy. The latter considered representatives only those who had been elected as such by a majority of the people of the district in which they lived; the former believed in a more restricted electorate, and the representation of districts and interests, rather than that of numbers.[13] Furthermore, almost from the founding of the colonies there was a court party consisting of the rich planters and favorites composing the coterie of royal officials generally opposed by a country party of men who, either denied certain privileges or unaccustomed to participation in the affairs of privileged classes, felt that the interests of the lowly were different. As the frontier moved westward the line of cleavage tended to become identical with that between the privileged classes and the small farmers, between the lowlanders and the uplanders, between capital and labor, and finally between the East and West.

The frontiersmen did not long delay in translating some of their political theories into action. The aristocratic East could not do things to suit the mountaineers who were struggling to get the government nearer to them. At times, therefore, their endeavors to abolish government for the people resulted in violent frontier uprisings like that of Bacon's Rebellion in Virginia and the War of Regulation in North Carolina. In all of these cases the cause was practically the same. These pioneers had observed with jealous eye the policy which bestowed all political honors on the descendants of a few wealthy families living upon the tide or along the banks of the larger streams. They were therefore, inclined to advance with quick pace toward revolution.[14] On finding such leaders as James Otis, Patrick Henry and Thomas Jefferson, the frontiersmen instituted such a movement in behalf of freedom that it resulted in the Revolutionary War.[15] These patriots' advocacy of freedom, too, was not half-hearted. When they demanded liberty for the colonists they spoke also for the slaves, so emphasizing the necessity for abolition that observers from afar thought that the institution would of itself soon pass away.[16]

In the reorganization of the governments necessitated by the overthrow of the British, however, the frontiersmen were unfortunate in that they lacked constructive leadership adequate to having their ideas incorporated into the new constitutions. Availing themselves of their opportunity, the aristocrats of the coast fortified themselves in their advantageous position by establishing State governments based on the representation of interests, the restriction of suffrage, and the ineligibility of the poor to office.[17] Moreover, efforts were made even to continue in a different form the Established Church against which the dissenting frontiersmen had fought for more than a century. In the other Atlantic States where such distinctions were not made in framing their constitutions, the conservatives resorted to other schemes to keep the power in the hands of the rich planters near the sea. When the Appalachian Americans awoke to the situation then they were against a stone wall. The so-called rights of man were subjected to restrictions which in our day could not exist. The right to hold office and to vote were not dependent upon manhood qualifications but on a white skin, religious opinions, the payment of taxes, and wealth. In South Carolina a person desiring to vote must believe in the existence of a God, in a future state of reward and punishment, and have a freehold of fifty acres of land. In Virginia the right of suffrage was restricted to freeholders possessing one hundred acres of land. Senators in North Carolina had to own three hundred acres of land; representatives in South Carolina were required to have a 500 acre freehold and 10 Negroes; and in Georgia 250 acres and support the Protestant religion.[18] In all of these slave States, suffering from such unpopular government, the mountaineers developed into a reform party persistently demanding that the sense of the people be taken on the question of calling together their representatives to remove certain defects from the constitutions. It was the contest between the aristocrats and the progressive westerner. The aristocrats' idea of government was developed from the "English Scion—the liberty of kings, lords, and commons, with different grades of society acting independently of all foreign powers." The ideals of the westerner were principally those of the Scotch-Irish, working for "civil liberty in fee simple, and an open road to civil honors, secured to the poorest and feeblest members of society."[19]

The eastern planters, of course, regarded this as an attack on their system and fearlessly denounced these rebellious wild men of the hills. In taking this position, these conservatives brought down upon their heads all of the ire that the frontiersmen had felt for the British prior to the American Revolution. The easterners were regarded in the mountains as a party bent upon establishing in this country a régime equally as oppressive as the British government. The frontiersmen saw in slavery the cause of the whole trouble. They, therefore, hated the institution and endeavored more than ever to keep their section open to free labor. They hated the slave as such, not as a man. On the early southern frontier there was more prejudice against the slave holder than against the Negro.[20] There was the feeling that this was not a country for a laboring class so undeveloped as the African slaves, then being brought to these shores to serve as a basis for a government differing radically from that in quest of which the frontiersmen had left their homes in Europe.

This struggle reached its climax in different States at various periods. In Maryland the contest differed somewhat from that of other Southern States because of the contiguity of that commonwealth with Pennsylvania, which early set such examples of abolition and democratic government that a slave State nearby could not go so far in fortifying an aristocratic governing class. In Virginia the situation was much more critical than elsewhere. Unlike the other Atlantic States, which wisely provided roads and canals to unify the diverse interests of the sections, that commonwealth left the trans-Alleghany district to continue in its own way as a center of insurgency from which war was waged against the established order of things.[21] In most States, however, the contest was decided by the invention of the cotton gin and other mechanical appliances which, in effecting an industrial revolution throughout the world, gave rise to the plantation system found profitable to supply the increasing demand for cotton. In the course of the subsequent expansion of slavery, many of the uplanders and mountaineers were gradually won to the support of that institution. Realizing gradually a community of interests with the eastern planters, their ill-feeling against them tended to diminish. Abolition societies which had once flourished among the whites of the uplands tended to decline and by 1840 there were practically no abolitionists in the South living east of the Appalachian Mountains.[22]

Virginia, which showed signs of discord longer than the other Atlantic States, furnishes us a good example of how it worked out. The reform party of the West finally forced the call of a convention in 1829, hoping in vain to crush the aristocracy. Defeated in this first battle with the conservatives, they secured the call of the Reform Convention in 1850 only to find that two thirds of the State had become permanently attached to the cause of maintaining slavery.[23] Samuel McDowell Moore, of Rockbridge County in the Valley, said in the Convention of 1829-30 that slaves should be free to enjoy their natural rights,[24] but a generation later the people of that section would not have justified such an utterance in behalf of freedom. The uplanders of South Carolina were early satisfied with such changes as were made in the apportionment of representation in 1808, and in the qualifications of voters in 1810.[25] Thereafter Calhoun's party, proceeding on the theory of government by a concurrent majority, vanquished what few liberal-minded men remained, and then proceeded to force their policy on the whole country.

In the Appalachian Mountains, however, the settlers were loath to follow the fortunes of the ardent pro-slavery element. Actual abolition was never popular in western Virginia, but the love of the people of that section for freedom kept them estranged from the slaveholding districts of the State, which by 1850 had completely committed themselves to the pro-slavery propaganda. In the Convention of 1829-30 Upshur said there existed in a great portion of the West (of Virginia) a rooted antipathy to the slave.[26] John Randolph was alarmed at the fanatical spirit on the subject of slavery, which was growing up in Virginia. Some of this sentiment continued in the mountains. The highlanders, therefore, found themselves involved in a continuous embroglio because they were not moved by reactionary influences which were unifying the South for its bold effort to make slavery a national institution.[27]

The indoctrination of the backwoodsmen of North Carolina in the tenets of slavery was effected without much difficulty because of less impediment in the natural barriers, but a small proportion of the inhabitants of the state residing in the mountainous districts continued anti-slavery. There was an unusually strong anti-slavery element in Davie, Davidson, Granville, and Guilford counties. The efforts of this liberal group, too, were not long in taking organized form. While there were several local organizations operating in various parts, the efforts of the anti-slavery people centered around the North Carolina Manumission Society. It had over forty branches at one time, besides several associations of women, all extending into seven or eight of the most populous counties of the State. This society denounced the importation and exportation of slaves, and favored providing for manumissions, legalizing slave contracts for the purchase of freedom, and enacting a law that at a certain age all persons should be born free.[28] That these reformers had considerable influence is evidenced by the fact that in 1826 a member of the manumission society was elected to the State Senate. In 1824 and 1826 two thousand slaves were freed in North Carolina.[29] Among the distinguished men who at times supported this movement in various ways were Hinton Rowan Helper, Benjamin S. Hedrick, Daniel R. Goodloe, Eli W. Caruthers, and Lunsford Lane, a colored orator and lecturer of considerable ability.[30] They constituted a hopeless minority, however, for the liberal element saw their hopes completely blasted in the triumph of the slave party in the Convention of 1835, which made everything subservient to the institution of slavery.

In the mountains of Kentucky and Tennessee conditions were a little more encouraging, especially between 1817 and 1830. The anti-slavery work in Kentucky seemed to owe its beginning to certain emancipating Baptists. Early in the history of that State six Baptist preachers, Carter Tarrant, David Darrow, John Sutton, Donald Holmes, Jacob Gregg, and George Smith, began an anti-slavery campaign, maintaining that there should be no fellowship with slaveholders.[31] They were unable to effect much, however, because of the fact that they had no extensive organization through which to extend their efforts. Every church remained free to decide for itself and even in Northern States the Baptists later winked at slavery. More effective than these efforts of the Baptists was the work of the Scotch-Irish. Led by David Rice, a minister of the Presbyterian Church, the anti-slavery element tried to exclude slavery from the State when framing its first constitution in the Convention of 1792.[32] Another effort thus to amend the fundamental law was made at the session of the legislature of 1797-98, and had it not been for the excitement aroused by the Alien and Sedition Laws the bill probably would have passed.[33]

Many successful efforts were made through the anti-slavery bodies. The society known as "Friends of Humanity" was organized in Kentucky in 1807. It had a constitution signed by eleven preachers and thirteen laymen. The organization was in existence as late as 1813. The records of the abolitionists show that there was another such society near Frankfort between 1809 and 1823.[34] Birney then appeared in the State and gave his influence to the cause with a view to promoting the exportation of Negroes to Liberia.[35] A number of citizens also memorialized Congress to colonize the Negroes on the public lands in the West.[36] In the later twenties an effort was made to unite the endeavors of many

wealthy and influential persons who were then interested in promoting abolition. Lacking a vigorous and forceful leader they appealed to Henry Clay, who
refused.[37] They fought on, however, for years to come. A contributor to the
Western Luminary said, in 1830, that the people of Kentucky were finding
slavery a burden.[38] Evidently a good many of them had come to this conclusion,
for a bill providing for the emancipation introduced in the Legislature was
postponed indefinitely by a vote of 18 to 11.[39] So favorable were conditions in
Kentucky at this time that it was said that Tennessee was watching Kentucky
with the expectation of following her lead should the latter become a free State
as was then expected.

The main factor in promoting the work in Tennessee was, as in Kentucky,
the Scotch-Irish Presbyterian stock. They opposed slavery in word and in deed,
purchasing and setting free a number of colored men. Among these liberal
westerners was organized the "Manumission Society of Tennessee," represented for years in the American Convention of Abolition Societies by Benjamin Lundy.[40] The Tennessee organization once had twenty branches and a
membership of six hundred.[41] Among its promoters were Charles Osborn,
Elihu Swain, John Underhill, Jesse Willis, John Cannady, John Swain, David
Maulsby, John Rankin, Jesse Lockhart, and John Morgan.[42] They advocated at
first immediate and unconditional emancipation, but soon seeing that the
realization of this policy was impossible, they receded from this advanced
position and memorialized their representatives to provide for gradual emancipation, the abolition of slavery in the District of Columbia, the prevention of
the separation of families, the prohibition of the interstate slave trade, the
restriction of slavery, the general improvement of colored people through church
and school, and especially the establishment among them of the right of
marriage.[43] To procure the abolition of slavery by argument, other persons of
this section organized another body, known as the "Moral Religious Manumission Society of West Tennessee."[44] It once had a large membership and tended
to increase and spread the agitation in behalf of abolition.

In view of these favorable tendencies, it was thought up to 1830 that
Tennessee, following the lead of Kentucky, would become a free State.[45] But
just as the expansion of slavery into the interior of the Atlantic States attached
those districts to the fortunes of the slaveholding class, it happened in some
cases in the mountains which to some extent became indoctrinated by the
teaching of the defenders of slavery. Then the ardent slavery debate in Congress
and the bold agitation like that of the immediatists led by William Lloyd
Garrison, alienated the support which some mountaineers had willingly given
the cause. Abolition in these States, therefore, began to weaken and rapidly
declined during the thirties.[46] Because of a heterogeneous membership, these
organizations tended to develop into other societies representing differing ideas
of anti-slavery factions which had at times made it impossible for them to
coöperate effectively in carrying out any plan. The slaveholders who had been
members formed branches of the American Colonization Society, while the
radical element fell back upon organizing branches of the Underground Railroad to coöperate with those of their number who, seeing that it was impossible
to attain their end in the Southern mountains, had moved into the Northwest

Territory to colonize the freedmen and aid the escape of slaves.[47] Among these workers who had thus changed their base of operation were not only such noted men as Joshua Coffin, Benjamin Lundy, and James G. Birney, but less distinguished workers like John Rankin, of Ripley; James Gilliland, of Red Oak; Jesse Lockhart, of Russellville; Robert Dobbins, of Sardinia; Samuel Crothers, of Greenfield; Hugh L. Fullerton, of Chillicothe, and William Dickey, of Ross or Fayette County, Ohio. There were other southern abolitionists who settled and established stations of the Underground Railroad in Bond, Putnam, and Bureau counties, Illinois.[48] The Underground Railroad was thus enabled to extend into the heart of the South by way of the Cumberland Mountains. Over this Ohio and Kentucky route, culminating chiefly in Cleveland, Sandusky, and Detroit, more fugitives found their way to freedom than over any other route.[49] The limestone caves were of much assistance to them. The operation of the system extended through Tennessee into northern Georgia and Alabama, following the Appalachian highland as it juts like a peninsula into the South. Dillingham, John Brown, and Harriet Tubman used these routes.

Let us consider, then, the attitude of these mountaineers toward slaves. All of them were not abolitionists. Some slavery existed among them. The attack on the institution, then, in these parts was not altogether opposition to an institution foreign to the mountaineers. The frontiersmen hated slavery, hated the slave as such, but, as we have observed above, hated the eastern planter worse than they hated the slave. As there was a scarcity of slaves in that country they generally dwelt at home with their masters. Slavery among these liberal people, therefore, continued patriarchal and so desirous were they that the institution should remain such that they favored the admission of the State of Missouri as a slave State,[50] not to promote slavery but to expand it that each master, having a smaller number of Negroes, might keep them in close and helpful contact. Consistently with this policy many of the frontier Baptists, Scotch-Irish and Methodists continued to emphasize the education of the blacks as the correlative of emancipation. They urged the masters to give their servants all proper advantages for acquiring knowledge of their duty both to man and to God. In large towns slaves were permitted to acquire the rudiments of education and in some of them free persons of color had well-regulated schools.[51]

Two noteworthy efforts to educate Negroes were put forth in these parts. A number of persons united in 1825 to found an institution for the education of eight or ten Negro slaves with their families to be operated under the direction of the "Emancipating Labor Society of the State of Kentucky." About the same time Frances Wright was endeavoring to establish an institution on the same order to improve the free blacks and mulattoes in West Tennessee. It seems that this movement had the support of a goodly number of persons, including George Fowler, and, it was said, Lafayette, who had always been regarded as a friend of emancipation. According to a letter from a clergyman of South Carolina, the first slave for this institution went from the York district of that State. Exactly what these enterprises were, however, it is difficult to determine. They were not well supported and soon passed from public notice. Some have said that the Tennessee project was a money-making scheme for the proprietors, and that the Negroes taught there were in reality slaves. Others have defended the work as a philanthropic effort so characteristic of the friends of freedom in Appalachian America.[52]

The people of eastern Tennessee were largely in favor of Negro education. Around Maryville and Knoxville were found a considerable number of white persons who were thus interested in the uplift of the belated race. Well might such efforts be expected in Maryville, for the school of theology at this place had gradually become so radical that according to the *Maryville Intelligencer* half of the students by 1841 declared their adherence to the cause of abolition.[53] Consequently, they hoped not only to see such doctrines triumph within the walls of that institution, but were endeavoring to enlighten the Negroes of that community to prepare them for the enjoyment of life as citizens in their own or some other country.[54]

Just as the people of Maryville had expressed themselves through *The Intelligencer,* so did those of Knoxville find a spokesman in *The Presbyterian Witness*. Excoriating those who had for centuries been finding excuses for keeping the slaves in heathenism, the editor of this publication said that there was not a solitary argument that might be urged in favor of teaching a white man that might not be as properly urged in favor of enlightening a man of color. "If one has a soul that will never die," said he, "so has the other. Has one susceptibilities of improvement, mentally, socially, and morally? So has the other. Is one bound by the laws of God to improve the talents he has received from the Creator's hands? So is the other. Is one embraced in the commands [to] search the scriptures? So is the other."[55] He maintained that unless masters could lawfully degrade their slaves to the condition of beasts, they were just as much bound to teach them to read the Bible as to teach any other class of their population.

From a group in Kentucky came another helpful movement. Desiring to train up white men who would eventually be able to do a work which public sentiment then prevented the anti-slavery minority from carrying on, the liberal element of Kentucky, under the leadership of John G. Fee and his co-workers, established Berea College. Believing in the brotherhood of man and the fatherhood of God, this institution incorporated into its charter the bold declaration that "God hath made of one blood all nations that dwell upon the face of the earth." This profession was not really put to a test until after the Civil War, when the institution courageously met the issue by accepting as students some colored soldiers who were returning home wearing their uniforms.[56] The State has since prohibited the co-education of the races.

With so many sympathizers of the oppressed in the back country, the South had much difficulty in holding the mountaineers in line to force upon the whole nation their policies, mainly determined by their desire for the continuation of slavery. Many of the mountaineers accordingly deserted the South in its opposition to the tariff and internal improvements, and when that section saw that it had failed in economic competition with the North, and realized that it had to leave the Union soon or never, the mountaineers who had become commercially attached to the North and West boldly adhered to these sections to maintain the Union. The highlanders of North Carolina were finally reduced to secession with great difficulty; eastern Tennessee had to yield, but kept the State almost divided between the two causes; timely dominated by Unionists with the support of troops, Kentucky stood firm; and to continue attached to the federal government forty-eight western counties of Virginia severed their connection with the essentially slaveholding district and formed the loyal State of West Virginia.

In the mountainous region the public mind has been largely that of people who have developed on free soil. They have always differed from the dwellers in the district near the sea not only in their attitude toward slavery but in the policy they have followed in dealing with the blacks since the Civil War. One can observe even to-day such a difference in the atmosphere of the two sections, that in passing from the tidewater to the mountains it seems like going from one country into another. There is still in the back country, of course, much of that lawlessness which shames the South, but crime in that section is not peculiarly the persecution of the Negro. Almost any one considered undesirable is dealt with unceremoniously. In Appalachian America the races still maintain a sort of social contact. White and black men work side by side, visit each other in their homes, and often attend the same church to listen with delight to the Word spoken by either a colored or white preacher.

Note: It has proven impossible to verify and complete some of the notes to this chapter, and they appear here approximately as they were originally published.

1. Thomas Jefferson Wertenbaker, *Patrician and Plebeian in Virginia; or, The Origin and Development of the Social Classes of the Old Dominion* (1910), p. 31.

2. Exactly how many of each race settled in the Appalachian region we cannot tell, but we know that they came in large numbers, after the year 1735. A few important facts and names may give some idea as to the extent of this immigration. The Shenandoah Valley attracted many. Most prominent among those who were instrumental in settling the Valley was the Scotchman, John Lewis, the ancestor of so many families of the mountains. The Dutchmen, John and Isaac Van Meter, were among the first to buy land from Joist Hite, probably the first settler in the Valley. Among other adventurers of this frontier were Benjamin Allen, Riley Moore, and William White, of Maryland, who settled in the Shenandoah in 1734; Robert Harper and others who, in the same year, settled Richard Morgan's grant near Harper's Ferry; and Howard, Walker, and Rutledge, who took up land on what became the Fairfax Manor on the South Branch. In 1738 some Quakers came from Pennsylvania to occupy the Ross Survey of 40,000 acres near Winchester Farm in what is now Frederick County, Va. In the following year John and James Lindsay reached Long Marsh, and Isaac Larne of New Jersey the same district about the same time; while Joseph Carter of Bucks County, Pa., built his cabin on the Oprequon near Winchester in 1743, and Joseph Hampton with his two sons came from Maryland to Buck Marsh near Berryville. But it is a more important fact that Burden, a Scotch-Irishman, obtained a large grant of land and settled it with hundreds of his race during the period from 1736 to 1743, and employed an agent to continue the work. With Burden came the McDowells, Alexanders, Campbells, McClungs, McCampbells, McCowans and McKees, Prestons, Browns, Wallaces, Wilsons, McCues, and Caruthers. They settled the upper waters of the Shenandoah and the James, while the Germans had by this time well covered the territory between what is known as Harrisonburg and the present site of Harper's Ferry. See Maury, "Physical Survey," 42; *Virginia Magazine,* 9 (1856), 337-52; *Washington's Journal,* pp. 47-48; Wayland, "German Element of the Shenandoah," p. 110.

3. Wayland, "German Element of the Shenandoah," pp. 28-30; *Virginia Historical Register* (Richmond, Va., 1850), vol. 3, p. 10.

4. See Meade, "Old Families of Virginia," *Transalleghany Historical Magazine,* 1 and 2; De Hass, "The Settlement of Western Virginia," pp. 71, 75; Samuel Kercheval, "History of the Valley," pp. 61-71; Faust, "The German Element in the United States."

5. Dunning, "The History of Political Theory from Luther to Montesquieu," 9, 10.

[6. Missing.]

7. George Buchanan, the most literary of these reformers, insisted that society originates in the effort of men to escape from the primordial state of nature, that in a society thus formed the essential to well-being is justice, that justice is maintained by laws rather than by kings, that the maker of the laws is the people, and that the interpreter of the laws is not the king, but the body of judges chosen by the people. He reduced the power of the ruler to the minimum, the only power assigned to him being to maintain the morals of the state by making his life a model of virtuous living. The reformer claimed, too, that when the ruler exceeds his power he becomes a tyrant, and that people are justified in rejecting the doctrine of passive obedience and slaying him. See *The Powers of the Crown in Scotland: Being a Translation with Notes and an Introductory Essay of George Buchanan's "De Jure Regni Apud Scotos,"* trans. C. H. Arrowood (Austin, Tex., 1949); Dunning, "History of Political Theory from Luther to Montesquieu"; and P. Hume Brown, *John Knox: A Biography* (London, 1895).

8. Just how much the racial characteristics had to do with making this wilderness a center of democracy, it is difficult to estimate. Some would contend that although the Western people were of races different from this aristocratic element of the East, their own history shows that this had little to do with the estrangement of the West from the East, and that the fact that many persons of these same stocks who settled in the East became identified with the interests of that section is sufficient evidence to prove what an insignificant factor racial characteristics are. But although environment proves itself here to be the important factor in the development of these people and we are compelled to concede that the frontier made the Western man an advocate of republican principles, heredity must not be ignored altogether.

Exactly how much influence the Scotch-Irish had in shaping the destiny of Appalachian America is another much mooted question with which we are concerned here because historians give almost all the credit to this race. Even an authority like Justin Winsor leaves the impression that Virginia cared little for the frontier, and that all honor is due to the Scotch-Irish. Their influence in shaping the destiny of other States has been equally emphasized. The facts collected by Hanna doubtless give much support to the claims of that people to the honor for the development of Appalachian America. His conclusions, however, are rather far-sweeping and often shade into imagination. On the other hand, a good argument may be made to prove that other people, such as the Germans and Dutch, deserve equal honor. Furthermore, few of the eulogists of the Scotch-Irish take into account the number of indentured servants and poor whites who moved westward with the frontier. Besides, it must not be thought that the East neglected the frontier intentionally simply because the Tidewater people could not early subdue the wilderness. They did much to develop it. The records of the time of the Indian troubles beginning in 1793 show that the State governments answered the call for troops and ammunition as promptly as they could, and their statute books show numerous laws which were enacted in the interest of the West during these troubles. The truth of the matter is that, whatever might have been the desire of the East to conquer the wilderness, the sectionalizing institution of slavery which the colony had accepted as the basis of its society rendered the accomplishment of such an object impossible. There was too great diversity of interest in that region.

9. Jefferson's Works, vol. 6, p. 484.

10. Kercheval, "History of the Valley," pp. 47 and 48.

11. It soon became evident that it was better to invest in slaves, who had much more difficulty than the indentured servants in escaping and passing as freemen.

12. Jefferson's Works, vol. 6, p. 484.

13. This statement is based on the provisions of the first State constitutions. See Thorpe's "Charters and Constitutions."

14. Grigsby, "Convention of 1788," pp. 15, 49.

15. The people living near the coast desired reform under British rule. The frontiersmen had to win them to the movement. A certain Scotch-Irish element in the Carolinas was an exception to this rule in that they at first supported the British.

16. The letters and speeches of most of the revolutionary leaders show that they favored some kind of abolition. Among the most outspoken were James Otis, John Adams, Alexander Hamilton, Thomas Jefferson, and John Laurens. See also Schoepf, "Travels in the Confederation," 149; and Brissot de Warville, "New Travels," [indecipherable].

17. See the various State constitutions in Thorpe's "Charters and Constitutions."

18. Ibid.

19. Foote, "Sketches of Virginia," p. 85.

20. Hart, "Slavery and Abolition," p. 73; Olmsted, "The Back Country," pp. 230-32; *Berea Quarterly,* 9, no. 3.

21. See the Speeches of the Western members of the Virginia Convention of 1829-30, *Proceedings and Debates of the Convention of 1829-30.*

22. This is proved by the reports and records of the anti-slavery societies and especially by those of the American Convention of Abolition Societies. During the thirties and forties the southern societies ceased to make reports. See Adams, "The Neglected Period of Anti-Slavery in America," p. 117.

23. The vote on the aristocratic constitution framed in 1829-30 shows this. See *Proceedings and Debates of the Convention of 1829-30,* p. 903.

24. *Proceedings and Debates of the Convention of 1829-30,* p. 226.

25. Thorpe, "Charters and Constitutions, South Carolina."

26. *Proceedings and Debates of the Convention of 1829-30,* pp. 53, 76, 442, 858.

27. See Calhoun's Works: "A Disquisition on Government," pp. 1 et seq.

28. Adams, "Neglected Period of Anti-Slavery," p. 138.

29. Ibid., p. 34.

30. Bassett, "Anti-Slavery Leaders of North Carolina," p. 72.

31. Adams, Neglected Period of "Anti-Slavery," pp. 100-101.

32. Speech of David Rice in the Constitutional Convention of Kentucky, 1792.

33. Birney, "James G. Birney," pp. 96-100.

34. Reports of the American Convention of Abolition Societies, 1809 and 1823.

35. Birney, "James G. Birney," p. 70.

36. Adams, "Neglected Period of Anti-Slavery," pp. 129-30. *Annals of Congress,* 17th Cong., 1st sess., 2d sess., 18th Cong., 1st sess.

37. Ibid., p. 20.

38. "The Genius of Universal Emancipation," vol. 11, p. 35.

39. Ibid., vol. 10, p. 145.

40. See *Proceedings of the American Convention of Abolition Societies.*

41. Adams, "Neglected Period of Anti-Slavery," p. 132.

42. Ibid., p. 131.

43. "The Genius of Universal Emancipation," vol. 1, p. 142; vol. 5, p. 409.

44. "The Genius of Universal Emancipation," vol. 4, pp. 76, 142; Birney, "James G. Birney," p. 77; Minutes of the American Convention of Abolition Societies, 1826, p. 48.

45. "The Genius of Universal Emancipation," vol. 11, pp. 65, 66.

46. See *The Minutes and Proceedings of the American Convention of Abolition Societies,* covering this period.

47. This statement is based on the accounts of a number of abolitionists.

48. Adams, "Neglected Period of Anti-Slavery," pp. 60, 61.

49. Siebert, "The Underground Railroad," vol. 10, p. 346.

50. Ambler, "Sectionalism in Virginia," pp. 107-108.

51. Woodson, "The Education of the Negro," pp. 120-21.

52. "The Genius of Universal Emancipation," vol. 5, pp. 117, 126, 164, 188, 275, 301, 324, 365; vol. 6, pp. 21, 140, 177.

53. *Fourth Annual Report of the American Anti-Slavery Society, 1837,* p. 48; *The New England Anti-Slavery Almanac for 1841,* p. 31.

54. Ibid.

55. *The African Repository,* vol. 32, p. 16.

56. *Catalogue of Berea College,* 1897.

5

Boyhood Days

BOOKER T. WASHINGTON

After the coming of freedom there were two points upon which practically all the people on our place were agreed, and I find that this was generally true throughout the South: that they must change their names, and that they must leave the old plantation for at least a few days or weeks in order that they might really feel sure that they were free.

In some way a feeling got among the coloured people that it was far from proper for them to bear the surname of their former owners, and a great many of them took other surnames. This was one of the first signs of freedom. When they were slaves, a coloured person was simply called "John" or "Susan." There was seldom occasion for more than the use of one name. If "John" or "Susan" belonged to a white man by the name of "Hatcher," sometimes he was called "John Hatcher," or as often "Hatcher's John." But there was a feeling that "John Hatcher" or "Hatcher's John" was not the proper title by which to denote a freeman; and so in many cases "John Hatcher" was changed to "John S. Lincoln" or "John S. Sherman," the initial "S" standing for no name, it being simply a part of what the coloured man proudly called his "entitles."

As I have stated, most of the coloured people left the old plantation for a short while at least, so as to be sure, it seemed, that they could leave and try their freedom on to see how it felt. After they had remained away for a time, many of the older slaves, especially, returned to their old homes and made some kind of contract with their former owners by which they remained on the estate.

My mother's husband, who was the stepfather of my brother John and myself, did not belong to the same owners as did my mother. In fact, he seldom came to our plantation. I remember seeing him there perhaps once a year, that being about Christmas time. In some way, during the war, by running away and following the Federal soldiers, it seems, he found his way into the new state of West Virginia. As soon as freedom was declared, he sent for my mother to come to the Kanawha Valley, in West Virginia. At that time a journey from Virginia over the mountains to West Virginia was rather a tedious and in some cases a painful undertaking. What little clothing and few household goods we had were placed in a cart, but the children walked the greater portion of the distance, which was several hundred miles.

I do not think any of us ever had been very far from the plantation, and the taking of a long journey into another state was quite an event. The parting from our former owners and the members of our own race on the plantation was a serious occasion. From the time of our parting till their death we kept up a correspondence with the older members of the family, and in later years we have kept in touch with those who were the younger members. We were several weeks making the trip, and most of the time we slept in the open air and did our cooking over a log fire out of doors. One night I recall that we camped near an abandoned log cabin, and my mother decided to build a fire in that for cooking, and afterward to make a "pallet" on the floor for our sleeping. Just as the fire had gotten well started a large black snake fully a yard and a half long drooped down the chimney and ran out on the floor. Of course we at once abandoned that cabin. Finally we reached our destination—a little town called Malden, which is about five miles from Charleston, the present capital of the state.

At that time salt-mining was the great industry in that part of West Virginia, and the little town of Malden was right in the midst of the salt-furnaces. My stepfather had already secured a job at a salt-furnace, and he had also secured a little cabin for us to live in. Our new house was no better than the one we had left on the old plantation in Virginia. In fact, in one respect it was worse. Notwithstanding the poor condition of our plantation cabin, we were at all times sure of pure air. Our new home was in the midst of a cluster of cabins crowded closely together, and as there were no sanitary regulations, the filth about the cabins was often intolerable. Some of our neighbours were coloured people, and some were the poorest and most ignorant and degraded white people. It was a motley mixture. Drinking, gambling, quarrels, fights, and shockingly immoral practices were frequent. All who lived in the little town were in one way or another connected with the salt business. Though I was a mere child, my stepfather put me and my brother at work in one of the furnaces. Often I began work as early as four o'clock in the morning.

The first thing I ever learned in the way of book knowledge was while working in this salt-furnace. Each salt-packer had his barrels marked with a certain number. The number allotted to my stepfather was "18." At the close of the day's work the boss of the packers would come around and put "18" on each of our barrels, and I soon learned to recognize that figure wherever I saw it, and after a while got to the point where I could make that figure, though I knew nothing about any other figures or letters.

From the time that I can remember having any thoughts about anything, I recall that I had an intense longing to learn to read. I determined, when quite a small child, that, if I accomplished nothing else in life, I would in some way get enough education to enable me to read common books and newspapers. Soon after we got settled in some manner in our new cabin in West Virginia, I induced my mother to get hold of a book for me. How or where she got it I do not know, but in some way she procured an old copy of Webster's "blue-back" spelling-book, which contained the alphabet, followed by such meaningless words as "ab," "ba," "ca," "da." I began at once to devour this book, and I think that it was the first one I ever had in my hands. I had learned from somebody that the way to begin to read was to learn the alphabet, so I tried in all the ways I could think of to learn it—all of course without a teacher, for I could find no one to teach me. At that time there was not a single member of my race anywhere near us who could read, and I was too timid to approach any of the white people. In some way, within a few weeks, I mastered the greater portion of the alphabet. In all my efforts to learn to read my mother shared fully my ambition, and sympathized with me and aided me in every way that she could. Though she was totally ignorant, so far as mere book knowledge was concerned, she had high ambitions for her children, and a large fund of good, hard, common sense which seemed to enable her to meet and master every situation. If I have done anything in life worth attention, I feel sure that I inherited the disposition from my mother.

In the midst of my struggles and longing for an education, a young coloured boy who had learned to read in the state of Ohio came to Malden. As soon as the coloured people found out that he could read, a newspaper was secured, and at the close of nearly every day's work this young man would be surrounded by a group of men and women who were anxious to hear him read the news contained in the papers. How I used to envy this man! He seemed to me to be the one young man in all the world who ought to be satisfied with his attainments.

About this time the question of having some kind of a school opened for the coloured children in the village began to be discussed by members of the race. As it would be the first school for Negro children that had ever been opened in that part of Virginia, it was, of course, to be a great event, and the discussion excited the widest interest. The most perplexing question was where to find a teacher. The young man from Ohio who had learned to read the papers was considered, but his age was against him. In the midst of the discussion about a teacher, another young coloured man from Ohio, who had been a soldier, in some way found his way into town. It was soon learned that he possessed considerable education, and he was engaged by the coloured people to teach their first school. As yet no free schools had been started for coloured people in that section, hence each family agreed to pay a certain amount per month, with the understanding that the teacher was to "board 'round" that is, spend a day with each family. This was not bad for the teacher, for each family tried to provide the very best on the day the teacher was to be its guest. I recall that I looked forward with an anxious appetite to the "teacher's day" at our little cabin.

This experience of a whole race beginning to go to school for the first time, presents one of the most interesting studies that has ever occurred in connection with the development of any race. Few people who were not right in the midst of the scenes can form any exact idea of the intense desire which the people of my race showed for an education. As I have stated, it was a whole race trying to go to school. Few were too young, and none too old, to make the attempt to learn. As fast as any kind of teachers could be secured, not only were day-schools filled, but night-schools as well. The great ambition of the older people was to try to learn to read the Bible before they died. With this end in view, men and women who were fifty or seventy-five years old would often be found in the night-school. Sunday-schools were formed soon after freedom, but the principal book studied in the Sunday-school was the spelling-book. Day-school, night-school, Sunday-school, were always crowded, and often many had to be turned away for want of room.

The opening of the school in the Kanawha Valley, however, brought to me one of the keenest disappointments that I ever experienced. I had been working in a salt-furnace for several months, and my stepfather had discovered that I had a financial value, and so, when the school opened, he decided that he could not spare me from my work. This decision seemed to cloud my every ambition. The disappointment was made all the more severe by reason of the fact that my place of work was where I could see the happy children passing to and from school, mornings and afternoons. Despite this disappointment, however, I determined that I would learn something, anyway. I applied myself with greater earnestness than ever to the mastering of what was in the "blue-back" speller.

My mother sympathized with me in my disappointment, and sought to comfort me in all the ways she could, and to help me find a way to learn. After a while I succeeded in making arrangements with the teacher to give me some lessons at night, after the day's work was done. These night lessons were so welcome that I think I learned more at night than the other children did during the day. My own experiences in the night-school gave me faith in the night-school idea, with which, in after years, I had to do both at Hampton and Tuskegee. But my boyish heart was still set upon going to the day-school, and I let no opportunity slip to push my case. Finally I won, and was permitted to go to the school in the day for a few months, with the understanding that I was to rise early in the morning and work in the furnace till nine o'clock, and return immediately after school closed in the afternoon for at least two more hours of work.

The schoolhouse was some distance from the furnace, and as I had to work till nine o'clock, and the school opened at nine, I found myself in a difficulty. School would always be begun before I reached it, and sometimes my class had recited. To get around this difficulty I yielded to a temptation for which most people, I suppose, will condemn me; but since it is a fact, I might as well state it. I have great faith in the power and influence of facts. It is seldom that anything is permanently gained by holding back a fact. There was a large clock in a little office in the furnace. This clock, of course, all the hundred or more workmen depended upon to regulate their hours of beginning and ending the day's work. I got the idea that the way for me to reach school on time was to move the clock hands from half-past eight up to the nine o'clock mark. This I found myself doing morning after morning, till the furnace "boss" discovered that something was wrong, and locked the clock in a case. I did not mean to inconvenience anybody. I simply meant to reach that schoolhouse in time.

When, however, I found myself at the school for the first time, I also found myself confronted with two other difficulties. In the first place, I found that all of the other children wore hats or caps on their heads, and I had neither hat nor cap. In fact, I do not remember that up to the time of going to school I had ever worn any kind of covering upon my head, nor do I recall that either I or anybody else had even thought anything about the need of covering for my head. But, of course, when I saw how all the other boys were dressed, I began to feel quite uncomfortable. As usual, I put the case before my mother, and she explained to me that she had no money with which to buy a "store hat," which was a rather new institution at that time among the members of my race and was considered quite the thing for young and old to own, but that she would find a way to help me out of the difficulty. She accordingly got two pieces of "homespun" (jeans) and sewed them together, and I was soon the proud possessor of my first cap.

The lesson that my mother taught me in this has always remained with me, and I have tried as best I could to teach it to others. I have always felt proud, whenever I think of the incident, that my mother had strength of character enough not to be led into the temptation of seeming to be that which she was not—of trying to impress my schoolmates and others with the fact that she was able to buy me a "store hat" when she was not. I have always felt proud that she refused to go into debt for that which she did not have the money to pay for. Since that time I have owned many kinds of caps and hats, but never one of which I have felt so proud as of the cap made of the two pieces of cloth sewed together by my mother. I have noted the fact, but without satisfaction, I need not add, that several of the boys who began their careers with "store hats" and who were my schoolmates and used to join in the sport that was made of me because I had only a "homespun" cap, have ended their careers in the penitentiary, while others are not able now to buy any kind of hat.

My second difficulty was with regard to my name, or rather *a* name. From the time when I could remember anything, I had been called simply "Booker." Before going to school it had never occurred to me that it was needful or appropriate to have an additional name. When I heard the school-roll called, I noticed that all of the children had at least two names, and some of them indulged in what seemed to me the extravagance of having three. I was in deep perplexity, because I knew that the teacher would demand of me at least two names, and I had only one. By the time the occasion came for the enrolling of my name, an idea occurred to me which I thought would make me equal to the situation; and so, when the teacher asked me what my full name was, I calmly told him "Booker Washington," as if I had been called by that name all my life; and by that name I have since been known. Later in life I found that my mother had given me the name of "Booker Taliaferro" soon after I was born, but in some way that part of my name seemed to disappear, and for a long while was forgotten, but as soon as I found out about it I revived it, and made my full name "Booker Taliaferro Washington." I think there are not many men in our country who have had the privilege of naming themselves in the way that I have.

More than once I have tried to picture myself in the position of a boy or man with an honoured and distinguished ancestry which I could trace back through a period of hundreds of years, and who had not only inherited a name, but fortune and a proud family homestead; and yet I have sometimes had the feeling that if I had inherited these, and had been a member of a more popular race, I should have been inclined to yield to the temptation of depending upon my ancestry and my colour to do that for me which I should do for myself. Years ago I resolved that because I had no ancestry myself I would leave a record of which my children would be proud, and which might encourage them to still higher effort.

The world should not pass judgment upon the Negro, and especially the Negro youth, too quickly or too harshly. The Negro boy has obstacles, discouragements, and temptations to battle with that are little known to those not situated as he is. When a white boy undertakes a risk, it is taken for granted that he will succeed. On the other hand, people are usually surprised if the Negro boy does not fail. In a word, the Negro youth starts out with the presumption against him.

The influence of ancestry, however, is important in helping forward any individual or race, if too much reliance is not placed upon it. Those who constantly direct attention to the Negro youth's moral weaknesses, and compare his advancement with that of white youths, do not consider the influence of the memories which cling about the old family homesteads. I have no idea, as I have stated elsewhere, who my grandmother was. I have, or have had, uncles and aunts and cousins, but I have no knowledge as to what most of them are. My case will illustrate that of hundreds of thousands of black people in every part of our country. The very fact that the white boy is conscious that, if he fails in life, he will disgrace the whole family record, extending back through many generations, is of tremendous value in helping him to resist temptations. The fact that the individual has behind and surrounding him proud family history and connection serves as a stimulus to help him to overcome obstacles when striving for success.

The time that I was permitted to attend school during the day was short, and my attendance was irregular. It was not long before I had to stop attending day-school altogether, and devote all of my time again to work. I resorted to the night-school again. In fact, the greater part of the education I secured in my boyhood was gathered through the night-school after my day's work was done. I had difficulty often in securing a satisfactory teacher. Sometimes, after I had secured some one to teach me at night, I would find, much to my disappointment, that the teacher knew but little more than I did. Often I would have to walk several miles at night in order to recite my night-school lessons. There was never a time in my youth, no matter how dark and discouraging the days might be, when one resolve did not continually remain with me, and that was a determination to secure an education at any cost.

Soon after we moved to West Virginia, my mother adopted into our family, notwithstanding our poverty, an orphan boy, to whom afterward we gave the name of James B. Washington. He has ever since remained a member of the family.

After I had worked in the salt-furnace for some time, work was secured for me in a coal-mine which was operated mainly for the purpose of securing fuel for the salt-furnace. Work in the coal-mine I always dreaded. One reason for this was that any one who worked in a coal-mine was always unclean, at least while at work, and it was a very hard job to get one's skin clean after the day's work was over. Then it was fully a mile from the opening of the coal-mine to the face of the coal, and all, of course, was in the blackest darkness. I do not believe that one ever experiences anywhere else such darkness as he does in a coal mine. The mine was divided into a large number of different "rooms" or departments, and, as I never was able to learn the location of all these "rooms," I many times found myself lost in the mine. To add to the horror of being lost, sometimes my light would go out, and then, if I did not happen to have a match, I would wander about in the darkness until by chance I found some one to give me a light. The work was not only hard, but it was dangerous. There was always the danger of being blown to pieces by a premature explosion of powder, or of being crushed by falling slate. Accidents from one or the other of these causes were frequently occurring, and this kept me in constant fear. Many children of the tenderest years were compelled then, as is now true I fear, in most coal-mining districts, to spend a large part of their lives in these coal-mines, with little opportunity to get an education; and, what is worse, I have often noted that, as a rule, young boys who begin life in a coal-mine are often physically and mentally dwarfed. They soon lose ambition to do anything else than to continue as a coal-miner.

In those days, and later as a young man, I used to try to picture in my imagination the feelings and ambitions of a white boy with absolutely no limit placed upon his aspirations and activities. I used to envy the white boy who had no obstacles placed in the way of his becoming a Congressman, Governor, Bishop, or President by reason of the accident of his birth or race. I used to picture the way that I would act under such circumstances; how I would begin at the bottom and keep rising until I reached the highest round of success.

In later years, I confess that I do not envy the white boy as I once did. I have learned that success is to be measured not so much by the position that one has reached in life as by the obstacles which he has overcome while trying to succeed. Looked at from this standpoint, I almost reach the conclusion that often the Negro boy's birth and connection with an unpopular race is an advantage, so far as real life is concerned. With few exceptions, the Negro youth must work harder and must perform his task even better than a white youth in order to secure recognition. But out of the hard and unusual struggle which he is compelled to pass, he gets a strength, a confidence, that one misses whose pathway is comparatively smooth by reason of birth and race.

From any point of view, I had rather be what I am, a member of the Negro race, than be able to claim membership with the most favoured of any other race. I have always been made sad when I have heard members of any race claiming rights and privileges, or certain badges of distinction, on the ground simply that they were members of this or that race, regardless of their own individual worth or attainments. I have been made to feel sad for such persons because I am conscious of the fact that mere connection with what is known as a superior race will not permanently carry an individual forward unless he has individual worth, and mere connection with what is regarded as an inferior race will not finally hold an individual back if he possesses intrinsic, individual merit. Every persecuted individual and race should get much consolation out of the great human law, which is universal and eternal, that merit, no matter under what skin found, is in the long run, recognized and rewarded. This I have said here, not to call attention to myself as an individual, but to the race to which I am proud to belong.

6

The Black South and White Appalachia

JAMES C. KLOTTER

Observers seemed to be depicting slave conditions in the antebellum South. One minister found the people "the worst housed, worst fed, most ignorant, most immoral" of any he had encountered. Others stressed the presence of homes that were mere hovels, of windowless log cabins with only one or two rooms. They told of a religious people, but one who believed in spells and witchcraft. Some writers termed the food deplorable and the speech patterns difficult to understand. Lazy, shiftless men and hard-working women inhabited this world. Their melancholy folk songs with origins across the ocean helped to lighten the burdens of everyday life and served as an emotional outlet. It was a closed, "peculiar" society.[1]

Yet these words were not written about blacks in slavery. Instead, these observers were describing Appalachian whites in the half-century following the end of Reconstruction. The fact that an important segment of the population viewed the two societies in a similar manner would have wide-ranging effects on both southern blacks and mountain whites. It would eventually result in the formation of an image that allowed many late-nineteenth-century reformers to turn their backs on the ex-slaves, as they told themselves that Appalachia needed aid as well. To them, mountain society differed from black society in only one important respect—it was white. That, however, was the crucial difference.

From 1870 to 1905 feuds stimulated interest in the Appalachian area. Family-oriented violence focused attention on the complex interplay of law and lawlessness, romance and sordidness, honor and deceit, and became eagerly read front-page copy. The region was "discovered" for the outside world by literary figures; then sociologists, folklorists, geographers, historians and the simply curious started to investigate the people and their lifestyle. These efforts resulted in similar accounts that in time became stereotypes.[2]

Blacks in slavery and freedom were often stereotyped by whites as a lazy but wily people who would not work hard if given the choice, as a superstitious folk who believed in spirits and witches, as an immoral race in which illegitimacy was not uncommon, as an inferior class that seemed to cower in subordination when talking with whites, and—paradoxically—as a violent, savage people who needed "civilization" and religion's guiding hand.[3]

In the period of their "discovery" Appalachian whites attracted very similar images. Novelist James Lane Allen told in 1886 of a "deferential, but . . . fearless" people, while another Kentuckian wrote in *Southern Bivouac* the next year that these "cunning" men and women deserved to be labeled our "later barbarians." At the turn of the century Ellen Churchill Semple (later the first woman president of the Association of American Geographers) described the "often inscrutable" faces of the mountaineers she encountered.[4] Two important 1913 studies used the words "crafty," "cunning," "secretive," and "inscrutable" to describe their subjects.[5] A *Journal of Geography* article noted the mountain man's "inexpressive face, which effectually conceals whatever he may feel or think." In 1935 Ann Wetzel Armstrong in the *Yale Review* said that mountain inhabitants masked themselves "in an almost unbelievably wily fashion." Substitute "Negro" for "mountaineer" in these accounts, and they would not differ greatly from those offered by the antebellum southern traveller or planter, or the postwar Bourbon.[6]

Witchcraft, ghosts, "haints," and magic existed not only as subcultural traits, but as a way of life for mountaineers who believed in signs, omens, and supernatural beings. An 1894 article in the *Journal of American Folk-Lore* described the presence of "magic and sorcery, witchcraft, shamanism, and fetishism" in the Appalachian area. Five years later a *Popular Science Monthly* study told of the "curious and persistent survival" of such beliefs in West Virginia, while John Fox, Jr., found his beloved hill people displaying various superstitious practices at the turn of the century.[7] A section in *The South in the Building of the Nation* also pointed out the presence of unusual beliefs mixed with "vague and confused notions of religion." Studies in the 1910s continued to emphasize those characteristics.[8]

When Arnold J. Toynbee took up the theme years later, he had ample precedent for his presentation. An earlier writer had argued, for example, that the mountaineer "is more of a genuine barbarian and closer related in instincts, habits, and morals to the Huns and Visigoths that hung on the girdle of Rome and drove arrows into the bosom of the Mother of the world, than would appear on first thought." Toynbee held to that view. His *Study of History* portrayed the Appalachian highlander as a person who had relapsed into illiteracy and superstition. "His agricultural calendar," wrote Toynbee, "is governed by the phases of the Moon; his personal life is darkened by the fear, and by the practice, of witchcraft. . . . In fact, the Appalachian 'Mountain People' at this day are no better than barbarians."[9]

In addition to the stereotype of a wily people who believed in witchcraft, observers also fashioned a prevailing image of mountain inhabitants that featured shiftless husbands and uncomplaining, overworked wives These men and women had "no respect for haste" and labored only when they needed money or food. One writer even explained that Kentucky mountaineers loved watermelons so much that they never counted them as part of the meal. Thus the stereotyped black reappeared in the Appalachian white.[10]

This similarity deserves further examination in two areas. The contradictory image of bondsmen as either the loving, peaceful "Sambo" or the violent, hating "Nat" could also be applied to postbellum mountain whites. The literature, almost without exception, agreed on Appalachian hospitality and openness toward visitors. At the same time, however, these families could be engaged in a feud of obscure origins and bloody results. The hospitable mountaineer might lie in ambush of an enemy, or commit bloody atrocities. Instead of "Sambo" and "Nat" came "Abner" and "Joab."[11]

White mountaineers and blacks appeared to share further characteristics. Arguing for the strength and stability of black families under difficult conditions, Herbert G. Gutman sought to show that "prenuptial intercourse and settled marriages were compatible." Presenting the slave's as a "premodern" culture," Gutman found similar examples in England, Germany, and West Africa. By inference, if not direct argument, he described a society where bridal pregnancies of slaves could be best explained as a part of "premodern" social values. If a settled union did not result, however, illegitimate offspring were not ostracized.[12]

Commentators on Appalachian society have noted a similar phenomenon. Investigators described the "low" domestic morality of the people generally and the "frail" virtue of the women particularly.[13] John C. Campbell of the Russell Sage Foundation said "baseborn" children did not receive the stigma given elsewhere. Later, Alfreda Withington observed that mountain families readily adopted illegitimate offspring into their households. Probably the most widely read portrayal of this aspect of Appalachian life appeared in Jack E. Weller's *Yesterday's People*, which suggested that contemporary Appalachian communities accepted illegitimacy without the ostracism often found in other regions of America.[14] As in other areas already examined, black life and mountain life have been viewed comparably in this respect.

Journalists', sociologists', and historians' descriptions of housing in the two societies indicate analogous perceptions of physical forms as well. Kenneth Stampp presented slave cabins as "cramped, crudely built, scantily furnished, unpainted, and dirty." Other historians of slavery have generally agreed that dwellings were limited to one or two small rooms with crude floors. Five or six members of one family unit shared the building.[15]

Similar descriptions appeared in regard to Appalachian homes. Visitors in both 1848 and 1858 used the adjective "cheerless" to describe the inhabitants' cabins.[16] Varied accounts of the 1870-1920 period pictured typical mountain "huts" of one to three rooms, with few or no windows, and either dirt or puncheon floors.[17] They reported large families as the norm. In point of fact, by 1870 Kentucky had the largest family units in the United States, and all other Appalachian state averages were large. Like blacks in their lifestyles, housing, and family make-up, Appalachian whites evoked parallel descriptions.[18]

But what does the similarity in descriptions of the two societies mean for the historian? After all, were not antebellum "poor whites" and blacks often compared in these same areas? Avery O. Craven noted, for example, that "the home of the poor white and the cabin of the Negro slave varied little in size or comfort." He found a "striking similarity" in the lifestyle of both groups.[19] Adjectives applied to "poor whites"—shiftless, immoral, violent—were common to black slaves and postwar Appalachian whites. As one writer noted: "Wherever one social class looks down upon another as inferior, members of the latter are regarded as brutish in nature and vulgar. . . . They are thickskulled, dull and unintelligent, primitive and childlike." Various aspects of this analysis apply to all three groups—blacks, poor whites, and Appalachian whites. All were viewed by one class as their inferiors, as part of a "premodern," traditionalist society.[20]

Perceptive commentators have questioned the Appalachian-"poor white" analogy, however, and the idea has gained few supporters. Mountain society remained historically apart from that of the southern "poor whites," and people who shaped opinion soon grasped this difference. This would in time prove a vitally important distinction, for mountaineers came to be considered a separate people worthy of uplift.[21]

Two schools of thought arose to explain distinctive Appalachian origins. One explanation was that the mountains so isolated the people that they continued to display customs, traits, and characteristics common to frontier America of the late eighteenth century. Forgotten by time, mountaineers of this *"New World"* were men and women of the age of the frontier suddenly come alive in a different era. They were "our contemporary ancestors."[22]

As early as the 1850s, John A. R. Rogers had maintained that the mountain people were as many as two centuries "behind the age."[23] By the 1880s numerous articles and books stressed Appalachian isolation. A writer for the *Magazine of American History* found in Appalachia citizens who "belong to the last century" and called them "a people *sui generis.*" Charles Willard Hayes, an Oberlin graduate and a member of the United States Geological Survey in 1895, presented an area "unaffected by the march of modern life," a primitive society displaying the characteristics of generations past.[24] By century's end, writers placed the people in a lifestyle comparable to that of the 1780s and 1790s.[25] The two decades after 1910 did not materially change the outlook, so that by 1930 a clear picture had emerged: "Cut off from the outside world, change penetrated the Mountains slowly or not at all, so that the group adhered to . . . pioneer standards of living and perpetuated the customs and expressions of a bygone day long after they had disappeared elsewhere."[26]

A fairly standard exposition of the process by which this isolation took place had also developed. According to this explanation, somewhere around 1820 in-migration ceased. Transportation routes changed, bypassing the area. Poor roads and lack of contact with the outside world left settlers "caught in an eddy" while the flood of civilization flowed around them. Their "Rip Van Winkle sleep"—interrupted only by war or a lumbering expedition to the flatlands—left them living in the past. In such an atmosphere and situation, a "marooned" people held fast to the ways of the eighteenth century.[27]

Despite the fact that some observers saw little good in the mountains— E. L. Godkin compared the mountaineer to a "New Guinea savage," while another writer labeled the region the "Balkans of America"—most pointed out that isolation had protected "our brothers in blood" from some of the destructive forces of change. This pure pioneer stock represented a potential for much good. One journalist wrote in 1896 that if George Washington returned to America, he would say of the area, "At last here I find a part of the world as I left it." Obviously, something good for the Father of Our Country was worth pursuing.[28]

A second outlook about the Appalachian past developed at almost the same time. According to this view, mountaineers displayed characteristics that went beyond late-eighteenth-century frontier America and went back instead to Elizabethan England or Scotland. Interest in the feuds brought initial stress on the Scotch-Irish, clannish origins of the Highlanders. Toynbee even used Appalachia as an example of regression—from Scotland and Ireland to America.[29] But the decline of the feuds after 1903 and the questionable statistical evidence for Scotch-Irish origins left this viewpoint with few adherents in the early twentieth century.[30]

Instead the English tradition prevailed in the fight over Appalachian origins. Supporters of this theory took their cue from early writers, such as one who, in discussing in 1882 the English nature of the people, said that with only "a change of costume and one wild bugle-call," he would have felt as if he were back in medieval times. Numerous studies emphasized that Appalachian natives spoke a purer English than the rest of America, that they preserved the dialects and phrases of the England of Shakespeare, and that they sang the songs of an older age. As folklorists and linguists studied and restudied the region, a whole new body of material became accepted fact.[31]

The literature became so voluminous and the image so commonplace that one former teacher in the mountains cried out in anguish that "writers . . . would have one believe that every-other mountaineer goes around singing quaint, beautiful sixteenth-century ballads as he plucks on a dulcimer." Despite his outcry, the prevailing pattern continued. Extremes surfaced. William Aspenwall Bradley discovered in 1915 that not only did the people speak old English but, when first learning to read, they preferred Shakespeare! A later writer predicted that if the Bard from Stratford-on-Avon "could revisit the earth today, he would feel more at home among our Mountain People than anywhere else." He and George Washington, no doubt.[32]

Why did Americans find Appalachia so interesting in this period? Why did the theories arise?[33] Part of the answer lies in the era's history. A nation that perceived that the Gilded Age was polluting America's moral fiber discovered a people untouched by the period's excesses. To an American public in search of order, the decades of the 1880s and 1890s gave birth to a multitude of organizations devoted to studying the past and tracing one's ancestors. The Daughters of the American Revolution in 1890, the Colonial Dames of America the next year, the United States Daughters of 1812 the year following, and the United Daughters of the Confederacy in 1894—all reflected this interest on the part of women. The Sons of the American Revolution in 1889 and a similar list of organizations provided an outlet for men's interest. As the history profession matured, organizations devoted to Clio developed more swiftly, sparked by the creation of the American Historical Association in 1884. As Robert H. Wiebe wrote, "Some idealized the past and the passing. A flood of fiction sighed over the lost virtues of another day: . . . the touching warmth between master and slave, . . . the happy innocence of the barefoot boy with cheek of tan." These people, he suggested, "fought . . . to preserve the society that had given their lives meaning." That lost society, that past, they rediscovered in the mountains.[34]

Added to this were the issues of race and religion. As large numbers of Eastern European immigrants settled in the United States, old-stock Americans, fearing the influx, saw the Appalachian area as a haven of refuge and a place of hope. In the *Missionary Review of the World* in 1895, Mrs. S. M. Davis brought these diverse themes together. She wrote about the mountain people's "deplorable" ignorance, their "dreadful" moral looseness, their "curious" customs, and their degraded hopelessness. "The visitor among them," she explained, "seems transported backward to the Elizabethan age." Hope remained, however. "Who knows whether these people be not a reserve force that God will bring out . . . for the coming crisis of conflict, a stalwart band to stand with us in defense of Protestantism!"[35] An article proclaimed in 1901 that this "purest Anglo-Saxon stock in all the United States" was "free from the tide of foreign immigrants which has been pouring in." In a book entitled *Christian Reconstruction in the South*, the author suggested that in this "arrested frontier" could be found the "largest and most valuable fragment" of original American stock. A North Carolina minister praised the "purest American type" whose ancestors had fought for the revolutionary cause and then for the Union. Now the nation needed them again, at a time when it was "overrun with a mob of strikers born in other lands."[36] Later, as the war in Europe raged, another observer found in the highlands the best qualities she sought to have preserved in the Anglo-Saxon race. Martha Sawyer Gielow, founder of both the National Historical Society and the Southern Industrial Education Association, called for conservation of a priceless possession—"the valorous stock of native-born Anglo-Saxons of our mountains." These purest, "truest" Americans formed the backbone of the race in the United States, she pointed out. Clearly, this isolated area offered opportunities for the concerned. Only one item was missing from the mixture of factors that would unite to open Appalachia to the world. That concerned the southern black's history since the Civil War.[37]

At the same time that mountain whites were being analyzed and stereotyped, actions outside Appalachia gave these developments added significance. A group who have been termed "neo-Puritan missionary teachers" within and without the abolitionist movement had come to the South during the Reconstruction period with many different and conflicting images of blacks. Many believed that schools would educate blacks while religion would improve their morality. The graces of civilization would make them competent citizens in white society. Disillusionment followed, and racism crept into their paternalistic efforts. Change was not so easy, smooth, or clearcut as it initially seemed. Nor did it come as quickly as expected. Within a decade, the northern white retreat from southern blacks was almost complete. With the exception of some support for black schools—segregated ones generally—the North seemed ready to accept blacks as second-class citizens. Acquiescence to Jim Crow followed. Richard N. Current has concisely gauged the mood:

By 1900 comparatively few whites inside or outside the South were in a mood to protest very strongly against what was happening to the Negroes in that section. Among Northerners the humanitarian concern for the freedmen which the Civil War had heightened—and which, along with other interests, had motivated Radical reconstruction—was at a low ebb. . . . Tired white idealists could at last retire from their labors with a good conscience, and when the Negro, even with the vote, failed to improve his lot very much, many of these idealists could but reflect that perhaps they all along had overestimated his capabilities.[38]

Similarly, John G. Sproat concluded: "Most Northerners, reformers included, showed an inordinate, premature impatience with the freedmen." The longer the problem of the freed Negro remained, the more discouraged these liberals became. Despite their "Puritan conscience," they turned away, "frustrated and fearful."[39]

Appalachia had been "discovered" by this time. Accounts made it clear that mountain whites in many ways resembled blacks in their needs, their lives, and their living conditions. Furthermore, the racism, frustration, and disappointment of white reformers who dealt with blacks after slavery would not be a factor in this society. Here were a people clearly Anglo-Saxon, retarded in their normal development only by their isolation and their history. They needed education, religion, and civilization. Bring in the towns, the railroads, the "civilizing influences" of modern America, and the highlanders would advance with the rest of the nation. This had not happened when dealing with blacks, but then—so thought white America—they were Negroes, an alien race. Perhaps southerners had been right about them after all.

Appalachian inhabitants were different. They were a self-contained people, nicely defined, and less numerous. To deal with them seemed only to step back to an earlier—if violent—Elizabethan age. As "scientific" thought had moved toward the theory of inferior races, and as white historians began to popularize a proslavery view of the South, Appalachian Anglo-Saxons began to replace blacks in the national awareness.[40] The white man's burden applied also to white Americans.

The missionary reform impulse did not, however, turn completely to Appalachia, for, as James M. McPherson notes, second-generation and third-generation "abolitionists" continued to aid blacks, generally in educational matters. But the condition and needs of white Americans in Appalachia were presented to the nation at an appropriate time for those disillusioned with black progress. Efforts previously devoted solely to blacks now could be partially redirected to mountain whites. Support that might have aided Negroes—even if the support was becoming half-hearted—now turned fully to mountain reform. As a result, the white effort to aid blacks was diluted at a crucial time.[41]

Change began gradually, then moved forward quickly. While the American Missionary Association (AMA) had sponsored missions in southeastern Kentucky before the Civil War, such attempts had been exceptional. Following the conflict and continuing into the twentieth century, more people began to turn their interest to the mountain area.[42] One of the earliest attempts to redirect white reform came from Ellen Myers, an AMA worker in the Kentucky and Tennessee mountains. In her October 1883 speech to the Woman's Meeting of the AMA, she began:

There is an unnoticed class of people dwelling almost in the very centre of the settled portion of the United States. "Our brother in black" has been held up to the view of two continents for the last fifty years. And what is America going to do with him and for him, has been a question which has interested the whole civilized world. . . . And right nobly has the Christian brotherhood evidenced its purpose to make men of these degraded classes. But until recently it has escaped the notice of these Christian workers that we have another class as needy perhaps as any.

Myers described the "natural" distaste for labor, large families, and almost universal log cabins of these "thriftless, improvident, and ignorant" people. Her appeal attracted sympathy and stimulated action.[43]

Two examples—the career of Oliver Otis Howard and the course of Berea College in Kentucky—most clearly show the redirection of missionary effort. Howard, the former commissioner of the Freedman's Bureau and past president of Howard University, personified the shift. On a business trip near Cumberland Gap, he visited the AMA-sponsored Harrow School, met the institution's leaders—A. A. Myers and his wife—found the situation promising, and in 1896 decided to work with them in building a university in Tennessee. Remembering how Abraham Lincoln had stressed the loyalty of the mountain people, Howard agreed to lend his talents to what became Lincoln Memorial University.[44]

The old general began to publicize the cause of Appalachian whites, "for the sake of Abraham Lincoln; for the sake of education; for the sake of industry; for the sake of humanity; . . . for the sake of . . . the whole mountain region." Writing for *Munsey's Magazine*, Howard made it clear that these people were not entirely like blacks, but rather "have our best blood in their veins, and yet . . . have been overlooked and left behind in all our educational privileges." He prescribed a program of industrial and domestic education for them. When discussing the feud spirit, Howard told of a "crude" society without hamlets or villages, roads or rails. Large families crowded into small cabins, without the benefit of teachers or clergy. Given post offices, stores, and other "civilizing factors," all this would change.[45] In a "labor of love" as managing director and then as president of the school's board of directors, he sought—and received— northern funds and moral support for the university. By 1909 contributors included Theodore Roosevelt, William Howard Taft, Charles Evans Hughes, Henry Cabot Lodge, Elihu Root, Alton B. Parker, William G. McAdoo, George B. Cortelyou, Lyman Abbott, Seth Low, and George Harvey. His appeals to them essentially repeated words used in Reconstruction—for blacks. Like others, Howard had redirected his efforts.[46]

Berea College's course is even clearer. Founded in the 1850s through the efforts of Kentucky abolitionist John G. Fee, the school was from the outset devoted to interracial education.[47] Despite attacks—one superintendent of public instruction called the school "a stench in the nostrils of all true Kentuckians"—the college did not retreat from its ideal. The Freedman's Bureau funded a building, Howard Hall, and growth began. In the first decade, blacks constituted over 60 percent of the student body. School regulations made no racial discriminations, and mixed dating, if discouraged, was still allowed. Until 1914 a Negro sat on the board of trustees of Berea. In short, the school remained true to its mission. It did not thrive, but did survive.[48]

In 1892 a new president was inaugurated. William Goodell Frost, descended from two generations of antislavery advocates, seemed a logical successor to the spirit of the founders. Extremely energetic, Frost doubled enrollment in five years, and when he stepped down in 1920, he had raised the value of Berea's plant and endowment from $200 thousand to $12 million. During that time he received significant contributions from Andrew Carnegie and Chicago philanthropist Daniel Kimball Pearsons as well as aid from former abolitionists such as Julia Ward Howe and Thomas W. Higginson. Frost spent much of his time in the field (168 days in one year), recruiting students and funds.[49]

Yet Frost faced major problems, and the cost of solving them came high. Initially, the existence of a new state-supported college for blacks threatened enrollment, as did the integration stigma that kept some white students away. Berea College had not prospered in almost three decades. An ambitious man, Frost decided to change the school's emphasis in order to rectify that situation and attract more students. In articles and speeches across the nation, he asked northerners to invest in Berea's dream of a mission to the Appalachian area. The mountain region—not interracial education—would become the school's focus of attention.

This was not completely new, for as early as 1873 the institution had called attention to education needs in the mountains. A decade later, when religious efforts began to turn consciously to southern mountain whites, Berea professor Charles G. Fairchild had supported the change of emphasis, arguing that although some hesitated to extend missionary work beyond blacks, "they need have little scruple here, for this section of the maps of our country is black through illiteracy. . . . Surely if the church at the North is sighing for new worlds to conquer, what more claim can there possibly be upon its attention and benevolence?"[50]

But if the idea was not new, the degree of effort and of emphasis was. In forceful terms, Frost began to stress modernist themes and the highlanders' need for northern leadership. For *Ladies' Home Companion* readers he portrayed the people as "a fine example of retarded development." Coming out of the same stock as the original settlers of America, these Appalachian citizens— "virtually picked out of the sixteenth century"—were but frontiersmen and women left isolated by environment. The post office, the railroad, and the telegraph would change this situation and bring progressive ideas to these traditionalists. Writing in the same period as Frederick Jackson Turner, Frost argued that in the mountains lay "the last piece of educational pioneering which America will have to do. Our western frontier has vanished, but here are three million people of our own blood and language." They too required guidance. After all, were not these Protestants placed here for a purpose: "to offset some of the undesirable foreign elements which are coming into our country?"[51]

In another article that year, Berea's president continued the same themes. "Uncontaminated with slavery," he wrote in the *Advance* in 1895, the mountaineers "are not Catholics, nor aliens, nor infidels," but rather "Americans of the Americas." Their soil could be made fertile for "New England ideas" of progress. A year later, Frost again pointed to these isolated people as the building blocks of a generation of sturdy yeomen who would offset the South's poor whites. Through his college, the "saving elements" of modern civilization would be taught. Appalachian America could then become "the New England of the South."[52]

In the half-decade from 1899 to 1903, Frost had his greatest impact as he combined the theme of the modernization of a retarded people with talk of the preservation of their more noble qualities. By January 1899, Princeton professor Woodrow Wilson had enlisted in the cause, telling a New York audience that

Berea College would teach "self-mastery" to the Appalachian people. That same year Frost's enormously influential "Contemporary Ancestors" article presented a persuasive picture in the *Atlantic*. A people living in pioneer conditions had slept like Rip Van Winkle for a century or more. Their frontier-like houses, their large families, their "startling survivals of Saxon speech" all pointed this out. Since the feuds that had sprung from Old World traditions had passed, the "latent ability" of a people much like "our forefathers on the bleak New England shore" would soon emerge.[53]

With some truth, Frost could call Berea "the discoverer of the mountain people." His article in the *American Monthly Review of Reviews* again told of colonial origins, of the mountaineers' need for "the right elements of advanced civilization in the right order," and of Berea's new mission. Frost added a fresh theme when he suggested that these recently discovered highlanders had such great potential that one of them might be a young Lincoln. Through some questionable reasoning, the Lincoln family became transposed into moun-taineers. Lincoln was one of them. By 1903 Berea's letterhead read, "In Lincoln's State—For Lincoln's People."[54]

While Berea emphasized the idea of the last American frontier and Frost stressed the mountaineers' Anglo-Saxon purity, blacks at the college faced new challenges. The president had initiated changes, some subtle, some significant, but all in line with his desire to make Berea more attractive to mountain whites. In one of his first moves Frost overturned the resolution approving interracial dating. He also discouraged social contacts between the races. Seeking a limited black enrollment approximating the state's overall black-white ratio, he suc-ceeded, for by 1903 only 157 of the 961 students were black. As Frost said later, "We frankly shifted emphasis, appealing more for the mountaineers."[55]

Probably not as inclined to racial equalitarianism as his predecessors, Frost reflected this in his actions. He called the blacks' decisions not to room with whites "the proper thing" and informed the faculty in 1894 that "the greatest peculiarity of Negro character which I have discovered is suspicion. This is a characteristic of all savage races." When discussing Reconstruction in 1896, Frost told how Negroes "naturally" abused the political powers given them. After a quarter-century as president, he openly admitted his motives. Since blacks attended Berea in adequate numbers when he arrived, he had felt they could be "relatively neglected."[56]

The angry, aging founder, John G. Fee, protested the transformation. Noting that "vigorous" attempts had been made to bring in white students, he asked why equal efforts had not been directed toward blacks. "The tendency now in Berea," said Fee, "is to run down to a mere white school." He added: "Ichabod will be written upon the face of Berea College—the glory is de-parted—that of maintaining into fair proportions the policy of educating the brotherhood of the race." Despite his pleas, the policy remained.[57]

In an appeal to both New South advocates and northern reformers, Frost stated that "the education of the Negro, momentous as that duty is, cannot solve the southern problem—we must deal with the white people of the South." In a plea for funding, Berea's president noted that the need of blacks "was univer-sally known and recognized, and all that has been given for his education has been abundantly repaid." The suggestion seemed to be that it was time to seek other fields of need. At a 1911 Carnegie Hall gathering in honor of Lincoln, Frost emphasized how mountain education could solve the "southern problem." Negro education, he said, "itself can never succeed, and the South can never be what it ought to be, until more is done for white education." Near the end of his presidency, he made a last strong plea to Bereans: "Search out that great army of the disadvantaged and unreached people who are our kin," then educate them. Frost's northern financial support made it clear that the national mood favored "our kin" more than blacks.[58]

But if not a racial equalitarian—few were in his era—Frost still lent eloquent pen and voice to the cause of the Negro race. While he apparently believed that Berea could prosper only with a reduced black attendance, Frost still felt strongly that the college should remain integrated, as an unique example off interracial education and cooperation. In his efforts to gain northern support for his beloved Appalachian people, however, he succeeded too well and stated his case too strongly. As a result, his words helped turn part of the "missionary reform impulse" away from southern blacks. The resulting change of sentiment—already a part of the national mood—allowed whites opposed to the Berea experiment the opportunity to rid themselves of "the one blot on an otherwise beautiful, moral, and social landscape." They moved quickly.[59]

In 1904 a legislator from the feud-ridden county called "Bloody Breathitt" introduced a bill to prohibit biracial education in all Kentucky schools, public and private. The Day Bill aimed directly at Berea College, the last integrated institution of higher learning in the South. If Frost supported the bill (as some blacks said at the time), then he might have been expected to offer mere token opposition. That he battled heart and soul to oppose passage indicates Frost's still lingering devotion to an ideal—one he had ignored and at times forgotten in the heady success of his mountain appeals.

In a report to the trustees, the president bitterly denounced the degrading spirit of caste behind the Day Bill. Berea had but one legal, moral, and historic course, he argued, and that was opposition. They agreed. Frost told supporters across the nation that the legislature's actions "deeply distressed" him: "We do not ask for approval, but for liberty." Yet even as he tried to rally support, the old prejudices appeared. To one friend, Frost told how Berea College offered the training needed by a still "irresponsible and unreliable" race. Speaking before the legislative committee considering the bill, he tried to silence criticism of the school's "radicalism" by stressing moderation. The college, said Frost, favored public school segregation as the "best arrangement" for Kentucky at the present time. Berea stood for keeping "the races pure," and through its efforts blacks would make contact with the "better element" of whites. Unimpressed, the legislature passed the bill. Tested by Berea College as far as the Supreme Court, it was upheld at all levels. Segregated education ended the Berea experiment.[60]

To meet the institution's historic commitment, Frost worked hard and successfully to raise money to set up another school for Kentucky blacks. He called it Lincoln Institute. But these efforts did not silence criticism from the Negro press. Finally, Frost's black ally James Bond defended his friends in *Alexander's Magazine;* he had never seen "a fairer or more sincere set of men" than those on Berea's board of trustees. Frost sincerely opposed the Day Law, even though he had failed in his attempts to stop it. Now blacks should end their attacks, said Bond, and support the new school.[61] The furor slowly subsided. Interracial higher education in the South ceased. Mountain whites continued to replace southern blacks as an attractive object of northern philanthropy.

Some of the forces and funds that might have eventually returned to southern Negroes went instead to southern Caucasians. The missionary reform impulse turned more and more to regional correction of "ethnically related people." Settlement schools, much like Freedmen's Bureau schools of the 1860s, but without their controversy, began to be built across Appalachia. By 1921 one survey located 192 mountain enterprises, and a decade later the number stood at 223. Many founders and, according to a 1930 study, "most" of the teachers came from the North.[62] But in time interest in Appalachia declined. The schools remained, but the force behind many of them faded. Periodic attempts at revitalization failed. The excitement of an earlier age could not be rekindled, and the expected army of "sound Americanism" remained in reserve.

And it remained in poverty. The "war" on that condition in the 1960s saw the reemergence of the forces at work at the turn of the century. John Alexander Williams has noted, for example, that "the youthful volunteers who staffed the anti-poverty and community action programs of the Kennedy-Johnson years were, like the religious benevolent workers of the last century, fleeing events in the lowland South, namely the rise of Black Power. . . . The liberal television commentators and welfare bureaucrats who displayed Appalachian poverty to the nation took obvious relish in the white skins and blue eyes of the region's hungry children."[63] A story from previous decades was being repeated.

But the most important story had already left its imprint on the nation's blacks. The "discovery" of a needy and "pure" people in the late nineteenth century had coincided with increased racism and northern disappointment over Reconstruction. Mountain "whiteness" together with the people's real needs—ironically similar to black ones—had allowed some reformers to turn with clear conscience away from blacks to aid Appalachia. In this way not only did late-nineteenth-century racism hinder black advancement, but so too did the increased dilution of white efforts by this alternative reform. For—to reverse Stampp's famous assertion—these highlanders had been, after all, only black people in white skins.[64]

1. John J. Dickey Diary, Dec. 5, 1895, Kentucky Historical Society, Frankfort; Emma Bell Miles, "Some Real American Music," *Harper's Monthly Magazine*, 109 (June 1904), 119; William Perry Brown, "A Peculiar People," *Overland Monthly*, 2d ser., 12 (Nov. 1888), 505-508.

2. Gordon B. McKinney, "Industrialization and Violence in Appalachia in the 1890's," in *An Appalachian Symposium: Essays Written in Honor of Cratis D. Williams*, ed. J. W. Williamson (Boone, N.C., 1977), p. 121; Robert F. Munn, "The Latest Rediscovery of Appalachia," *Mountain Life and Work*, 41 (Fall 1965), 11; Ronald D. Eller, "Industrialization and Social Change in Appalachia, 1880-1930: A Look at the Static Image," in *Colonialism in Modern America: The Appalachian Case*, ed. Helen Mathews Lewis, Linda Johnson, and Donald Askins (Boone, N.C., 1978), p. 35.

3. Stereotypes are presented in Claude H. Nolen, *The Negro's Image in the South: The Anatomy of White Supremacy* (Lexington, Ky., 1967); George M. Fredrickson, *The Black Image in the White Mind: The Debate on Afro-American Character and Destiny, 1917-1914* (New York, 1971); and the voluminous slavery literature.

4. James Lane Allen, "Through Cumberland Gap on Horseback," *Harper's New Monthly Magazine*, 63 (June 1886), 57; Young E. Allison, "Moonshine Men," *Southern Bivouac*, n.s., 2 (Feb. 1887), 528; Ellen Churchill Semple, "The Anglo-Saxons of the Kentucky Mountains: A Study in Anthropogeography," *Bulletin of the American Geographical Society*, 42 (Aug. 1910), 567. A. S. Elliott noted "a certain stolidity of expression" in mountaineers (A. S. Elliott, "The Kentucky Mountaineer," *Bibliotheca Sacra*, 63 [July 1906], 492).

5. Horace Kephart, *Our Southern Highlanders* (New York, 1913), pp. 214, 205, 341; Josiah Henry Combs, *The Kentucky Highlanders from a Native Mountaineer's Viewpoint* (Lexington, Ky., 1913), p. 18. Combs's work first appeared in *Watson's Jeffersonian Magazine* in 1912.

6. D. H. Davis, "The Changing Role of the Kentucky Mountains and the Passing of the Kentucky Mountaineer," *Journal of Geography*, 24 (Feb. 1925), 47; Anne W. Armstrong, "The Southern Mountaineers," *Yale Review*, 24 (Mar. 1935), 541.

7. Hampden Porter, "Notes on the Folk-Lore of the Mountain Whites of the Alleghanies," *Journal of American Folk-Lore*, 7 (Apr.-June 1894), 106-107; Frances Albert Doughty, "Folklore of the Alleghanies," *Appletons' Popular Science Monthly*, 55 (July 1899), 391; John Fox, Jr., *Bluegrass and Rhododendron: Out-doors in Old Kentucky* (New York, 1901), p. 13. See also Wilbur G. Ziegler and Ben S. Grosscup, *The Heart of the Alleghanies or Western North Carolina* (Raleigh, N.C., 1883), pp. 298-311; Mrs. D. L. Pierson, "The Mountaineers of Madison County, N.C.," *Missionary Review of the World*, n.s., 10 (Nov. 1897), 828; and Sadie F. Price, "Kentucky Folk-Lore," *Journal of American Folk-Lore*, 14 (Jan.-Mar. 1901), 30.

8. Frederick W. Neve, "Social Settlements in the South," in *The South in the Building of the Nation*, 12 vols. (Richmond, Va., 1909), vol. 10, p. 617. On the 1910s, see Hubert Gibson Shearin, "Some Superstitions in the Cumberland Mountains," *Journal of American Folk-Lore*, 24 (July-Sept. 1911), 319-22; William Aspenwall Bradley, "In Shakespeare's America," *Harper's Monthly Magazine*, 131 (Aug. 1915), 440-42; and D. L. Thomas, "The Awakening of the Kentucky Mountains," *Kentucky Magazine*, 2 (Jan. 1918), 78-79.

9. Allison, "Moonshine Men," p. 528; Arnold J. Toynbee, *A Study of History*, 12 vols. (London, 1934-61), vol. 2, p. 311. Toynbee admitted in a July 27, 1948, letter to James Brown that his knowledge of the area came not from books but rather only from "a number of visits to a friend of mine" in east-central Kentucky, plus a trip to the region "once or twice" (James S. Brown, "An Appalachian Footnote to Toynbee's *A Study of History*," *Appalachian Journal*, 6 [Autumn 1978], 29-32).

10. Alfreda Withington, "The Mountain Doctor," *Atlantic Monthly*, 150 (Sept. 1932), 265; Thomas Hughes, *Rugby, Tennessee: Being Some Account of the Settlement Founded on the Cumberland Plateau by the Board of Aid to Land Ownership Limited* (New York, 1881), p. 63; "Poor White Trash," *Eclectic Magazine*, n.s., 36 (July 1882), 132.

11. John W. Blassingame, *The Slave Community: Plantation Life in the Antebellum South* (New York, 1972), pp. 133-43. Many of the generalizations are based on Cratis D. Williams, "The Southern Mountaineer in Fact and Fiction," ed. Martha H. Pipes, *Appalachian Journal*, 3 (1975-76), 8-61, 100-63, 186-261, 334-92; and Henry D. Shapiro, *Appalachia on Our Mind: The Southern Mountains and Mountaineers in the American Consciousness, 1870-1920* (Chapel Hill, N.C., 1978).

12. Herbert G. Gutman, *The Black Family in Slavery and Freedom, 1750-1925* (New York, 1976), pp. 64, 65-75, 557n; Daniel Scott Smith and Michael S. Hindus, "Premarital Pregnancy in America, 1640-1971; An Overview and Interpretation," *Journal of Interdisciplinary History*, 5 (Spring 1975), 559.

13. *New York Times*, July 26, 1885, p. 3; Allen, "Through Cumberland Gap on Horseback," p. 60; Ellen Churchill Semple, "A New Departure in Social Settlements," *Annals of the American Academy of Political and Social Science*, 15 (Mar. 1900), 304; Semple, "Anglo-Saxons of the Kentucky Mountains," p. 589; John H. Ashworth, "The Virginia Mountaineers," *South Atlantic Quarterly*, 12 (July 1913), 195.

14. John C. Campbell, *The Southern Highlander and His Homeland* (Lexington, Ky., 1921), p. 132; Withington, "Mountain Doctor," p. 266; Jack E. Weller, *Yesterday's People: Life in Contemporary Appalachia* (Lexington, Ky., 1965), pp. 70-71.

15. Kenneth M. Stampp, *The Peculiar Institution: Slavery in the Ante-Bellum South* (New York, 1956), p. 294; Eugene D. Genovese, *Roll, Jordan, Roll: The World the Slaves Made* (New York, 1974), p. 524; Robert William Fogel and Stanley L. Engerman, *Time on the Cross: The Economics of American Negro Slavery,* 2 vols. (Boston, 1974), vol. 1, pp. 115-16; Blassingame, *Slave Community,* p. 159.

16. Charles Lanman, *Letters from the Alleghany Mountains* (New York, 1849), p. 154; J. A. R. Rogers, "Letters from Kentucky," *Independent,* 10 (Sept. 23, 1858), 2.

17. Frederick Law Olmsted, *A Journey in the Back Country* (New York, 1860), p. 230; Porte Crayon [David Hunter Strother], "The Mountains," *Harper's New Monthly Magazine,* 45 (Aug. 1872), 352; John Esten Cooke, "Owlet," ibid., 57 (July 1878), 200; *Louisville Courier-Journal,* Dec. 9, 1878, p. 1; "Poor White Trash," p. 129; Hughes, *Rugby,* p. 62; Allen, "Through Cumberland Gap on Horseback," p. 61; Allison, "Moonshine Men," p. 531; James Mooney, "Folk-Lore of the Carolina Mountains," *Journal of American Folk-Lore,* 2 (Apr.-June 1889), 96; Adelene Moffatt, "The Mountaineers of Middle Tennessee," ibid., 4 (Oct.-Dec. 1891), 316; Julian Ralph, *Dixie; or, Southern Scenes and Sketches* (New York, 1886), pp. 302, 329; Leonidas Hubbard, Jr., "The Moonshiner at Home," *Atlantic Monthly,* 90 (Aug. 1902), 237-39; Edward Owings Guerrant, *The Galax Gatherers: The Gospel among the Highlanders,* ed. Grace Owings Guerrant (Richmond, Va., 1910), p. 231; William Aspenwall Bradley, "Hobnobbing with Hillbillies," *Harper's Monthly Magazine,* 132 (Dec. 1915); Arthur W. Spaulding, *The Men of the Mountains* (Nashville, Tenn., 1915), p. 67; Elizabeth Wysor Klingberg, "Glimpses of Life in the Appalachian Highlands," *South Atlantic Quarterly,* 14 (Oct. 1915), 372. The correct spelling of Arthur W. Spaulding's name is Spalding.

18. Francis A. Walker, comp., *Ninth Census* (1870), vol. 1: *The Statistics of the Population of the United States, Embracing Tables of Race, Nationality, Sex: Selected Ages, and Occupations* (Washington, D.C., 1872), p. 595.

19. Avery O. Craven, "Poor Whites and Negroes in the Ante-Bellum South," *Journal of Negro History,* 15 (Jan. 1930), 16; Eugene D. Genovese, "Rather Be a Nigger than a Poor White Man: Slave Perceptions of Southern Yeomen and Poor Whites," in *Toward a New View of America: Essays in Honor of Arthur C. Cole,* ed. Hans L. Trefousse (New York, 1977).

20. Lewis C. Copeland, "The Negro as a Contrast Conception," in *Race Relations and the Race Problem,* ed. Edgar T. Thompson (Durham, N.C., 1939), p. 157. See Richard Jensen, "Modernization and Community History," Newberry Papers on Family and Community History, paper 78-6, Newberry Library (Chicago, 1978), p. 18; and Samuel P. Hayes, "Modernizing Values in the History of the United States," *Peasant Studies,* 6 (Apr. 1977), 69-79.

21. [Edward H. Fairchild], *Berea College, Ky.: An Interesting History* (Cincinnati, 1875), p. 85; Mooney, "Folk-Lore of the Carolina Mountains," p. 95; Kephart, *Our Southern Highlanders,* p. 359; Richard B. Drake, "Appalachian Whites in the Era of Slavery . . . . ," *Appalachian Notes,* 4 (4th quarter, 1976), 61.

22. Edward A. Pollard, *The Virginia Tourist Sketches of the Springs and Mountains of Virginia* (Philadelphia, 1870), p. 3; William Goodell Frost, "Our Contemporary Ancestors in the Southern Mountains," *Atlantic Monthly,* 83 (Mar. 1899), 311.

23. Rogers, "Letters from Kentucky," p. 2.

24. Allen, "Through Cumberland Gap on Horseback," p. 57; Milton T. Adkins, "The Mountains and Mountaineers of Craddock's Fiction," *Magazine of American History,* 24 (Oct. 1890), 305; Charles Willard Hayes, "Eastern Kentucky: Its Physiography and Its People," *Berea Quarterly,* 1 (May 1895), 7.

25. Charles G. Mutzenbergh, *Kentucky's Famous Feuds and Tragedies* (Hyden, Ky., 1899), pp. 20-21; Semple, "New Departure in Social Settlements," p. 301. See also Charles Dudley Warner, "Comments on Kentucky," *Harper's New Monthly Magazine,* 77 (Jan. 1889), 268. In a later edition, "Mutzenbergh" correctly appeared as Mutzenberg.

26. D. H. Davis, "A Study of the Succession of Human Activities in the Kentucky Mountains, a Dissected Highland Area," *Journal of Geography,* 24 (Mar. 1930), 90-91. On the 1910-20 period, see also the *Louisville Courier-Journal,* May 12, 1912, sec. 4, p. 4; Kephart, *Our Southern Highlanders,* pp. 18, 211; Bradley, "Hobnobbing with Hillbillies," p. 92; Olive Dame Campbell and Cecil J. Sharp, comps., *English Folk Songs from the Southern Appalachians* (New York, 1917), p. iv; and Mabel Brown Ellis, "Children of the Kentucky Coal Fields," *American Child,* 1 (Feb. 1920), 289.

27. J. Stoddard Johnston, "Romance and Tragedy of Kentucky Feuds," *Cosmopolitan,* 207

(Sept. 1899), 552; Samuel Tyndale Wilson, *The Southern Mountaineers* (New York, 1914), pp. 8-9; Kephart, *Our Southern Highlanders*, p. 373. See also George E. Vincent, "A Retarded Frontier," *American Journal of Sociology*, 4 (July 1898), 16. George E. Vincent, a member of the University of Chicago department of sociology, later was head of the Rockefeller Foundation.

28. *Nation*, 38 (May 22, 1884), 436; William Aspenwall Bradley, "The Folk Culture of the Kentucky Cumberlands," *Dial*, 64 (Jan. 31, 1918), 98; Henderson Daingerfield Norman, "Social Settlement and Educational Work in the Kentucky Mountains," *Journal of Social Science*, 39 (Nov. 1901), 174, 186; Ralph, *Dixie*, p. 312.

29. Johnston, "Romance and Tragedy of Kentucky Feuds, p. 553, Daingerfield, "Social Settlement and Educational Work," p. 177; Julian Ralph, "Our Appalachian Americans," *Harper's Monthly Magazine,* 107 (June 1903), 33; Toynbee, *Study of History*, 2:312.

30. On the origins of mountaineers, see attacks on the Scotch-Irish school in Combs, *Kentucky Highlanders*, pp. 10-12; Harry M. Caudill, "Anglo-Saxon vs. Scotch-Irish—Round 2," *Mountain Life and Work,* 45 (Mar. 1969), 18-19; Harry M. Caudill, *A Darkness at Dawn: Appalachian Kentucky and the Future* (Lexington, Ky., 1976), p. 9; James H. Siler, "Anglo-Saxon vs. Scotch-Irish—Round 4," *Mountain Life and Work,* 45 (June 1969), 16; and Virginia Clay McClure, "The Settlement of the Kentucky Appalachian Highlands" (Ph.D. diss., University of Kentucky, 1933), pp. 121-25.

31. "Poor White Trash," p. 129. Some of these views appear in Allison, "Moonshine Men," p. 529; Johnston, "Romance and Tragedy of Kentucky Feuds," p. 556; N. S. Shaler, "The Peculiarities of the South," *North American Review,* 151 (Oct. 1890), 484; Semple, "Anglo-Saxons of the Kentucky Mountains," p. 561; Henderson Daingerfield Norman, "The English of the Mountaineer," *Atlantic Monthly*, 105 (Feb. 1910), 276; Emerson Hough, "Burns of the Mountains: The Story of a Southern Mountaineer Who Is Remaking His Own People," *American Magazine*, 75 (Dec. 1912), 13; Bruce Barton, "Children of the Feudists," *Collier's,* 51 (Aug. 23, 1913), 8; Campbell and Sharp, *English Folk Songs*, p. iv, dust jacket; Bradley, "Folk Culture of the Kentucky Cumberlands," p. 97; Thomas D. Clark, *The Kentucky* (Lexington, Ky., 1969), p. 122.

32. John F. Day, *Bloody Ground* (Garden City, N.Y., 1941), p. 242; Bradley, "In Shakespeare's America," p. 436; James W. Raine, *The Land of Saddle-bags: A Study of the Mountain People of Appalachia* (New York, 1925), p. 4.

33. Henry D. Shapiro in a discerning study suggests that Appalachian violence brought a redefinition stressing the British background of Appalachians even more. Otherwise, he notes, America's pioneer ancestors were merely "brawlers and brigands." Change placed the origins of violence in Europe rather than America. Such a redefinition, however, is not as clear-cut as Shapiro suggests. See Shapiro, *Appalachia on Our Mind*, p. 106.

34. Sophonisba P. Breckinridge, *Women in the Twentieth Century: A Study of Their Political, Social, and Economic Activities* (New York, 1933), p. 23; Robert H. Wiche, *The Search for Order, 1877-1920* (New York, 1967), pp. 39, 44.

35. Mrs. S. M. Davis, "The 'Mountain Whites' of America," *Missionary Review of the World*, n.s., 8 (June 1895), 424, 426, 423.

36. Semple, "Anglo-Saxons of the Kentucky Mountains," p. 566; H. Paul Douglass, *Christian Reconstruction in the South* (Boston, 1909), pp. 19-20; Junius M. Horner, "Educational Work in the Mountains of North Carolina," *Outlook*, 94 (Mar. 12, 1910), 590.

37. Klingberg, "Glimpses of Life in the Appalachian Highlands," p. 378; Martha Sawyer Gielow, "The Call of the Race," *Journal of American History*, 11 (2d quarter, 1917), 216-17.

38. James M. McPherson, *The Abolitionist Legacy: From Reconstruction to the NAACP* (Princeton, 1975), p. 161; Richard N. Current, ed., *Reconstruction in Retrospect: Views from the Turn of the Century* (Baton Rouge, La., 1969), p. vi.

39. John G. Sproat, *"The Best Men": Liberal Reformers in the Gilded Age* (New York, 1968), pp. 31, 33, 30, 36.

40. See John S. Haller, Jr., *Outcasts from Evolution: Scientific Attitudes of Racial Inferiority, 1859-1900* (Urbana, Ill., 1971), pp. 153-202; John David Smith, "The Formative Period of American Slave Historiography, 1890-1920" (Ph.D. diss., University of Kentucky, 1977), pp. 62-75.

41. McPherson, *Abolitionist Legacy*, pp. 3, 143-49.

42. Ibid., p. 240, Fannie W. Dunn, "Missionary and Philanthropic Schools," in Elizabeth R. Hooker, *Religion in the Highlands* (New York, 1933), pp. 243-50, 308-16.

43. Mrs. A. A. Myers, *Mountain White Work in Kentucky* (New York, 1883), pp. 3-6.

44. A. A. Myers to H. S. Howard, June 9, 1896, Oliver Otis Howard Papers, Bowdoin College Library; Oliver Otis Howard, "The Negro as a Free Man," *Alexander's Magazine*, 6 (Sept. 15, 1908), 206. On Howard's career see John A. Carpenter, *Sword and Olive Branch: Oliver Otis Howard* (Pittsburgh, 1964); William S. McFeely, *Yankee Stepfather: General O. O. Howard and the Freedmen* (New Haven, 1968).

45. Oliver Otis Howard to Cyrus Kehr, Aug. 25, 1898, Howard Papers, Bowdoin College; Oliver Otis Howard, "The Folk of the Cumberland Gap," *Munsey's Magazine*, 27 (July 1902), 508; Oliver Otis Howard, "The Feud Spirit in Kentucky," *Interior*, 34 (Nov. 5, 1903), 1435. See also Oliver Otis Howard, "Lincoln's Monument in the Mountains," *National Magazine*, 22 (June 1905), 299-304.

46. Oliver Otis Howard, *Autobiography*, 2 vols. (New York, 1908), vol. 2, p. 569; Kehr to Oliver Otis Howard, Feb. 25, 1897; Oliver Otis Howard to D. K. Pearsons, Feb. 9, 1899, Howard Papers, Bowdoin College; unidentified clipping, 1905, Oliver Otis Howard Papers, Berea College Archives; Lincoln Memorial Endowment Association to Warren C. Deem, Sept. 9, 1909, General Oliver Otis Howard Letters, Lincoln Memorial University, Harrogate, Tenn.; John S. Allen, "The Door through the Barrier," *Harper's Weekly*, 53 (Oct. 30, 1909), 12.

47. John G. Fee, "Home Missions: Kentucky," *American Missionary*, 10 (Dec. 1855), 13-14; "From Rev. J. G. Fee," ibid., n.s., 3 (May 1859), 114; "Rev. John G. Fee," ibid. (Dec. 1859), 275-77.

48. [Fairchild], *Berea College*, pp. 41, 53; McPherson, *Abolitionist Legacy*, pp. 244-46; Elisabeth S. Peck, *Berea's First Century, 1855-1955* (Lexington, Ky., 1955), p. 47.

49. William Goodell Frost, *For the Mountains: An Autobiography* (New York, 1937), pp. 10-13, 110, 116, 88; William Goodell Frost, "God's Doings in My Time," *Berea Alumnus*, 1 (June 1931), 13.

50. "Acclimating Northern Principles," *American Missionary*, n.s., 17 (Mar. 1873), 58-59; "Address of Prof. C. G. Fairchild," ibid., n.s., 36 (Dec. 1883), 391-92.

51. William Goodell Frost, "Appalachian America," *Ladies' Home Companion*, 23 (Sept. 1896), 3-4, 21.

52. William Goodell Frost, "New England in Kentucky," *Advance*, June 6, 1895, p. 1285; William Goodell Frost, "An Educational Program for Appalachian America," *Berea Quarterly*, 1 (May 1896), 12-14; Frost, "Appalachian America," p. 4.

53. Woodrow Wilson, "Our Last Frontier," *Berea Quarterly*, 4 (May 1899), 6; Frost, "Our Contemporary Ancestors," pp. 311, 313, 318, 317.

54. William Goodell Frost, "The Southern Mountaineer: Our Kindred of the Boone and Lincoln Type," *American Monthly Review*, 21 (Mar. 1900), 308-11. In a speech at Berea College, Mar. 8, 1923, William E. Barton said that if Lincoln were alive he would "strain every effort" to attend Berea. William E. Barton, *Abraham Lincoln, Kentucky Mountaineer* (Berea, Ky., 1923), p. 13.

55. Paul David Nelson, "Experiment in Interracial Education at Berea College, 1858-1908," *Journal of Negro History*, 59 (Jan. 1974), 19-22, 25; William Goodell Frost to G. W. Mallow, May 11, 1907, cited in ibid., p. 20.

56. Frost, *For the Mountains*, p. 63; "Berea College President's Quarterly Report—Feb. 3, 1894," William G. Frost Papers, Berea College Archives; Frost, "Appalachian America," p. 12; William Goodell Frost, "Twenty-five Years at Berea," sermon to graduates, June 3, 1917, Frost Papers.

57. Clipping from *Union Herald*, July 22, 1899, and John G. Fee, "A Word to the Convocation," n.d., John G. Fee Papers, Berea College Archives.

58. William G. Frost, "Berea College," *Berea Quarterly*, 1 (May 1895), 22; Frost, "The Southern Mountaineer," p. 308; "Address of President Frost," *Berea Quarterly*, 15 (Apr. 1911), 18; Frost, *For the Mountains*, p. 325.

59. Frost, *For the Mountains*, p. 334; William Goodell Frost, "Berea's Re-Adjustment," speech, ca. 1910, Frost Papers; Harry V. McChesney to Robert Lloyd Jones, Feb. 27, 1905 [copy], Harry V. McChesney Papers, Kentucky Historical Society.

60. "To Trustees of Berea College, May 28, 1904," Frost to William B. Smith, Feb. 4, 1904, Frost to James Speed, Feb. 6, 1904, and Frost to R. N. Roark, Feb. 12, 1904, Frost Papers; William Goodell Frost, "Before the Senate Committee," *Berea Quarterly*, 8 (Apr. 1904), 23-24. In 1950 the school was allowed to re-admit blacks for the first time. Peck, *Berea's First Century*, pp. 60-61.

61. James Bond to Frost, Mar. 9, 1907, in *Alexander's Magazine,* 3 (Mar. 15, 1907), 227-28. James Bond was the grandfather of Julian Bond. On the attacks, see McPherson, *Abolitionist Legacy,* pp. 256-58; *New York Age,* July 20, 1905, p. 4; "Berea College: Has It Become a Fraud?" *Alexander's Magazine,* 3 (Jan. 15, 1907), 125; and "Berea and Its President Still a Puzzle," ibid. (Feb. 15, 1907), 176.

62. Richard B. Drake, "Documents Relating to the Mission to Appalachia," *Appalachian Notes,* 3 (3d quarter, 1975), 34-35; Olive D. Campbell, comp., *Southern Highland Schools Maintained by Denominational and Independent Agencies* (New York, 1921), pp. 3-16; Mary K. Jasper, "Social Value of Settlement Schools in the Kentucky Mountains" (Master's thesis, University of Kentucky, 1930), p. 17. See also Richard B. Drake, *Mountaineers and Americans* (Berea, Ky., 1976), pp. 51-55.

63. John Alexander Williams, "Henry Shapiro and the Idea of Appalachia: A Review/Essay," *Appalachian Journal,* 5 (Spring 1978), 353. See a similar view in F. Scott Rogers, "The Missionaries' Effect on the Appalachian Self-Image," *Appalachian Notes,* 1 (4th quarter, 1973), 2.

64. Stampp, *Peculiar Institution,* p. vii.

PART THREE

Community Studies

Part 3 focuses on black Appalachia as a geographical and cultural unit. James T. Laing outlines an area-specific Appalachian context (West Virginia), rendering the structural conditions of blacks at the point of origin, their plane-of-living/ quality-of-life, and their general status in the coal-mining sector of the southern Appalachian region where most Appalachian blacks lived.

Russell Parker's look at "boom years" in a non-coal-mining town in East Tennessee considers the role of black leadership in a setting much like that of coal towns. Parker's community investigation shows that company towns have certain characteristics which transcend the nature of the dominant industry. Blacks had been used initially as strikebreakers in the early development of the aluminum industry of the area and were depended upon to undertake work not acceptable to whites. The story of ALCOA blacks ends as they move on to accept jobs in the defense industries that grew after the start of World War II.

According to David Corbin's award-winning analysis of class and race in company-dominated towns, the social structure(s), as planned and maintained by the companies, mitigated the potential conflicts between the races. Corbin explains how the symbiotic relations between blacks, whites, and European immigrants in the coal towns were based on a tenuous collective discontent with "the Company"—not with each other.

7

The Negro Miner in West Virginia

JAMES T. LAING

Although studies of Negro migration of the past two decades have pointed out the fact that every large exodus of Negroes from the south has contained a number whose destination was the mining fields of West Virginia[1] no sociological study has appeared of the Negro in this area.[2] Here Negroes occupy a unique position; more Negro miners work in the coal mines of West Virginia[3] than in those of any other state. Although they formed only 6.6 per cent of the population of the state in 1930 they constituted 21.8 per cent of all miners.

The purpose of the study, of which this article is a brief summary, is to provide sociological data concerning this group, first, by discussion of the origin, development, and present status of the Negro miners of West Virginia, and, second, by describing in some detail certain aspects of the Negro culture in the mining fields.

METHOD

Information was obtained by personal interviews with employers, miners, Negro teachers, preachers, and other persons who could furnish factual material concerning the Negroes in the mining fields; by extensive correspondence with persons not available for interview; by wide reading, especially in the West Virginia State Library; and by study of coal company records. Two schedules were used, an employer's schedule and a miner's schedule, in Logan, Kanawha, McDowell, Raleigh, and Fayette, counties where 74.6 per cent of all Negro miners live. Six hundred miners' schedules were taken, while the schedules of 44 operators employing almost half of the Negro miners in the state were obtained.

HISTORICAL BACKGROUND

Negroes have probably been employed in the mines of West Virginia since the early years of the nineteenth century after coal supplanted wood as the fuel used in the Great Kanawha Valley salt furnaces in 1819. In the late ante-bellum years Negro slaves were largely used in the coal mines and cannel coal oil factories of Kanawha County. With the building of the Chesapeake and Ohio Railroad and consequent opening of the New River coal field in 1873 the Negro population of the southern counties increased rapidly. These newcomers, coming mostly from Virginia to work on the railroad,[4] remained to work in the mines. The transition from railroad workers to miners was duplicated in the building of the Norfolk and Western Railroad from 1883 to 1892, the Virginian in 1909, and in the later extensions of these railroads.

In the state as a whole Negroes and native whites constituted the bulk of the mining population until the great expansion of the industry after 1892. Following the great strike in 1902 both Negroes and native whites were supplanted by foreigners,[5] the percentages of native whites and Negroes in 1907 being only 36.3 and 17.6 respectively.[6] The foreigners outnumbered the Negroes every year until 1925. Since then, however, the Negroes have been more numerous than they, the percentages of native whites, Negroes, and foreigners in 1931 being 61.1, 21.9 and 17.0.[7]

MIGRATION

The Negro miners are largely a migrated group. Only 14.0 per cent of the 600 miners interviewed were born in West Virginia; 47.8 per cent came from Virginia; 11.8 per cent from North Carolina; 11.2 per cent from Alabama; 4.5 per cent from Tennessee; 3.3 per cent from Georgia; 2.5 per cent from South Carolina; and the remaining 4.9 per cent from five southern and six northern states. Various reasons were given by the migrated miners for coming to West Virginia. Chief among these were economic, the "pull" of higher wages and increased opportunity being almost universal. Crop failures and bad conditions of the farms from which many of them came constituted a "push" which rendered the economic "pull" of the mining fields more effective. Economic reasons, however, while powerful, were by no means the only ones given. Better schools for their children and a greater opportunity for civic and personal liberty were also named, particularly by the more articulate migrants. Crises of various kinds which interfere with the accustomed tenor of life influenced others to leave their native states and wander. Death of a relative or a wife and offenses against the law by them or their parents were not infrequently given as personal reasons for migration. Desire for travel and new experience led many young men to "venture out."

The movements of migrants may be classified into nine directional types: (1) From states south of Virginia direct to West Virginia. (2) From southern states north of Alabama to that state and thence north to West Virginia. (3) From the southern states northward with one or more stops the last of which was in Virginia from which the migrant came to West Virginia. (4) From southern states with one or more stops the last being in Kentucky from which state the migrant came to West Virginia. (5) From states south of Virginia direct to northern states and thence back to West Virginia. (6) From northern states directly to West Virginia. (7) From southern states to the western states such as Kansas or Missouri and thence to West Virginia. (8) From Virginia to West Virginia direct. (9) From Virginia to Kentucky, thence to West Virginia.

FUNCTIONS PERFORMED BY THE NEGRO MINER

Negroes occupy all of the labor positions in the industry, both skilled and unskilled, but rarely a position of authority. The greatest number of Negroes are employed in underground positions, or "inside labor." Of the 2,411 Negroes concerning whom detailed information was obtained, 96.3 per cent were employed in these occupations. Coal loaders constituted 75.7 per cent of all Negroes in the group. Negroes choose this occupation not only because it is the most available of all but it is one of the most lucrative and provides the least supervision with the greatest amount of personal freedom in work hours. Other jobs and the percentage of the Negro group in each are as follows: brakeman, 6.8; trackman, 5.5; motorman, 4.9; and machine man, 2.3. Only 3.2 per cent were employed in "outside labor," a term applied to surface work in preparing the coal for shipment and in maintenance of equipment. Only 11, 0.5 percent of the 2,411 Negroes studied, were in positions which, even by the most liberal stretching of the term, could be called positions of authority. The position of mine foreman was the highest held by a Negro unless that of the one Negro safety director with the State Department of Mines be counted as a mining position.

EFFICIENCY OF THE NEGRO MINER

So far as employer opinion is an index, Negroes are efficient workers in most of the positions they occupy. Race prejudice on the part of whites and jealousy of other Negroes have greatly limited the success of Negro bosses. They must face the opposition of white workers, the suspicion of employers, and the antagonism of members of their own group who expect special favors. While the opinions of employers varied widely, the average opinion rated Negroes higher than native whites as coal loaders and brakemen and higher than the foreigners as machine men, motormen, and tipple men. They were considered inferior to the native whites as machine men, track men, motormen, and tipple men, and to the foreigners as coal loaders and track men. In all-round desirability, however, the Negroes for many employers are preferable because they are, in addition to being good workers, good company customers and "more easily handled" than other workers.

WAGES OF NEGRO MINERS

The daily wage of Negro miners appears high; the irregularity of work, however, cuts down the amount of annual wages recorded. Study of payrolls of three companies revealed that in 1929 the average semi-monthly wage of 142 Negroes was $59.15, or about $118.30 a month. By 1931, however, wages in three Kanawha County mines dropped 50.9 per cent from the 1929 figures, a condition somewhat typical of mines in every county. In 1932 conditions were more depressed than in 1931. With the operation of the NRA over several months of 1933 the earnings were undoubtedly higher.

Negroes in the mines studied paid back to the company in charges of some kind 71.9 per cent of their earnings. Foreigners spent only 32.5 per cent of their earnings with the company, while native whites spent 51.4 of theirs. Foreigners, although receiving an average wage of $18.86 each semi-monthly period more than the Negroes, spent an average of $17.15 less with the company. The chief items of expenditure are for groceries, furniture, and supplies at the company-store; rent, powder, and miners' tools; doctor and hospital fees; fuel; light; and burial fund. In spite of the large part of their earnings spent with the company 119, or 19.8 per cent of the 600 miners interviewed reported ownership of real estate. One hundred and twenty-three, or 20.5 per cent, owned automobiles, while 43.8 per cent either owned an automobile or had previously owned one.

THE COMPANY-OWNED TOWN

Coal development in isolated areas has forced coal companies to build houses for shelter and to provide all other resources necessary to even the simplest and rudest life. The resulting "company-owned" towns vary from those in which the state of disrepair, in the words of the United States Coal Commission, "runs beyond the power of verbal description,"[8] to those with paved streets and running water in the houses superior to many non-mining rural communities.

In all of these towns a sort of feudalistic paternalism on the part of the company inevitably exists. Company stores found at every operation as a rule enjoy a monopoly since no other store is allowed on company property. The building of good roads, however, has provided the miners with some outside markets. The health of the miners is cared for by "company doctors" who, although paid by the workers, usually consider themselves employees of the company and identify themselves with its interests. Miners live in "company houses" for which they must sign contracts which specifically state that they do not create the relationship of landlord and tenant but only of master and servant. They further stipulate that the miner will allow no one on the premises objectionable to the company. By these means, and a local police system under company pay in some localities, the companies have made most difficult the organization of miners by labor unions.[9]

THE FAMILY

In the drab life of the mining fields are to be found comparatively few unmarried Negroes. Of the miners interviewed, 76.0 per cent were married and 6.5 per cent more were either separated, widowed, or divorced. The traditional Negro family in which the mother is the stable quantity is tending, under the influence of mining conditions, toward standards of the white majority group. The miner must be working for a company in order to hold his house. Employment opportunities for wives are limited; hence, the man is necessarily a more stable element in family life than in many other occupations.

Birth rates for Negroes in mining counties are lower than for whites.[10] The reason for this fact probably lies not in the absence of large families but in the frequency of childless marriages. Of the 495 married miners, 22.2 per cent were childless, while 37.2 per cent had more than three children. The largest family contained 17 children. Scarcity of large houses in the mining fields has resulted in 64.6 per cent of the people in Negro miners' families living under what are ordinarily considered as overcrowded conditions.

In the early days Negro migrants took up with women and maintained them as common-law wives. Some of these unions are still to be found although the requirement of a marriage license by the state in order for a wife to receive "compensation" for the death of a husband led most of them to marry. Negro sex and family mores are slowly approaching the standards of the white group.

EDUCATION

Of the Negro miners interviewed 9.5 per cent had no schooling; 12.8 per cent finished the eighth grade; 4.4 per cent finished high school; while six, or 1.2 per cent, had some college work. Their children are provided with comparatively good schools, since the state spends practically the same amount per capita for Negro and white education. The children of Negro miners are taking advantage of their opportunities; a slightly larger percentage of all Negroes in the mining fields between 5 and 20 years of age are enrolled in school than of native whites of the same ages.[11] A larger proportion of the Negroes in school remain for the high school years than in any other southern or border state.[12] A large proportion of the students in the two Negro state colleges are children of miners, forming according to the Dean of the Bluefield State Teachers College 93.9 per cent of their 232 students and a somewhat smaller proportion of those of West Virginia State College.[13]

A heightened racial self-respect is given the children of Negro miners by race-conscious teachers. The different rates at which children and their parents assimilate white standards create a wide gap between them; some are bewildered by the conflict of standards and family tensions increase. Hypersensitivity concomitant with the developing racial psychosis leads many children to see in the mining situation only racial exploitation. They leave to face deadlines of other industries. Some are successful; others return in defeat to add their more articulate voices to the undertone of discontent which is always present.

RECREATION

Recreational facilities are definitely lacking in the mining fields. Much of the enforced leisure is spent in time killing rather than in activities likely to promote individual or social improvement. Loafing, "visiting," gossip, pool, checkers, and horseshoes take much of the miners' time. Baseball is also popular with the young people of both sexes. In more prosperous times automobile riding was greatly enjoyed by Negro miners, but many of them have lost their cars or can not buy gasoline for them during the depression. Fishing is indulged in to a very limited extent since not all mines are on streams where fish are plentiful. Many Negroes keep "hunting dogs" which they use upon occasion.

Negro churches and lodges have traditionally filled the need for recreation. Funerals, weddings, and "baptizings" are well attended. Schools have also seen their responsibility and provide programs of various sorts, particularly for adolescents. Negro musical organizations are prevalent, especially vocal quartettes. These quartettes represent different mining towns [and] compete for prizes.

RELIGION

Most of the Negro miners are church members, 71.6 per cent of those interviewed belonging to some denomination. Baptists are most numerous, constituting upwards of 80 per cent of all church members in the coal fields.[14] Fifteen and seven-tenths per cent of the miners whose schedules were taken were Methodists, while 3.7 per cent were adherents of the "Holiness" Church. Negro preachers range all the way from college and seminary graduates to uneducated "preaching" miners. Some "professional" jealousy exists between these groups.

All gradations between the extremely emotional, uninhibited, rhythmic service[15] and that identical with urban white churches exist. Study of the Negro churches in the mining fields indicates that diverse cultural elements, even in a group with racial homogeneity and bonds of common disadvantages, may not have their religious needs met in the same way. Simple Negro peasants lately from the south, caught in the maelstrom of economic maladjustment, desiring the ecstacy which only a certain type of religion can give them, complain that they cannot "understand" the preacher. Educated and race-conscious Negro ministers, for whom the adoption of white standards constitutes the most important desideratum complain because they must "talk down" to their congregations. Both are unsatisfied.

SOCIAL CLASSES

Negroes in the mining fields are by no means a homogeneous group. Social rank among Negro miners rests not so much upon economic bases as upon cultural differences, sharp distinctions being made between West Virginia and Virginia natives and those from further south. The Virginians and West Virginians consider the southerners "crude," emotional, and "mean," and tend to avoid them. Alabamans particularly are objectionable. Isolated by the majority group of Virginians and West Virginians the southerners either become "clannish" or attempt to escape discrimination by denying their origin and passing as Virginians or West Virginians. Other bases of social status are church membership and, in some places, denominational adherence. Upper classes further hold aloof from the "criminals" as they term them, meaning thereby those who habitually run afoul of the law.

RACE RELATIONS

Race relations are relatively intimate and friendly even though whites and Negroes work in closest contact. The stable equilibrium of the present time comes as one stage in a cycle the other stages of which may be said to be isolation, economic welcome by employers, industrial and social conflict, accommodation and quiescence.[16] Race consciousness is present to a limited extent among miners and to a greater extent among their children, teachers, and preachers. Sporadic growth of Garveyism in the mining fields, however, was concomitant with the growth of the Ku Klux Klan.

The interracial situation in the mining fields provides sufficient evidence for questioning the extent of applicability of the common generalization that race prejudice exists in inverse proportion to the status of the white person. Ordinarily acculturation of the white has led him to expect the Negroes to be necessarily lower; when Negroes approximate the position of the white, prejudice is aroused. Under the stimuli of controlled competition of the company-owned town the white no longer expects the Negro to receive lower wages or occupy a definitely lower plane. Negroes and whites receive equal pay in the same positions; their respective numbers are determined by company policy to which both races must become accommodated. Over a period of years the status of the groups has become, thus, more nearly identical, with eventual decrease rather than an increase of race prejudice, quite contrary to the usual generalization.

PROSPECT

Although their proportion in the mining industry of West Virginia has increased during the depression, owing to the departure of thousands of whites,[17] Negro miners are, as a whole, a dissatisfied and downcast group whose future depends pretty largely on the fate of the coal industry itself. Attempts have recently been made, after a favorable decision of the Supreme Court, to stabilize conditions by means of coöperative sales organizations of competing operators,[18] and some gains have been made by labor under the NRA. It is too early yet to say just what the ultimate results will be. If the Negroes remain while whites leave and through some means order replaces chaos they may be able to preëmpt for themselves a place in the mining industry superior to any they have yet occupied. If, on the other hand, the new control devices mean only anarchistic competition and production by larger units the conclusion seems inescapable that the Negro youth of the mining fields will continue its exodus to other parts, the void will be filled by recruits from the South, brief periods of prosperity will alternate with squalor, and Negro miners will continue, as in the past, to be "more easily handled."

1. See, for example, C. G. Woodson, *A Century of Negro Migration* (1918); *Negro Migration in 1916-17*, U.S. Dept. of Labor, Division of Negro Economics (Washington, D.C., 1919).

2. Greene and Carter G. Woodson's *The Negro Wage Earner* (Washington, D.C., 1930); Charles S. Johnson's *The Negro in American Civilization* (Washington, D.C., 1930); and Sterling D. Spero and Abram L. Harris's *The Black Worker, 1915-1930* (New York, 1931) contain valuable material but are limited largely to economic discussion. Additional material is to be found in the reports of the West Virginia Bureau of Negro Welfare and Statistics from 1921 to 1932.

3. According to the West Virginia Department of Mines there were 25,335 Negro miners in 1927, 23,987 in 1928, 23,941 in 1929, 23,521 in 1930, and 21,514 in 1931. Later figures are not

yet available. [See chapter 21, this volume, for recent figures.] In spite of the decline in their numbers during the depression, Negroes have lost a smaller proportion than either native whites or foreigners.

4. The Negro legendary hero John Henry was supposed to have worked at the Big Bend Tunnel on the C. & O. Railroad during its construction, 1870-72. (See Guy B. Johnson, *John Henry* [Chapel Hill, N.C., 1929], p. 54.)

5. *Reports of the U.S. Immigration Commission, 1911* (Washington, D.C., 1911), vol. 7, p. 151.

6. West Virginia Department of Mines, *Annual Report, 1907*. No reports prior to 1907 contained any data on racial or national groups in the mining population.

7. West Virginia Department of Mines, *Annual Reports, 1907-31*.

8. *Reports of the U.S. Coal Commission, 1923* (Washington, D.C., 1923), pt. 3, p. 1431.

9. The "freedom" of the companies has been somewhat limited by the NIRA. See Title 1, sec. 72.

10. *Birth, Stillbirth, and Infant Mortality Statistics for Birth Registration Area of the U.S.* (Washington, D.C., 1929), pp. 127-28.

11. U.S. Bureau of the Census, *West Virginia, Composition and Characteristics of the Population, 1930* (Washington, D.C., 1931), p. 9.

12. U.S. Bureau of Education, bulletin no. 20 (1931), p. 73.

13. Information secured through correspondence and interview with the officials of the two institutions.

14. *Religious Bodies: 1926*, vol. 1, p. 69. Further information was secured from J. J. Turner, State Director of Religious Education and Missions of the Baptist Church.

15. Cf. H. W. Odum, *Social and Mental Traits of the Negro*, p. 54ff.; E. T. Kreuger, "Negro Religious Expression," *American Journal of Sociology*, 38 (July 1932); N. N. Puckett, *Folk Beliefs of the Southern Negro* (Chapel Hill, N.C., 1926), chap. 8.

16. Cf. E. S. Bogardus, "A Race Relations Cycle," *American Journal of Sociology*, 35 (1940), 612ff.

17. Between 1930 and 1931 there was a decrease of 9.2 per cent in the number of miners employed, while the proportion of Negroes employed increased 0.1 per cent (West Virginia Department of Mines Reports, 1930 and 1931). Study of Company pay rolls indicated that a much larger percentage of whites left in 1932, while Negroes tended to remain.

18. See *Coal Age*, 36 (1931), pp. 65, 648; 37 (1932), pp. 34, 85, 123. *Coal Mining*, 9 (1919), p. 97; 10 (1920), p. 24.

8

The Black Community in a Company Town: Alcoa, Tennessee, 1919-1939

RUSSELL D. PARKER

For almost four decades, from the time of its incorporation in 1919 to 1956, when the first "outsider" was brought in as city manager, Alcoa, Tennessee, was a company town. There was a progressive facade, but neither city manager nor commission could "sharpen a pencil without getting approval from a Company official."[1]

The purpose of this article is to consider the function of the black community within that framework and to identify such leadership as demonstrated itself in the twenty-year span of Alcoa's development before the advent of World War II, although it should be stressed at the outset that the climate was not the most salubrious for expression of leadership, black or white.

The terminal point is not one of mere convenience. By 1939, blacks were leaving Alcoa as new job opportunities developed in defense industries about the country. It seems also that ALCOA's enthusiasm for black workers had waned. Negroes had been useful to discourage unionization in the early twentieth century: they could be depended upon to work under less than ideal conditions. But unionization succeeded in the 1930's and blacks could no longer be arbitrarily calculated to do the "dirtier" work or to do the same work as a white man for less pay.[2] This is not to say that unionization at that point wrought a miracle for black workers, but it did make a difference, as will be demonstrated.

The insights presented here are drawn from interviews with Alcoa residents of that generation, as well as their progeny; close examination of the municipal archives, which were opened to my scrutiny; and an understandably restricted perusal of the archives of the Aluminum Company of America, Tennessee Operations. The *Aluminum Bulletin,* an in-house monthly which had its beginning in October, 1918, furnished valuable perceptions into what life was like in the black community of that era. There was a separate section entitled "Colored Notes" usually prepared by John Brice, teacher-minister. Regrettably, the *Bulletin* expired in December, 1920. After a 27-year gap, The *Tennessee Alcoan* began publication in 1947. But the *Alcoan* does not match the *Bulletin* as a resource. In fairness, this is partially explained by the space limitation. Whereas the *Bulletin* usually ran around twenty pages, the *Alcoan* is an 8-page sheet, on occasion cut to four.

ALCOA's venture into East Tennessee can be explained principally in terms of quest for low cost power. The average rainfall of the region is the highest in the United States outside the Puget Sound area, and the mountains bordering the Little Tennessee River system rise to 6000 feet. The concept of an integrated network of dams to utilize the full electrical potential of a total watershed was a new one in 1910 when ALCOA began buying riparian rights along the Little Tennessee.[3] Three years later, they reached a decision regarding location of a plant site and quietly bought up land in North Maryville—they would ultimately purchase 3300 acres—some thirty-five miles north of their hydroelectric power source.

By 1914 construction of a reduction plant and about 150 houses got under way. In 1917 the extensive townsite construction was begun; the city plan was predicated on 7500 acres with provision for an eventual population of forty to sixty thousand and consideration for separation of residential and industrial facilities. Parks and playgrounds were to be allocated an acre to each one hundred population.[4] By a special act of the Tennessee Assembly, Alcoa, Tennessee, was incorporated, its charter effective July 1, 1919. By 1920 it was a townsite of 700 houses with a population of 3358 and a labor force of 3672, and ALCOA's payroll was running $3,150,000.[5]

The plan of 1922 divided the City into four sections: (1) Vose, the maiden name of Mrs. C. L. Babcock. Babcock Lumber and Land Company had built about 150 houses for its employees at a sawmill and finishing mill shortly before ALCOA's location in the area, also a general store, clubhouse, dormitory and school; Babcock was the first mayor of Alcoa; (2) Bassel, for G. M. Bassel, ALCOA engineer employed in construction of the reduction plant; (3) Springbrook, for the stream that ran through that section; and (4) Hall, for Charles M. Hall, discoverer of the electrolytic process for reduction of aluminum from its ore.[6]

The latter section was the black community and the terminology is suggestive of the fact—that blacks were to be involved in the reduction process at the South Plant, which was the earliest construction. A fabricating or sheet mill (West Plant) was in operation by August, 1920.[7]

In the reduction process, bauxite ore is mixed with a solution of caustic soda and heated under pressure. The hydrated alumina (aluminum hydroxide) dissolves; solid impurities are filtered out. The filtered solution is heated in a revolving kiln to 1800° F; it becomes pure alumina, a white powder. Metallic aluminum is produced by electrolysis, which separates alumina into its components, oxygen and aluminum. Alumina is dissolved in a bath of molten cryolite in electrolytic furnaces called reduction pots. By means of a carbon anode suspended into the bath, electric current is passed through the mixture, causing metallic aluminum to be deposited on the cathode; alumina is added as necessary to keep the process continuous. At intervals, aluminum is siphoned from the pots to be cast into ingots. Aluminum oxide combines with the anode as CO and CO_2.

The potrooms were extremely hot, as was the carbon plant, where the anodes were baked for setting in the pots. In the full knowledge that this task would be most unpleasant and would require a considerable work force, ALCOA sent recruiters into Alabama, Georgia, and Mississippi to obtain unskilled black labor.[8] Workers came in on rail "transportation," their fares paid—it was later deducted from their wages.[9] They came in a steady stream at a time when blacks were being pressed back from whatever prosperity they had enjoyed in the extraordinary conditions resultant from World War I. For all the unpleasantness of their work assignment, it was generally viewed as a great opportunity.[10]

A recruiting pamphlet, widely circulated, painted an enticing picture:

ALCOA offers to reliable colored workmen a fair wage, a bonus for good workmanship, short hours, excellent working conditions, and a chance for promotion. In addition, the city of Alcoa offers modern well-built homes, progressive churches, and an excellent public school system.[11]

The schools, it was pointed out, offered in addition to regular subjects "cooking, sewing, carpentry, and bricklaying." Four-room houses rented for $7.50-$9.00 per month; three-room houses for $6.50; all were equipped with "running water, electric lights, and a toilet in the house."[12] It was stressed that ALCOA employees must be in top physical condition—"a man must weigh at least 150 pounds; he must be over 5 feet, 7 inches tall; and he must have two good eyes . . . arms, and . . . legs. He must be free from ruptures, hernia, varicose veins, venereal disease, and all other disabling defects. . . ."[13]

In 1920, with the City barely a year old, the black population did not lag far behind that of the white—1482 to 1708—and there were 130 Mexicans. By 1930, the white population had risen to 3647, with that of blacks stabilized at 1587. The Mexicans had all departed. The 1940 census indicates a considerable drop in black population—to 1209—while the white figure at 3917 was still rising.[14]

During the construction period in 1913, before the City plan was drawn, blacks were housed in two- and three-room temporary tarpaper shacks on the low ground near Pistol Creek Pump Station which came to bear the title "Black Bottom." When those houses were destroyed, the title was applied to the Montgomery and Americus Avenue sections of Hall, reflecting the heavy influx from Alabama and Georgia. Those houses were early removed and the street names changed to honor famous world inventors. The whole black section was first termed by its inhabitants "Peniel," a Biblical derivation, then "Walnut Hill" before the "Hall" designation.[15]

Two buildings which would serve as the nucleus for black community activity were completed in 1918-19 on Hall Road, the City's main thoroughfare: the Negro Community Building, a one-story structure 31 × 91 with recreation hall and auditorium, and the Commercial Building, a two-story brick 107 × 101 with businesses on the first floor and the seven rooms of the top floor serving as the black school until construction of Charles M. Hall School in 1926.[16]

Once established, black workers were urged to buy homes at cost from the Aluminum Company Property Sales Office.[17] A cartoon in the April, 1919, *Bulletin* depicts blacks coming from their humble homes and whites from their larger dwellings converging on the office. One black exclaims, "Here's where we share alike." And another, "Wait, white folks. Ise gwine, too."[18]

The Real Estate Department reproduced an exact copy of a deed to assure prospective buyers that they were not simply leasing, as had been rumored. Along with clauses restricting building investment, requiring connection to City water and sewage systems, and forbidding livestock was a provision that "none of these premises shall be sold, leased or transferred to a member of the Colored race."[19] Blacks could buy lots also, so long as they stayed in their Hall sector.[20] While there were rental and lot options, the Company preferred to sell house and lot, and in time, allowing for replacements and relocations, there were some 1200 such parcels available.[21] In an open statement that lacked something in psychological insight a Company spokesman explained that homeowners were "the last to go on strike and the first to return to work." And "a contented workman is a more efficient workman. . . . Mr. Colored Man: Buy yourself a home in the most promising colored community in the country. Watch it Grow."[22]

In the townsite the person with whom citizens must reckon was Victor J. Hultquist, a New Yorker of Swedish extraction who hired on with ALCOA in 1913 and as construction engineer developed the towns of Calderwood (the original Alcoa); Badin, North Carolina; and finally Alcoa. He was appointed city manager in 1919 and proceeded to serve "longer than any other person who has managed a city in this country."[23] He was simultaneously superintendent of ALCOA's Construction Division in charge of plant and townsite construction, maintenance of townsite housing, collection of rents, sale of real estate, operation of the Knoxville Power Company Light and Water Departments (an ALCOA subsidiary), ALCOA Terminal Railroad, Brick and Tile Works, Farms and Dairy, Quarry and Concrete Mixing Plant, Lumbering Operation and Woodworking Shop, Trucking Department, and Landscape and Gardening Nursery. Amazingly, he seems to have recognized no necessary contradiction or conflict of interest in his divided loyalties. A true believer in the free enterprise system and in the moral soundness and responsibility of industry, his stirring remarks to a civic club are an index to his commitment:

If Mr. Hall and Mr. Davis [ALCOA's first president] with the help of a few associates were able to create the great accomplishments we look back upon today, each one of us has the power to make contribution by our minds and hands not only to our own Alcoa, but to the greater ALCOA, that it may lead the world in aluminum production for the betterment of us all.[24]

Hultquist's partner was Arthur B. Smith, a local product, the city recorder, treasurer, and judge, who served the same lengthy term then succeeded (1948-56) Hultquist as city manager. He was simultaneously bookkeeper for the Construction Division. Given the nature of the city charter and the areas of activity they controlled through their Company employment, these two men, or more properly the Company through them, dominated virtually every facet of every Alcoan's life. If, for example, there was any delinquency in payment of rents, fines, taxes, utility bills, etc., Smith simply wrote deduction notices to the Payroll Department of the Company, which withheld the charges without question.[25]

On his part, Hultquist was a genius at planning City construction projects to coincide with periods of slack employment at the plant so as to obtain labor at a low wage and hold workers in the community until such time as they might be called back by ALCOA.[26] Such a policy discouraged many blacks from moving on to Detroit, Michigan, or Lynch, Kentucky, where, it was rumored, there were better prospects in the automobile and coal industries.[27]

Education was a realm in which Hultquist's administration touched the total black community most intimately. As city manager, he appointed the superintendent of schools and hired all teachers. But the Company had brought in a remarkable black leader, John T. Arter, to serve as principal of the black school before the City was incorporated. A close examination of Arter's earlier career is essential to an understanding of what he had in mind to do at Alcoa.

John T. Arter was born July 18, 1867, in Pickens County, South Carolina. His parents moved to Greeneville, Tennessee, while he was a small boy. In 1885, at the age of sixteen or seventeen, he entered Knoxville College and received his BA degree in 1895; he attended Pittsburgh Theological Seminary in 1899.[28] In 1903, Arter and his wife Minnie went to Arlington or Annemanie, one of the five mission schools the United Presbyterian Church had established through its Freedmen's Board in Wilcox County, Alabama. During their fifteen-year stay the enrollment grew to over 150 with a faculty of 25-30.[29]

It was a boarding school-home model based on the Arters' experience at Knoxville College; students and faculty came together for meals in the dining room and for communion in the large chapel. Arter was, moreover, a conscious imitator of Booker T. Washington. He visited Tuskegee periodically to observe its operation and desired that at Arlington, as at Tuskegee, students should pursue a trade or occupation in addition to their academic courses. Female students were trained in homemaking, sewing, and dressmaking; the young men in brickmaking, carpentry, blacksmithing, mill work, and scientific farming.[30]

The school's growth and reputation were so impressive that the Freedmen's Board in 1908 permitted Arter to open an office in Pittsburgh from which to solicit funds for expansion. He was hired by ALCOA in the fall of 1918 with duties that went beyond those of school principal. His philosophy apparently agreed with that of B. L. Glascock, the first works manager at ALCOA's Tennessee Operations, who said in 1922 in a eulogy delivered at the time of Arter's untimely death from a heart attack,

Our idea was and is that we should have such a colored community that our men would be satisfied and would become permanent citizens. To that end we set aside a very large portion of our town site as a village for Negro people. . . . Our idea was that we would have a community that would grow naturally in numbers and that we would, therefore, be able to get our employees from our own town as the boys came into manhood. This plan coincided exactly with what Professor Arter had in mind and had been doing in Alabama. . . .[31]

If Arter's philosophy smacks of accommodation, it should be noted that he was a man of keen perception, doubtless aware that progress within a system is unlikely without first gaining acceptance. He was experienced and polished and generally gained his objective, sometimes by devious means. When the City of Maryville announced in the summer of 1918 that its facilities would not accommodate the increased school population resultant from ALCOA's precipitate location in the area, it was decided that the upstairs of the large Commercial Building in process of construction would serve admirably as a temporary school for blacks. White students would be obliged to attend temporarily a renovated "Mule Barn," the building which had housed equipment and animals during the construction process. There was some trepidation in Pittsburgh at the racial implications,[32] a tenseness which was not relieved when Arter clashed with Hultquist's first choice as school superintendent, Ben W. Frazier. Frazier became disturbed when the Commercial Building was put to a variety of uses at Arter's order.[33] On his part, Arter complained that the building was not adequately heated and that Frazier had refused his requisition for toilet paper. Further, he charged that the superintendent had reneged on a promise to hire two teachers from Knoxville College, with which he was seeking to establish a strong tie. The latter charge was undoubtedly a dig at Hultquist, who, he surely realized, had the final word in hiring and firing of teachers.[34] Hultquist released Frazier abruptly with the observation, "We are satisfied that things are not as well knit together as they should be, and we want to endeavor to fill this position with someone who is a little older in experience in handling the various elements we have to contend with in this city."[35]

One cannot but wonder if Arter could have stayed on in view of his strong personality, had his tenure not been cut short by his death. An observer reckons that had he been permitted another ten years, he would have achieved a miracle for blacks; he was a "Moses."[36] But there is evidence of abrasiveness in his dealings with Hultquist at the turn of the decade when it seemed that the ALCOA venture into Tennessee would not prosper and the hierarchy were cutting back on some of their high-flown promises (which had attracted Arter in the first place) regarding what the black community might become. As the World War I prosperity faded and orders fell off, the total Tennessee Operations was shut down from August, 1921, to February, 1922.[37]

Arter had been hired, he said, on a twelve-months basis at a salary of $125 per month. His pay had been cut to $100 per month, and he was receiving no pay at all for the summer months of 1920. P. W. Moore, Hultquist's townsite lieutenant, was sent to bear the tidings, but the decision must have been Hultquist's. Arter thereupon advised the city manager by letter that he had a family of eight to support, and that for his services he deserved and expected $2400—or $900 more than the $1500 he wasn't getting![38] He checked the ALCOA installation at Badin, North Carolina, to see what the prospects might be for black teachers and reported the authority there had informed him that "he would employ as few as they could get along with, and pay them as little as they would work for."[39]

Hultquist was likewise spending as little as he could to procure black teachers—$75-$80 per month, while white teachers drew around $125.[40] Thomas P. Marsh, who had come to Alcoa at Arter's bidding, complained of inadequate pay and threatened to return to Alabama.[41] Arter interceded and procured teaching positions for Marsh and his wife—Marsh had been employed in a tree-planting project. It is quite evident that Arter was attempting to build a power base with a cadre of people who held views similar to his own. Marsh, John Brice, Frank W. Woodfin, and Dr. Walter S. E. Hardy were among his chosen leadership circle and he demonstrated a willingness to challenge any competing authority in the black community.

A case in point is his letter to Hultquist proposing that T. P. Marsh be placed in charge of the athletic program. Suits and supplies had become scattered and Rufus Lenoir, the Company's choice in the black community, lacked something in managerial ability, said Arter. Marsh, he suggested, would render a responsible accounting in matters of gate receipts and concessions.[42]

That Hultquist was suspicious of Arter's design is indicated by his letter to Harry Clark, Professor of Secondary Education at the University of Tennessee, inquiring into the degree of radicalism that might be expected from teachers matriculated from Knoxville College. Clark was reassuring: "There is practically no radicalism. . . . You know there is some of it everywhere among the Negroes now."[43]

Arter intended that the schools should serve as the nucleus for a community that must be more closely knit. Hultquist quickly advised him that children under six should not attend school. "We had never figured on running a nursery . . . nor had we . . . felt able to establish a kindergarten."[44] Arter was utilizing the schools to bring together those over, as well as under, school age. He defended his summer school program—and gained his point—even in the face of economic recession and argued that programs must be maintained if the morale of disillusioned blacks was to be lifted: "An element of Negroes and whites around here have taken advantage of the slump, and are trying to discourage the colored people and make them believe that the Company has a program to discard all Negroes and Mexicans. . . ."[45] He was probably probing with this letter, since the Company was at that time in fact engaged in "discarding" the Mexican element.

The church was also envisaged by Arter as a unifying device. He requested of B. L. Glascock a truck to transport "our people" to the Second Presbyterian Church in Maryville; he, Hardy and Brice would be responsible. In the same note he complained that "there is so much prejudice around here we are not allowed to ride in any of the public conveyances and our workers have been forced to walk. . . ."[46] He got the truck.

The major consideration, it would seem, is to what degree the black community responded to Arter's leadership and philosophy. John Brice, whose utterances are extant through the medium of the *Bulletin,* expressed from time to time an impatience with the masses, which is perhaps typical of an elitist leader. A graduate of the Knoxville College Normal School (1899), baccalaureate program (1904), and seminary (1907), Brice had pastored an Athens, Tennessee, mission church and served as a chaplain with the AEF in France. His job description with ALCOA was "Personal Relations" and he was Arter's right arm.[47] He upbraided his fellows: "We clamor for opportunities, for privileges, advantages, and when they come we carelessly pass them by."[48]

Brice was convinced that education was the key to a better life for Negroes and he hammered away at the need to make the most of what he considered a unique opportunity. Black school enrollment in 1919 exceeded that of whites; of the 522 total, 205 were white, 278 black (including 74 in adult night classes), and 39 Mexican.[49] A year later, however, with the fabricating plant in operation (it employed essentially whites) the enrollment ran 891—537 white, 318 black, and 36 Mexican.[50] Brice assured his readers that ALCOA intended to accomplish no less than "the best graded school for Negroes in the South. They are paying good salaries to secure the services of some of the best prepared teachers in the race."[51]

The teachers were of high calibre and there was a scramble for positions, reflecting not so much the high level of salaries as a dearth of possibilities where educated blacks were concerned. Arter counted forty-eight applications for seven vacancies as the system was organized.[52] In 1926, after two schools for whites—Springbrook (1921) and Bassel (1923)—had been constructed, the City provided Charles M. Hall School for Colored Children, of comparable quality.[53] When the decision came to build the latter school, Hultquist feared a "backlash" from the elements of the City outside the Company, particularly Babcock Lumber Company, at the tax hike that would inevitably result. Alcoa's current rate was $1.65 and he calculated the building would elevate it fifteen cents. Maryville's tax rate was $1.75 and he didn't want to exceed that level. On the other hand, there was "considerable complaint" from blacks for the failure to offer high school courses and he feared "we cannot stave this off longer than next year. . . ."[54] His most common correspondent, Edwin Stanton Fickes, ALCOA's vice-president in charge of engineering with office in Pittsburgh, looked to stepped up production as an outgrowth of additional power from the completed Santeetlah Dam project and saw a need "to keep the colored population contented, in view of the increased demand for potroom labor which we will have at the end of 1927."[55]

Knoxville College was close by and John Brice optimistically forecast that an interurban [bus] would soon be transporting Alcoa blacks to the college on a regular basis.[56] This projection was doubtless at odds with the Company's own plan, which was to move grade school graduates directly to the potrooms. City manager Hultquist, who perennially addressed the eighth grade graduating class, said it in so many words with a regularity that became extremely tiresome to his auditors.[57]

Next to Brice, T. P. Marsh was Arter's closest associate. A graduate of Knoxville College, he had worked with Arter in the mission school at Arlington. Arter sent for him at what might appear to be an unlikely time—the height of the 1920-22 recession. But Arter had operated a cannery at Arlington and the Company had installed a cannery in the Hall community as a relief measure in the crisis period. Marsh would operate the cannery and free Arter for other activities.[58]

Hultquist was supportive of any self-help program, so long as the cost was minimal to Company and City. In consistent fashion he deplored the relief strategy of the New Deal Democrats when the Great Depression took hold in the 1930's:

The popular posture of the day seems to be to cuss and discuss the large industries, and popular opinion seems to be directed more and more toward governmental planning of our society, but I believe we have an excellent opportunity at Alcoa to plan an industrial order that will . . . show . . . better results than much of the work the government is attempting to carry on.[59]

In that spirit Glascock announced early that the Company would plow vegetable gardens and furnish seed at cost,[60] and Hultquist reported in the mid-30's that 199 white and 94 black families had been assigned 103 acres for garden plots.[61]

Dr. W. S. E. Hardy, from Charleston, South Carolina, a graduate of Meharry Medical College, Nashville, had been in the Medical Reserve during World War I and was practicing in Jefferson City at the time the Company invited him to Alcoa. He was not, however, a Company doctor. The Company briefly operated a hospital and the Medical Director, J. Walter McMahan, noted that blacks were not using the segregated facility, although "we always strive to make our patients feel that the hospital is a place where color does not make any difference."[62] He complained that "some persons have been practicing medicine and mid-wifery in our colored village who are not licensed by the State Board to practice in Tennessee" and urged blacks to use Hardy.[63]

There is indicated here an insular tendency, which, if understandable, was antithetical to what Arter was attempting to accomplish; he was insistent on participation in the system. A high point of sorts in this aim to draw attention to black achievement was (in the Booker T. Washington tradition) a School and Community Fair in the Commercial Building for a full week in June, 1919. On display were quilts, garments, crochet, cakes, rolls, bread, pies, canned fruit and manual training furniture products. Brice reported, "The good feeling existing between the races was evidenced by the presence at all our exercises of some of the best whites of the community."[64]

The clouds of recession were clearing in the summer of 1922 when Arter was struck with a fatal heart attack. His wife Minnie applied for his position for the coming year;[65] she was succeeded briefly by T. P. Marsh. But the administrative structure her husband had been struggling to fashion quickly fell apart. Mrs. Arter turned to teaching in the Knoxville school system; Marsh made his way back to Alabama; Brice took a teaching job in North Carolina. One member of the circle around Arter stayed on, a paradoxical figure. F. W. Woodfin, a graduate of the Knoxville College Normal School (1880) was a master brickmason and woodworker, skilled in the manual arts. In 1910 he had been principal of the United Presbyterian School in Bristol; later he had run the brickyard at Arlington. In Alcoa, while he trained young people in his capacity as public school teacher, he was a major influence upon those who strove to rise above a future in the potrooms.[66]

With Arter's circle removed, the principal's post ceased to be the seat of power. This was due in part to the character of the successor who emerged after the stumbling efforts to perpetuate the Arter dynasty. Samuel E. Gosby had worked his way through Knoxville College. He has been described as a "stern disciplinarian" but at the same time gentle and sensitive, "almost effeminate."[67] He was an excellent pastry cook, played piano and taught voice. He lived with his mother, where he raised flowers and kept a model lawn. For all these accomplishments, from the time he became principal in 1925 Company and City administrators called him "Sam"—his predecessor had been "Professor" Arter. He lacked the commanding demeanor of the prior occupant of his post. Too, that post had become somewhat circumscribed; his was a narrower responsibility than Arter's. Life went on, but at a more pedestrian pace. Absent was the inspirational drive, briefly available, that might have made Alcoa unique.

The Commercial Building remained a center of activity, but the "improvement" programs of Arter lapsed. Brice in particular had pressed for black enterpreneurs in the downstairs business stalls, but of the "modern stores, pharmacy, meat market, barber shop, and tailer shop," only the barber was black.[68]

Masons, Knights of Pythias and Odd Fellows with their respective Eastern Star, Ruths, and Court of Calanthe auxiliaries maintained active schedules, meeting in the Commercial Building.[69] There had been talk of a black Boy Scout troop—Fickes had suggested to Glascock early that this would "keep them out of mischief and make better citizens of them"[70]—but that project languished.

Whereas Arter had been able to obtain jobs in the fabricating plant for a select few,[71] the community was obliged to look, at his passing, to a different breed of fixer. Starling Henry and, more particularly, Rufus Lenoir owned influence with the Personnel Department.[72] Lenoir was a convivial type who administered the athletic program since Arter was no longer present to question his qualification. He attended church and the lodges, was highly visible and accessible. He was a "company man" and all knew it, but he was no mere tool. Both Company and community paid a price for his services.[73]

Unionization in the mid-1930's reduced the vulnerability of black workers. With qualifications and wage scales set, Company capriciousness in these areas was checked.[74] Still, black reaction to unionization was ambivalent; they well knew that their place in the labor force was dependent on their manipulative function. Nonetheless, blacks were actively involved in the labor agitation that ended in violence in 1937 and the eventual establishment of the principle of collective bargaining.[75] Although they were encouraged to join the union, blacks did not enjoy equal opportunities in the 1930's and 40's. Rest-rooms, water fountains, and cafeteria facilities remained segregated and relegation to less desirable jobs continued. The union hall was integrated, but the membership perpetuated inequities and the Company did nothing to discourage them.[76] A proper share of union benefits and Company initiative in the field of equal rights were developments of the 1950's.[77]

Near the close of the second decade of the City's existence, after Arter's firm policy had given way to expediency and accommodation, Alcoa blacks rallied around an unconventional young college student and sought to revive community spirit. Hendrika Tol, of Dutch descent, attended Maryville College and with National Youth Administration funding supervised in 1935 playground activities at Hall School. At the same time and without compensation she opened a library in the basement of the Second Presbyterian Church (black) in Maryville. Tol called on H. C. Bristol of the Alcoa Rent Department, who in turn requested of his superior, Hultquist, that she be permitted to move the library's holdings to a dwelling on Hall Road. Hultquist agreed to the plan; the City paid light and water bills, furnished tables and chairs, and paid Tol $4.50 per week as a supplement to her government stipend.[78]

At the time she moved to Alcoa, Tol's shelf list included 1500 books and 2000 magazines. She showed 369 books issued to 133 readers in the month of October and reported gifts of books from various publishers—Harper Brothers, Alfred A. Knopf, Funk & Wagnalls, Doubleday Doran, and Viking, as well as contributions from individuals and such institutions as Lend-a-Hand Book Mission of Boston.[79] Hultquist, as the Company's representative, became concerned at the content and tone of her letters; the inference might be drawn that ALCOA was not doing everything necessary for the well-being of its black workers.[80]

Buoyed up by community support, Tol organized adult education classes and a black Boy Scout troop, both calculated from her point of view to inspire initiative for a higher level of existence. Hultquist cooperated for a time because her programs kept the youth occupied and the cost to the City was minimal.[81] She embarrassed him when she went to the top to inquire if the Mellon Foundation, in view of the banking family's considerable interest in ALCOA, might lend support to her projects.[82]

ALCOA vice-president I. W. Wilson (he would become president of the corporation in 1951) did not choose to answer directly but advised Hultquist that the Mellon Foundation was not set up "for any such purposes as are served by this Hall Community Library. . . ."[83] Wilson passed Tol's letter to C. C. Carr, ALCOA's public relations manager in Pittsburgh, with a note that he should do what he could to assist. Carr responded that he was sending a display chart on the aluminum manufacturing process which "ought to satisfy them."[84]

Tol apparently went too far when she proposed a Negro Health Center.[85] Dr. A. J. Alexander, a black physician, would conduct a prenatal and pediatric clinic. Dr. Charles Davis, also black, of Knoxville, would conduct a dental clinic. These services would be available to Alcoa blacks, whether they worked at the plant or not. There were 309 blacks employed by ALCOA at the time, Tol said, and a minimal deduction of fifteen cents per week from their paychecks would support the clinic; it could be based in the library building. Tol conceived of the plan as a "common venture," a "socializing factor" that would bring Alcoa's blacks together.[86]

Hultquist shelved the plan and instructed Tol not to organize a health campaign in the black community "before discussing it with me"; nor should she "allow the library building to be used for any purpose other than has been approved by me. . . ."[87] Alcoa Police Chief Arthur Lively, who kept close vigil over Tol's movements, warned her to get the black clinic idea out of her mind or to get out of town.[88]

Hultquist demonstrated considerable alacrity in accepting Tol's resignation from the library post in June 1939, even though no resignation was in fact tendered.[89] She had by this time graduated from college and was supervising black youth funded by NYA to administer the program.[90] It seems that Hultquist was ridding himself of periphery concerns so as to devote his full attention, as construction superintendent, to a massive expansion of the aluminum plant. The developing war in Europe had established that the airplane would be a prime weapon and defense orders were already pouring in. The Alcoa North Plant, erected in 1940-41, would cover over 65 acres—the largest plant under one roof in the world—and ALCOA's local work force would swell to an all-time high of 12,000.[91]

In the post-war era ALCOA, in a move to improve its public image, divested itself of the various townsite operations which had been Hultquist's province and which had made Alcoa a "company town" prototype. The benignly paternal oversight of the City was abandoned. Alcoa blacks benefitted from this change and more particularly from the civil rights initiative of the Truman administration. It is axiomatic that in the post-World War II period advances by Alcoa blacks came about primarily through changing institutions, by law, rather than by force of strong personalities. But there was a brief point in time at the city's inception when a strong leadership demonstrated itself—John T. Arter was a man with a plan. And surrounding him were a number of exceptional individuals to assist in the realization of that plan. At his death in 1922, the succession faltered, then collapsed. Although no absolute power vacuum resulted, there was lacking a leader disposed to prod City and Company officialdom and the citizenry to undertake great things.

1. Roy Fisher, Tennessee Operations Manager, "Speech to Maryville Kiwanis Club" (Aug. 12, 1969), ALCOA Archives, Tennessee Operations.

2. Fred Wetmore, AFL-CIO organizer, private interview in Alcoa, Tenn., Apr. 11, 1975; Archie Simpson, private interview in Alcoa, Tenn., Feb. 26, 1975.

3. "Development of Power," pp. 1-2, ALCOA Archives, Tennessee Operations.

4. Robert F. Ewald, "City Plan for Alcoa, Tennessee" (Nov. 15, 1922), pp. 3-7, City of Alcoa, General File.

5. Maryville-Alcoa Times, Oct. 28, 1960.

6. Victor J. Hultquist, City Manager of Alcoa, "Speech to Alcoa Rotary Club" (Jan. 14, 1959), Hultquist Papers.

7. Ibid.

8. G. R. Swany, who became reduction and carbon works manager in 1925, recalls that it was thought "they would be better for the pots" ("G. R. Swany," p. 6, ALCOA Archives, Tennessee Operations); Iva McMahan Moore, Dr. Mac: A Beloved Physician (Douglas, Ga., 1974), p. 70. The daughter of ALCOA's first local Medical Director states that "it was very hot work and the Aluminum Company found that Black and Mexican men could stand the intense heat better than anyone else." She observes that "these men would wear large aprons of some sort of protective material, wrap their feet in burlap or gunny sacks of some other, hopefully, protective material and they would wear gloves. If, by chance, some of the hot molten aluminum splashed on the body, hands, arms, feet or legs it made a very deep painful and hard-to-heal burn. One of the best way to treat such a burn was to force liquid parawax over the bruised area" (Moore, Dr. Mac, p. 70).

9. Archie Simpson, interview, Feb. 26, 1975; C. H. Sudderth, private interview in Alcoa, Tenn., May 23, 1975.

10. Ibid.

11. "ALCOA's Advantages for the Colored Workman" (Alcoa, Tenn., n.d.), p. 2.

12. Ibid., pp. 3-4.

13. Ibid., p. 9.

14. U.S. Bureau of the Census, Census Reports, 1920-1940, (Washington, D.C., 1921-1941). According to Swany, the Mexican labor, which was recruited on a tentative basis, was driven out due to conflict with blacks during the 1920-22 recession ("Swany," p. 6). This contention

is totally rejected by black residents, who maintain it was ALCOA initiative that sent the Mexicans on their way (Fred Brown, private interview in Alcoa, Tenn., Apr. 14, 1975; Lee Byrd, private interview, Alcoa, Tenn., May 19, 1975).

15. Victor J. Hultquist, "Chronological History of Construction Department, Alcoa Works, 1913-1946," p. 14, ALCOA Archives, Tennessee Operations.

16. Ibid., p. 15.

17. Although the Company purported to make no profit, over a ten-year span—most purchases were made on a "120-month plan"—the buyer would pay 60% of the base price in interest.

18. *Aluminum Bulletin,* 1 (Apr. 1919), 12.

19. Ibid., 3 (Dec. 1920), 15.

20. That blacks were serious about settling in Alcoa on a permanent basis is indicated by their early commitments. In the period April 1919 to June 1920, 62 lots were sold in the white community with 7 cancellations. In the black community 15 lots were sold with no cancellations (ibid., 2 [Aug. 1920], 3).

21. Otto Cochran, ALCOA Properties Manager, Tennessee Operations, private interview in Alcoa, Tenn., Mar. 4, 1975.

22. *Aluminum Bulletin,* 2 (Aug. 1920), 11; ibid., 1 (Mar. 1919), 4-5.

23. *Knoxville News-Sentinel,* June 16, 1948.

24. Hultquist, "Speech to Alcoa Rotary Club."

25. As a consequence, delinquency was virtually non-existent. In the decade 1925-35, delinquent City taxes ranged from a low of $29.70 to a high of $197.88 (City of Alcoa, General File, passim).

26. Victor J. Hultquist to Edwin S. Fickes, Dec. 31, 1920; Hultquist to I. W. Wilson, Feb. 19, 1938, City of Alcoa, General File.

27. *Aluminum Bulletin,* 2 (July 1920), 15.

28. "Tribute to the Life and Work of Rev. John T. Arter, AB '95, by the Synod of the Presbyterian Church, U.S.A.," *Aurora,* 36 (1923), 28.

29. Minnie Jenkins Arter, "A Narrative of the Work of the United Presbyterian Mission School at Arlington from the Year 1900 through the Spring of 1918" (1950), p. 10.

30. Ibid., pp. 3, 7.

31. "Tribute," p. 31.

32. Charles H. Moritz to Edwin S. Fickes, Sept. 9, 1981, City of Alcoa, General File.

33. Ben W. Frazier to Hultquist, n.d., ibid.

34. John T. Arter to Hultquist, June 19, 1920, Nov. 5, 1920, ibid.

35. Hultquist to Frazier, Apr. 27, 1921, ibid.

36. Archie Simpson, interview, Feb. 26, 1975.

37. Hultquist, "Speech to Alcoa Rotary Club"; C. F. Hord, "Speech to Alcoa Rotary Club" (Mar. 10, 1965), ALCOA Archives, Tennessee Operations.

38. Arter to Hultquist, June 19, 1920, City of Alcoa, General File.

39. Arter to Hultquist, n.d., ibid.

40. Hultquist to William H. Carey, June 23, 1922, ibid.

41. T. P. Marsh to Hultquist, June 23, 1922, ibid.

42. Arter to Hultquist, Apr. 25, 1921, ibid.

43. Harry Clark to Hultquist, Dec. 20, 1919, ibid.

44. Hultquist to Arter, Sept. 16, 1921, ibid.

45. Arter to Hultquist, May 16, 1921, ibid.

46. Arter to B. L. Glascock, May 28, 1921, ibid.

47. *Aluminum Bulletin,* 2 (Feb. 1920), 17. The *Bulletin* reported Arter and Brice attending a two-day farmers' conference at Tuskegee.

48. Ibid., 3 (Oct. 1920), 22.

49. Ibid., 1 (Feb. 1919), 7.

50. Ibid., 3 (Nov. 1920), 7.

51. Ibid., 1 (Mar. 1919), 8; ibid., 3 (Dec. 1920), 19.

52. Ibid., 2 (Nov. 1919), 18.

53. "Comparative Cost of School Buildings" (Jan. 8, 1926), City of Alcoa, General File. Springbrook cost the City $68,079.70; Bassel $61,108.73; and Hall $64,028.95. There were subsequent additions and improvements, but the basic building program was completed insofar as

the limits of this study are concerned when Alcoa High School was built in 1939 at a cost of $106,135 of which WPA furnished $47,781. With completion of the first three buildings, Hultquist boasted as Brice had anticipated that "we have the reputation of having the best schools in East Tennessee, and one of the best colored schools in the South" (Hultquist to Fickes, June 15, 1929, City of Alcoa, General File).

54. Hultquist to Fickes, Jan. 5, 1926, ibid.

55. Fickes to Hultquist, Dec. 26, 1925, ibid.

56. *Aluminum Bulletin,* 2 (Apr. 1920), 15.

57. Archie Simpson, interview, Feb. 26, 1975; Ruth Matthews, private interview in Alcoa, Tenn., Mar. 5, 1975.

58. *Aluminum Bulletin,* 2 (May 1920), 19; ibid., 3 (Oct. 1920), 23.

59. Hultquist to Fickes, Jan. 23, 1934, City of Alcoa, General File.

60. *Aluminum Bulletin,* 2 (Mar. 1920), 1-2.

61. Hultquist to Fickes, Apr. 6, 1935, City of Alcoa, General File.

62. *Aluminum Bulletin,* 1 (Nov. 1918), 2.

63. Ibid., 2 (Feb. 1920), 19.

64. Ibid., 1 (June 1919), 9-10.

65. Minnie Jenkins Arter to Hultquist, June 29, 1922, City of Alcoa, General File.

66. Archie Simpson, interview, Feb. 26, 1975; Ruth Matthews, interview, Mar. 5, 1975.

67. Beulah Brown, private interview in Alcoa, Tenn., Apr. 14, 1975; Hendrika Tol, private interview in Alcoa, Tenn., Mar. 19, 1975.

68. *Aluminum Bulletin,* 1 (July 1919), 15; ibid., 2 (Sept. 1920), 49. City policy did not bar black proprietors but restrictions were such that black capital was insufficient to gain a foothold. Archie Simpson, interview, Feb. 26, 1975.

69. *Aluminum Bulletin,* 1 (July 1919), 15.

70. Fickes to Glascock, Mar. 24, 1920, City of Alcoa, General File.

71. Archie Simpson, interview, Feb. 26, 1975; Ruth Matthews, interview, Mar. 5, 1975.

72. C. H. Sudderth, interview, May 23, 1975; Beulah Brown, interview, Apr. 14, 1975.

73. Beulah Brown, interview, Apr. 14, 1975.

74. Archie Simpson, interview, Feb. 26, 1975; Fred Wetmore, interview, Apr. 11, 1975.

75. Sammy E. Pinkston, "History of Local 309, United Steelworkers of America; Alcoa, Tennessee" (master's thesis, University of Tennessee, 1970), p. 43; Fred Wetmore, interview, Apr. 11, 1975.

76. Pinkston, "History of Local 309," pp. 43-44.

77. Ibid., 88.

78. H. C. Bristol to Hultquist, Aug. 20, 1935, City of Alcoa, General File.

79. Hendrika Tol, "Report of the Library Project for Colored People in Alcoa, Tennessee, Sept. 16-Oct. 31, 1935," ibid.

80. Hendrika Tol, interview, Mar. 19, 1975.

81. C. H. Sudderth, interview, May 23, 1975.

82. Tol to ALCOA, Pittsburgh, Oct. 13, 1938, City of Alcoa, General File. By 1920, Andrew W. and Richard B. Mellon, who had bankrolled ALCOA in its early expansion, owned one-third of the stock. Charles C. Carr, *ALCOA: An American Enterprise* (New York, 1952), p. 44.

83. Wilson to Hultquist, Oct. 17, 1938, City of Alcoa, General File.

84. Memorandum attached to ibid.

85. Hendrika Tol, "Report Concerning Negro Health Center" (Aug. 19, 1937), City of Alcoa, General File.

86. Ibid.

87. Hultquist to Tol, Oct. 15, 1937, ibid.

88. Hendrika Tol, interview, Mar. 19, 1975.

89. Ibid. See also Hultquist to Tol, June 1, 1939, City of Alcoa, General File.

90. Tol to Hultquist, Jan. 31, 1936, ibid.

91. *Maryville-Alcoa Times,* Aug. 29, 1969.

9

Class over Caste: Interracial Solidarity in the Company Town

DAVID A. CORBIN

> You live in a company house
> You go to a company school
> You work for this company,
> according to company rules.
>
> You all drink company water
> and all use company lights,
> The company preacher teaches us
> what the company thinks is right.
>
> Carl Sandburg,
> "The Company Town"

Although the UMWA made little headway in the southern West Virginia coal fields between 1890 and 1911, a powerful social force was already producing a collective mentality among the miners. By its contrived and rigid structure, the company town, while giving the coal operators extraordinary forms of power over the miners, precluded the development of a social and political hierarchy based on color ethnicity, that is, a caste system, within the working class community. Its standardized living and working conditions prohibited socioeconomic competition and mobility, and its highly rigid capitalistic structure established distinct class lines, based not on an ethnicity or race, but on occupation. The company town quickly and ruthlessly destroyed old cultures and stimulated the development of a new one. The nature of the company town focused the workers' discontent, not on each other nor on a racial or ethnic group, but upon the employer—the coal operator—enabling the miners to develop that sense of group oppression necessary for class feeling and behavior. As Jeremy Brecher explains, "Class consciousness involves more than an individual sense of oppression. It requires the sense that one's oppression is a function of one's being part of an oppressed group, whose position can be dealt with by the action of the entire group."[1]

The influence of the company town in producing interracial harmony was evident in the earliest stages of the creation of the southern West Virginia work force. Under the impact of the migration of blacks, northern cities exploded in racial conflict, as thousands of blacks became economic and social competitors with whites. Between 1890 and 1900 alone, northern white workers conducted over thirty strikes protesting the hiring of black workers, and hundreds of northern labor unions declared themselves "lily-white" by prohibiting blacks from membership. Later thousands of northern white workers joined the Ku Klux Klan, and race riots between black and white workers flared in East St. Louis, Illinois, Newark, New Jersey, Philadelphia and Chester, Pennsylvania, Washington, D.C., Omaha, Nebraska, and Chicago, Illinois.[2]

In contrast, racial troubles remained conspicuously absent in southern West Virginia. Recognizing the migration of thousands of blacks into southern West Virginia, the U.S. Department of Labor reported that "the tradition of harmony and reciprocal good will remains, and intense and bitter race feelings have not developed in West Virginia."[3]

Part of the explanation lies in the type of migrant that the coal fields attracted. Black migration to the north was essentially a rural to urban movement, of farmers and sharecroppers accustomed to the southern agrarian way of life moving into industrial cities.[4] The migration into southern West Virginia, the only state below the Mason-Dixon line to have an increase in black population between 1890-1910, was a movement into a rural area, apparently equally from two sources.[5] Southern industrial black workers, as well as agrarian blacks, flooded the state's coal fields, seeking escape from southern racism. An elderly black miner recalled that he moved from Alabama to West Virginia in 1902 because "the Negro counted for nothing in the south, the south wasn't like these [West Virginia] coal camps." Similarly, a migrant black miner in Omar, West Virginia, wrote a friend in Alabama that a "collered [sic] man stands just as good as a white man here." A black miner in southern West Virginia wrote the *UMWJ* that he was glad he had left Alabama because "there is none so hampered as the colored toilers in the Alabama coal fields. The colored man is so badly treated and browbeaten he hardly knows which way to turn for real friendship." Southern industrialists recognized this cause for defection. The president of Bessemer Coal, Iron and Land Company, angered over the loss of his black employees, told the Chamber of Commerce in Birmingham, Alabama, "I don't blame the Negroes for leaving Birmingham. The treatment that these unfortunate Negroes are receiving from the police is enough to make them depart for Kentucky or West Virginia."[6]

The blacks who moved from the southern farms to the southern West Virginia coal fields migrated generally for economic purposes. A black miner in McDowell County, who had been a sharecropper in Virginia, stated that he moved to West Virginia because he "could see it [money] better. The miner got paid once or twice a month. On the farm you had to wait till the fall of the year when you gathered your crops, and then the other fellows, the landowner, merchants, etc. got it all and that way we didn't make nothing." The migrants were even more impressed with the "high pay." "On the farm I was no[t] making anything," explained Bill Deering, "[but] in West Virginia I made a dollar on my first day and I thought I was rich!" Another miner recalled that he made two dollars on his first day and declared, "I'll never go back to farmin'." A black migrant miner in Holden, Logan County, wrote his former minister in

Alabama that he now "made money with ease. I am saving my money while spending part of it." Rumors spread throughout southern farmlands, "You can get rich in the West Virginia coal mines."[7]

That the black migrants from southern industrial areas had been accustomed to more oppressive conditions and that the migrants from the farms were content with economic conditions in their new homes may account for the white miners' initial hostility to them during the early formation of the southern West Virginia work force. A white miner in Oak Hill, Fayette County, angrily declared that he did not care for a recently hired group of blacks because "it is a class of labor that meets the approval of the operators here. . . . They are used to low wages and therefore grateful for the increase in pay and they dare not breathe a word without permission from the company."[8]

The controlled conditions of the company town, however, contained the hostility of the whites to the blacks. When four white miners in a company town in McDowell County, for example, struck in protest of the hiring of a black motorman, the superintendent immediately fired and blacklisted them. In a letter to the coal operator, the superintendent explained, "I had to show them who was boss." An elderly black miner supported this observation: "If the company felt a black man could do a job better, cause they wanted profits, they put the black man on the job and nothing was said. It was up to the company. . . . I don't know if the whites resented it, if they did, it didn't matter cause they couldn't do anything about it."[9]

The controlled and standardized economics of the company town prevented the economic competition between the races that produced so much racial strife in the northern cities. Because of hostility of northern whites, blacks were segregated and kept away from the better jobs. The great majority of them were forced to work at menial, dirty, and poorly paid positions that the native American or Americanized immigrant did not want. Racial conflicts erupted when black workers attempted to rise above these jobs or follow their trade, thus entering into competition with white workers and appearing to depress the job market. [10]

In the company towns blacks did not compete economically with the white workers, nor did they depress the job market. The black migration coincided with the meteoric rise of West Virginia as a coal-producing state. Although thousands of blacks entered the coal fields, the demand for miners, at least till 1920, was greater than the supply. In 1910 the number of miners in the state was triple that of the previous decade (62,189 versus 20,287 in 1900). Yet the companies were still 15,000 miners short of their needs.

The companies' standardized economic policies insured future economic racial parity. The companies' system of payment, for instance, did not allow discriminatory practices. Over 90 percent of the miners in southern West Virginia were paid on the "piece-rate basis"; less than 50 percent of the rest of the nation's miners were paid this way. West Virginia miners were paid according to the amount of coal they mined, not according to the color of their skin.[11]

Furthermore, in the company town the miners worked side by side inside the coal mine. Writing about West Virginia, one labor historian has noted that "segregation either by occupation or by place of work, unlike most factory industries in the South, is conspicuous by its absence in the coal mines." Such economic togetherness undoubtedly contributed to interracial unity. A team of psychiatrists explained that working inside a coal mine produces a peculiar social cohesion among miners. Inside the mine, they have suggested that

the miner finds himself in a world of tension . . . [he is] potentially expendable, close to danger . . . under protracted tension because he may be the next man to get it. . . . Thus while on the job, both potential and actual threats are all around the miner, and this has to be dealt with in such a way as to minimize "wear and tear." Miners, like other groups, deal with such stress by strong social cohesion on the job. An example of such unity under stress may be seen in army and civilian groups during war-time. When such groups face dangers, prejudice, selfishness, pettiness, hatred and other frailties of personality melt in a "common defense." There is a "social security" among men who team up, not only to keep working, but to keep alive.[12]

The migration of southern blacks into the southern West Virginia coal fields differed from the northern migration in its familial patterns and its effects upon the migrant's family. The move to the industrial cities of the north, according to E. Franklin Frazier, caused the migrants to suffer a deep sense of loss in migration because "customary familial attachments were broken." Between 70 and 80 percent of the black migrants in the north, one observer estimated, were without family ties. Black families were further weakened after settlement. Because of the ethnic pecking order of the American job market and other discriminatory, economic policies (e.g., low wages), black women were forced to become breadwinners while their husbands cared for the children and house, thus producing unstable family arrangements.[13]

Unlike the migration to the North, the migration to southern West Virginia was primarily a family movement. The migrant black miners brought their families with them to the company town. In the Elkhorn District of McDowell County, family structure (husband and wife) characterized 68 percent (431 of 660) of the black households. Of the remaining 32 percent, almost one-half were married men who had left their families in their native state until they could earn enough money to bring them to West Virginia. It took Walter Hale thirteen years of mining during the winter and returning home during the summer to earn enough money to bring his family to West Virginia, but he was eventually successful.[14]

The company town stabilized the already family-oriented black migrants—as the company town sustained the patriarchal family—because the pecking order of the job market in the coal fields was sexual, not racial. Both company policy and superstition prevented women from working in the mines; therefore, other than doing laundry for the single miners or company officials or taking in boarders, the miner's wife was housewife and mother. Unlike the situation in the northern industrial areas, the black male in the southern West Virginia company town was always the breadwinner.[15]

The coal companies pursued policies that further secured the family unit. Managers preferred married men because they worked harder and longer under the piece-rate system to feed their families, and they were also less mobile than single men. The U.S. Women's Bureau reported that "only the presence of the family can keep the mine worker in the area. . . . The bunk house and the lodging house long ago proved themselves inadequate to attract a requisite number of workers to maintain a stable labor supply . . . [because] the mine worker cannot at will substitute the restaurant for the family table as can the wage earner in other industries." Because of their preference for married men, the coal companies generally laid off workers during slack periods according to marital status rather than seniority or color. Herbert Spencer, a single black miner in Gary, McDowell County, recalled being laid off with a number of single white miners while his father and other married miners, both black and white, retained their jobs. [16]

Stable family structures became extremely important as the black migrants remained in southern West Virginia. Not only did married men make the best miners, they later made good union men. Single miners often left struck coal fields for more peaceful areas where they could make more money. The married miner viewed the coal fields as more of a permanent home. They found it more difficult to move and recognized that they had a vested interest in improving their working conditions. Consequently, it was the married miner who stuck out the strikes and fought the hardest for the union, and their families helped sustain them. [17]

Company housing promoted a class over caste perspective. When the southern blacks flooded the northern cities, the housing situation was one of the gravest problems they encountered. Throughout the North, the black newcomers were jammed together in the worst houses, forced to pay excessively high rent, and suffered from an inequality of public services. [18] In the southern West Virginia company towns, the migration of miners was neither haphazard nor excessive. The companies regulated the influx according to their needs of a work force and the availability of houses; hence, overcrowding never became a problem. [19]

Most of the company towns were integrated, although some of them, depending on company policy, were segregated. Even when segregated, the town was too small, its population too familiar, and social interaction too great to allow racial stereotyping and social distance and, hence, a culture of discrimination to flourish. The population of a company town usually ranged from 200 to 500 people. When the company town was segregated, blacks never lived more than a few hundred yards "up the hollow" from the whites, and they still worked together in the integrated mines and went on picnics or played baseball together on Sunday afternoon in the company ball park. On Saturday night black and white miners went to integrated whorehouses or drank homebrew together in front of the company store. Assuredly their children played together in the company playground or in the company streets. [20]

Segregation, where it existed, was not an ironclad rule, as coal companies often violated their own segregation policies when it was convenient or necessary. For example, when a coal operator in the Winding Gulf coal field obtained the services of white cokemen, who were difficult to obtain, he placed them in the empty houses in the black section of the town because the houses for whites were filled. The extreme geographic mobility of the coal miners and the ease of employment because of the labor shortage allowed the black miner, if bothered by residential segregation, to move to a company town with integrated housing. Rogers Mitchell lived in eleven different company towns during his forty years as a coal miner in southern West Virginia. Only one of the towns, Ed Wight, was segregated. In that town, Mitchell explained, "all the coloreds lived on the hill, the whites lived on the bottom. I felt different so I didn't stay. . . . I drew one paycheck then left."[21] Likewise, if a white person objected to living beside blacks in an integrated town, he had two choices: to tolerate the situation or leave. There was no other section of town where he could move.

Whether voluntary or coerced, integration worked remarkably well among the various ethnic, racial, and religious groups in the company towns, where the miners and their families developed a strong community spirit and neighborly comradeship. An aged black miner related that his family had lived beside an Italian family, and "we were great friends." The Italian miner's wife "would cook Italian dishes and bring them over to our family to eat. And my wife would bake corn bread for both families and took part over to them. . . . Our young people had great times together. They would play and dance together. We helped each other out like good neighbors."[22]

The coal companies' standardized housing practices insured social and racial parity, for housing conditions in the company town did not consider race, religion, creed, or previous condition of servitude. The coal companies built all their houses alike, usually an A-frame, Jenny Lind-type, with the intention of housing the most people possible at the lowest cost. The result was some rather shabby, poorly built houses. John Schofield, a black miner, recalled the time when, during a heavy rainstorm, the roof of his house collapsed, hitting his wife on her head and knocking her unconscious for several minutes. Sydney Box, a white migrant from England, remembered that on his arrival in southern West Virginia he thought the miners' shacks were chicken houses, because they were so small and poorly built. The black and white miners' houses were equally bad. Further, the black migrants were not hampered by excessively high discriminatory rent, as the coal companies charged a standardized rent based on the number of rooms to a house, and not on the color of the occupant.[23]

Black and white miners suffered equally from the same insecurity with regard to keeping their housing once they had it. The housing contract, which created a relationship of "master to servant," was, as the U.S. Coal Commission claimed, "obnoxious and inconsistent with the spirit of free local communities," but it served to create friendliness and solidarity among the miners.[24] It limited a miner's friends to his fellow workers because of the companies' suspicion of strangers in the company towns, and it created a common anger against the employer.

Lack of home ownership had other important effects. Neither white nor black miners cared to invest, financially or physically, in the repair or improvement of their homes; therefore, housing competition did not exist between neighbors. Because both races lived in the same style of house and neither bothered to upgrade the houses, investigators reported that even in the segregated towns both black and white sections of the town consisted of "rows of frame houses monotonously similar" and that the houses of blacks were "as good as those of the white people."[25] Because there was no home ownership, there was no fear of lowering of property values when blacks moved into a company town.

In the company town there was no discrepancy in the quality or quantity of public services between the black and white miners. In Iaeger, McDowell County, for example, black families lived about one-third of a mile "up the road" from the whites. But both races received the same public services—or suffered from the lack of them. In 1922 Iaeger had no telephones, sidewalks, paved roads, electricity, or garbage collection. (Garbage was "thrown to the pigs.") Outdoor water service was available to all miners free—only company officials had inside water. Outdoor privies in both sections were cleaned once a year without charge—only company officials had indoor toilets. The company provided free coal for fuel to all employees, but charged fifty cents per delivery. Both races supplemented their income by raising gardens and poultry on the vacant land that the company provided for those purposes. The only store from which the miners could purchase their needs was the company store—the closest commercial store was fifteen miles away and off-limits to the miners.[26]

The company town quickly and ruthlessly dissolved the traditional cultures and the time-honored social institutions of the migrant miners (whether native white, immigrant white, or southern black) that might have encouraged the continuation of ethnic or racial, instead of class, perspectives in the newly created work force. This aspect of life in the company town is most vividly illustrated by the fact that the company town broke down one of the most important and enduring institutions for blacks in American society—the black church and the black preacher.

Even during slavery blacks had constantly looked to their ministers for secular as well as spiritual guidance. When the southern blacks moved to the North, they brought their church and its leadership patterns with them. Denied access to most of the intellectual, political, and commercial channels of expression in the northern communities, black migrants, George Haynes explained, "found an untrammeled outlet in their churches. They built up its form, made its rules and traditions, handled its finances and picked its leaders unhindered by the surrounding [white] world."[27]

In southern West Virginia the black preacher and the black church suffered a "fall from grace." In the company town, the coal company, not the blacks, built the church, "made its rules and traditions, handled its finances and picked its leaders." The minister in the company town church retained the pulpit at the sufferance of the company, which meant the preacher dared not address himself to the immediate material needs and wants (for example, unionism) of his congregation, or he would lose his job, if not his life. After a black minister, the Reverend Alfred Eubanks, made a pro-union talk in a Saturday night sermon in McDowell County, he was attacked by mine guards on his way to Sunday service the next morning, "severely beaten over the head with a pistol," and then arrested on the charge of resisting an officer. In Logan County, after a black minister advised members of his flock to join the UMWA, he was attacked by the county sheriff, punched in the ribs, and warned, "be the ——— ——— sure you don't do anything here but preach." In the majority of the cases, the coal company simply fired the pro-union minister or prohibited him from preaching on company property.[28]

If the black preacher wanted to remain in the coal fields, he not only had to preach what the company desired but also had to serve as a company "lick." During week days or slack season, the black preacher served as a labor agent who went south to recruit miners for his company. At times the preacher spied for the company and, during strikes, served as a mine guard. A black miner in southern West Virginia complained:

We have some negro preachers in the district who are nothing more than stool pigeons for the coal operators, and instead of preaching of the Gospel of the Son of God, they preach the doctrine of union hatred and prejudice, but I thank God the tide is fast changing and we are beginning to see the light for ourselves and realize the fact that they are only selling us out to the bosses for a mere mess of the porage.[29]

The black preacher's affiliation with the company earned him the disrespect, if not the contempt, of his congregations. The minister often had to maintain order during services "at the point of a pistol." Frequently, gambling and liquor selling took place in church, even during services. Probably the most revealing incident occurred when a group of black miners got drunk on a Saturday night and went to church. Halfway through the service, the inebriated churchgoers stood up and began shooting at the minister, who ran across the room and jumped out the window eight feet above the ground, breaking a leg and an arm. Rather than rising to the defense of their minister, the remainder of the congregation broke out in laughter and went home. On another occasion, a black minister literally "died of fright" when he saw his flock arm themselves during a strike. The mine superintendent in the town lamented the minister's death because, as he wrote to the coal operator, "he was one of the best leaders we [the coal company] had." Consequently, in the company towns the black miners as well as immigrants and native whites developed new social institutions, new patterns of leadership and prestige, and a new religion.[30]

One of the most conspicuous, integrative institutions in the company towns was, paradoxically, the segregated school system. This contention is difficult to argue because, as Raymond Mack points out, "most Americans now alive have grown up with the assumption that citizens opposed to desegregation are anti-Negro."[31] In effect, the Supreme Court's reasoning in *Brown v. Board of Education* ("To separate them from others of similar age and qualifications solely because of their race generates a feeling of inferiority as to their status in the community that may affect their hearts and minds in a way unlikely ever to be undone") has become generally accepted throughout the land.

In 1872 West Virginia enacted a provision to its constitution that called for racially segregated schools. For the next twenty years, the state's schools remained separate and unequal. In the 1890s, however, as the coal companies began to dominate both the people of southern West Virginia and the state government, they ushered in what elderly black teachers today call the "Golden

Age of Negro education in West Virginia." Concerned with the need for a more literate work force to reduce accidents, to increase productivity, and to stabilize a very mobile work force, the coal establishment secured the passage of progressive educational legislation. Largely because of the efforts of the coal industry, teachers' salaries became based on qualifications, not color. Because black teachers, especially those in the coal fields, were better qualified, the salaries for black teachers were, on the average, higher than for whites. Further, West Virginia was one of the few states in the nation that paid more per black pupil ($111.47) than for white ($100.63) for education.[32]

Black spokesmen in West Virginia were not reticent in pointing out the state's separate but equal educational policies and the advantages that they offered to black students. The director of the Bureau of Negro Welfare and Statistics for West Virginia remarked, "For thirty years West Virginia has been busily engaged in educating Negroes whose education had been sadly neglected by their native states." The black West Virginian and professor at West Virginia State College, Thomas Posey, while recognizing that the state constitution "provided for separate schools," pointed out that "the people of the state have fought for equal facilities under the law. The success they have achieved is evident by the fine educational and eleemosynary institutions in the state." Posey was no Uncle Tom; he had earned a Ph.D. in economics from the University of Wisconsin, where he had studied under Selig Perlman, and was a member of the Socialist Party of America.[33]

The coal companies exercised their greatest influence on educational policy at the local level. Taking advantage of the decentralized school system, the coal companies funneled tremendous amounts of aid into the local schools. They subsidized the building of schools and provided them with equipment. Public education in McDowell County in 1885 consisted of nine log-cabin schools, worth less than $100 each, and the school term was only three months a year. In 1904, largely as a result of the efforts of the coal companies, the county had seventy-eight schools, worth between $300 and $600 each, and the school term was eight months. The coal companies in Logan County spent nearly $100,000 on education within a four-year period.[34]

The coal companies also supplemented the teachers' incomes with a monthly bonus, to induce the better teachers to remain in the coal fields. Coal companies in McDowell County subsidized the teachers' salaries by almost $20 a month. In Logan County the coal companies gave the teachers monthly bonuses that amounted to $6,000 over a four-year period. Combined with the state's equal-pay policies for teachers, the subsidization of salaries made the pay for teachers high. Consequently, well-qualified black teachers throughout the eastern United States (including the son of a U.S. Senator B. K. Bruce of Mississippi) went to the southern West Virginia coal fields to teach.[35]

The contribution of the coal companies to public education in southern West Virginia was recognized throughout the country. Winthrop Lane, a New York journalist and no friend of the coal operators, conceded that "one respect in which the mining companies . . . are trying to improve conditions is in regard to schools." The black leader and scholar Carter G. Woodson praised the black schools in the McDowell County company towns as "well-equipped" and having as "well-qualified" teachers as any black schools throughout the country. The state supervisor of Negro Schools in West Virginia annually praised "the willingness of companies operating mines to provide adequate school facilities for children living in their camps."[36]

The children of black miners took advantage of the educational opportunities that the coal companies offered. In 1910 nearly 80 percent (1,639 of 2,067) of the black children between the ages of six and fourteen in McDowell County attended school. Native white children of the same age in the county had an attendance rate of 75 percent, and the children of white immigrants had an attendance rate of 78.6 percent. The editor of the *McDowell Times*, a black newspaper, claimed that the blacks' higher rate of attendance was an indication of the aspirations of black boys and girls when they were given "the advantage of the very best common school education."[37]

The separate but equal educational facilities were important in the lives of the black miners and their children. Although the educational level of the coalfield school remained relatively low as compared to northern education (high schools, for example, were conspicuously absent in the coal fields), the schools provided blacks with the sense of dignity and pride that comes with the knowledge of one's past and helped to make it possible for the blacks to live, work, and cooperate with whites on an equal basis. As long as the black teachers did not discuss labor affairs, they had complete control over their schools on the administrative level as well as in the classroom. As a result, reported a former teacher in Wyoming County, "The segregated school offered the opportunity to teach black history and culture and to emphasize the positive contributions of blacks to American society and to instill racial pride." Able to select their own texts, teachers used books such as Booker T. Washington's *Up from Slavery*. The black teachers in the southern West Virginia coal fields were in constant communication with Woodson and used his ideas, materials, and books in their classes. One of these ideas was the staging of annual "Negro History Week," for which teachers had their students make posters that illustrated the history of blacks in American society and place the posters throughout the town, in the mine offices, company stores, and the school. "Negro History Week" culminated with a large parade with floats, and students dressed as famous black Americans.[38]

This was the "proper education of the Negro race" that W. E. B. Du Bois claimed could not be obtained in the integrated, but white-dominated, northern schools. He pointed out that he had graduated from the great white institution of Harvard "without the slightest idea that Negroes ever had any history." A graduate of the coal-field education tells of going to Temple University to work for his master's degree and being astonished at the northern blacks' lack of knowledge of their own history: "Why they had no idea who Crispus Attucks and John Henry were, people we learned about in grade school!"[39]

The presence of schools in the coal fields offered another important benefit to the black miners. Ever cognizant of the problems and needs of members of their race, the black teachers, without pay, offered free night courses to the illiterate blacks working in the mines. Columbus Avery, born in 1871 in Alabama, had never attended school and was illiterate when he came to the West

Virginia coal field in the 1890s. In Mingo County he took night classes and worked in the mines during the day. Avery learned to read and write, and he eventually held office in the union.[40]

Black teachers had the respect of both the whites and blacks in the town, but like black preachers, they could never serve as leaders because they also could not address themselves to the miners' economic needs. If black (or white) school teachers discussed labor affairs, they lost their monthly bonus and jobs, because the coal operators, who often controlled the local school boards, had the right to fire as well as hire teachers. Where the coal companies did not control the school board, they controlled the school. The coal companies, after building the school on company property, leased or deeded the land to the county under the condition that "if used for any other purpose than educational or religious services, the land shall revert to the owner [the coal company]."[41]

As differences in housing, religion, and education existed between the North and southern West Virginia, so were there differences in politics. After settling in the North, the black migrants found a source of protection, prestige, and mobility in politics. Residential segregation in the northern industrial cities produced voting blocs of blacks, which enabled the blacks to elect members of their race into office who, to a limited extent, were able to respond to the wants and needs of the black community. Ambitious blacks became party bosses because of their ability to exploit the voting blocs for their personal advancement.[42]

Partly because of the Appalachian tradition—"mountaineers are always free"—partly because of the number and proportion of blacks in West Virginia at the time, but most important because their support gave the Republicans a majority in the legislature, blacks in West Virginia also obtained some political power. Several commentators and historians have emphasized the political rights and power of blacks in this state. Posey, for instance, acknowledged that "there is no state in the Union where the Negro has a larger share in the party councils or enjoys the political prestige of our own colored citizens." Because of their political power, blacks were elected to state offices and won considerable concessions from the Republicans, including state colleges for blacks, several state orphanages, and the formation of the Bureau of Negro Welfare and Statistics. Blacks were appointed to national as well as state offices. And blacks became political bosses in several commercial towns.[43]

It may be too easy to exaggerate the influence of black miners on the Republican party and erroneous to write of their political consciousness. If blacks enjoyed such political acuteness and power as other writers have claimed, surely the Republican party would have passed progressive mining laws, especially safety legislation, and would have abolished the hated mine-guard system. It is much more likely that neither the black nor white miners possessed enough political power to threaten, even remotely, the power of the coal companies. Officers and managers of these companies still rendered politics meaningless to the miner. Denied access to political information (other than what the companies supplied) and ordered how to vote or given a ballot already marked, the miners did not have a political voice in southern West Virginia.[44]

Consequently, politics did not provide opportunities for mobility and prestige, nor did it produce any black leaders in the company town.

The role of middle-class blacks in state politics and in the Republican party did have some beneficial consequences for the black miners that should not be ignored. Their influence made the Republican party a bulwark against "Jim Crow" laws in West Virginia, led to the passage of progressive legislation, helped to ban *Birth of a Nation* and other movies that would "arouse racial feeling," and aided the establishment of important black institutions.[45]

Little is known about the role of social clubs and fraternities in the lives of the black miners in the company towns, but it must have been significant. In 1915 over 10,000 blacks belonged to at least one fraternal organization, and by 1922 the total membership reached 33,000, or one-half of the black population in West Virginia. One observer noted that it was "the exceptional Negro miner who did not belong to at least one of the various lodges."[46]

Many blacks joined the social organizations for practical reasons. The director of the state's Bureau of Negro Welfare and Statistics explained that large numbers of blacks joined because three-fourths of the blacks in West Virginia were "engaged in the hazardous occupation of coal mining" and therefore unable to obtain life insurance. "The only provision which a large number of them can make for sickness and death and care for dependents . . . is to become a member of one or more fraternal and benevolent societies." In the year from July 1, 1924, to June 30, 1925, these organizations paid out $32,640 in death benefits to black miners' families. Many black miners joined simply because "it was the thing to do in the coal fields."[47]

The coal companies encouraged fraternities and often allowed them to use space on company ground for their meetings; a few companies even provided buildings for the social clubs. These fraternities relieved the monotony of life in the company town and provided "moral uplift" (immorality, adultery, or drunkenness, for example, was reason for expulsion). The lodges were usually headed by the more established, middle-class, anti-union conservative blacks from commercial towns; the coal operators undoubtedly hoped that their black workers would emulate the officers of the lodge. A black state official and an ardent supporter of the coal companies explained that the lodges were valuable for black miners because "they stand for a high degree of morality, for peace, law and order and progress. They teach industry and thrift. . . . More than any other agency working among Negroes, they have taught them the value of unity."[48] Herein lay another inherent contradiction in the operators' efforts to control their miners.

In the social clubs the blacks, especially those from the southern farms, learned and experienced the values of cooperation and the principles of brotherhood. A. L. Booker, a charter member of the local union at Helen, Raleigh County, claims that belonging to the Masons helped him and probably other miners to "become good union men because both organizations taught many of the same values; that a person should not hurt a fellow miner, he should not discriminate nor take another man's job. The Masons taught us to aid your brother in the time of need." George Hairston joined the Masons at War Eagle, Mingo County, a few years before the violent labor war in that county. He recalls that belonging to the Masons helped make him a "better union man" and helped prepare both black and white miners for the conflict because "it drawed us closer together; it brought us together in brotherhood and taught us not to mistrust or mistreat your brother." At a massive Thanksgiving service of the Colored Odd Fellows Lodge at Eckman, McDowell County, the principal speaker, a middle-class black from Keystone, instructed his audience of miners on the values of coal capitalism by quoting from Psalm 133: "Behold how good and how pleasant it is for brethren to dwell together in unity."[49]

Within the constraints of the company town, socioeconomic class lines became distinct and solidified. Florence Reese's classic labor song, "Which Side Are You On," vividly describes the class arrangements in the company town as a man, either black or white, was either a miner or a company "lick." Several observers and scholars have commented on this aspect of the company town, and the National Coal Association probably analyzed it best when it urged the abolition of the company town, believing that the "influence of small-town life will be most beneficial to the miners and their families. . . . It will be the best thing in the world for the miners' children to mingle with the children of the carpenter and the storekeeper and the doctor and also for the miners to participate and take an interest in civic affairs." The result would be to "create a civic rather than a class consciousness."[50]

The class structure in a company town prevented the development of a middle-class black leadership with conservative, racially conscious tendencies. Middle-class professional blacks (e.g., dentists, doctors, and ministers) who lived in company towns were not looked upon as symbols of individual or racial progress, but as company "licks" and spies, neither to be trusted nor emulated. Moreover, professional blacks did not live among the miners, even in the segregated towns; rather they lived on "silk-stocking row" in the company town or moved to commercial towns and traveled daily to work. There was no inspiration for social mobility that has so often splintered the American working class and prevented solidarity.[51]

The black miners developed antagonisms toward the middle-class blacks who lived in the commercial towns. Black organizations, such as the National Association for the Advancement of Colored People, were held in contempt because they represented "upper colored groups and not the common miner." The black miners also despised the anti-union attitudes of middle-class blacks. The black newspaper the *McDowell Times* was decidedly in favor of the coal operator and proclaimed that the black miners in West Virginia possessed the "best working conditions" and "most comfortable homes" and received higher pay than any other black workers in the country. It urged the black miners to eschew the union and not to strike because the operators were "their best friends." The superintendent of the Winding Gulf Coal Company described the editor of the *West Virginia Clarion,* another black newspaper, as a "real friend of the coal industry . . . who does more to keep us posted as to conditions than any agent [labor spy] covering the field."[52]

With the decline in influence and prestige of the black preacher and cut off from politics and distrustful of the middle-class, professional blacks, the black (and white) miners in the southern West Virginia coal company towns developed new sources of prestige and leadership patterns. One source proved to be on the job, that is, down in the coal mine, where the miners who displayed an "ability to meet emergencies" and "efficiency in performance" were most admired.[53] By the 1910s the miners accorded their highest prestige to the men who held office in the only institution that the miners regarded as their own and the one that promised to end the exploitation and oppression of the company town—the UMWA. When the union came to southern West Virginia, it would reflect the interracial harmony and egalitarian brotherhood that the miners had developed in the company towns. Blacks would hold office throughout the District 17 organization; they would be represented on the District's Executive Board, would work as District organizers, and would commonly hold office in the local union. In one instance, the president, vice-president, and secretary-treasurer of a local would all be blacks.[54]

More significant was the spirit of those locals. A miner in Mount Claire wrote the *UMWJ* that "we have 150 miners in our local and among them are white and Negro Americans, Horvats, Hungarians, Slavs, Croatians, Italians. We get along well in our local for having so many nationalities and races represented in our membership." Fred Ball, the president of the UMWA local at Silush, a white man, wrote the journal telling about the members' cooperation and success during a strike. He finished the letter by exclaiming, "So brothers you can call [us] . . . Negroes, or whites or mixed. I call it a darn solid mass of different colors and tribes blended together, woven, bound, interlocked, tongued and grooved and glued together in one body."[55]

That cohesive union spirit promised to abolish the system that held all miners, regardless of race, nationality, or religion, in industrial slavery. The southern blacks who migrated to the West Virginia coal fields may have been initially content with their higher wages and the lack of discriminatory practices, but after several years of living and working in the company town, their attitudes and values changed dramatically. The exploitation and oppression that they encountered, as a class and not a race, in the company town, and the social, political, and economic power that the coal operators exercised over them reminded the black miners of the darkest pages in black history in the United States—slavery—but this time the slaves were whites as well as blacks.

This comparison of conditions in the company town to those in slavery may be exaggerated, but it was real to the miners who lived and worked in the southern West Virginia coal fields; they constantly compared their plight to slavery. One black miner called the company town a "damnable, slave-driving system" and asked for the return of "Grant's Army" to emancipate the miners from the "greatest octopus of serfdom encompassing any set of men on the American continent." A miner from Raleigh County wrote:

> The boss said stand up boys
> And drive away your fears,
> You are sentenced to slavery
> For many long years.
>
> So pick up your shovels
> And do your work well.

You are right here where we want you
And we'll work you like hell.[56]

The most revealing comparisons came from black miners who had been slaves or who were children of slaves. George Echols, a black miner in Mingo County and a former slave, told a U.S. Senate committee:

I know the time when I was a slave and I feel just like *we* feel now. . . . My master and my mistress called me and I had to answer. We claim that we are citizens of the United States of America according to the amendment in the Constitution. You know that that guarantees us free and equal rights and that is all we ask.

The chairman of the committee asked, "Just what rights do you feel are getting away from you?" Echols responded:

If we get together and are talking, we are ordered to scatter and move out. If we go out for a walk, two by two, we are ordered to scatter and move out. If we go to town . . . we have to tell our wives good-bye for we know we might not come back. . . . [It is like it was] before the Constitution prohibited slavery. Let us be free men. Let us stand equal and I do not mean that there is any prejudice against colored people here.[57]

Columbus Avery stated that "miners possibly had it worse than the colored folk under slavery, if I understood my parents [who] had been slaves right." Walter Hale recalled discussions with his parents, who were former slaves, who had told him he had it worse as a miner than they did under slavery.[58]

The black miners realized, however, that there was a major difference between plantation slavery and company-town industrial slavery. Plantation slavery was based on color, company-town industrial slavery was based on class. A black miner in southern West Virginia, who described himself as a union miner "from my head to my feet" wrote,

The American white miner is in a worse state today than the Negro was in slavery. He has to feed himself and family. The Negro did not have to do all that. When he wanted to go for a long distance he went to his master and asked for a mule to ride and it was all right. He has a full stomach to sleep on. No man working for a coal operator ever has a full stomach. Abe Lincoln signed a proclamation to set the colored slave free. Now the white miner is in slavery. Who will set him free?[59]

The black miners also recognized that because this time they were aligned with working whites, they had the opportunity to fight for their freedom. A black miner in southern West Virginia explained, "There was a time when we colored people could not fight for our freedom, but I thank God that the day is come that every man can fight for his own rights. My dear colored friends let us all stand firm and show the world that we have grown to be men of America, and that we are not afraid to fight for our rights."[60]

And fight for those rights they did, on Paint Creek and Cabin Creek. They fought with, not against, their fellow white workers, on a working-class basis, for the one institution that offered them power, prestige, leadership, and escape from bondage. The company town was not the only force in southern West

Virginia conducive to racial harmony and working-class solidarity. However, it prevented the black migration of the 1890s from creating in southern West Virginia many of the racial antagonisms that affected other coal fields and the northern cities. Nor would the UMWA's egalitarian union policies have been as successful without these necessary preconditions.

1. Jeremy Brecher, *Strike!* (San Francisco, 1972), p. 247. Both numerically and proportionally, more miners in West Virginia lived in company towns than in any other state in the nation—94 percent. The number of blacks employed in the southern West Virginia coal industry was substantially higher than in any other state. In 1920, for example, 18,371 West Virginia coal miners were black. Second to West Virginia was Alabama, with 11,723 black miners, and third was Pennsylvania, with 2,288. Indeed, in 1920, 43 percent of all black miners employed in the bituminous coal industry worked in West Virginia. See Sterling D. Spero and Abram L. Harris, *The Black Worker, 1915-1930* (1931; reprint ed., New York, 1974), p. 208; Edward Hunt, F. G. Tryon, and Joseph Willits, eds., *What the Coal Commission Found* (Baltimore, 1925), pp. 136-40; Donald T. Barnum, *The Negro in the Bituminous Coal Mining Industry* (Philadelphia, 1970), pp. 1-10; West Virginia Bureau of Negro Welfare and Statistics, *Annual Reports, 1925-29*, pp. 22-24; James T. Laing, chapter 7, this book, and "Negro Migration to the Mining Fields of West Virginia," *Proceedings of the West Virginia Academy of Science*, 10 (1936), 171-81; U.S. Department of Labor, Women's Bureau, *Home Environment and Employment Opportunities of Women in Coal-Mine Workers' Families*, Women's Bureau, bulletin no. 45 (Washington, D.C., 1925), pp. 12, 51-55.

2. William Tuttle, *Race Riot: Chicago in the Red Summer of 1919* (New York, 1974), pp. 108-55; Allan Spear, *Black Chicago: The Making of a Negro Ghetto* (Chicago, 1974), pp. 201-22; Spero and Harris, *Black Worker*, pp. 57-62, 162; Kenneth Jackson, *The Ku Klux Klan in the City, 1915-1930* (New York, 1967); Henderson Donald, "The Negro Migration of 1916-1918," *Journal of Negro History*, 6 (Oct. 1921). Sociologists claim that it is a "socio-cultural law" that the migration of a "visibly different group" into a given area increases prejudice, discrimination, and the "likelihood of conflict" (Gordon Allport, *The Nature of Prejudice* [Reading, Mass., 1954], pp. 227-29); Robin Williams, *The Reduction of Inter-Group Tensions* (New York, n.d.), pp. 57-58; Gerhart Soenger, *The Social Psychology of Prejudice* (New York, 1953), p. 99.

3. "Industrial Relations and Labor Conditions: Economic Condition of the Negro in West Virginia," *Monthly Labor Review*, 16 (Apr. 1923), 713. The coal fields generally experienced less racial strife than other industrial areas. Some labor historians have claimed that the egalitarian, industrial union policies of the UMWA were the determining factor. See, for example, Herbert Northrup, *Organized Labor and the Negro* (New York, 1944); Herbert G. Gutman, "The Negro and the United Mine Workers," in *The Negro and the American Labor Movement*, ed. Julius Jacobson (Garden City, N.Y., 1968); Spero and Harris, *Black Worker;* Charles Simmons, John Rankin, and U. G. Carter, "Negro Coal Miners in West Virginia," *Midwest Journal*, 54 (Spring 1954); Barnum, *Negro in Coal Mining*, p. 1. This explanation, while useful, is not definitive as racial turmoil hindered the success of the UMWA in many coal fields. In northern West Virginia racial conflict broke out in the early 1920s. One mine was wrecked because of the employment of blacks, while another mine was named "the Ku Kluxer's mine" because the superintendent and white mine workers allegedly had an agreement against employing blacks. A district official in northern West Virginia declared that racial intolerance among the native whites constituted "a serious menace to the United Mine Workers"; a rank-and-file miner from Clarksburg in northern West Virginia lamented that "in our miners' union there is not enough of that spirit of oneness. The union must lay aside the color of the skin and count men as men who honestly struggle to play the part of a man" (Boris Emmet, *Labor Relations in the Fairmont, West Virginia Bituminous Coal Field*, U.S. Department of Labor, Bureau of Labor Statistics, bulletin no. 361 [Washington, D.C., 1924], pp. 24-26); T. H. Seals, letter to the editor, *UMWJ*, Sept. 15, 1924, p. 7. For racial strife among Illinois miners, see Agnes Wieck, "Ku Kluxing in the Miners' Country," *New Republic*, 38 (Mar. 26, 1924), and Carter Goodrich, *The Miners' Freedom* (Boston, 1925), p. 113. For Alabama, see Robert David Ward and William Rodgers, *Labor Revolt in Alabama* (Tuscaloosa, Ala., 1965), p. 21, and

UMWJ, Jan. 15, 1919, p. 5, for a description of how the Alabama operators played black and white miners against each other. For the problems in Pennsylvania, see William Donovan, letter to the editor, *UMWJ,* Dec. 15, 1932, p. 11, and Aug. 9, 1917, p. 4. For Tennessee and Kentucky, see chapter 14, this book.

4. P. O. Davis, "Negro Exodus and Southern Agriculture," *American Review of Reviews,* 68 (Oct. 1923). Also see George Haynes, "The Movement of Negroes from Country to City," *Southern Workman,* 42 (Apr. 1913); Donald, "Negro Migration," p. 407; Abram Harris, "Negro Migration to the North," *Current History,* 20 (Sept. 1924). For a discussion of the difficulty that agrarian blacks had in adjusting to northern industrial norms, see Spero and Harris, *Black Worker,* pp. 163-65. For a general discussion of this problem, see Herbert Gutman, "Work, Culture, and Society in Industrializing America, 1815-1919," *American Historical Review,* 78 (June 1973).

5. This view is purely impressionistic and is based on interviews with elderly black miners and other research. Because the company towns were unincorporated, they were not labeled by census enumerators, and therefore an accurate statistical study of the black migration into southern West Virginia is impossible. Because the 1900 census shows the black migrants were from Virginia, North Carolina, and Alabama, it is easy to assume that they had been sharecroppers. See Jerry Bruce Thomas, "Coal County: The Rise of the Smokeless Coal Industry and Its Effect on Area Development, 1872-1910" (Ph.D. diss., University of North Carolina, 1971), p. 76. For a similar view about the patterns of black migration as given in this chapter, also based on interviews, see Peter Gottlieb, "Making Their Own Way: Southern Black Migration to Pittsburgh" (Ph.D. diss., University of Pittsburgh, 1977).

6. Interview with Rogers Mitchell, Institute, W. Va., May 17, 1975; W. L. McMillian to R. L. Thorton, Nov. 2, 1916, Straight Numerical File 182363-231, Record Group 60, General Records of the Department of Justice, National Archives, Washington, D.C.; T. H. Seals, letter to the editor, *UMWJ,* Sept. 15, 1924, p. 17. The President of Bessemer Coal, Iron and Land was Henry L. Budland, and his speech of Sept. 22, 1916, is in Migration Study, Negro Migrants Letters, FRB, 1916-18, Papers of the National Urban League, Manuscript Room, Library of Congress, Washington, D.C. (hereafter cited as Negro Migrants Letters, National Urban League Papers).

7. Interviews with Thomas Cannady, Anawalt, W. Va., Abe Helms, Eckman, W. Va., and Bill Deering, Williamson, W. Va., summer 1975; [no name] to Dr. [no name], [n.d.], Negro Migrants Letters, National Urban League Papers. Also see the letters and testimonies in Straight Numerical File 182363, Record Group 60, General Records of the Department of Justice.

8. W. F. Larrison, letter to the editor, *UMWJ,* Jan. 9, 1908. For other accounts of early racial antagonisms, see John R. Williams to William Thomas Brynawel, Nov. 10, 1895, in Alan Conway, ed., *The Welsh in America: Letters from Immigrants* (Minneapolis, Minn., 1961), pp. 204-10, and Gutman, "Negro and the United Mine Workers," pp. 49-127. In this early period there was still much cooperation between black and white miners. See, for example, *UMWJ,* May 17, 1894, p. 6, and Kenneth R. Bailey, "Tell the Boys to Fall in Line," *West Virginia History,* 32, no. 4 (July 1971).

9. W. J. Elgin to Justin Collins, May 9, 1912, Justin Collins Papers, West Virginia University Library, Morgantown, W. Va.; interviews with John Drew, Williamson, W. Va., Curt Smith, Mullins, W. Va., and John Schofield, Alpoca, W. Va., summer 1975. Other elderly miners, both black and white, made similar statements.

10. Emit Frankel, "Occupational Classes among Negroes in Cities," *American Journal of Sociology,* 35 (Mar. 1930); Spero and Harris, *Black Worker,* pp. 155-57; Guy Johnson, "Negro Migration and Its Consequences," *Social Forces,* 11 (Mar. 1924).

11. See chapter 7, this book. For discussion on types of payment in the bituminous coal fields, see Hunt, Tryon, and Willits, *What the Coal Commission Found,* pp. 164-229.

12. Northrup, *Organized Labor,* p. 159; Lewis Field, Reed Ewing, and David Wayne, "Observations on Relations of Psychosocial Factors to Psychiatric Illness among Coal Miners," *International Journal of Social Psychiatry,* 3 (Autumn 1957).

13. Gilbert Osofsky, *Harlem: The Making of a Ghetto* (New York, 1966), pp. 147-48; E. Franklin Frazier, *The Black Community: Diversity and Unity* (New York, 1975), chaps. 2 and 3; Charles A. Valentine, *Culture and Poverty: Critique and Counter-Proposals* (Chicago, 1968); Donald, "Negro Migration," pp. 407-408.

14. U.S. Bureau of the Census, Population Census, McDowell County, Elkhorn District, 1900 (manuscript), National Archives. All the towns in this census district were coal company towns. Interview with Walter Hale, Eckman, W. Va., summer 1975. It appears that most of the single

black migrants into West Virginia went to the coal fields in the northern part of the state; see West Virginia Bureau of Negro Welfare and Statistics, *Annual Reports, 1923-24,* pp. 8-9. For the role of the single black miner in southern West Virginia, see Randall G. Lawrence, "Here Today, Gone Tomorrow: Coal Miners in Appalachia, 1880-1940," paper presented at the meeting of the Organization of American Historians, Detroit, Mich., April. 1-4, 1981.

15. In 1924 West Virginia had the highest percentage of black males employed in the United States, and the lowest percentage of black females. West Virginia Bureau of Negro Welfare and Statistics, *Annual Report, 1924,* p. 25; Women's Bureau, *Home Environment,* pp. 37-55.

16. Women's Bureau, *Home Environment,* pp. 16-19; Nettie McGill, *The Welfare of Children in Bituminous Coal Mining Communities in West Virginia,* Children's Bureau, U.S. Department of Labor, publication no. 117 (Washington, D.C., 1923), pp. 8-10; interview with Herbert Spencer, Keystone, W. Va., summer 1975. For the company preference of hiring by families, see George Wolfe to Collins, May 18, 1916, and A. H. Herndon to Collins, Dec. 15, 1909, Collins Papers; Josiah Keeley, "The Cabin Creek Consolidated Coal Company," *West Virginia Review* (June 1926), p. 349. Similarly, see the letters and testimonies in Straight Numerical File 182363, Record Group 60, General Records of the Department of Justice, especially the testimony of George Bowman, Oct. 23, 1916.

17. Interview with Willie Anderson, Holden, W. Va., summer 1975.

18. Spero and Harris, *Black Worker,* p. 162; George Haynes, "Negro Migration," *Opportunity,* Oct. 1924, pp. 303-306; Donald, "Negro Migration," pp. 436-38; Eli Ginzberg and Dale Hiestand, *Mobility in the Negro Community,* U.S. Commission on Civil Rights, Clearinghouse Publications, no. 11 (New York, 1968), p. 21.

19. This was only a southern West Virginia company town experience, for the black migrants who moved into the commercial cities (e.g., Charleston) and northern West Virginia encountered the same housing problems as did the migrants who moved into the northern industrial centers. See West Virginia Bureau of Negro Welfare and Statistics, *Negro Housing Survey of Charleston, Keystone, Kimball, Wheeling, and Williamson* (Charleston, W. Va., 1938).

20. Jack Rodgers, "I Remember That Mining Town," *West Virginia Review,* 15 (Apr. 1938), pp. 203-205); interviews with Willie Betz, Keystone, W. Va., Tom Cannady, Anawalt, W. Va., and John Schofield, Alpoca, W. Va., summer 1975; Mary Simmons, interview with Pauline Haga, *Beckley* (W. Va.) *Post Herald* (Diamond Jubilee Edition), Aug. 2, 1975; Louise Coffee interviewed in *Charleston Gazette,* July 28, 1975. Sociologist Raymond Mack has pointed out that the most damaging aspect of segregation is that it "minimizes one's exposure to members of a minority who do not conform to the stereotype of what they should be like," thus producing a "culture of discrimination" and race prejudice ("Riot, Revolt, or Responsible Revolution: Of Reference Groups and Racism," *Sociological Quarterly,* 10 [Spring 1969], 151). In the same vein, Sidney Mintz has explained that it is not race nor segregation but the "perception of race differences" that accounts for the absolute as well as relative well-being of a minority within a given society ("Toward an Afro-American History," *Journal of World History,* 13 [1971], and his foreword to *Afro-American Anthropology,* ed. Norman Whitten and John Szwed [New York, 1970]).

21. W. J. Elgin to Collins, May 9, 1912, Collins Papers, and interviews with John Drew, Williamson, W. Va., and Rogers Mitchell, Institute, W. Va., summer 1975.

22. Ralph D. Minard, "Race Relations in the Pocahontas Coal Field," *Journal of Social Issues,* 8 (1952), 37.

23. W. P. Tams, Jr., *The Smokeless Coal Fields of West Virginia* (Morgantown, W. Va., 1963), p. 51; interviews with John Schofield, Alpoca, W. Va., and Sidney Box, Glen White, W. Va., summer 1975; R. H. Hamil, "Design of Buildings in Mining Towns," *Coal Age,* 11 (June 1917), 1045-48.

24. Committee on Coal and Civil Liberties, "A Report to the U.S. Coal Commission," Aug. 11, 1923, U.S. Department of Labor Library, Washington, D.C.

25. Women's Bureau, *Home Environment,* pp. 9, 29; Tams, *Smokeless Coal Fields,* p. 52; Thomas J. Morris, "The Coal Camp: A Pattern of Limited Community Life" (master's thesis, West Virginia University, 1950), pp. 9-11, 18, 19.

26. U.S. Coal Commission, 1923, Records of the Division of Investigation of Labor Facts, Living Conditions Section, Mining Communities Schedules, A, Schedule for Iaeger, box 30, Record Group 68, Records of the United States Coal Commission, National Archives.

27. George Haynes, "Negro Migration," *Opportunity,* Sept. 1924, p. 273, and Oct. 1924, pp.

304, 305. See also Charles Hamilton, *The Black Preacher* (New York, 1972), esp. pp. 12-13, and W. E. B. Du Bois, *The Souls of Black Folk* (1903; reprint ed., New York, 1961), p. 141, who noted that "the black preacher is the most unique personality developed by the Negro on American soil. A leader, a politician, an orator, a 'boss,' an intriguer, an idealist—all these he is, and ever too, the center of a group of men, now twenty, now a thousand in number."

28. *UMWJ*, Jan. 1, 1925, p. 3, and Jerome Davis, "Human Rights and Coal," *Journal of Social Forces*, 3 (Nov. 1924), 103-106.

29. Spero and Harris, *Black Worker*, p. 378; West Virginia, Bureau of Negro Welfare and Statistics, *Report, 1921-22*, p. 77; Laing, "Social Status," p. 563, and chapter 7, this book; letter to the editor, *UMWJ*, June 1, 1916, p. 9. Also see the resolution passed by the UMWA local at Morrisvale, W. Va., to protest the companies' ousting of a nearby pro-union minister, *UMWJ*, July 15, 1922, p. 7.

30. West Virginia Bureau of Negro Welfare and Statistics, *Report, 1921-22*, pp. 77-78; interview with Columbus Avery, Matewan, W. Va., summer 1975; Jarius Collins to Justin Collins, June 8, 1916, Collins Papers; Laing, "Social Status," pp. 563-66.

31. Mack, "Riot, Revolt," p. 155.

32. Interview with Mr. and Mrs. Carl Hazzard, Mullins, W. Va., summer 1975. Charles Ambler, *History of Education in West Virginia* (Huntington, W. Va., 1951), chap. 7; "Biennial Survey of Education in the United States, 1944-1946," in Mark Rich, *Some Churches of Coal Mining Communities of West Virginia* (New York, 1951), p. 12; W. W. Sanders, "Report of the Division of Negro Schools," West Virginia State Superintendent of Free Schools, *Annual Report, 1930*, pp. 84-86; Wolfe to Justin Collins, July 14, 1913, Collins Papers; U.S. Senate, Committee on Education and Labor, *West Virginia Coal Fields: Hearings . . . to Investigate the Recent Acts of Violence in the Coal Fields of West Virginia*, 67th Cong., 1st sess., 2 vols. (Washington, D.C., 1921-22), vol. 1, p. 27 (hereafter cited as West Virginia Coal Fields); Edwin Cubby, "The Transformation of the Tug and Guyandot Valleys" (Ph.D. diss., Syracuse University, 1962), pp. 296-97; John Peters and F. Carden, *A History of Fayette County* (Fayetteville, W. Va., 1962), pp. 326-28.

33. West Virginia Bureau of Negro Welfare and Statistics, *Annual Report, 1926*, p. 6, and *Annual Report, 1932*, p. 17.

34. Walter Thurmond, *The Logan Coal Field of West Virginia* (Morgantown, W. Va., 1964), pp. 81-82; Ambler, *History of Education*, chap. 7; Superintendent, McDowell County, "Report," in West Virginia State Supervisor of Free Schools, *Annual Report, 1906*, pp. 17, 217; West Virginia State Supervisor of Free Schools, *Annual Report, 1914*, pp. 75, 217, and *Annual Report, 1930*, p. 47; interview with Mr. and Mrs. Carl Hazzard, Mullins, W. Va., summer 1975.

35. Ibid.

36. Winthrop Lane, *Civil War in West Virginia* (New York, 1921), p. 34; W. W. Sanders, Supervisor of Negro Schools, "Report," in West Virginia Bureau of Negro Welfare and Statistics, *Annual Report, 1926*, p. 140. Also see Raymond Murphy, "A Southern West Virginia Mining Community," *Economic Geography*, 9 (Jan. 1933), 48-50.

37. *McDowell* (W. Va.) *Times*, May 9, 1913.

38. Interviews with Mr. and Mrs. Carl Hazzard, Mullins, W. Va., Mrs. A. L. Booker, Mullins, W. Va., and John Drew, Williamson, W. Va., summer 1975. For a discussion on the importance of "Negro History Week," see Carter G. Woodson, "The Celebration of Negro History Week, 1927," *Journal of Negro History*, 12 (Apr. 1927).

39. W. E. B. Du Bois, "Does the Negro Need Separate Schools?" *Journal of Negro History*, 10 (July 1925), and interview with John Drew, Williamson, W. Va., summer 1975. In the 1960s, progressive black leaders and radicals were making similar arguments for segregated schools; Roy Innis, assistant director of the Congress of Racial Equality, acknowledged that "people today talk about control of their community schools. Integration is contrary to the mood of the black people;" the Black Panthers argued that black students "should be taught black economics and black history in black schools, with black teachers" (quoted in Mack, "Riot, Revolt," pp. 154-55).

40. Interview with Columbus Avery, Williamson, W. Va., summer 1975. For the importance of these night schools in decreasing black illiteracy, see Director of Extension Work among Colored Schools, "Report," in West Virginia State Superintendent of Free Schools, *Annual Report, 1916*, pp. 89-91, and Ambler, *History of Education*, p. 213.

41. Testimony of M. T. Davis in U.S. Senate, Committee on Education and Labor, *Conditions*

in the Paint Creek District, West Virginia, 63d Cong. 1st sess., 3 vols. (Washington, D.C., 1913), vol. 2, p. 1280; Wolfe to Justin Collins, July 14, 1913, Collins Papers; Homer Morris, *The Plight of the Bituminous Coal Miner* (Philadelphia, 1934), p. 94. For an example of a public school teacher losing his job for supporting a strike, see *West Virginia Coal Fields,* vol. 1, pp. 27, 33. For the miners' early resentment of the company-controlled school, see Henry Stephenson, letter to the editor. *UMWJ,* July 21, 1898, p. 17. As late as 1933, when the UMWA called an organizing meeting at a Mingo County school, the superintendent of U.S. Coal and Coke at Gary, W. Va., informed the county board of education that holding the meeting in the school "will automatically and immediately cancel the lease on the lot on which this school house is built. . . . It is not a question as to whether or not the Board of Education grants . . . permission for the holding of a labor meeting in this school house, or on these school grounds, but the crucial fact is whether or not such a meeting is held" (William Stratton to Mingo County Board of Education, July 10, 1933, District 17 Correspondence Files, UMWA Archives, UMWA Headquarters, Washington, D.C. [copy in author's files]).

42. John Hope Franklin, *From Slavery to Freedom* (New York, 1967), pp. 524-26.

43. Spero and Harris, *Black Worker,* pp. 370-74; *McDowell* (W. Va.) *Times,* May 6 and 16, 1913; Thomas Posey, "Political Activity of West Virginia Negroes," West Virginia Bureau of Negro Welfare and Statistics, *Annual Report, 1929-32,* pp. 40-45; Kenneth Bailey, "A Judicious Mixture," *West Virginia History,* 34 (Jan. 1972), 152-54; Fred Barkey, "Socialist Party of West Virginia from 1898-1920" (Ph.D. diss., University of Pittsburgh, 1971), p. 168.

44. For a discussion on the backwardness of mine-safety legislation in West Virginia, see William Graebner, *Coal-Mining Safety in the Progressive Era* (Lexington, Ky., 1973), chap. 1. For individual examples of political corruption, see the interview with Oscar Roebuck, Cabin Creek, W. Va., summer 1975; Wolfe to Justin Collins, Feb. 27, 1913, Collins Papers; *UMWJ,* Jan. 1, 1925, p. 3.

45. West Virginia Bureau of Negro Welfare and Statistics, *Annual Report, 1922,* pp. 72-73; Spero and Harris, *Black Worker,* pp. 37-74; Bailey, "Judicious Mixture," p. 155.

46. *McDowell* (W. Va.) *Times,* Aug. 20, 1915; West Virginia Bureau of Negro Welfare and Statistics, *Annual Report, 1924;* Laing, "Social Status," p. 566.

47. West Virginia Bureau of Negro Welfare and Statistics, *Annual Report, 1922,* pp. 59, 83; *Annual Report, 1924,* p. 81; [no name] to Dr. [no name], [n.d.], Negro Migrants Letters, National Urban League Papers.

48. C. A. Vabell, "Building a Mining Community," *West Virginia Review* (Apr. 1927), p. 210; interviews with Frank Hunt, former vice-president of the Winding Gulf Coal Operators' Association, Beckley, W. Va., and Oscar Pennel, Mead, W. Va., summer 1975; West Virginia Bureau of Negro Welfare and Statistics, *Annual Report, 1922,* p. 5.

49. Interviews with A. L. Booker, Mullins, W. Va., and George Hairston, Mead, W. Va., summer 1975; *McDowell* (W. Va.) *Times,* May 16, 1913. Similarly, Barkey discovered many socialist miners who belonged to social lodges ("Socialist Party," p. 104).

50. National Coal Association, bulletin no. 725, Aug. 13, 1927 (copy in author's files). Also see Goodrich, *Miners' Freedom,* pp. 47, 38; Archie Green, *Only a Miner* (Urbana, Ill., 1974); George Korson, *Coal Dust on the Fiddle* (Philadelphia, 1943), pp. 20, 31; Winthrop Lane, "The Black Avalanche," *Survey,* 47 (Mar. 25, 1922). For similar interpretations about company towns in England, see A. L. Lloyd, *Come All Ye Bold Miners* (London, 1952), and G. D. H. Cole, *Labour in the Coal Mining Industry* (London, 1924), pp. 6-7.

51. Minard, "Race Relations," pp. 29-44; Spero and Harris, *Black Worker,* pp. 304-306; Seymour Lipset and Reinhart Bendix, *Social Mobility in Industrial Society* (Berkeley, Calif., 1963), p. 106.

52. M. L. Shrumm, letter to the editor, *McDowell* (W. Va.) *Times,* May 30, July 4, Aug. 28, 1913; Laing, "Social Status," p. 567.

53. See chapter 7, this book; Minard, "Race Relations," pp. 31, 32, 36; Morris, *Plight,* p. 28.

54. Testimony of Frank Ingham, *West Virginia Coal Fields,* vol. 1, pp. 26-30; interviews with Rogers Mitchell, Institute, W. Va., George Hairston, Mead, W. Va., Columbus Avery, Williamson, W. Va., and Carl Hazzard, Mullins, W. Va., summer 1975; Helen Norton, "Feudalism in West Virginia," *Nation* 123 (Mar. 1931), pp. 154-55; Fred Mooney, *Struggle in the Coal Fields,* ed. Fred Hess (Morgantown, W. Va., 1967), pp. 26-29.

55. Ball, letter to the editor, *UMWJ,* Sept. 1, 1921, p. 15, and A. R. Grimes, letter to the

editor, *UMWJ,* Mar. 15, 1921, p. 17. See also Anthony Gray, letter to the editor, *UMWJ,* Oct. 15, 1913, p. 15.

56. George Edmunds, Paint Creek, W. Va., letter to the editor, *UMWJ,* June 20, 1912, p. 5. The ballad cited in text was written by Fred Niswander of Freeman, W. Va.; it was found in his letter to John L. Lewis, Nov. 12, 1934, District 17 Correspondence Files, UMWA Archives. For another example in which the southern West Virginia miners compared their plight to the slaves, see Artie Surber, letter to the editor, *UMWJ,* Jan. 15, 1922, p. 7. For other ballads, see "Miner's Lifeguard," and Arville Jenks, "In the State of McDowell," in *Coal Dust,* ed. Korson, pp. 304-305, 414-15. During the "armed march on Logan," a reporter asked one of the miners, "What do you boys really think you can do?" The marcher-miner replied, "Well, John Brown started something at Harpers Ferry, didn't he?"; Heber Blankenhorn, "Marching through West Virginia," *Nation,* 113 (Sept. 14, 1921), 288.

57. Testimony of George Echols, *West Virginia Coal Fields,* vol. 1, pp. 469-71.

58. Interviews with Columbus Avery, Williamson, W. Va., and Walter Hale, Eckman, W. Va., summer 1975.

59. Anthony Gray, letter to the editor, *UMWJ,* Apr. 1, 1931, p. 9.

60. Emmett Lemons, letter to the editor, *UMWJ* May 15, 1931, p. 15.

PART FOUR

Race Relations

Does the history of respect for the individual so pervade Appalachia that whites in the region are less troubled by issues of race and are less prejudiced than their counterparts farther south? Kenneth Bailey and John Stanfield address this question.

"A Judicious Mixture" explores the melting pot theme, examining the ways in which coal companies recruited blacks in order to forestall unionism by playing one group off against another. The essay concludes that while the descendants of the miners work in industries other than mining, the present population of the state has a solid history of relatively harmonious race relationships.

John Stanfield of Yale University, who was formerly at the University of Tennessee, offers a sociological study of resolving the "problems of the black community" of Knoxville, Tennessee, and of attempts to solve them. Historical in method, his essay reviews a series of studies of the city's black community in an Appalachian context of political and economic conservatism.

10

A Judicious Mixture: Negroes and Immigrants in the West Virginia Mines, 1880-1917

KENNETH R. BAILEY

In the first years of West Virginia's coal mining industry the labor force was made up primarily of native, white Americans who left their poor farms to work for the high wages available in the mines.[1] There were also some Negroes used in the mines either as slave labor or as free men. The use of Negroes became particularly widespread after the railroad companies brought many of them to the Mountain State for use in railroad construction. The Negroes often chose to remain in West Virginia as coal miners rather than to return to their homes in the South.[2] Negroes, however, were not as numerous in West Virginia as the native whites or foreigners until the 1920s.[3] Instead, the bulk of the labor force between 1880 and 1917 was primarily made up of native whites and white foreigners but with a sizable minority of Negro miners.

The present composition of West Virginia's population is evidence of the foreigner in the development of the Mountain State. Men from nearly every country in Western and Southern Europe have been employed in the coal mines of the State. Their arrival in such an out of the way area was sometimes due to chance or desire, but just as often was the result of a deliberate effort to attract foreign labor to the coal fields.

In the early 1870s, West Virginians became interested in attracting immigrants to the State. The first individuals who were sought were farmers to help develop the agricultural potential of the State. A state immigration commissioner was appointed in 1871 and the first commissioner, Joseph H. Diss Debar, attempted to attract farmers from his native Switzerland.[4] Diss Debar was somewhat successful as evidenced by the settlements of Swiss farmers in such towns as Helvetia. *The Virginias,* a magazine devoted to the study of Virginia and West Virginia, reported that Swiss commissioners visited West Virginia in 1880 to investigate the conditions that their countrymen would have to live under if they migrated to the State.[5]

Encouragement for immigration to West Virginia came also from the American Legate at Copenhagen, Denmark. M. J. Cramer wrote West Virginia Governor Henry Mason Matthews that he held real estate interests in the State and desired to stimulate the migration of many of the industrious, prosperous and moral Danes to West Virginia. He requested that the Governor furnish him with maps and information to be disseminated to prospective immigrants.[6]

As more and more of Europe's people came to America, bureaus were created to distribute the laborers among the states. Governor Matthews received several letters from immigration agents offering to represent West Virginia at the ports of debarkation. One M. Primer of New York was particularly desirous of representing West Virginia among the hordes of new arrivals in that port.[7] Matthews also received a letter from William G. Sleeman of Birmingham, England who offered to work to send immigrants to West Virginia since he had visited the State and was familiar with it.[8]

As early as 1882, *The Virginias* carried an article describing a new group of coal miners settling in West Virginia. The Winifrede Coal Company of Kanawha County, West Virginia, employed twenty-six Belgian miners who, with their wives and children, comprised a group of forty individuals. The magazine emphasized that the men were of good character and would be an asset to the Kanawha Valley.[9]

The twenty-six Belgian miners represented a very small proportion of the waves of immigrants which would arrive in the Mountain State in later years. Until 1890 there were few foreigners in the entire State, let alone working in the coal mines. According to census figures, West Virginia had only twenty-five foreigners out of a total work force of 4,497 men in 1880. This increased to 151 foreigners out of a total work force of 9,952 in 1890. The number of aliens increased ten fold by 1901, when there were an estimated 1,792 immigrant workmen in the State. That, however, was still a very small part of the work force totaling 23,914.[10] To use just one county as an example, Marion County in the Fairmont coal district had an almost entirely American work force until 1890. By 1900 the work force was still 97 per cent American but had received enough foreign workmen to make up 3 per cent of the laboring force.[11]

An even larger number of immigrants settled in West Virginia, principally to work in the coal mines, between 1900 and 1917. In 1915 figures were published showing that West Virginia had 28,583 foreign miners compared to 49,458 native miners. The numbers of miners from abroad had grown to more than half the entire work force. The importance of the foreign element in the State was noted in the article accompanying the figures. Coal mining towns, it was stated, had a polyglot culture as a result of the mixing of the nationalities. While most of the immigrants seemed to stick close together and avoided mixing to any great degree, the men were considered to be hardworking and an asset to the State.[12]

The thousands of immigrant miners found their way to the isolated coal regions of West Virginia in a variety of ways. Some of the miners were encouraged to come to the mines by relatives who had gone before them. The main drawing feature was usually reports of the high wages that the relatives were receiving.[13] Others were attracted to West Virginia even before they left their native lands by agents of the coal companies or labor companies who had been sent to lure them to the mines. Companies often prepared glowing brochures detailing the advantages to be obtained by working in the coal pits of West Virginia. In addition to the promise of good wages, such inducements as the promise of citizenship, free transportation to the New World and an advance on wages were offered.[14]

TABLE 10.1   National Origins of West Virginia Miners

	1880	1900	1907	1909	1911	1913	1915	1917
American White	2,777	12,028	20,409	24,696	30,094	33,612	37,918	48,237
Austrian	--	915	832	631	1,276	1,292	2,109	1,833
Belgian	--	--	7	17	--	--	--	--
Bohemian	--	--	4	17	10	--	--	--
Bulgarian	--	--	--	--	28	5	--	--
Canadian	--	14	--	--	--	--	--	--
Croatian	--	--	--	--	12	55	--	--
Danish	--	--	1	8	33	--	--	--
English	447	1,053	280	327	505	--	--	--
French	--	--	1	10	71	30	--	--
German	159	368	291	303	451	801	--	--
Greek	--	--	167	208	446	388	--	--
Granish	--	--	--	--	--	5	--	--
Horwat	--	--	--	--	2	23	--	--
Hungarian	--	--	2,753	3,183	4,106	4,615	5,120	4,346
Italian	--	554	5,965	--	8,184	10,698	8,495	7,388
Irish	274	520	149	96	558	266	--	--
Litvitch	--	--	148	64	237	186	--	--
Lithuanian	--	--	419	391	346	329	--	--
Macedonian	--	--	10	8	--	--	--	--
Negro American	--	4,620	9,908	10,550	11,950	14,506	11,835	18,128
Polish	--	220	1,540	1,512	2,181	2,324	2,723	2,117
Roumanian	--	--	40	205	370	232	--	--
Russian	--	275	543	706	1,267	1,315	2,208	1,362
Scandinavian	2	7	--	--	--	--	--	--
Scotch	--	--	120	186	221	155	--	--
Slav	--	--	394	1,596	1,841	1,827	2,042	1,215
Spanish	--	--	--	--	18	100	--	--
Swedish	--	--	37	52	45	32	--	--
Syrian	--	--	24	81	22	60	--	--
Turks	--	--	--	--	--	16	--	--
Welsh	--	--	31	96	41	6	--	--
Others	25	113	--	--	--	--	6,675	4,039
Totals	3,701	20,287	56,209	62,189	70,644	70,321	81,328	88,665

Source: Various reports of the West Virginia Department of Mines and United States Census Reports.

Some labor companies waited until the immigrants reached New York City or, later, Ellis Island and then contacted them through agents who were often recent immigrants themselves. Italian laborers [often accompanied new arrivals] to the company for which they worked. In most cases, the immigrants, whether Italian or some other nationality, were duped into believing that West Virginia was only a short distance from New York. Once on the labor trains, however, they were locked in for the journey.[15]

The coal companies often employed a technique called bringing men "on transportation" to the mines. This meant that the coal company provided free transportation to the prospective coal miner from New York or other port of entry to West Virginia. Once in the coal fields, the companies tried to keep the men at work as long as possible in order to get their money's worth from them. In many cases this was difficult because the agents in New York would trick men who were barbers, writers and waiters into signing contracts to work in the mines.[16]

One labor contract was entered into between a labor company, George

William Labor Contractors, and an Italian immigrant named Hemuri Sandro. The contract pledged Sandro to work for a coal company for two years as a blacksmith at $5.50 per day.[17] Another example of a labor contract was made between the Cabin Creek Coal Association and Rudolf Krivosik to bring him from New York to Cabin Creek, West Virginia, as a strikebreaker. The contract read:

I hereby acknowledge that I have read the foregoing schedule [of wages] and I have agreed to go to West Virginia to work in or about the mines of the members of the Cabin Creek Coal Association according to this scale of prices set forth in said schedule. I also acknowledge that I have been informed that a labor strike is now, and has been for sometime in force on Cabin Creek, West Virginia, and that the mines of the said Cabin Creek Coal Association are involved in said strike.

The company agrees to pay my transportation to the place of my employment and the amount of such transportation to be deducted from my wages at the rate of twenty-five per cent per month until paid, and if I leave the employ of the company before all of the transportation is collected on a deducting basis, the balance due shall forthwith become due and I must work 60 days to be entitled to free transportation.

Signed the 21 day of November, 1912.   Rudolf Krivosik[18]

Although most of the immigrants undoubtedly accepted the "free" transportation to West Virginia with the intention of remaining on the job long enough to pay it off, there were some who did not desire to remain in the employ of the coal companies. In such cases, there were reports that the immigrants would often be held against their will until they worked off the debt. This "debt peonage" was reported several times, but proven in only two cases.[19]

One of the first instances of "debt peonage" was reported to Governor A. B. Fleming by the Austrian-Hungarian Consul at Richmond, Virginia on March 11, 1891. The Consul wrote that newspaper clippings which had been sent to him from New York claimed that Bohemians were being held against their will at Purcell's Camp, a railroad construction camp, and that the story had been brought out of West Virginia by two men who had escaped. Although the Governor doubted the validity of the story, he requested the Mercer County Circuit Court to investigate the incident which had taken place in its jurisdiction although actually near Elkhorn in McDowell County. An investigation was made but no substantiation of the charges could be made.[20] However, the fact that such charges were again made on several occasions made it likely that if such an allegation was not true in this case, it may have been in others.

In 1894 Governor William A. MacCorkle was asked to investigate the living conditions of 350 Italians who worked for the Randolph Company. The Vice Consul for Italy at Cincinnati, A. Raooglia, made the request for the men who were working at Homelsdorf, West Virginia, and who claimed that they had not been paid by the company for two months. Again, no evidence was gathered that the men were actually being mistreated, but the fact that they hadn't been paid for two months was certainly justification for complaints.[21]

More evidence of mistreatment of immigrants was gathered in 1906 when the Italian Ambassador to the United States complained to Secretary of State Elihu Root that his countrymen were being held captive in West Virginia. The

Ambassador explained that at the Raleigh Lumber Company at Raleigh, West Virginia, there were 15 Italian laborers of a party of 21 workers who had left New York in November, 1906, supposedly for work on the railroads. Instead, they found that they were expected to work in the mines. When they protested and attempted to leave, they were stopped by armed men. The Italian foreman was manacled with handcuffs and the others were subjected to such "brutal threats that 3 or 4 young and weak ones fainted." The men were allowed to pool their resources and were able to collect $164. with which they paid the company for the transportation costs of the weakest five or six men, who were sent back to New Jersey. The others were held by force and kept under surveillance. They were locked in a railroad car for six days and given nothing but bread and water. Only by "stealth and subterfuge were they able to communicate indirectly with their friends and call for help." Secretary Root forwarded the story to Governor William M. O. Dawson and asked for a complete investigation.[22]

Dawson employed two detectives and an Italian interpreter to investigate the charges. The men discovered that the Italians had indeed been held against their will because they were accused of "defrauding" the lumber company of $12. each which they had been advanced as the cost of their transportation. The investigators could discover nothing about the food the men had been given, but did discover that the box car in which they were kept was heated. They returned the Italian laborers to the State Capitol, Charleston, to await someone from New York to take charge of them.[23]

Governor Dawson received more information about "debt peonage" in January 1907, and again hired detectives to investigate. They discovered that both Americans and foreigners had been held by force by the William Ritter Lumber Company in Wyoming County, West Virginia. The men had been recruited by the Southern Immigration Bureau from the slums and dives of New York and from the ranks of the immigrants. When the men desired to leave before working off their transportation, they were prevented from doing so by force. One of the men, known only by his number, 288, given to him by the immigration bureau, tried to leave by taking the train from Estelle, Wyoming County. He was apprehended, however, at Prince, Fayette County, by a company guard, Elias Hatfield. Number 288 tried to resist arrest and was struck on the jaw by Hatfield's pistol. Hatfield returned 288 to William Lolliver, another guard of the company, who testified to the investigators that he had forcefully kept workers at the lumber camp until they had paid off their transportation.[24] There were evidently no charges filed against Hatfield for his assault on the laborer, and the records do not show if the men who were being held were released.

In another incident in which Governor Dawson's administration became involved: two Italian laborers were killed near Wriston, Fayette County, on May 23, 1906. Investigation showed that W. D. Auxier, "walking boss" for the Dunn's Construction Company on a private railroad project (probably a spur being built to a mine), killed Dominick Masuleo and Frank Leper. Masuleo and his son owed a small amount of money on their transportation fare to West Virginia. The men desired to leave the employ of the company but they and Auxier disagreed over the fare of the young boy. Auxier wanted Masuleo to pay the full fare for the boy but Masuleo protested that he still owed only $1.50 for his son's transportation. In the argument that followed, Auxier pulled a pistol and shot the men, killing them instantly. Auxier fled to Kentucky but returned to defend himself against murder charges in a justice of the peace court and was acquitted, even though it was shown that the two Italians were unarmed.[25]

In light of the accusations of debt peonage and the murders, Governor Dawson recommended to the 1907 session of the West Virginia Legislature that an immigration bureau be created in order that a better class of immigrants could be attracted to West Virginia. He emphasized that the bad publicity resulting from the foregoing incidents could be alleviated by attracting more responsible men to the coal fields.[26]

The new immigration bureau which was created was intended to resurrect the activities of the first immigration commissioner which had largely been neglected since Diss Debar had left the post. The first man appointed to the new post was John H. Nugent, who began to expand his search for new laborers to the native countries. He personally visited England and Wales seeking miners for the Mountain State.[27]

Nugent was not given an official salary; instead, his expenses and salary were provided by the coal companies. From 1907 to 1909 the New River Coal Company bore the expense of Nugent's activities and, it can be assumed, reaped a great deal of the benefit of his labors in bringing miners into the State. From 1909 to 1913 the huge Consolidation Coal Company supported the Immigration Commissioner.[28]

During a United States Senate investigation of the 1912-13 Paint Creek strike, it was revealed that advertisements from the Immigration Commissioner seeking laborers bore the "official endorsement of the State Commissioner—Immigration, State of West Virginia," and gave no indication that he was the special agent of the coal companies.[29]

WANTED

Two thousand (2000) Coal Miners and Helpers, either experienced miners, with their
    families, or green laborers to learn coal mining under competent instructor (sic).
All drift mines in the Monongahela Valley.
Average wages of experienced miners $3.50 to $5.00 per day;
Average wages of Helpers from $2.00 to $3.00 per day;
Average wages Machine Runners $3.50 to $6.00 per day.
No Shaft Mines; All drift, located at Fairmont and Clarksburg, West Virginia on the
    Baltimore and Ohio Railroad.
Height of coal seam eight feet. Practically free from explosive gasses.

                                              The Consolidation Coal Co., Inc.

I have investigated the conditions outlined in the above letter and find them true as claimed. I find there are no labor troubles or difficulties in the Fairmont field and that the statement of average wages earned is correct.

I think the above offer of employment a splendid opportunity for men with families seeking employment. The dwelling houses are comfortable and rent charges I find reasonable.

                                              John Nugent
                                              Immigration Commissioner
                                              State of West Virginia[30]

The investigation into Nugent's activities by the Senate investigating committee revealed that the Federal Government did not consider West Virginia's mines safe enough to recommend miners to them. Nugent had visited Washington, D.C., to ask the United States Commissioner General of Immigration, Daniel J. O'Keefe, for some 2,000 miners. Nugent was informed that the United States government would refuse his request and any further requests from West Virginia for miners until the mines of the State complied with the requirements of the United Mine Workers of America. The Commissioner General also made it plain that all miners would be discouraged from choosing West Virginia as their new home.[31]

Following his rebuff at Washington, Nugent then traveled to England and Wales in search of miners. For an ordinary immigration commissioner, the fact that miners would be sought after such a scathing rebuke on the part of the Federal Government might not be too unusual. However, Nugent had been, prior to the appointment as Immigration Commissioner, an organizer and then President of District 17, United Mine Workers of America.[32] One labor newspaper complained that Nugent was now enticing men to work under the very conditions that he once bitterly opposed.[33] Regardless of the attacks upon him, Nugent continued attracting miners to the State with great success.

As the numbers of immigrants coming to West Virginia grew in the latter part of the 19th century and the early part of the 20th, opinions both pro and con as to the value of the immigrant's labor were voiced. Many of the West Virginia newspapers praised the foreign element for being industrious and honest. However, some people in the State felt that immigration was having a detrimental effect on the American population. An editorial in the *Wheeling Daily Intelligencer,* in 1888, held that some 19,000 foreign persons per day were arriving in the United States from foreign countries. The editorial expressed the opinion that this tremendous influx of workers would lower the wages and living standards of the native Americans.[34]

The impact of the foreign worker on the West Virginia miner was also the subject of one of the questions put to the State's miners by the First Commissioner of Labor in 1889. Some of the miners, at Coalburg, Palatine, Elm Grove and Simon's Creek, reported that immigration was detrimental to them because the foreigners would work for lower wages than they. At Simon's Creek, the miner wrote, the Hungarians would put up with anything and so were hired instead of American miners.[35] On the other hand, miners at Coal Valley, and Bramwell, both in Fayette County, West Virginia, reported that immigration was not yet hurting them.[36] Considering that Coalburg and Coal Valley are approximately only eight miles apart there doesn't seem to be any geographical significance to where the miners were being affected by immigration.

Opinions as to the worth of the foreign worker and his effect on the native worker changed with the growing need for labor, regardless of its source, and the leveling effect that the union organization had on wages. Newspapers in the early 20th century as well as the Commissioner of Labor praised the alien workers in glowing terms as being industrious, hardworking, etc.[37]

However, there were still many incidents in which nativism reared its head, particularly in times of labor strife. An article in *The Charleston Mail* in 1912 reported that foreign miners at Boomer, Fayette County, West Virginia, were going out on strike and threatening American miners who worked on nearby Paint and Cabin creeks. "It seems unfortunate that foreign speaking people, neither citizens of West Virginia, nor even of the United States, should be allowed to conduct themselves as to render it necessary to fill the Kanawha Valley with special officers for the purpose of protecting West Virginia miners who are willing and want to work for the support of their families."[38]

In 1917, shortly after the United States had entered World War One, there were several work stoppages in the Fairmont fields that involved both American and foreign workers. On the surface, the strikes appeared to be mostly the work of foreign miners, Austrians and Italians predominating. Telegrams from State Labor Commissioner Samuel Montgomery and the superintendent of one of the affected mines to Governor John J. Cornwell indicated that they felt the foreigners were primarily responsible for the difficulty. "All or most all are not citizens," Montgomery wired Cornwell after his offer of arbitration in the strike was turned down by the miners.[39]

One might surmise that the Austrians, particularly, were unhappy with the entry of the United States into the war against the Central Powers. Later telegrams, however, from local officials on the scene indicated that what the miners, both foreign and native, desired was recognition of their union. The men were universally desirous of obtaining bargaining rights through the United Mine Workers of America and, according to local reports, were using the national emergency and need for coal as a bargaining position to achieve their goal.[40]

Another reason why the strikes in 1917 may not have been in sympathy for the Central Powers or other European countries was that the European countries had already called for their reservists living in West Virginia and other states to return home. As early as August 7, 1914, one West Virginia newspaper was predicting that the European war would cause a large number of vacancies in the West Virginia mines. The paper noted that there were many miners who were members of the Austrian Reserve and it was estimated that about 90 per cent of them would answer a call for mobilization. The figure was based on an interview with the Austrian-Hungarian Vice Consul von Reuter at Charleston. The same newspaper article predicted that West Virginia coal sales would mount since the coal mining in Europe would be disrupted by the war.[41]

About a year later, in May 1915, figures were published showing that there were nearly two million Italian nationals in the United States, of whom about forty-five per cent were reservists. In McDowell County, West Virginia, Hungarians made up about a fourth of all the miners and Italians another fourth. With so much foreign labor in the Norfolk and Western coal area, fears were expressed that there would be a serious shortage of mine labor if the number of reservists nationwide was correspondingly accurate for West Virginia.[42]

Predictions of the number of men who would return to Europe were evidently fairly accurate, for Van A. Bittner, president of the United Mine Workers at Pittsburgh, reported that many Slav miners had left the region for Europe in 1915 and since Italy had entered the war, Italian miners would probably follow. Bittner estimated that the Pittsburgh District had lost some 7500 men and some 3000 more were expected to leave.[43] In June, 1915, another estimate was made that West Virginia and Pennsylvania had lost about 15,000 miners combined. The loss would not normally be a problem, one newspaper noted, but the war had shut off immigration and there was no possibility of replacing the lost laborers.[44]

In spite of the many estimates that were made of the number of men who returned to Europe, there are few concrete figures available on the subject. However, some representative numbers are available. On June 16, some 30 Italian-American reservists were enlisted into the Italian Army by the Charleston based Italian Consul, T. Luigi, and left for Italy at once.[45] Fifty Italian miners from Cabin Creek and the New River coal fields left Charleston for New York to embark for Italy on July 22, 1915.[46] Also, on October 31, 1915, it was reported that within the previous sixty days, some 1200 Greek miners left for the war in Europe and some 2000 Italian miners had preceded them, creating a very serious labor shortage in the State.[47] To make up for the shortage of labor, Negroes were imported from the South, a subject which will be dealt with presently.

Although many of the foreign miners left West Virginia, many remained throughout the war and on into the 20th century. The life style of the immigrant miner was much like that of the native West Virginia coal miner, but there were some differences in attitudes toward work, problems associated with strange customs and language and also some criminal matters which are alien to the native.

Many of the immigrants who came in the first groups were either single or had left their families behind in the Old World. Often one of their greatest desires was to save enough money to pay the passage of their wives and children to America.[48] Sometimes, though, the immigrants brought their wives and children with them. The man who had a wife was occasionally able to rent a four-room home and go into business renting rooms and furnishing meals to other miners. Usually the man and his wife would rent two rooms to sixteen men who would sleep eight to a room in four beds per room. One room was kept for the family itself and the fourth was used as the kitchen and dining room. The woman would cook and wash for all the men, divide up the cost of food and charge each man, including her husband, equal amounts. Usually, the husband got his laundry done free.[49]

The entire household would often join in the purchase of beer on pay days. The beer was poured into a large galvanized tub, probably used during the week for bathing and washing clothes, and then the night would be spent drinking and singing songs of the Old Country. The various Saints Days, called "Big Sundays," were also occasions for celebration. Even though they liked to celebrate, the foreigners generally spent less on liquor and gambling than did Negroes or white Americans.[50]

One Lithuanian resident of Fayette County, West Virginia, recalled that the foreign families in his home town of Minden were diligent and hard-working. He related the incident of a Polish lady who, along with her husband, ran a boarding house for Polish miners. The lady was expecting a child but didn't let her delicate condition interfere with her duties as mistress of a boarding house. On the day of the child's birth, the lady retired to her bed, gave birth at 3 o'clock in the morning and then was up at 6 o'clock preparing breakfast for her thirteen ravenous boarders and fixing lunches for their dinner buckets.[51]

As with the American miners, tragedy stalked the working hours of the immigrants. In the case of the immigrants, however, it often seemed doubly heartbreaking for a man, whose wife and children were still in Europe, to be killed. For example, Adam Pacis, a 55-year-old miner was killed in a slate fall on April 26, 1915, at the Sycamore Coal Company mine at Cinderella, West Virginia. Pacis left a wife and five children who lived in Russia. Fortunately, even though his wife and children were thousands of miles away, they were eligible for workmen's compensation payments which were mailed to them each month.[52]

Mrs. Joe Mika, the wife of a coal miner, desired to return with her children from West Virginia to Hungary to visit relatives in July, 1914. Before she and her children could return to the State, the First World War broke out. To add to the tragedy of separation for what must have seemed like an interminable period, Mrs. Mika received word that her husband had been killed in the mines. Since she and her children were also entitled to workmen's compensation, the Austrian-Hungarian Consul in Wheeling handled the necessary paperwork with the Compensation Commission for her.[53]

Ignorance and misunderstanding also caused grief for the families of the miners. In one incident the widow of a Bohemian miner refused to give up her marriage certificate, which was necessary to validate her claims for compensation payments after her husband was killed in the mines. The lady, a Mrs. Flegler, was married in 1895 in Bohemia and came to Ellis Island with her husband. They contracted to come to West Virginia to work in the mines at Layland, Fayette County. Both her husband and son were killed in an explosion at Layland in March, 1915. It took neighbors, the manager of the Pocahontas Consolidated Coal Company and Workmen's Compensation officials to entice Mrs. Flegler to part with her marriage certificate which was written in Bohemian so that it could be translated and her payments could be authorized. When her marriage certificate was translated it was quickly returned along with her first month's payment of $25.00 for the loss of her husband and $12.00 for the loss of her son.[54]

Although many of the newspapers and officials emphasized the honesty and diligence of the immigrants, there were some who tried to make their living by preying on their fellows. In the Pocahontas and Fairmont fields there were frequent reports of "Blackhand" activities. The "Blackhand" tried to extort money from an Italian miner in Mercer County in the Pocahontas field on one occasion. The miner, fearful for his life, agreed to pay the extortionists $1,000 in order to be left alone. When the same individuals again warned the miner to prepare $1,000 for them, he decided to go to the Prosecuting Attorney of Mercer County with the story. The Prosecuting Attorney, Howard B. Lee, told the miner to take an empty shoe box to the rendezvous with the members of the "Blackhand" and when the men came to collect the money, to shoot them. Following the instructions, the miner met the extortionists in a deserted railroad yard and shot and killed two of them. According to the Prosecuting Attorney, that was the last of the difficulty with the "Blackhand" in Mercer County.[55]

In the Fairmont field, a murder took place on May 22, 1915, which was attributed to the "Blackhand." Dominick Ferara shot Fueriro Rome five times while the latter was at work in the mines. The murderer then escaped his would-be pursuers by holding them off with several shots from his revolver. The reason for the murder was not clear, but was attributed to a long standing feud between the two men who had come from the same town in Italy but who had belonged to rival Mafia organizations there. The incident which touched off the shooting was reported to be because the two men had been assigned to work together in the mine.[56]

Also in the Fairmont field, Luigi Olivero received a letter from the "Black-hand" threatening his family and himself if he didn't pay some $200.00 to the organization. He, instead, reported the matter to the police.[57] There were undoubtedly many other incidents of extortion and murder or beatings which were not reported due to fear. The number of incidents that were reported, however, does indicate that the Mafia was probably fairly widespread although probably not as organized or as successful as in some of the urban areas of the country.

Immigrants, before the 1920s, made up the second largest group of miners in West Virginia and then the next largest group, after the native whites and immigrants, was Negroes. Negroes were often preferred as employees over both the immigrants and native whites, because they seemed to be more resistant to unionization and less likely to complain.[58] But, there were few Negro miners before 1900. Many of the men who were in the State before 1900 had originally been brought to West Virginia to work on the railroads which were being constructed in the 1870s. Once the railroads were finished, they often remained to find employment in the mines. The early railroad on which the Negroes worked was the Chesapeake and Ohio which was completed across the State to Huntington, West Virginia, in 1873. Later, construction on the Norfolk and Western Railroad and the Virginia Railroad again brought large numbers of Blacks to the State in 1883 and 1892, respectively.[59] The earliest figures available list some 4,620 Negro miners in West Virginia in 1900.[60]

Like the immigrants from Europe, the Negroes came to the State for a variety of reasons. Some were brought as strikebreakers during times of labor unrest, others came of their own free will because of the opportunity for good wages in the mines, and others were sought out by labor contractors who were employed by coal companies to bring Negroes to the State. Of the miners who came to West Virginia on their own, what the sociologists call "push" and "pull" factors played a large part in the decision to emigrate. The "pull" factors were such things as the promise of high wages, less discrimination, better educational systems for their children, etc. "Push" factors included droughts, bad harvests, brushes with the law, deaths of relatives or wives and desires for travel and new experiences.[61]

The coal companies often desired to recruit Negro miners in order to have a "judicious mixture" of white native miners, Negroes and immigrants in order to forestall unionism by playing one group off against another. In one coal mine a white owner used Blacks exclusively to forestall unionization attempts. The Negro workers came under attack from the white miners of their region when they refused to join in strikes seeking union organization. In this and other cases, the differences between the races led to bloodshed.[62]

In order to attract Negro miners, agents were often employed to travel to the South to recruit the men.[63] Some of the companies employed tough "Baldwin-Felts guards" to be agents. They usually traveled in pairs, were well armed, and carried a large amount of cash to use in enticing the miners to come to the State. The mine guards were accompanied by two colored recruiters "who were skillfully selected for their persuasive eloquence and conscienceless disregard of the truth."[64] At their destination, the agents would disappear while the colored recruiters held mass meetings in such places as churches where the "spellbinders" described the advantages and opportunities of working in the West Virginia mines. Those who were persuaded to come to the State were told to bring enough food for six meals and when to meet the labor train that would be traveling throughout the South picking up the prospective miners. Once on the train, the men were placed under the control of the Baldwin-Felts men who kept the coach doors locked until it arrived at its destination. The reason given for the locked doors was that many of the men were taking their first train ride and might fall from the train if they wandered too far.[65] Perhaps just as likely, the doors were locked to keep those who had changed their minds about mining from leaving the train.

In most of the coal mine towns, Negro miners and their families were segregated into areas bearing names like "Colored Town."[66] In addition to living areas, most of the recreation was segregated. The Negroes had their own churches, dances and lodges.[67]

The fact that Negroes were segregated in most towns did not mean that they were in all coal mine towns or that they lacked influence.In the Flat Top coal field in Mercer and McDowell counties there were more Negro miners than native white or foreigners combined. One of the towns in that region, Keystone, McDowell County, was predominantly black and even had a newspaper owned and operated by Blacks. While the living arrangements in this town were not segregated by race, there were separate facilities for blacks and whites. The schools, for example, were segregated and in different sections of the town. There were two white and two colored drug stores, several white and two or three Negro lawyers. There were also segregated restaurants, saloons and musical groups. Although the town officials were white, they catered to Negro demands, because the Negroes were in a majority and the prominent members of the Negro community wielded much influence.[68]

Keystone had a notorious red-light district called "Cinder Bottom" for which the minute town is still infamous. In "Cinder Bottom" there were houses of prostitution for the white miners, the black miners, and some which catered to both. Reportedly, the largest and best run of the houses was for blacks and was run by a huge madam named Mary Miller, a Negro. This same individual became the object of a court trial for holding girls by force in her house. The trial scandalized both the black and white communities of West Virginia.[69]

Despite the segregation of many facilities in the Flat Top field, the black Keystone newspaper ran an article expounding on the advantages to the colored miner who settled in that region. The newspaper reported that the men had very good working conditions, good pay and well built, comfortable homes. The rents which were paid for the homes were reasonable and a man was often able to obtain land for a garden at no extra cost. The company stores were also honestly run and generally earned less profit than privately owned stores in the area.[70]

The *McDowell Times* article also noted that there were good schools in the area. The schools obtained the best teachers who were paid the highest salaries in the State. There were only a few schools which had school terms of less than seven months per year. Further, the paper noted that the political conditions were good since the men were permitted to vote for whomever they pleased, with no danger of losing their jobs. The article concluded by claiming that if the coal companies and railroads wished to prevent labor trouble they should employ Negroes. The Negro was not susceptible to the persuasions of the labor agitator as was the white and foreign miner, since "labor agitators, socialists and demagogues have never found much favor with the Negro."[71]

The Negro miners of the Flat Top region also had the opportunity of joining the Golden Rule Beneficial and Endowment Association, which held meetings, socials, provided entertainment for its members and more importantly served as a mutual benefit society. One advertisement for the Association pleaded for up to 2,000 new members for the first six months of 1914, indicating that the membership must have been substantial. The rates for membership were 50 cents per year for children from 3 to 16, $2.50 per year for those 16 to 50 years old, and $5.50 for those who were between 50 and 60 years old. The Association paid sick benefits of $.20 per week to $1.00 per week for children and from $1.50 to $3.00 per week for adults. The death benefits were scaled from $15.00 to $38.00 in a lump sum for children and $56.00 to $110.00 for adults. The advertisement claimed that the Association was founded for and operated by the Negro race and could boast of chapters in many mining communities.[72] The Association provided a needed service before the passage of Workmen's Compensation and as an important supplement to it after the law was enacted.

Another region in which the Negro miners had some influence was Boone County, West Virginia. On October 30, 1914, the Young Men's Christian Association building was dedicated at Ramage. The board of directors for the YMCA was made up of both black and white miners and no discrimination was permitted at the activities at the "Y." At the dedication ceremonies, Governor Henry Hatfield and ex-Governor William A. MacCorkle appeared on the same stage as speakers as Professor Byrd Prillerman, an instructor at the West Virginia Colored Institute. The three gentlemen made speeches to help celebrate the opening of the "Y" which was a two story frame building with showers and lavatories in the basement, facilities for serving refreshments on the first floor as well as room for "social games" and a second floor reserved for religious services.[73]

At Montgomery, West Virginia, further evidence of the Negro's standing in some communities was the formation of a Negro-owned coal company. The Eagle Coal Company was created by a group of colored businessmen of Montgomery in order to buy the mining property of a defunct Eagle Coal Company. The new owners put the property in shape by building a new tipple, installing electric pumps, buying electric cars for hauling coal in the mine and building a new spur from the Chesapeake and Ohio Railroad to the new tipple.[74]

An obituary in the *McDowell Times* also gives some insight into the status of some of the black miners. J. O. S. Leftwich, described as a prominent citizen of Anawalt, was killed at work in the mines on May 13, 1915. Among his survivors were his wife, brother and sister. "He had been both industrious, economical and a strong provider, had saved considerable money and could boast of owning one of the best homes in Anawalt. Mr. Edward Crews, his 'buddy,' was with him when he met with this most fatal accident." The dead man had no insurance and had belonged to no fraternal organizations. He "was a man who attended to his own business and had high ideals about how men should live." Leftwich was buried in Virginia and the newspaper noted that many of the men who had migrated from the South were taken back to their home states for burial.[75]

Although the coal towns, often had segregated facilities, the men usually worked side by side in the mines.[76] One reason for having the men work together, particularly in union mines, was that the United Mine Workers emphasized the equality of the races in their organizing efforts.[77]

There were at least two important reasons why the union desired equality for the black miners. First, it was more difficult to make a contract if the union desired to have separate wage scales for black and white workers. Secondly, it was very difficult to conduct a successful strike if a large part of the miners were excluded from the union. Consequently, pains were taken to assure Negroes equality as members of the rank and file, but not necessarily as officers of the union.

One example of efforts to create unity among black and white workers was the selection of speakers at a rally at Montgomery, West Virginia, in 1894. The United Mine Workers of America were trying to win a strike against several coal companies but were having difficulty in keeping the black miners away from work. One of the speakers at the rally was John Carter, a black miner, who had worked himself up to be a lawyer. He appeared on the stage with the representatives of the national union in their attempt to maintain a solid front against the employers.[78]

Some further evidence of the attempts to treat all men equally in the union was an incident in 1914 at Boomer, West Virginia, where 1200 miners mostly foreign, went out on strike because a Negro miner, Fletcher Norwood, had been fired for an alleged violation of the work rules.[79] Also, the newspapers which were supported by the labor elements, and the *United Mine Worker's Journal* gave space to stories about Negro miners.[80] Unlike some of the West Virginia newspapers, the labor papers never called Negroes darkies or "niggers."[81]

The present polyglot population of West Virginia can be traced in large measure to the attraction of the coal mines with their high wages and the needs of a fiercely expanding coal industry. Many of the descendants of the coal miners no longer work in that industry, but they have remained in the State as employees in many of the other industries that have grown up. Racial and ethnic prejudice has never been as strong in West Virginia as in many other more southerly states. This may be partly attributable to the efforts of the United Mine Workers of America to enlist all men into the union and the integrated working conditions in the mines.

1. Walter R. Thurmond, *The Logan Coal Field of West Virginia* (Morgantown, W. Va., 1964), p. 59.

2. See chapter 7, this book.

3. Ibid.

4. Arthur E. Suffern, *Conciliation and Arbitration in the Coal Industry of America* (Boston, 1915), p. 74.

5. *Virginias*, 1, no. 5 (May 1880), 1.

6. M. J. Cramer to Governor Henry M. Matthews, Nov. 1, 1880, Governor Matthews Collection, State Department of Archives and History, State Capitol, Charleston, W. Va., box 36 (a). All collections of papers in the State Capitol, Charleston, hereafter cited with individual's name and, the city, e.g., Matthews Papers, Charleston.

7. M. Primer to Governor Henry M. Matthews, May 26, 1879, Matthews Papers, Charleston, box 36(b).

8. William G. Sleeman to Governor Henry M. Matthews, Mar. 22, [no year], Matthews Papers, Charleston, box 36(b).

9. *Virginias*, 3, no. 11 (Nov. 1882), 172.

10. Suffern, *Conciliation and Arbitration*, p. 36.

11. Katherine Harvey, *The Best Dressed Miners* (Ithaca, N.Y., 1969), p. 23.

12. *Charleston Post*, Mar. 19, 1915, p. 8.

13. Thurmond, *Logan Coal Field*, p. 61.

14. Howard B. Lee, *Bloodletting in Appalachia* (Parsons, W. Va., 1969), p. 6; Thurmond, *Logan Coal Field*, p. 60.

15. Suffern, *Conciliation and Arbitration*, p. 73.

16. Ibid.

17. Collection of documents pertaining to the Paint Creek Coal Field, microfilm, no. 1383, West Virginia University Library (hereafter cited as Paint Creek Coal Field).

18. Ibid.

19. Lawrence R. Lynch, "The West Virginia Coal Strike," *Political Science Quarterly*, 29, no. 4 (1914), 644.

20. J. W. Ewing, Secretary to Governor Fleming, to Louis Bourchers, Mar. 21, 1891, Fleming Papers, Charleston, box 85.

21. A. Raooglia to Governor William A. MacCorkle, Dec. 11, [no year], MacCorkle Papers, Charleston, Box 90.

22. Elihu Root to Governor William M. O. Dawson, telegram, Dec. 29, 1906, *West Virginia Governor's Messages Submitted to the Legislature of 1907* (Charleston, W. Va., 1907), vol. 1, p. 3.

23. Ibid., p. 5.

24. Ibid., p. 23.

25. Ibid., pp. 28-31.

26. Ibid., p. 31.

27. U.S. Senate, Committee on Education and Labor, *Conditions in the Paint Creek District, West Virginia*, 63d Cong., 1st sess., 3 vols. (Washington, D.C., 1913), vol. 3, p. 2076 (hereafter cited as *Conditions in the Paint Creek District*).

28. Suffern, *Conciliation and Arbitration*, p. 74.

29. Ibid.

30. Paint Creek Coal Field.

31. *Conditions in the Paint Creek District*, vol. 3, p. 2078.

32. Ibid., p. 2081.

33. *Labor Argus* (Charleston), Oct. 31, 1907.

34. *Wheeling Daily Intelligencer*, May 7, 1888.

35. West Virginia State Commissioner of Labor, *First Report, 1890*, p. 56.

36. Ibid., p. 68.

37. Ibid., passim; W. P. Tams, Jr., *The Smokeless Coal Fields of West Virginia* (Morgantown, W. Va., 1963), p. 61; Thurmond, *Logan Coal Field*, p. 63.

38. *Charleston Mail*, Apr. 26, 1912, p. 4.

39. Samuel B. Montgomery to Governor John J. Cornwell, telegram, May 9, 1917, Cornwell Papers, Charleston, box 150.

40. Ibid., several telegrams and letters in boxes 130 and 131.

41. *McDowell Times*, Aug. 7, 1914.

42. *Charleston Post*, May 25, 1915, p. 9.

43. Ibid., May 29, 1915, p. 3.

44. Ibid., June 4, 1915, p. 5.

45. Ibid., June 16, 1915, p. 2.

46. Ibid., July 22, 1915, p. 8.

47. Ibid, Oct. 31, 1915, p. 16.

48. Thurmond, *Logan Coal Field*, p. 63.

49. Tams, *Smokeless Coal Fields*, p. 61.

50. Ibid.

51. Jack Rodgers, "I Remember That Mining Town," *West Virginia Review*, 15 (Apr. 1938), 204.

52. *Charleston Post*, Apr. 27, 1915, p. 2.

53. Ibid, Apr. 22, 1915.

54. Ibid,. June 14, 1915, p. 4.

55. Lee, *Bloodletting in Appalachia*, p. 47.

56. *Charleston Post*, May 22, 1915, p. 3.

57. Ibid.

58. *McDowell Times*, May 30, 1913, p. 1.

59. See chapter 7, this book.

60. U.S. Bureau of the Census, *The Twelfth Census of the United States* (Washington, D.C., 1904), p. 412.

61. See chapter 7, this book.

62. Donald T. Barnum, *The Negro in the Bituminous Coal Mining Industry* (Philadelphia, 1970), pp. 16, 19; Kenneth R. Bailey, "Tell the Boys to Fall In Line," *West Virginia History*, 32, no. 4 (July 1971), 226.

63. William Livingston, "Coal Miners and Religion" (Master's thesis, Union Theological Seminary, Richmond, Va., 1931), p. 29.

64. Lee, *Bloodletting in Appalachia*, p. 4.

65. Ibid.

66. Interview with Mrs. Gladys Lowe of London, W. Va., July 27, 1972 (hereafter cited as Lowe interview).

67. See chapter 7, this book.

68. Virginia Lad, *History of Keystone, West Virginia* (n.p., 1912), unpaginated.

69. Ibid.

70. *McDowell Times*, May 30, 1913, p. 1.

71. Ibid.

72. Ibid., Jan. 16, 1914, p. 2.

73. Ibid., Oct. 30, 1914, p. 1.

74. Ibid., Aug. 27, 1915, p. 1.

75. Ibid., May 14, 1915, p. 1.

76. Loew interview.

77. Barnum, *Negro in Coal Mining*, p. 15.

78. Bailey, "Tell the Boys to Fall In Line," p. 233.

79. *McDowell Times*, Aug. 21, 1914, p. 3.

80. See such newspapers as the *Charleston Labor Argus*, the *Montgomery Miner's Herald*, and the *UMWJ*.

81. *Logan County Banner*, July 14, 1892, p. 3.

11

The Sociohistorical Roots of White/Black Inequality in Urban Appalachia: Knoxville and East Tennessee

JOHN H. STANFIELD

The low-caste position of Knoxville's native black today can best be understood in sociohistorical terms. Racial inequality cannot be examined adequately without consideration of forces such as industrial development, migration patterns, and geographical location as well as racial ideologies. When these factors are studied, it becomes clear why Knoxville's blacks, and those of East Tennessee in general, have lagged behind those of other southern cities both economically and politically.

For nearly 200 years, Knoxville, Tennessee, has been a major Appalachian city, mainly because of its central location with relation to a number of southern regions: East Tennessee, east Kentucky, West Virginia, northern Alabama, northern Georgia, and more broadly, the Tennessee Valley. Historically, Knoxville has prospered as a result of being a bridge between the Southeast and other southern subregions. In turn, the city has served as a regional center for wholesale trade, railroads, manufacturing, and liquid fuel deposit. The establishment of Tennessee Valley Authority (TVA) headquarters in Knoxville during the 1930s bears witness to the strategic importance of the city.

Even though its location and resources made many late nineteenth-century observers predict that Knoxville would eventually develop into a great wealthy inland city, it has yet to develop a "national city" image and has not experienced the population explosion of other major southern cities. The low-keyed, sometimes negative image of Knoxville apparent in academic and popular literature can be attributed to the long-time local orientation of major leaders. The parochial biases of local politicians, journalists, and civic leaders have been shared by native-born historians who portray Knoxville as "one big happy family."[1]

It would not be overstating the case to say that Knoxville has always been a small private city. Knoxville's traditional leaders have been business families extensively related through kinship ties. A close examination of the social origins of nineteenth-century and early twentieth-century Knoxville bears out these observations.[2] Although there have recently been indications that power is shifting to "nonnatives," the problems encountered by the Knoxville Expo '82 Commission in attracting corporate support suggest the city's low-key image and the parochial biases of contemporary native leaders.

During the period 1870-1970, Knoxville's population growth did not keep pace with that of other cities in and on the fringe of the Appalachian South, because the city performed an auxiliary role in the industrial development of Louisville, Chattanooga, Atlanta, and Birmingham. This auxiliary function was especially apparent between 1870 and 1920, when Atlanta, Birmingham, and Chattanooga were developing industries through the use of Cumberland coal, transported through the major railroad terminal point of Knoxville. Meanwhile, though Knoxville also industrialized rapidly during that period of time and afterward, its activity was not the kind which stimulates quick growth. The local biases of Knoxville's major leaders, which did not encourage the development of heavy-production industry, have contributed to Knoxville's remaining a "small city" in both ethos and population.[3]

BLACKS IN APPALACHIA

Scholars concerned with the races in the South have greatly neglected the social, political, and economic dimensions of white/black inequality in the Appalachian region. Appalachia has been considered an "open" subregion with regard to race, since it did not have an extensive plantation slavery system and has always had a small post-Civil War black population. This academic assumption has been reinforced through popular regional folk wisdoms about "liberal" race relations in Appalachia.[4] Certainly, the optimistic assumptions made about blacks in Appalachia ignore questions and problems such as why this region, which is sandwiched between the Deep South, the Midwest, and the Middle Atlantic, has remained so predominantly white, while surrounding areas have traditionally attracted large black populations.

The subject of race relations in Appalachia has typically been approached from a "folklore" perspective rather than with an orientation toward serious research. The several folklore accounts of black Appalachians may vividly describe particular attributes of black Appalachian culture, but they do little to shed light on the structure and dynamics of racial inequality. Also, the focus on folklore instills a rural bias in the literature, since folklore has always stressed the lifestyles of black mountaineers. Besides government census reports and sketchy survey reports, little is known about white/black inequality in Appalachian cities such as Chattanooga; Charleston, West Virginia; and Knoxville and the Tri-Cities (Kingsport, Johnson City, and Bristol, Tennessee). Exceptions to this traditional pattern of neglect are the numerous critical studies of Birmingham, Alabama, which is on the southern fringe of the Appalachian subregion. I have no space to discuss Birmingham as a special case in the Appalachian region.

SOCIOHISTORICAL BACKGROUND:
KNOXVILLE AND EAST TENNESSEE

Tennessee is divided into three subdivisions on the basis of political, economic, geographical, and cultural factors, with a major urban area in each: West

Tennessee (Memphis); Middle Tennessee (Nashville); and East Tennessee (Knoxville). Unlike the rest of the state, East Tennessee is very hilly and replete with creeks, rivers, lakes, and valuable minerals, such as coal and marble. It is the poorest region in the state and the least politically influential and is often stereotyped as "hillbilly" country. The culture of its mountaineers has a profound, if not predominant, influence on both rural and urban life.

Historians and public officials of Knoxville and other parts of East Tennessee have long considered this city and all of East Tennessee an area apart from the rest of the state and from the South. What a Knoxvillian trade group proclaimed in 1869 is still conventional wisdom today.

The people of East Tennessee are at peace. The outrages of which strangers may read are in Middle and West Tennessee. There are no Ku Klux Klan outrages here. During the late Civil War a very large majority of our people sympathized with the National Government. Those who took the opposite side in East Tennessee are totally law abiding and peaceful citizens quietly engaged in legitimate business. . . . Let not East Tennessee be confounded with other divisions of this state or with other parts of the South. We are a distinct and peculiar people.[5]

The Unionist sympathies and Republicanism of East Tennessee have been used to support the idea that white/black relations were peaceful, but such rhetoric does little to explain the realities of race relations. Though it is true that the terrain and climate of East Tennessee made extensive plantation slavery impossible, the region did have substantial household and dirt-farming slave systems. As Creekmore notes in *Early East Tennessee Taxpayers,* a substantial number of taxpayers owned slaves in Knoxville and in other parts of East Tennessee. Slaves were also used in iron factories in East and Middle Tennessee. More than plantation slavery, household and dirt-farming slavery produced intimate ties between master and slave. Especially in the city, household slaves were given freedom of movement and sometimes freedom to choose their residence.[6]

Household and dirt-farming slave systems produced assumed and actual biracial kinship ties, which resulted in a less conflict-oriented type of slavery. In fact, the first slave manumission society in Tennessee originated not far from Knoxville, and Quaker abolitionists were quite active in what is now the Knoxville Standard Metropolitan Statistical Area. In the small town of Knoxville, in the antebellum period, the prevalence of household slavery blurred status lines between slaves and free blacks.[7] Several factors made this situation unique to Knoxville before the war: (1) household slavery was not just an extension of plantation slavery in the surrounding countryside; (2) because of the geographic isolation of Knoxville, there was no large influx of whites and free blacks, and the slave regime thus developed a high degree of stability; and (3) the local bias of Knoxvillian leaders, and the presence of a small, largely light-skinned free black population, fostered a paternalism which encouraged a belief in the goodness of native blacks as well as informal tolerance of racial miscegenation. The close master-slave relations fostered by household slavery originally led to racial miscegenation and its tolerance. Although this surface harmony has continued, it periodically breaks down, revealing tense undercurrents of racism, which seem to "make no sense," such as the rise of the Ku Klux Klan and the 1919 race riot.

The traditional antebellum black middle class comprised slave and free artisans. A large, well-organized, and assertive black middle class did not form, as it did in Nashville, Memphis, Atlanta, and Birmingham, because black and white leaders were accustomed to working out problems in a personalized framework. With reference to black efforts at progressivism early in the twentieth century, Lamon's telling comparative analysis of differences in black leadership styles in Tennessee's major cities gives credence to the argument advanced above.[8]

Because blacks tended to migrate to centers of heavy industry, the geographic isolation of Knoxville and its light industrial base have perpetuated the low economic and political status of Knoxville's stable black population. Thus, the city never received large influxes of black migrants seeking employment opportunities and admission into labor unions. In fact, between 1870 and 1970, Knoxville's black population was either static or decreased in proportion to the white population, unlike black populations in other major southern cities, which were exploding. The unattractiveness of Knoxville resulted in traditions and relationships between blacks and whites which have persisted well into the twentieth century.

INDUSTRIAL DEVELOPMENT AND RACE RELATIONS IN KNOXVILLE AND EAST TENNESSEE

Even though trade groups in Knoxville began lobbying for Yankee capital to develop manufacturing in the years immediately following the Civil War, the more prominent local leaders resisted the movement of industry into their city until near the end of the nineteenth century. They feared that heavy manufacturing would ruin the environment and would attract "undesirable" persons to the community. Not until 1901 could a trade representative boldly proclaim victory over this resistance and announce the coming of the age of industrialism in Knoxville:

Just now the citizens of Knoxville are more interested in manufacturing industries than they were ever known to be in the history of the city. The time was when some of the best citizens of the old town were sincerely opposed to the location of a factory in their midst because they thought smoke would begrime the city and an undesirable element would be added to the population. This book is sufficient evidence that such ideas no longer exist.[9]

The major antebellum and post-Civil War industrial base was wholesale trade, though iron factories and mills certainly employed more people and had higher levels of capital investment. Wholesale commercialism was congenial to the city, since it grew from Knoxville's strategic location, and more importantly, because it was rooted in family ownership and local capital. Indeed, most of the more prominent Knoxvillian civic leaders in the nineteenth and early twentieth centuries were affluent wholesale businessmen or came from families involved in such industries. The wholesale sector declined during the Great Depression because of the production problems of the midwestern farmers and manufacturers on whom the industry depended. In the 1930s textiles became the prime model industry.[10]

The interest in more diversified light manufacturing in Knoxville became quite apparent between 1900 and 1930. In fact, between 1900 and 1930, Knoxville had the greatest expansion of manufacturing of any city in the urban South. This growth lagged about thirty years behind that of Birmingham, Atlanta, and Chattanooga. Knoxville, East Tennessee, and the Tennessee Valley in general became attractive areas for industrial relocation and development for several reasons: (1) the area's ample water supply provided abundant and inexpensive power; (2) wages could be kept low; and (3) workers were likely to be nonunion.[11] (In the midst of union controversies in the late nineteenth and early twentieth centuries in the North, capitalists began to search for areas such as the South where union problems would be minimal or nonexistent.) The Appalachian South was particularly attractive to industrialists who had enterprises which were extraordinarily sensitive to national and world markets. It is not surprising to find the U.S. Census Bureau reporting that flour and textile mills were the most important industries in the city (in terms of employment and capital investment), at least through World War II, or that three out of four of Tennessee's rayon mills were in East Tennessee. The Tri-Cities and Elizabethton in East Tennessee experienced phenomenal growth after World War I due to the establishment of paper and textile mills.

Another reason Knoxville attracted light industry is that the manufacturing plants were labor intensive. The geographic location of Knoxville made it quite accessible to white mountain people, especially those residing in the hills of the Smoky Mountains. Local businessmen and industrialists considered mountain people ideal for their factories; they saw them as hard-working and virtuous white American citizens who were nonunion. In a 1927 industrial survey, a representative of the Tennessee Electric Power Company put the matter this way:

One of the greatest assets in the development of industry in the South is the abundance and character of the native white labor. The hill labor of the Piedmont section of the South—of which Middle and East Tennessee are a part and about which so much has been said and written—is particularly well suited by heritage to engage in industrial pursuits. This is an exceptional advantage that accrues to manufacturing enterprises located in this section. The greatest percentage of this labor, being of English, Scotch, Irish, and Welsh origin, is genuinely American and is characterized by such attributes as reliability, industry, tractability and intelligence. Managers and operatives in southern textile mills speak the same language and there is better understanding and spirit of cooperation prevailing between employer and employee. It is also of importance to know that practically no trade unionism exists among the textile workers in Tennessee.[12]

The emphasis on white labor in the development of textile mills and other light industries has been well documented. After the Civil War, a dual economy emerged in the South: a cotton tenancy for blacks and mill industries for poor whites.[13] The adherence to this idea of dual economy was apparent in Knoxville. In selling their city to industrialists, Knoxvillian trade groups stressed the smallness of the black population and the abundance of docile native white labor.

Because of the availability of mill jobs, the white population grew rapidly in the first quarter of the twentieth century. In 1880, the black population was 32.5 percent of the total city population, but it dropped to 22.5 percent in 1890. In general, between 1880 and 1940 the in-migration of whites led to a dramatic decrease in the proportion of blacks in the population, though in absolute terms the black population continued to increase.[14]

Comparative census data indicate that between 1910 and 1920, Knoxville's 114 percent population growth rate (85 percent of which was white) was the highest in the urban South and one of the greatest in the nation. Certainly this swift in-migration of whites could not be readily absorbed into the city's political and economic spheres, especially during World War I, which, like all American wars, stimulated production but did not facilitate social integration of diverse groups. It can be conjectured that many poor white migrants were unable to compete with native whites for skilled industrial labor and were locked out of the black-dominated unskilled nonindustrial sector, especially domestic-service-related employment. Also, since the end of the Civil War, blacks were passive (if not factionalized) participants in local political machines dominated by affluent whites, while poor whites were greatly excluded. These structural factors point to the possibility that the Knoxville race riot of 1919 was a mob incident incited by poor and working-class whites. Paternalistic white leaders were embarrassed by the incident and in many ways wrote off the riot and its aftermath as a lower-class activity. (The jury at the trial of the white rioters was composed entirely of poor and working-class whites.) Also, the rapid population growth in the city in the first quarter of the century suggests the reason why so many insecure white natives of Knoxville joined an eventually flourishing Ku Klux Klan chapter in the early 1920s.[15]

The confinement of most blacks to domestic servitude and marginal industrial occupations in a cohesive biracial community facilitated passive racial accommodation in the urban industrialization process. Simply stated, blacks seldom collectively protested the lack of employment opportunities in the skilled or professional sector. In fact, Knoxville and other East Tennessee cities were known to have great employment opportunities for blacks as compared with the other regions of the state, but such opportunities were in the nonindustrial and unskilled occupations.[16] In a 1926 survey of the black community (sample size: 3,151 families), the director of Knoxville's black public library reported an employment distribution which documents the point.

Category	Number
Skilled	15
Semiskilled	96
Unskilled	1,253

The relegation of blacks to menial work similar to that found during the antebellum period resulted in the limited development of a black petty bourgeoisie, which never became a highly visible and prosperous middle class.[17] As early as 1926, Daves noted that the Negro Board of Trade was "inactive" and that blacks had business problems, which persist to the present.

A more fundamental reason for the economic underdevelopment of the black community is that because blacks were able to patronize most white commercial enterprises (except certain restaurants, hotels, and store lunch counters) and could sit anywhere on public transportation, blacks in Knoxville, unlike those in other major southern cities, did not feel impelled to organize their own extensive business sector. Also, white politicians and other leaders were quite willing to "look after their blacks" by establishing black theatres and public schools and by supporting the businesses of their former slaves and house servants. [18]

During the Jim Crow era and afterward, some social traditions were aspects of the superstructure of the kinship qualities of white/black relations. For instance, Knoxville's black population has not used educational institutions to develop an articulate, indigenous black middle class. In Atlanta and Nashville, on the other hand, local black colleges served as training grounds for natives, who eventually became community leaders and actively campaigned for black rights. Indeed, colleges such as Fisk in Nashville and Atlanta University in Atlanta were intertwined with black churches in the development of aggressive local black leadership. Martin Luther King, Jr., is a good example of a leader whose advancement resulted from such traditional interinstitutional relationships. At most, Knoxville has shown a highly individualized pattern of accommodative black leadership which has denied the importance of black community development, black mobility and rights, and the effects of racism on the quality of life for blacks. Cansler's dedication speech in 1918 for the establishment of Knoxville's first black library exemplifies an early variant of this passive attitude:

I like to contemplate the thought that the Negro race, unlike the white race, has not reached the zenith of its greatness and its glory, but that it is now making a beginning. No doubt many of you have heard the story of the three young men of different races and ancestry who met upon one occasion, and as young men have always done and always will do, talked of the mighty heroes of the past and the great achievement they themselves hoped to accomplish in the future. Said he whose racial type indicated him to be an Asiatic and a Jew: "I come from a strong and powerful race. Before Europe was overrun with the barbarous hordes, before America was known to the map of the world, my ancestors were mighty in the temples and on the throne." And said he of Anglo-Saxon birth and of European lineage: "My ancestors were warriors of mighty deeds and renown. The blood of Vikings flows in my veins. I belong to a race which has overthrown kingdoms and upon the ruins of empires has erected the greatest monuments of civilization, a race which has built up the waste places of the earth and the glory of whose deeds is to live forever in story and song." He of African descent was silent. And he of Asiatic birth and he of European lineage said to him of African descent: "And what of your race and ancestry?" "Alas!" said he, "I can boast for my race few mighty deeds of prowess. I belong to one of the humblest races that God has created, a dark people with a dark past full of sad memories. But," said he, as he drew himself up to his full height, "you boast of your proud ancestry, tracing it back to kings and priests, I can boast of more than you, for I *am* an ancestor, and the germ of a mighty people yet to be."[19]

The personalized relationships between whites and blacks in Knoxville prevented the extensive use of local schools, churches, and traditional civil rights organizations as means of developing a broad, assertive native middle class. The history of black leadership has been individually, not collectively based, for example reflecting the role of the Cansler family, W. Porter, and Reverend James rather than that of formal groups and associations.[20] This tradition has been reinforced through the historical exclusion of the native black population from local colleges and universities. Knoxville College, a black institution which has been in the city for more than 100 years, has usually recruited outside the urban area, and though the University of Tennessee is entering its second decade of gradual desegregation, it too recruits most black students from other areas. The history of "no education" for poor blacks, obviously, not only has produced great social cleavages in the black community but also has perpetuated a highly undereducated black underclass, thereby also continuing the cycle of unemployment or marginal employment and residence in public housing.

WHITE/BLACK INEQUALITY IN POST-WORLD WAR II KNOXVILLE

In the first twenty-five years following the end of World War II, Knoxville remained an invisible small city snuggled next to the Smoky Mountains. Census reports show that the city grew from 124,769 (12 percent black) in 1950 to 190,502 (8 percent black) in 1970. Even the presence of Tennessee Valley Authority headquarters in the city and of neighboring Oak Ridge, the atomic research center, did not move city leaders to convert their community into a "national city."

By the late 1960s and early 1970s things had begun to change. First, the completion of an interstate highway made Knoxville and all of East Tennessee more accessible.[21] Second, the expansion of three local institutions—the University of Tennessee, Oak Ridge, and the Tennessee Valley Authority—greatly increased in-migration, particularly by professional workers. West Knoxville, which is currently the principal commercial area in the city and the residence of many young professional "outsiders," was farmland fifteen years ago. Many contemporary political controversies regarding the annexation of surrounding areas and Expo '82 are really power struggles between old native Knoxvillians and an economic elite crystallizing on the west side.

Third, and most important, the desegregation of the University of Tennessee, Oak Ridge, the Tennessee Valley Authority, and other local institutions has stimulated the in-migration of blacks with values, beliefs, and life-styles different from those in the native black community. The exact number of such migrants cannot be accurately assessed in this paper, but their impact has materialized in intraracial and interracial conflicts, such as church splits in the black community, and a black students' sit-in in 1982 at the University of Tennessee.[22] There is a growing awareness among traditional white and black leaders that something other than accommodation and resignation must take place to maintain order in a city which seems to be developing an assertive black middle class and a racially conservative white populace.

Brooks and Banner mention several persistent problems related to white/

black inequality, including employment, housing, medical care, and garbage collection.[23] Problems in employment are due to the facts that the native black population is still highly underskilled and that qualified blacks are unable to find work in local industries. As in the past, many blacks move to other urban areas to find employment. I should mention that TVA, like most federal agencies, has been slow to violate the norms of local race relations; blacks are usually hired in menial and clerical positions. TVA has only recently established an Equal Employment monitoring office as required by the 1964 Civil Rights Act. Certainly, the persistence of this dual economy in Knoxville is the product of traditional race relations in a city long geographically and ideologically isolated from changes in the rest of the country.

The undereducation and underemployment of the black population have aggravated housing problems in Knoxville's black community, which are extensive. As in most inner cities, housing for blacks has always been poor and limited. Prior to World War II, dire conditions existed which have not yet been fully resolved. Brooks and Banner speak of real estate agencies in the city that still discriminate between the races.[24]

During the World War II era, much poor housing in the two predominantly black areas was torn down and was replaced with city-controlled public housing. Since most recent industrial development has been outside the city, or at least far from the black communities, housing project dwellers have little employment opportunity, and thus they remain dependent on the state. Since the solution to black poverty chosen by Knoxville's elite has been the development of housing projects, the black underclass has continued barely to subsist on the state. Thus residence predominantly in housing projects completes a vicious cycle of black undereducation, unemployment and underemployment, and almost absolute powerlessness. This pattern reproduces racial accommodation and hinders the development of a native black middle class which would be assertive and aggressive on civil rights issues and would advocate progressive community development.

SOME THEORETICAL OBSERVATIONS

Knoxville is an old principal city in the Appalachian South. Its geographical location has made it the urban hub of East Tennessee, east Kentucky, West Virginia, northern Alabama, and northern Georgia. The rapid urbanization of Atlanta and Birmingham has created the interesting interdependency of Knoxville and these two cities. Ever since the turn of the century, Knoxville has been important to Atlanta and Birmingham as a fuel transport terminal. Heavy industry has developed little in Knoxville partly because city leaders have long considered such industry a menace.

Though it is true that Knoxville and other Appalachian cities have much in common with other southern urban areas, significant differences affect patterns of white/black inequality in urban Appalachia. First, cities in the Deep South and Southeast, such as Richmond, New Orleans, Memphis, and Nashville, industrialized through the manufacturing of cash-crop commodities. On the other hand, Knoxville, Tri-Cities, Birmingham, Wheeling, and other Appalachian cities industrialized through the development of extractive and textile processing and manufacturing plants.

Second, though all southern cities have experienced population growth through native white and black in-migration rather than through influxes of European immigrants, there is an important qualitative difference between Appalachian and other southern cities. Historically, most of the migrants to Appalachian cities have been white mountain people uprooted by coal-mining or lumber companies or attracted to economic and social opportunities in the city.[25] Indeed, there are striking parallels between the dislocation of hill people and urban population explosions. For instance, the appeals of early Knoxvillian businessmen and industries for mountain people to work in expanding light industries coincided with the increasing activity of lumber companies in East Tennessee and of coal corporations in east Kentucky and West Virginia and with the commercialization of the Smoky Mountains. A similar case can be made for the parallel between the mechanization of the coal industry in the 1950s and 1960s and the rapid growth of Knoxville's poor white population in the post-World War II era.

As a result of this migration, many problems of the white underclasses in Appalachian cities reflect the clash of values between traditional mountaineers and native urban dwellers. For example, most problems related to family violence, juvenile delinquency, and social conflict in Knoxville occur in the southern area, which has the highest rate of poor white in-migration.

Because of the geographic location of Appalachia, the regional and local elites have been interested in maintaining it as an area in which a conservative poor white underclass is concentrated; this underclass, when the need arises, can be tapped for labor-intensive industries. This attitude does not benefit the economic and political ambitions of blacks. Thus even when black populations in other southern cities were numerically and proportionally exploding, black populations in urban and rural Appalachia were either stabilizing or decreasing. The trend has not been helped by the traditional employment policies of TVA, which stipulated that it would hire blacks in proportion to their percentage in a locale. This policy concentrated the black population and did not encourage migration, since white hill communities were required to hire only white TVA employees.[26]

In conclusion, racial inequality can be adequately considered only when pertinent economic, political, legal, and social factors are taken into account. White/black inequality in Knoxville and in other Appalachian cities can be understood only when we consider factors such as the impact of household and dirt-farming slave systems; the development of extractive and textile manufacturing, the personalization of race relations, and the stabilization and decrease of black populations. Only then can we understand why, on the one hand, Knoxville is portrayed as a city with tolerant race relations and why, on the other hand, it exhibits the realities of a passive native black population which is highly undereducated, economically underdeveloped, politically invisible, and intimately dependent upon the state.

1. J. B. Killebrew, *Introduction to the Resources of Tennessee* (Nashville, Tenn., 1874); Willson, Whitman, *God's Valley: People and Power along the Tennessee River* (New York, 1939); Kenneth T. Jackson, *The Ku Klux Klan in the City, 1915-1930* (New York, 1967); Blaine A. Brownell, *The Urban Ethos in the South 1920-1930* (Baton Rouge, La., 1975); William Rule, *Standard History of Knoxville, Tennessee* (Chicago, 1900); Mary U. Rothrock, *The French Broad-Holston County* (Knoxville, Tenn., 1946); Betsey B. Creekmore, *Knoxville* (Knoxville, Tenn., 1967).

2. Rothrock, *French Broad-Holston County*, p. 39; Goodspeed Publishing Company, *Goodspeed's History of Tennessee* (Nashville, Tenn., 1887); Great Smoky Mountains Publishing Company, *Knoxville Men and Women of Affairs* (Knoxville, Tenn., 1929).

3. Knoxville Industrial Association, *Facts and Figures Concerning the Climate, Manufacturing Advantages, and the Agricultural and Mineral Resources of East Tennessee* (Knoxville, Tenn., 1869); Brownell, *Urban Ethos*, p. 57; "Knoxville, Knox County Lags Far Behind in New Industry," *Knoxville Journal*, Mar. 5, 1968.

4. See chapter 1, this book; Knoxville Industrial Association, *Facts and Figures*, p. 12; Merrill Proudfoot, *Diary of a Sit-in* (Chapel Hill, N.C., 1954); Creekmore, *Knoxville*, p. 188.

5. Knoxville Industrial Association, *Facts and Figures*, p. 17.

6. Rothrock, *French Broad-Holston County*, p. 40; Creekmore, *Knoxville*, p. 193; Pollyanna Creekmore, *Early East Tennessee Taxpayers* (Easley, S.C., 1980); Stanley J. Folmsbee, Robert E. Corlew, and Enoch L. Mitchell, *Tennessee: A Short History* (Knoxville, Tenn., 1969); Charles W. Cansler, *A Library Milestone* (Chicago, 1946); Lester C. Lamon, *Black Tennesseans, 1900-1930* (Knoxville, Tenn., 1977); Richard C. Wade, *Slavery in the Cities: The South, 1820-1860* (New York, 1967).

7. Folmsbee, Corlew, and Mitchell, *Tennessee*, p. 213; Charles W. Cansler, *Three Generations: The Story of a Colored Family of Eastern Tennessee* (Kingsport, Tenn., 1939).

8. William E. B. Du Bois, *The Negro Artisan* (Atlanta, Ga., 1903); Hollis R. Lynch, *The Black Urban Condition: A Documentary History 1866-1971* (New York, 1973); Howard N. Rabinowitz, *Race Relations in the Urban South 1865-1870* (New York, 1978); Lamon, *Black Tennesseans*, p. 219.

9. W. H. Kephart, *Manufacturers of Knoxville, Tennessee* (Knoxville, Tenn., 1901).

10. Charles E. Allfred and Samuel W. Atkins, *Human and Physical Resources of Tennessee* (Knoxville, Tenn., 1974).

11. Brownell, *Urban Ethos*, p. 131; Allfred and Atkins, *Human and Physical Resources*, p. 144.

12. Tennessee Electric Power Company, *Industrial Survey of Territory Served by the Tennessee Power Company, Chattanooga, Tennessee*, Commission no. 1712 (Atlanta, Ga., 1927).

13. Melvin T. Copeland, *The Cotton Manufacturing Industry of the United States* (Cambridge, Mass., 1917).

14. Knoxville City Planning Commission, "Knoxville's People," preliminary draft, 1950.

15. Larry W. Dunn, *Knoxville Negro Voting and the Roosevelt Revolution, 1928-1936*, East Tennessee Historical Society Publication no. 43, (Knoxville, Tenn., 1971); Lamon, *Black Tennesseans*, p. 34; Jackson, *Ku Klux Klan*, pp. 59-65.

16. J. H. Daves, *Social Study of the Colored Population of Knoxville, Tennessee* (Knoxville, Tenn., 1926); William H. Wesson, Jr., "Negro Employment Practices in the Chattanooga Area" in *Selected Studies of Negro Employment in the South* (Washington, D.C., 1955); J. Harvey Kerns, *Social and Economic Conditions in Knoxville, Tennessee, as They Affect the Negro* (Atlanta, Ga., 1967).

17. Du Bois, *Negro Artisan*, p. 211.

18. "Interesting Stories Are Recalled about City Soap Making Industry," *Knoxville Journal*, Feb. 21, 1943; "Knoxville's First Mattress Plant Operated on South Central Street," *Knoxville Journal*, June 20, 1954.

19. Cansler, *Three Generations*, p. 20.

20. Sharyn Owen, "Mount Zion Baptist Church, Knoxville, Tennessee: 1860-1975," *Black Tennessean*, Fall 1976.

21. Allen Booz and Ive Hamilton, *Study of the Utilization of Scientific, Technical, and Professional Resources in the Economic Development of EGST in Tennessee* (Washington, D.C., 1968).

22. I thank Professors Ira Harrison and Riggins Earl of the University of Tennessee for helping me develop this point.

23. J. Michael Brooks and Mae Guyer Banner, "The Search for Power: A Sociohistorical Perspective on the Persistence of Black Grievances in Knoxville," *Black Tennessean,* Fall 1976.

24. William E. Cole, *Knoxville Community Audit on Human Relationships* (Knoxville, Tenn., 1949); Brooks and Banner, *Search for Power,* p. 13.

25. Helen M. Lewis, L. Johnson and D. Askins, *Colonialism in Modern America: The Appalachian Case* (Boone, N.C., 1978).

26. Whitman, *God's Valley.*

PART FIVE

Black Coal Miners

Part 5 focuses on Alabama, Kentucky, Tennessee, Virginia, and West Virginia—the southern Appalachian region known for its abundant reserves of bituminous coal, in which blacks have historically been a major source of labor. The lead article is a part of Du Bois's monumental research into the central pattern of blacks' role in America's industrial development, their racial domination and economic exploitation as "the dark proletariat." Black mine laborers are central to the Marxian view of racism, linking it to social structure (of which it is a part) and offering confirmation that the race problem is determined in economic organization and the fight for power in society.

Herbert R. Northrup's article is a detailed account of the split labor market thesis as it accounts for the differences in union effectiveness between blacks in the northern and southern Appalachian coal fields. Following this macro-analysis are some letters written by William Riley, one of the first black organizers for the UMWA. He clearly establishes that some blacks joined the debate over white racism and black antiunionism in the UMW. His letters attest to the conflicting demands and cross pressures on black organizers whose loyalty to race *and* unionism cast them between progressive idealism and the social realities of the day. Richard Straw seems to reject the simplistic account of the race problem in the UMW "as a reflex of the class struggle." On the other hand, his research supports the idea that ethnic antagonisms are a "strategem of owners for dividing and weakening the working class (union) movement." His case study of racial antipathy finds it originating from and resulting in fierce competition between groups of laborers that produces a wage differential for labor and a disadvantage for labor unionism. The great feature of this milestone in UMWA history was "that old race antagonism."

12

The Black Worker

W. E. B. DU BOIS

Easily the most dramatic episode in American history was the sudden move to free four million black slaves in an effort to stop a great civil war, to end forty years of bitter controversy, and to appease the moral sense of civilization.

From the day of its birth, the anomaly of slavery plagued a nation which asserted the equality of all men, and sought to derive powers of government from the consent of the governed. Within sound of the voices of those who said this lived more than half a million black slaves, forming nearly one-fifth of the population of a new nation.

The black population at the time of the first census had risen to three-quarters of a million, and there were over a million at the beginning of the nineteenth century. Before 1830, the blacks had passed the two million mark, helped by the increased importations just before 1808, and the illicit smuggling up until 1820. By their own reproduction, the Negroes reached 3,638,808 in 1850, and before the Civil War, stood at 4,441,830. They were 10% of the whole population of the nation in 1700, 22% in 1750, 18.9% in 1800 and 11.6% in 1900.

These workers were not all black and not all Africans and not all slaves. In 1860, at least 90% were born in the United States, 13% were visibly of white as well as Negro descent and actually more than one-fourth were probably of white, Indian and Negro blood. In 1860, 11% of these dark folk were free workers.

In origin, the slaves represented everything African, although most of them originated on or near the West Coast. Yet among them appeared the great Bantu tribes from Sierra Leone to South Africa; the Sudanese, straight across the center of the continent, from the Atlantic to the Valley of the Nile; the Nilotic Negroes and the black and brown Hamites, allied with Egypt; the tribes of the great lakes; the Pygmies and the Hottentots; and in addition to these, distinct traces of both Berber and Arab blood. There is no doubt of the presence of all these various elements in the mass of 10,000,000 or more Negroes transported from Africa to the various Americas, from the fifteenth to the nineteenth centuries.

Most of them that came to the continent went through West Indian tutelage, and thus finally appeared in the United States. They brought with them their religion and rhythmic song, and some traces of their art and tribal customs. And after a lapse of two and one-half centuries, the Negroes became a settled working population, speaking English or French, professing Christianity, and used principally in agricultural toil. Moreover, they so mingled their blood with white and red America that today less than 25% of the Negro Americans are of unmixed African descent.

So long as slavery was a matter of race and color, it made the conscience of the nation uneasy and continually affronted its ideals. The men who wrote the Constitution sought by every evasion, and almost by subterfuge, to keep recognition of slavery out of the basic form of the new government. They founded their hopes on the prohibition of the slave trade, being sure that without continual additions from abroad, this tropical people would not long survive, and thus the problem of slavery would disappear in death. They miscalculated, or did not foresee the changing economic world. It might be more profitable in the West Indies to kill the slaves by overwork and import cheap Africans; but in America without a slave trade, it paid to conserve the slave and let him multiply. When, therefore, manifestly the Negroes were not dying out, there came quite naturally new excuses and explanations. It was a matter of social condition. Gradually these people would be free; but freedom could only come to the bulk as the freed were transplanted to their own land and country, since the living together of black and white in America was unthinkable. So again the nation waited, and its conscience sank to sleep.

But in a rich and eager land, wealth and work multiplied. They twisted new and intricate patterns around the earth. Slowly but mightily these black workers were integrated into modern industry. On free and fertile land Americans raised, not simply sugar as a cheap sweetening, rice for food and tobacco as a new and tickling luxury; but they began to grow a fiber that clothed the masses of a ragged world. Cotton grew so swiftly that the 9,000 bales of cotton which the new nation scarcely noticed in 1791 became 79,000 in 1800; and with this increase, walked economic revolution in a dozen different lines. The cotton crop reached one-half million bales in 1822, a million bales in 1831, two million in 1840, three million in 1852, and in the year of secession, stood at the then enormous total of five million bales.

Such facts and others, coupled with the increase of the slaves to which they were related as both cause and effect, meant a new world; and all the more so because with increase in American cotton and Negro slaves, came both by chance and ingenuity new miracles for manufacturing, and particularly for the spinning and weaving of cloth.

The giant forces of water and of steam were harnessed to do the world's work, and the black workers of America bent at the bottom of a growing pyramid of commerce and industry; and they not only could not be spared, if this new economic organization was to expand, but rather they became the cause of new political demands and alignments, of new dreams of power and visions of empire.

First of all, their work called for widening stretches of new, rich, black soil—in Florida, in Louisiana, in Mexico; even in Kansas. This land, added to cheap labor, and labor easily regulated and distributed, made profits so high that a whole system of culture arose in the South, with a new leisure and social philosophy. Black labor became the foundation stone not only of the Southern social structure, but of Northern manufacture and commerce, of the English factory system, of European commerce, of buying and selling on a world-wide scale; new cities were built on the results of black labor, and a new labor problem, involving all white labor, arose both in Europe and America.

Thus, the old difficulties and paradoxes appeared in new dress. It became easy to say and easier to prove that these black men were not men in the sense that white men were, and could never be, in the same sense, free. Their slavery was a matter of both race and social condition, but the condition was limited and determined by race. They were congenital wards and children, to be well-treated and cared for, but far happier and safer here than in their own land. As the Richmond, Virginia, *Examiner* put it in 1854:

Let us not bother our brains about what *Providence* intends to do with our Negroes in the distant future, but glory in and profit to the utmost by what He has done for them in transplanting them here, and setting them to work on our plantations. . . . True philanthropy to the Negro, begins, like charity, at home; and if southern men would act as if the canopy of heaven were inscribed with a covenant, in letters of fire, that *the Negro is here, and here forever; is our property, and ours forever;* . . . they would accomplish more good for the race in five years than they boast the institution itself to have accomplished in two centuries. . . .

On the other hand, the growing exploitation of white labor in Europe, the rise of the factory system, the increased monopoly of land, and the problem of the distribution of political power, began to send wave after wave of immigrants to America, looking for new freedom, new opportunity and new democracy.

The opportunity for real and new democracy in America was broad. Political power at first was, as usual, confined to property holders and an aristocracy of birth and learning. But it was never securely based on land. Land was free and both land and property were possible to nearly every thrifty worker. Schools began early to multiply and open their doors even to the poor laborer. Birth began to count for less and less and America became to the world a land of economic opportunity. So the world came to America, even before the Revolution, and afterwards during the nineteenth century, nineteen million immigrants entered the United States.

When we compare these figures with the cotton crop and the increase of black workers, we see how the economic problem increased in intricacy. This intricacy is shown by the persons in the drama and their differing and opposing interests. There were the native-born Americans, largely of English descent, who were the property holders and employers; and even so far as they were poor, they looked forward to the time when they would accumulate capital and become, as they put it, economically "independent." Then there were the new immigrants, torn with a certain violence from their older social and economic surroundings; strangers in a new land, with visions of rising in the social and economic world by means of labor. They differed in language and social status, varying from the half-starved Irish peasant to the educated German and English artisan. There were the free Negroes: those of the North free in some cases for many generations, and voters; and in other cases, fugitives, new come from the South, with little skill and small knowledge of life and labor in their new environment. There were the free Negroes of the South, an unstable, harried class, living on sufferance of the law, and the good will of white patrons, and yet rising to be workers and sometimes owners of property and even of slaves, and cultured citizens. There was the great mass of poor whites, disinherited of their economic portion by competition with the slave system, and land monopoly.

In the earlier history of the South, free Negroes had the right to vote. Indeed, so far as the letter of the law was concerned, there was not a single Southern colony in which a black man who owned the requisite amount of property, and complied with other conditions, did not at some period have the legal right to vote.

Negroes voted in Virginia as late as 1723, when the assembly enacted that no free Negro, mulatto or Indian "shall hereafter have any vote at the elections of burgesses or any election whatsoever." In North Carolina, by the Act of 1734, a former discrimination against Negro voters was laid aside and not reënacted until 1835.

A complaint in South Carolina, in 1701, said:

"Several free Negroes were receiv'd, & taken for as good Electors as the best Freeholders in the Province. So that we leave it with Your Lordships to judge whether admitting Aliens, Strangers, Servants, Negroes, &c, as good and qualified Voters, can be thought any ways agreeable to King Charles' Patent to Your Lordships, or the English Constitution of Government." Again in 1716, Jews and Negroes, who had been voting, were expressly excluded. In Georgia, there was at first no color discrimination, although only owners of fifty acres of land could vote. In 1761, voting was expressly confined to white men.[1]

In the states carved out of the Southwest, they were disfranchised as soon as the state came into the Union, although in Kentucky they voted between 1792 and 1799, and Tennessee allowed free Negroes to vote in her constitution of 1796.

In North Carolina, where even disfranchisement, in 1835, did not apply to Negroes who already had the right to vote, it was said that the several hundred Negroes who had been voting before then usually voted prudently and judiciously.

In Delaware and Maryland they voted in the latter part of the eighteenth century. In Louisiana, Negroes who had had the right to vote during territorial status were not disfranchised.

To sum up, in colonial times, the free Negro was excluded from the suffrage only in Georgia, South Carolina and Virginia. In the Border States, Delaware disfranchised the Negro in 1792; Maryland in 1783 and 1810.

In the Southeast, Florida disfranchised Negroes in 1845; and in the Southwest, Louisiana disfranchised them in 1812; Mississippi in 1817; Alabama in 1819; Missouri, 1821; Arkansas in 1836; Texas, 1845. Georgia in her constitution of 1777 confined voters to white males; but this was omitted in the constitutions of 1789 and 1798.

As slavery grew to a system and the Cotton Kingdom began to expand into imperial white domination, a free Negro was a contradiction, a threat and a menace. As a thief and a vagabond, he threatened society; but as an educated property holder, a successful mechanic or even professional man, he more than threatened slavery. He contradicted and undermined it. He must not be. He must

be suppressed, enslaved, colonized. And nothing so bad could be said about him that did not easily appear as true to slaveholders.

In the North, Negroes, for the most part, received political enfranchisement with the white laboring classes. In 1778, the Congress of the Confederation twice refused to insert the word "white" in the Articles of Confederation in asserting that free inhabitants in each state should be entitled to all the privileges and immunities of free citizens of the several states. In the law of 1783, free Negroes were recognized as a basis of taxation, and in 1784, they were recognized as voters in the territories. In the Northwest Ordinance of 1787, "free male inhabitants of full age" were recognized as voters.

The few Negroes that were in Maine, New Hampshire and Vermont could vote if they had the property qualifications. In Connecticut they were disfranchised in 1814; in 1865 this restriction was retained, and Negroes did not regain the right until after the Civil War. In New Jersey, they were disfranchised in 1807, but regained the right in 1820 and lost it again in 1847. Negroes voted in New York in the eighteenth century, then were disfranchised, but in 1821 were permitted to vote with a discriminatory property qualification of $250. No property qualification was required of whites. Attempts were made at various times to remove this qualification but it was not removed until 1870. In Rhode Island they were disfranchised in the constitution which followed Dorr's Rebellion, but finally allowed to vote in 1842. In Pennsylvania, they were allowed to vote until 1838 when the "reform" convention restricted the suffrage to whites.

The Western States as territories did not usually restrict the suffrage, but as they were admitted to the Union they disfranchised the Negroes: Ohio in 1803; Indiana in 1816; Illinois in 1818; Michigan in 1837; Iowa in 1846; Wisconsin in 1848; Minnesota in 1858; and Kansas in 1861.

The Northwest Ordinance and even the Louisiana Purchase had made no color discrimination in legal and political rights. But the states admitted from this territory, specifically and from the first, denied free black men the right to vote and passed codes of black laws in Ohio, Indiana and elsewhere, instigated largely by the attitude and fears of the immigrant poor whites from the South. Thus, at first, in Kansas and the West, the problem of the black worker was narrow and specific. Neither the North nor the West asked that black labor in the United States be free and enfranchised. On the contrary, they accepted slave labor as a fact; but they were determined that it should be territorially restricted, and should not compete with free white labor.

What was this industrial system for which the South fought and risked life, reputation and wealth and which a growing element in the North viewed first with hesitating tolerance, then with distaste and finally with economic fear and moral horror? What did it mean to be a slave? It is hard to imagine it today. We think of oppression beyond all conception: cruelty, degradation, whipping and starvation, the absolute negation of human rights; or on the contrary, we may think of the ordinary worker the world over today, slaving ten, twelve, or fourteen hours a day, with not enough to eat, compelled by his physical necessities to do this and not to do that, curtailed in his movements and his

possibilities; and we say, here, too, is a slave called a "free worker," and slavery is merely a matter of name.

But there was in 1863 a real meaning to slavery different from that we may apply to the laborer today. It was in part psychological, the enforced personal feeling of inferiority, the calling of another Master; the standing with hat in hand. It was the helplessness. It was the defenselessness of family life. It was the submergence below the arbitrary will of any sort of individual. It was without doubt worse in these vital respects than that which exists today in Europe or America. Its analogue today is the yellow, brown and black laborer in China and India, in Africa, in the forests of the Amazon; and it was this slavery that fell in America.

The slavery of Negroes in the South was not usually a deliberately cruel and oppressive system. It did not mean systematic starvation or murder. On the other hand, it is just as difficult to conceive as quite true the idyllic picture of a patriarchal state with cultured and humane masters under whom slaves were as children, guided and trained in work and play, given even such mental training as was for their good, and for the well-being of the surrounding world.

The victims of Southern slavery were often happy; had usually adequate food for their health, and shelter sufficient for a mild climate. The Southerners could say with some justification that when the mass of their field hands were compared with the worst class of laborers in the slums of New York and Philadelphia, and the factory towns of New England, the black slaves were as well off and in some particulars better off. Slaves lived largely in the country where health conditions were better; they worked in the open air, and their hours were about the current hours for peasants throughout Europe. They received no formal education, and neither did the Irish peasant, the English factory-laborer, nor the German *Bauer;* and in contrast with these free white laborers, the Negroes were protected by a certain primitive sort of old-age pension, job insurance, and sickness insurance; that is, they must be supported in some fashion, when they were too old to work; they must have attention in sickness, for they represented invested capital; and they could never be among the unemployed.

On the other hand, it is just as true that Negro slaves in America represented the worst and lowest conditions among modern laborers. One estimate is that the maintenance of a slave in the South cost the master about $19 a year, which means that they were among the poorest paid laborers in the modern world. They represented in a very real sense the ultimate degradation of man. Indeed, the system was so reactionary, so utterly inconsistent with modern progress, that we simply cannot grasp it today. No matter how degraded the factory hand, he is not real estate. The tragedy of the black slave's position was precisely this; his absolute subjection to the individual will of an owner and to "the cruelty and injustice which are the invariable consequences of the exercise of irresponsible power, especially where authority must be sometimes delegated by the planter to agents of inferior education and coarser feelings."

The proof of this lies clearly written in the slave codes. Slaves were not considered men. They had no right of petition. They were "devisable like any other chattel." They could own nothing; they could make no contracts; they

could hold no property, nor traffic in property; they could not hire out; they could not legally marry nor constitute families; they could not control their children; they could not appeal from their master; they could be punished at will. They could not testify in court; they could be imprisoned by their owners, and the criminal offense of assault and battery could not be committed on the person of a slave. The "willful, malicious and deliberate murder" of a slave was punishable by death, but such a crime was practically impossible of proof. The slave owed to his master and all his family a respect "without bounds, and an absolute obedience." This authority could be transmitted to others. A slave could not sue his master; had no right of redemption; no right to education or religion; a promise made to a slave by his master had no force nor validity. Children followed the condition of the slave mother. The slave could have no access to the judiciary. A slave might be condemned to death for striking any white person.

Looking at these accounts, "it is safe to say that the law regards a Negro slave, so far as his civil status is concerned, [as] purely and absolutely property, to be bought and sold and pass and descend as a tract of land, a horse, or an ox."[2]

The whole legal status of slavery was enunciated in the extraordinary statement of a Chief Justice of the United States that Negroes had always been regarded in America "as having no rights which a white man was bound to respect."

It may be said with truth that the law was often harsher than the practice. Nevertheless, these laws and decisions represent the legally permissible possibilities, and the only curb upon the power of the master was his sense of humanity and decency, on the one hand, and the conserving of his investment on the other. Of the humanity of large numbers of Southern masters there can be no doubt. In some cases, they gave their slaves a fatherly care. And yet even in such cases the strain upon their ability to care for large numbers of people and the necessity of entrusting the care of the slaves to other hands than their own, led to much suffering and cruelty.

The matter of his investment in land and slaves greatly curtailed the owner's freedom of action. Under the competition of growing industrial organization, the slave system was indeed the source of immense profits. But for the slave owner and landlord to keep a large or even reasonable share of these profits was increasingly difficult. The price of the slave produce in the open market could be hammered down by merchants and traders acting with knowledge and collusion. And the slave owner was, therefore, continually forced to find his profit not in the high price of cotton and sugar, but in beating even further down the cost of his slave labor. This made the slave owners in early days kill the slave by overwork and renew their working stock; it led to the widely organized interstate slave trade between the Border States and the Cotton Kingdom of the Southern South; it led to neglect and the breaking up of families, and it could not protect the slave against the cruelty, lust and neglect of certain owners.

Thus human slavery in the South pointed and led in two singularly contradictory and paradoxical directions—toward the deliberate commercial breeding and sale of human labor for profit and toward the intermingling of black and white blood. The slaveholders shrank from acknowledging either set of facts but they were clear and undeniable.

In this vital respect, the slave laborer differed from all others of his day: he could be sold; he could, at the will of a single individual, be transferred for life a thousand miles or more. His family, wife and children could be legally and absolutely taken from him. Free laborers today are compelled to wander in search for work and food; their families are deserted for want of wages; but in all this there is no such direct barter in human flesh. It was a sharp accentuation of control over men beyond the modern labor reserve or the contract coolie system.

Negroes could be sold—actually sold as we sell cattle with no reference to calves or bulls, or recognition of family. It was a nasty business. The white South was properly ashamed of it and continually belittled and almost denied it. But it was a stark and bitter fact. Southern papers of the Border States were filled with advertisements:—"I wish to purchase fifty Negroes of both sexes from 6 to 30 years of age for which I will give the highest cash prices."

"Wanted to purchase—Negroes of every description, age and sex."

The consequent disruption of families is proven beyond doubt:

"Fifty Dollars reward—Ran away from the subscriber, a Negro girl, named Maria. She is of a copper color, between 13 and 14 years of age—bareheaded and barefooted. She is small for her age—very sprightly and very likely. She stated she was *going to see her mother* at Maysville. Sanford Tomson."

"Committed to jail of Madison County, a Negro woman, who calls her name Fanny, and says she belongs to William Miller, of Mobile. She formerly belonged to John Givins, of this county, who now owns *several of her children*. David Shropshire, Jailer."

"Fifty Dollar reward.—Ran away from the subscriber, his Negro man Pauladore, commonly called Paul. I understand Gen. R. Y. Hayne *has purchased his wife and children* from H. L. Pinckney, Esq., and has them on his plantation of Goosecreek, where, no doubt, the fellow is frequently *lurking*. T. Davis." One can see Pauladore "lurking" about his wife and children.[3]

The system of slavery demanded a special police force and such a force was made possible and unusually effective by the presence of the poor whites. This explains the difference between the slave revolts in the West Indies, and the lack of effective revolt in the Southern United States. In the West Indies, the power over the slave was held by the whites and carried out by them and such Negroes as they could trust. In the South, on the other hand, the great planters formed proportionately quite as small a class but they had singularly enough at their command some five million poor whites; that is, there were actually more white people to police the slaves than there were slaves. Considering the economic rivalry of the black and white worker in the North, it would have seemed natural that the poor white would have refused to police the slaves. But two considerations led him in the opposite direction. First of all, it gave him work and some authority as overseer, slave driver, and member of the patrol system. But above and beyond this, it fed his vanity because it associated him with the masters. Slavery bred in the poor white a dislike of Negro toil of all sorts. He never regarded himself as a laborer, or as part of any labor movement. If he had any ambition at all it was to become a planter and to own "niggers." To these Negroes he transferred all the dislike and hatred which he had for the whole slave system. The result was that the system was held stable and intact by the

poor white. Even with the late ruin of Haiti before their eyes, the planters, stirred as they were, were nevertheless able to stamp out slave revolt. The dozen revolts of the eighteenth century had dwindled to the plot of Gabriel in 1800, Vesey in 1822, of Nat Turner in 1831 and crews of the *Amistad* and *Creole* in 1839 and 1841. Gradually the whole white South became an armed and commissioned camp to keep Negroes in slavery and to kill the black rebel.

But even the poor white, led by the planter, would not have kept the black slave in nearly so complete control had it not been for what may be called the Safety Valve of Slavery; and that was the chance which a vigorous and determined slave had to run away to freedom.

Under the situation as it developed between 1830 and 1860 there were grave losses to the capital invested in black workers. Encouraged by the idealism of those Northern thinkers who insisted that Negroes were human, the black worker sought freedom by running away from slavery. The physical geography of America with its paths north, by swamp, river and mountain range; the daring of black revolutionists like Henson and Tubman; and the extra-legal efforts of abolitionists made this more and more easy.

One cannot know the real facts concerning the number of fugitives, but despite the fear of advertising the losses, the emphasis put upon fugitive slaves by the South shows that it was an important economic item. It is certain from the bitter effort to increase the efficiency of the fugitive slave law that the losses from runaways were widespread and continuous; and the increase in the inter-state slave trade from Border States to the deep South, together with the increase in the price of slaves, showed a growing pressure. At the beginning of the nineteenth century, one bought an average slave for $200; while in 1860 the price ranged from $1,400 to $2,000.

Not only was the fugitive slave important because of the actual loss involved, but for potentialities in the future. These free Negroes were furnishing a leadership for the mass of the black workers, and especially they were furnishing a text for the abolition idealists. Fugitive slaves, like Frederick Douglass and others humbler and less gifted, increased the number of abolitionists by thousands and spelled the doom of slavery.

The true significance of slavery in the United States to the whole social development of America lay in the ultimate relation of slaves to democracy. What were to be the limits of democratic control in the United States? If all labor, black as well as white, became free—were given schools and the right to vote—what control could or should be set to the power and action of these laborers? Was the rule of the mass of Americans to be unlimited, and the right to rule extended to all men regardless of race and color, or if not, what power of dictatorship and control; and how would property and privilege be protected? This was the great and primary question which was in the minds of the men who wrote the Constitution of the United States and continued in the minds of thinkers down through the slavery controversy. It still remains with the world as the problem of democracy expands and touches all races and nations.

And of all human development, ancient and modern, not the least singular and significant is the philosophy of life and action which slavery bred in the souls of black folk. In most respects its expression was stilted and confused; the rolling periods of Hebrew prophecy and biblical legend furnished inaccurate but splendid words. The subtle folk-lore of Africa, with whimsy and parable, veiled wish and wisdom; and above all fell the anointing chrism of the slave music, the only gift of pure art in America.

Beneath the Veil lay right and wrong, vengeance and love, and sometimes throwing aside the veil, a soul of sweet Beauty and Truth stood revealed. Nothing else of art or religion did the slave South give to the world, except the Negro song and story. And even after slavery, down to our day, it has added but little to this gift. One has but to remember as symbol of it all, still unspoiled by petty artisans, the legend of John Henry, the mighty black, who broke his heart working against the machine, and died "with his Hammer in His Hand."

Up from this slavery gradually climbed the Free Negro with clearer, modern expression and more definite aim long before the emancipation of 1863. His greatest effort lay in his coöperation with the Abolition movement. He knew he was not free until all Negroes were free. Individual Negroes became exhibits of the possibilities of the Negro race, if once it was raised above the status of slavery. Even when, as so often, the Negro became Court Jester to the ignorant American mob, he made his plea in his songs and antics.

Thus spoke "the noblest slave that ever God set free," Frederick Douglass in 1852, in his 4th of July oration at Rochester, voicing the frank and fearless criticism of the black worker:

What, to the American slave, is your 4th of July? I answer: a day that reveals to him, more than all other days in the year, the gross injustice and cruelty to which he is the constant victim. To him your celebration is a sham; your boasted liberty, an unholy license; your national greatness, swelling vanity; your sounds of rejoicing are empty and heartless; your denunciation of tyrants, brass-fronted impudence; your shouts of liberty and equality, hollow mockery; your prayers and hymns, your sermons and thanksgivings, with all your religious parade and solemnity, are, to him, mere bombast, fraud, deception, impiety and hypocrisy—a thin veil to cover up crimes which would disgrace a nation of savages. . . .

You boast of your love of liberty, your superior civilization, and your pure Christianity, while the whole political power of the nation (as embodied in the two great political parties) is solemnly pledged to support and perpetuate the enslavement of three millions of your countrymen. You hurl your anathemas at the crown-headed tyrants of Russia and Austria and pride yourselves on your democratic institutions, while you yourselves consent to be the mere *tools* and *bodyguards* of the tyrants of Virginia and Carolina. You invite to your shores fugitives of oppression from abroad, honor them with banquets, greet them with ovations, cheer them, toast them, salute them, protect them, and pour out your money to them like water; but the fugitives from your own land you advertise, hunt, arrest, shoot, and kill. You glory in your refinement and your universal education; yet you maintain a system as barbarous and dreadful as ever stained the character of a nation—a system begun in avarice, supported in pride, and perpetuated in cruelty. You shed tears over fallen Hungary, and make the sad story of her wrongs the theme of your poets, statesmen, and orators, till your gallant sons are ready to fly to arms to vindicate her cause against the oppressor; but, in regard to the ten thousand wrongs of the American slave, you would enforce the strictest silence, and would hail him as an enemy of the nation who dares to make those wrongs the subject of public discourse![4]

Above all, we must remember the black worker was the ultimate exploited;

that he formed that mass of labor which had neither wish nor power to escape from the labor status, in order to directly exploit other laborers, or indirectly, by alliance with capital, to share in their exploitation. To be sure, the black mass, developed again and again, here and there, capitalistic groups in New Orleans, in Charleston and in Philadelphia; groups willing to join white capital in exploiting labor; but they were driven back into the mass by racial prejudice before they had reached a permanent foothold; and thus became all the more bitter against all organization which by means of race prejudice, or the monopoly of wealth, sought to exclude men from making a living.

It was thus the black worker, as founding stone of a new economic system in the nineteenth century and for the modern world, who brought civil war in America. He was its underlying cause, in spite of every effort to base the strife upon union and national power.

That dark and vast sea of human labor in China and India, the South Seas and all Africa; in the West Indies and Central America and in the United States—that great majority of mankind, on whose bent and broken backs rest today the founding stones of modern industry—shares a common destiny; it is despised and rejected by race and color; paid a wage below the level of decent living; driven, beaten, prisoned and enslaved in all but name; spawning the world's raw material and luxury—cotton, wool, coffee, tea, cocoa, palm oil, fibers, spices, rubber, silks, lumber, copper, gold, diamonds, leather—how shall we end the list and where? All these are gathered up at prices lowest of the low, manufactured, transformed and transported at fabulous gain; and the resultant wealth is distributed and displayed and made the basis of world power and universal dominion and armed arrogance in London and Paris, Berlin and Rome, New York and Rio de Janeiro.

Here is the real modern labor problem. Here is the kernel of the problem of Religion and Democracy, of Humanity. Words and futile gestures avail nothing. Out of the exploitation of the dark proletariat comes the Surplus Value filched from human beasts which, in cultured lands, the Machine and harnessed Power veil and conceal. The emancipation of man is the emancipation of labor and the emancipation of labor is the freeing of that basic majority of workers who are yellow, brown and black.

> Dark, shackled knights of labor, clinging still
> Amidst a universal wreck of faith
> To cheerfulness, and foreigners to hate.
> These know ye not, these have ye not received,
> But these shall speak to you Beatitudes.
> Around them surge the tides of all your strife,
> Above them rise the august monuments
> Of all your outward splendor, but they stand
> Unenvious in thought, and bide their time.
> LESLIE P. HILL

1. Compare A. E. McKinney, *The Suffrage Franchise in the Thirteen English Colonies in America* (Philadelphia, 1905), p. 137.

2. *A Picture of Slavery Drawn from the Decisions of Southern Courts*, p. 5.

3. Compare Bancroft, *Slave-Trading in the Old South;* Weld, *American Slavery as It Is.*

4. Quoted in Carter G. Woodson, *Negro Orators and Their Orations* (Washington, D.C., 1925), pp. 218-19.

13

The Coal Mines

HERBERT R. NORTHRUP

The bituminous coal industry has served as a laboratory for the development of many trade union policies. Of considerable importance is the manner in which the United Mine Workers has met the problem posed by the presence of large numbers of both white and Negro workers in the coal industry. The "miners' formula" for resolving this question has been adopted by many of the CIO unions, which it helped to bring into existence, and in which the influence of the experiences of collective bargaining in the coal industry is still strong, although the UMW has now dissociated itself from the CIO.

This chapter discusses the effects of the UMW's racial policies on the welfare of Negro miners. Before turning to the main topic, however, it will be necessary to examine briefly the trend of employment and the racial-occupational pattern in the industry.[1]

THE TREND OF EMPLOYMENT

Tables 13.1 and 13.2 show the number of workers attached to the industry, and the proportional strength of colored miners, in the country as a whole, and in the coal-producing states of the Southern Appalachian region, for the years 1890-1940. The data for 1890 and 1900 cannot, of course, be strictly compared with those of the four succeeding census years, as they include metal miners and, in the case of 1900, quarrymen as well. But since coal is the predominant mineral produced in all these states, these figures do convey the idea of the rapid increase in the number of coal mines employed during the two decades before 1910.

Taking first the figures for the entire country, both the absolute number of miners and the proportion of Negroes showed marked increases during the first decade after 1910. Most striking, however, is the fact that between 1920 and 1930 the number of Negro miners rose by 5 per cent in the face of a 14 per cent decrease in total employment in the industry; and then, in the next ten years, the Negroes' gains were more than wiped out: the total number of coal miners decreased by 16 per cent, whereas the number of Negroes decreased by 33 per cent. The circumstances under which these gains and losses of colored miners took place will be described in detail below.[2]

Turning next to the data for the individual states, we find that in 1940 approximately 90 per cent of all the Negroes in the industry were located in the five southern and border states of Alabama, Kentucky, Tennessee, Virginia, and

TABLE 13.1 Negro Workers in the Coal Industry in the United States and in the
Principal Coal-Producing States of Southern Appalachia, 1890-1910

	1890[a]			1900[b]			1910		
	All Workers	Negroes	% Negro	All Workers	Negroes	% Negro	All Workers	Negroes	% Negro
Total, United States	--	--	--	--	--	--	644,500	40,584	6.3
Total, So.Appalachia	31,475	9,148	29.1	66,253	22,304	33.7	112,358	29,642	26.4
Alabama	7,966	3,687	46.3	17,898	9,735	54.3	20,779	11,189	53.8
Kentucky	5,091	976	19.2	9,299	2,206	23.7	18,310	3,888	21.3
Tennessee	4,889	769	15.7	10,890	3,092	28.4	11,094	1,609	14.5
Virginia	3,924	1,700	43.3	7,369	2,651	35.9	7,291	1,719	23.6
W.Virginia	9,605	2,016	21.0	20,797	4,620	22.2	54,884	11,237	20.5

Note: Total U.S. figures for 1890 and 1900 would be without meaning because of inclusion
of metal miners and quarrymen. U.S. totals in subsequent years include 100,000 to 150,000
anthracite miners.

[a]Includes all miners.
[b]Includes all miners and quarrymen.

TABLE 13.2 Negro Workers in the Coal Industry in the United States and in the
Principal Coal-Producing States of Southern Appalachia, 1920-1940

	1920			1930			1940[a]		
	All Workers	Negroes	% Negro	All Workers	Negroes	% Negro	All Workers	Negroes	% Negro
Total, United States	733,936	54,597	7.5	621,661	57,291	9.2	519,420	38,560	7.4
Total, So.Appalachia	182,845	42,666	23.3	197,162	44,266	22.5	214,253	34,793	16.0
Alabama	26,204	14,097	53.8	23,956	12,742	53.2	23,022	9,605	41.8
Kentucky	44,269	7,407	16.7	54,307	7,346	13.3	54,676	5,474	10.0
Tennessee	12,226	913	7.5	8,765	578	6.6	9,534	168	1.8
Virginia	12,418	2,450	19.8	12,629	1,511	12.0	20,086	1,190	5.9
W.Virginia	87,728	17,799	20.3	97,505	22,089	22.7	106,935	18,356	17.2

[a]Before 1940, the figures are those "gainfully occupied," i.e., attached to the industry. The 1940 figures are those actually employed. But the difference between these
terms is not substantial. It is highly probable that most people in 1930 reported not
their usual status, but their actual status at the time of enumeration, and the latter
is just the point stressed by the 1940 census.

Source: U.S. Census of Occupations, 1890-1940.

West Virginia, the so-called Southern Appalachian region, where 16 per cent of
the workers were colored. In no other state did Negroes comprise as much as 3
per cent of the total number of coal miners.

In three Southern Appalachian states—Kentucky, Tennessee, and Virginia—the percentage of Negroes declined by approximately one-half between
1910 and 1930. In Alabama, during this period, the proportion of Negro miners
remained quite stable. In West Virginia, however, the proportion of Negroes
remained constant from 1910 to 1920, but during the next ten years almost one-
half of the new job opportunities created by the expansion of the industry went to
Negro miners despite the fact that they comprised but one-fifth of the labor force
in the state in 1920. It was in West Virginia, then, that the aforementioned rise in
Negro employment was concentrated, a gain which was large enough to out-
weigh significant losses in three other southern states.

Between 1930 and 1940, the proportion of Negro miners in each Southern Appalachian state declined sharply, despite the fact that employment in that region, although not in the total industry, took a turn for the better. The downward trend, observed since 1910 in Kentucky, Tennessee, and Virginia, continued at an accelerated rate; for the first time since 1890, the proportion of Negroes in Alabama mines fell below 50 per cent; and in West Virginia, the gains of the Negroes during the 1920's were more than swept away.

THE DEVELOPMENT OF THE
SOUTHERN APPALACHIAN REGION

The causes of these shifts in the racial-employment pattern are found, first, in the comparatively late exploitation of the southern coal fields and their subsequent rapid development and, second, in the displacement of men by machines. Both are inextricably entwined with the story of collective bargaining in the industry.

Because of their greater distance from the centers of coal consumption, and because of inferior transportation facilities, the rich coal deposits of West Virginia and Kentucky were not exploited on a large scale before 1900. Since then, however, they have been developed at a rapid rate; nor is this difficult to explain. "The coal seams of these states are unusually thick and contain an exceptionally high grade coal." But, most important, "the southern coal industry was from its inception, and with a few years excepted, for nearly forty years thereafter, strictly non-union; whereas the central competitive field, composed of the mine fields of Illinois, Indiana, Ohio, and Pennsylvania, was to a large extent organized as early as 1900. Since labor costs constitute the principal element in total costs of production, the non-union coal operators in the southern fields were able to encroach steadily on the markets of the union employers in the North by paying lower wages than the union scale."[3]

The gradual infringement of the southern coal industry upon that of the North was noticeable even before World War I, but because of the expanding market and a still favorable freight rate structure[4] the northern operators were able to market increased quantities of coal until 1920. After that date, however, both these favorable factors were lost to them. In addition, they became involved in a series of costly strikes and lockouts with the United Mine Workers, mainly over the issue of whether age rates should be reduced. Although the UMW was able to maintain the wage structure, one group of operators after another went non-union until 1927 when the entire collective bargaining system in the central competitive field collapsed.

The consequences of these events were that production in the Southern Appalachian region increased as fast as that in the North fell off, until in 1927 the former area was producing as much as the latter. After the collapse of collective bargaining in that year, the northern operators succeeded in regaining a slight supremacy by drastic wage and price reductions, and since then they have been able to maintain their top position, either by further wage slashes or, since 1933, because of government stabilization of the industry.

The sharp gain of the Southern Appalachian field, particularly West Virginia, at the expense of the northern coal-producing states during the twenties accounts for the already observed fact that Negro coal miners were able to increase their share of employment between 1920 and 1930 despite the fact that the number of white workers decreased by nearly one-sixth. Of special interest is the fact that in West Virginia, the state in which all the employment gains of colored miners were made during this decade, the coal operators imported Negro labor primarily for strikebreaking and anti-union purposes. But in Kentucky, Tennessee, and Virginia, the coal operators found the white "mountaineers" and recent immigrants from southeastern Europe less likely to catch the union contagion, and consequently the number of white employees was increased at the expense of the Negroes in these three states.[5]

THE RACIAL-OCCUPATIONAL PATTERN

The decline in importance of Negroes in the coal industry since 1930 is attributable primarily to the displacement of men by machines. To understand this clearly, it is necessary to discuss briefly the racial-occupational pattern of the industry.

The range of occupations in coal mining is comparatively narrow. Except for a few maintenance men, there are in the average coal mine no jobs which require more than a modicum of skill. Over 50 per cent of the personnel "consist of hand coal loaders, and most of the other workers are machine operators of one sort or another. While the former are paid by the piece, and the latter by the day, there is seldom any great difference in the earnings of the two groups."[6]

Segregation either by occupation or by place of work, unlike most factory industries in the South, is conspicuous by its absence in the coal mines. In mines where the two races are employed, they invariably work side by side and at the same occupations. Negroes are used in all capacities, but their share of work varies from occupation to occupation. Thus, in a sample study of some twenty southern West Virginia mines in 1932, it was found that only 2 per cent of the Negroes were undercutting-machine operators as against 6 per cent of the white. In all the "indirect labor" jobs, except that of brakemen (one of the most dangerous jobs in a coal mine), and in all jobs carrying a supervisory function, the whites were more heavily represented than the Negroes. On the other hand, however, 77 per cent of the colored miners were found to be hand loaders, but only 60 per cent of the whites were engaged in this occupation.[7] The field work of the present writer, carried on in southern West Virginia and Alabama during the summers of 1940 and 1941, confirms the general tenor of these findings.[8]

Despite this uneven distribution of jobs between the two races, the fact remains that the outstanding characteristic of the southern coal industry from a racial-occupational standpoint is the comparatively high degree of mixing of the races. Besides, since the earnings of piece- and day-workers are usually about equal, no wage differential based on race is present in the industry.[9]

On the other hand, the relatively heavy concentration of Negroes in hand loading jobs has made them especially vulnerable to technological displacement. Since World War I, mechanical loaders of various types have been put on the market, which perform these operations and in so doing displace a substantial number of hand loaders. Before 1933, mechanization of loading operations was confined almost without exception to the high-wage North. Together with the competition of other fuels, and the introduction of more efficient methods of fuel utilization, it contributed to the already noted 14 per cent decline in employment in the industry.[10] With the advent of collective bargaining and high wages after 1933, the introduction of loading machines went forward at a rapid rate in the South. It is to this fact that the sharp decline of Negro miners in the industry is mainly attributable. For Negroes not only suffered heavily by reason of being concentrated in the occupation which the machines eliminated, but they also failed to receive a proportionate share of employment as machine operators. Since the causes of this last event are explicable only if one understands the Negro-union relationships in the industry, further discussion of the subject will be postponed until we have examined the racial policies of the United Mine Workers.[11]

THE NEGRO AND THE DEVELOPMENT
OF COLLECTIVE BARGAINING

The United Mine Workers of America was founded in 1890 by a merger of the Progressive Miners' Union with Knights of Labor District Assembly No. 135. From its beginning the UMW was organized on an industrial basis, taking into membership all those who worked "in and around the mines," regardless of race, color, creed, or nationality. To what was left of the Knights of Labor's "take in anybody" philosophy was added the special feeling of unity among all mine workers engendered by the isolation of the mining towns. Usually cut off from direct communication with the outside world, these communities rarely developed more than two classes: the "company" with its manager, mine guards, and all-pervasive authority, on the one hand, and the workers, whether machinists, coal loaders, or what not, on the other.[12] The workers' solidarity was also strengthened by the narrow wage differential between the highest and lowest paid. Race and nationality differences remained the primary disturbing element, and this, as we shall see, the UMW leaders strenuously combated.

In the early years of its existence, the UMW was quite successful in organizing the miners of Illinois, Indiana, Ohio, and to a lesser extent, Pennsylvania—the central competitive field—and the small southwestern area, composed of Arkansas, Kansas, and Oklahoma. Attempting to forestall unionism, the coal companies of these areas frequently staffed their mines with "judicial mixtures" of native whites, recent immigrants, and Negroes. As early as 1880, and as late as 1927, southern Negroes, fresh from the cotton fields and totally ignorant of industrial conflict, were imported as strikebreakers. Although this resulted in serious racial outbreaks on several occasions, the UMW officials did not attempt to fight the operators by drawing the color line. Had they done so, they would undoubtedly have encouraged the importation of more colored strikebreakers. Instead, they encouraged the Negroes to join the union and guaranteed them full privileges of membership. Racial friction and discrimination in the central competitive and southwestern fields did not vanish, to be sure. But the methods used by the UMW to combat the importation of Negro strikebreakers kept it at a minimum.[13]

In the Southern Appalachian region, where Negro labor was used from the beginning of mining operations, the UMW found the going much rougher, as its experiences in Alabama and West Virginia illustrate.

Labor organization among Alabama coal miners dates as far back as 1883; and a decade later the United Mine Workers first entered the region. Progress was at first slow, but by 1902 the union had entered into compacts with most of the operators in the region. Two years later, however, some of the larger producers denounced the agreement and, despite a series of strikes, the Alabama miners' unions were completely destroyed by 1908.[14]

The next attempt at organization of Alabama came some ten years later. Aided by the federal government's World War I labor policy, which officially approved of collective bargaining, the UMW succeeded in organizing several thousand miners—again, as previously, mainly Negroes. Although the operators refused to recognize the union, they did accept successive arbitration awards by federal officials, and thus stoppages during the war were prevented. In the fall and winter of 1920-21, however, the UMW was defeated after a bitter strike, and coal unionism disappeared from Alabama till 1933.

In both the 1908 and the 1920-21 strike, the employers and their supporters found the race issue a valuable ally. In the former year, the tent colony, in which the strikers lived after they had been evicted from the company-owned houses, was burned to the ground in order to prevent the "mobilization of Negroes in union camps." In addition a committee of citizens threatened a race riot unless the president of the UMW ordered the miners to return to work. The UMW executive was informed that "no matter how meritorious the union cause, the people of Alabama would never tolerate the organization and striking of Negroes along with white men." The union officials then proposed to transfer all of the Negroes out of the state and make the strike a "white man's affair." But the governor of Alabama stated that he "would not permit white men to live in camps under the jurisdiction" of the UMW. The apparent hopelessness of the struggle, plus the fact that there had occurred no little violence and bloodshed, undoubtedly induced the miners' president to terminate the strike.

In the 1920-21 struggle, the race issue was given no less prominence. Over 76 per cent of the strikers were Negroes. To this the operators declared the success of the strike to be due, because "southern Negroes . . . are easily misled, especially when given a prominent and official place in an organization in which both races are members." A citizens' committee stressed the fact that *northern* Negro and white organizers spoke from the same platform. And the strike was featured by violence as primitive and brutal as in any of the earlier coal mining tragedies of the North and West, with Negroes being especially singled out for savage treatment.

While there is every likelihood that racial friction would not have been absent in an atmosphere so tense as that of an Alabama coal strike, it is clear that the coal operators and their friends were responsible for bringing the question of color to the forefront and making it a central issue of the industrial conflicts of both 1908 and 1920-21. The attempts of the UMW to organize the coal fields of West Virginia further demonstrate the difficulties encountered by unions which attempt to build effective organizations where the labor force is represented by large numbers of both races.

The UMW first entered West Virginia a few months after it was founded in 1890, but its efforts were for the most part unsuccessful until the period during and immediately following World War I. Then the heads of the miners' union realized that the very existence of their organization was threatened by the low wage and price schedules of the non-union southern fields. After a strenuous campaign, the UMW secured contracts with about 80 per cent of the producers in northern West Virginia, and with the operators in the southern counties of Fayette, Kanawha, and Raleigh, but failed to secure even a foothold in Logan, Mingo, Mercer, and MacDowell, the counties along the southeastern rim of the state. Within a few years after the war, the UMW was driven entirely from southern West Virginia, and from most of the northern part of the state as well.[15]

Likewise, the miners' union obtained a precarious footing in eastern Kentucky during the war, but was driven out soon thereafter.[16]

The failure of the miners' union to organize the workers in the southernmost counties of West Virginia is not difficult to understand. The operators in this section of the state employed practically every device known to anti-unionists, including race-hatred propaganda, to defeat the union, which often also resorted to extreme measures.[17]

In their attempts to organize the miners of West Virginia, as in Alabama, the leaders of the UMW adhered to the policy of organizing both white and colored workers into the same local bodies. Although the union was successful in bringing large numbers of both white and colored miners into the fold, the presence of a large number of workers of both races played into the hands of the operators. The white miners, themselves divided between native "mountaineers" and recent immigrants from southeastern Europe, were loath to make common cause with the Negroes. The employers were quick to capitalize upon this situation by spreading rumors that, should the United Mine Workers be successful, the black miners would lose their jobs. In addition, the West Virginia operators, as in past labor disputes, imported large numbers of Negro agricultural workers from neighboring states farther South. The effect was both to supply a labor force with which strikes were defeated and to add to the antagonism between the races.

The failure of the United Mine Workers to organize the Southern Appalachian fields put it on the defensive during the remainder of the twenties. Unable either to compete with the low-wage South or to induce the UMW to make wage concessions, company after company broke with the union in order to cut wages, until in 1927, after the wholesale shift of production from North to South, the entire collective bargaining machinery in the central competitive field collapsed. The next five years were featured by vicious price and wage slashes, and by internal dissension within the shattered UMW.[18]

The organizing opportunity afforded by the NRA was taken advantage of by the UMW as by no other union. When the law went into effect, organizers were already in the field. Within three months, 90 per cent of the nation's coal miners had been enrolled by the UMW. The desperate conditions in which the miners found themselves as a result of the depression caused them to embrace unionism with such unanimity as to make opposition on the part of even the most bitter anti-union operator largely futile. Besides, after the experience of the preceding five years, many of the operators questioned the desirability of unrestricted wage and price competition in the industry.[19]

That is not to say that the majority of the southern coal mine owners welcomed the UMW. Company unionism, some violence, and race prejudice were used in an endeavor to stem the tide. This time, however, even the last-named failed. The terrible privations of the depression imbued both races with mutual understanding and tolerance. The arguments of the UMW organizers, both white and colored, that no union could succeed unless it had the support of both white and black miners, were heeded. When, in Alabama, the Ku-Klux Klan was revived to fight the union, white miners joined it, won control of it, and destroyed its effectiveness.[20]

With the assistance of President Roosevelt and the NRA machinery, the UMW won an agreement covering the entire Appalachian area in September 1933. Bolstered by federal regulation of competition in the industry, the UMW has steadily raised wages and extended its control until in 1941 it established a $7 basic wage rate for both North and South, and secured the union shop for almost the whole working force in the industry.[21] Since then more wage concessions have been obtained.

The Alabama mining field has never been included in the Appalachian agreements because of unique local conditions.[22] At present the basic wage in Alabama is approximately $1.50 below that of the Appalachian agreement.

AN APPRAISAL OF THE MINERS' FORMULA OF EQUALITARIAN UNIONISM

The revival of unionism in the bituminous coal industry and the subsequent establishment of industry-wide collective bargaining have, then, meant a substantial increase in the standard of living of the Negro, as well as of the white, miners in the South. But the consequences of organization to the thousands of colored miners in the South cannot be judged solely on the basis of immediate gain. What unionism has meant to them in other respects and whether they stand to gain from it in the long run are equally important questions.

It must be re-emphasized at this point that the UMW has an enviable record of practicing, as well as preaching, racial equality in its organization ever since it began to function. It is true that there have been instances of discrimination against Negroes in particular locals, both in the North and in the South. But the officials of the national union have never, to the writer's knowledge, condoned such action, and have not hesitated to chastise individual locals for failing to live up to the letter of the nondiscrimination policy.[23] Moreover, the UMW has always conducted both its organizing campaigns and its day-to-day union affairs without prejudice to any race.

When the 1933 organizing campaign was initiated in the South, the UMW did not deviate from its equalitarian policies. The success of the campaign was indeed a tribute to the forthright manner in which its representatives faced the race issue and preached the necessity of interracial co-operation.

More important than the success of the organizing campaign, however, has been the ability of the UMW district leaders in the South to devise a workable system whereby the two races could co-operate effectively and yet not antagonize the public by encroaching too sharply upon the customs of the communities. In West Virginia, where rigid separation is not the rule, and where race patterns are relatively fluid, the problem was not so serious; but in Alabama a good deal of both tact and courage was required.

For example, when the time came for the election of local officers, the Alabama district leaders advocated the selection of whites as president and Negroes as vice-presidents, and this procedure was followed in locals even where the Negroes were in a majority. "This device was designed to facilitate good employer-employee relations, for the local president usually heads the 'pit' committee which meets with the representatives of management for the joint settlement of grievances arising from working conditions in the mines." It was felt that the employers should be accustomed to the novelty of joint grievance committees before being subject to the still more novel experience of having to deal with Negroes as equals. At the same time, the election of Negro vice-presidents and of other Negro officers provided the colored miners with representation in the policy-making decisions of the locals.

The results of this policy of gradualism are already discernible. According to a number of informants of both races, "Negro members of grievance committees, who a few years ago would have risked physical violence had they raised their voices in joint union-management meetings, now argue their cases quite as freely as their fellow white members." Local meetings are no longer featured by such "formal" relationships between the races as, according to Dr. G. S. Mitchell, was the case in 1934-35. White members no longer hesitate to call a Negro unionist "brother," or to shake hands with Negro delegates without displaying embarrassment. And, now, Negro delegates contribute rather freely to discussions.[24]

In West Virginia, it was not found necessary to adhere to a policy of strict gradualism. Negroes are usually well-represented among the local and district officers and in some cases have been elected local union presidents even though white miners are in the majority. In many mines where there are a large number of foreign-born workmen, it is the custom to elect on a three-man pit committee one from this group, one native white, and one Negro. By such means, the UMW has been able to weld into a united front that conglomerate mixture of races and nationalities which many coal operators once thought was an insurmountable bar to unionism.

The machinery for the settlement of grievances constitutes one of the major gains which unionism has brought to southern miners. Undoubtedly, Negroes have benefited more from it than whites. "Colored miners are more heavily concentrated in the hand loading jobs, where payment is computed on a tonnage basis. Output on these jobs is frequently seriously interfered with by unusual mining conditions and other unavoidable circumstances." It was not until the advent of unionism and its grievance machinery that equitable adjustments were made in such instances. In addition, the power of mine foremen to discharge without cause or to assign to the poorer workplaces—treatment which these petty officials have been more inclined to inflict upon Negroes than upon whites—is now subject to joint union-management review, where the aggrieved can seek, and find, redress. The results of grievance machinery have been material, as well as psychological.[25]

By far the most difficult problem which confronts the equalitarian program of the United Mine Workers involves the disposal of employment problems incident to the introduction of labor-saving machinery, nowadays principally loading machines. Coal loading machines were introduced into the mines on a large scale soon after World War I, but before 1933 their use was largely confined to the high-wage areas of the North. Since then, under the impetus of unionism and high wages, mechanical loading machinery has made rapid strides in the Southern Appalachian region. In West Virginia, for example, less than 1 per cent of the total production was loaded by machines in 1933; by 1940, however, the proportion had jumped to 70.2 per cent. Likewise in the other Southern Appalachian states, less than 1 per cent of the total output was mechanically loaded in 1933; but in 1940, the relevant figures were, for Alabama, 32 per cent; for Kentucky, 76.8 per cent; for Tennessee, 13.1 per cent; and for Virginia, 64.2 per cent.[26] Since then, the percentage of coal loaded by machinery has continued to increase in the Southern Appalachian region.[27]

It has been estimated by competent experts that 46 men working with mobile loaders can do the work of 100 hand loaders.[28] Along with unemployment attributable to declining markets, this technological displacement has meant a real hardship to the miners. Moreover, there is no doubt but that Negroes have borne the brunt of the unemployment, for it is to the introduction of these loading machines that the already noted sharp drop in the proportion of Negroes in the industry since 1930 is primarily ascribable.[29] Indeed, this was to be expected since Negroes are more heavily concentrated in the hand loading jobs than are whites. In addition, however, Negroes have not received a proportionate share of jobs as machine operators. There are several reasons for this.

The introduction of machinery, or the substitution of a new technique for an old, has often meant in the South the displacement of Negro handworkers by white machine operators. Thus when undercutting machines and other mechanical devices were installed in southern coal mines earlier in the century, whites were assigned in disproportionately large numbers to operate them, and most black workers remained hand loaders. This was the pattern *before* the advent of UMW and collective bargaining. Hence, when loading machines were installed, the employers gave white workers preference as a matter of course.

This, of course, is in direct conflict with the equalitarian policies of the UMW, but until recently the district officials of the union have hesitated to take a firm stand on the question. For the very reason that machine jobs have been traditionally "white man's work," the UMW officials, pursuing a policy of gradualism, did not attempt a quick break with the past. More important, it is at least questionable whether, before 1939, the heads of the UMW had given the question of technological unemployment the serious attention that it deserved.

The UMW has not opposed the introduction of machinery; it has merely insisted that the benefits therefrom be shared with its members.[30] But before 1939 few of the district agreements in the South contained clauses providing that workers who had been displaced by machines should be rehired, if possible, before newcomers could be employed.[31] Indeed, it was not until 1941 that such provision was written into the basic Appalachian agreements.[32] But since the qualifications for machine loading jobs are not possessed by all hand loaders, strict seniority cannot be observed in the transfer from handwork to machine operation, and so the way is still open for discrimination unless the national and district officials of the UMW are vigilant and the employers co-operative.

A further point should be brought out. Because the white workers had performed the bulk of the machine jobs before the introduction of mechanical loaders, they often have been in a better position to learn how to operate the mobile loading machines. This, of course, has counted in their favor, and against Negroes.

THE FUTURE

In sum, then, because, for various reasons, the UMW has not obtained equal treatment for Negroes in the allocation of job opportunities, white miners may be said to have benefited from unionism to a somewhat greater extent than Negroes, although the advantages to the latter in the form of increased wages, better working conditions, and protection from arbitrary treatment on the job have been substantial. To what extent this will hold true in the future, depends upon the outcome of postwar adjustments.

Because of the war boom, current demands for coal exceed those in any previous period since World War I. In addition, the draft and the migration of miners to more lucrative jobs have depleted the industry's working force. Consequently, miners displaced by machinery at the present time have little difficulty in finding employment.

When the war is over, however, the abnormally large demand for coal may be expected to subside and, as a result, employment in the industry will decline. Moreover, the employment problem is likely to be aggravated by mechanization, by the use of more efficient methods of fuel utilization, and by the competition of substitute fuels, all of which adversely affected employment in the industry between the two World Wars. Especially are these three economic forces likely to threaten the stability of the industry if the UMW officials continue to use their great bargaining power to gain ever higher wages and shorter hours, for such a policy will probably accelerate the substitution of machines for men and the introduction of improved methods of fuel utilization, as well as worsen the competitive position of coal in relation to other fuels.[33]

If, as predicted, employment in the bituminous coal industry declines when peace returns, and if past experience is any guide, Negroes will suffer disproportionately heavy losses in jobs. This is particularly likely to occur in instances where machines replace men. These postwar adjustments will put the equalitarian policies of the UMW to their severest tests. If Negroes continue to bear the brunt of technological unemployment, the UMW will no longer be able to claim that it adheres to a policy of racial equality as steadfastly as any other American labor union.

1. Only bituminous coal mining will be considered in this chapter. There never have been more than a few score Negroes in the anthracite mining region of Pennsylvania. The terms "coal mining" and "bituminous coal mining" will be used interchangeably hereafter.

2. See below, under "Racial-Occupational Pattern."

3. For a more complete account of the North-South competition, see F. E. Berquist, et al., *Economic Survey of the Coal Industry under Free Competition and Code Regulation*, NRA Work Materials no. 69, 1936, pp. 13-78, mimeograph. Quotations are from P. H. Norgren, "The Negro Coal Mine Worker," report made to the Carnegie Corporation of New York's Negro in America survey, 1940.

4. For an analysis of the effect of freight rate structure on coal production and mine location, see Glen L. Parker, *The Coal Industry* (Washington, D.C., 1940), pp. 43-50.

5. Sterling D. Spero and Abram L. Harris, *The Black Worker, 1915-1930* (New York, 1931), pp. 213-14, 217-25, 374-75.

6. The discussion in this section owes much to an unpublished manuscript by P. H. Norgren.

7. See chapter 7, this book. Also see Homer L. Morris, *The Plight of the Coal Miner* (Philadelphia, 1934), pp. 66-67; Norgren, "Negro Coal Mine Worker."

8. The author of this study maintains that the relatively heavy concentration of Negroes in hand loading jobs is, to a large extent, a matter of choice. Negro miners, he claims, prefer piecework jobs because such work allows them a relatively high degree of freedom from supervision and permits them to take an occasional day off if they so desire. A like conclusion was reached by the author of another study, which was based on a survey of some fifty mining communities in Kentucky and West Virginia, conducted at approximately the same time as the former's investigation.

It should also be emphasized, however, that hand loading requires the greatest amount of physical effort of any of the occupations in coal mining. When one considers that it is a general custom to assign such tasks to Negroes, it seems likely that other factors besides the desires of the colored workers are involved. E.g., it has long been customary to assign machine jobs to whites, and leave the hand loading for Negroes, and usually the preferences considered have been those of the white workers, and not of the Negroes.

9. The fact that in the past, earnings of Negroes have been, on the average, below those of whites is attributable to the concentration of the former in the low wage, non-union areas of the South.

10. For an authoritative discussion of mechanization and its effects, see W. E. Hotchkiss, et al., eds. *Mechanization, Employment and Output Per Man in Bituminous-Coal Mining* (Philadelphia: WPA, National Research Project, 1939).

11. See below, under "An Appraisal of the Miners' Formula of Equalitarian Unionism."

12. Herbert Harris, *American Labor* (New Haven, 1937), pp. 113-14.

13. Spero and Harris, *Black Worker*, pp. 210-13, 355-57; F. L. Ryan, *The Rehabilitation of Oklahoma Coal Mining Communities* (Norman, Okla., 1935), pp. 39, 46-49, 64-68, 89, 98-99.

14. *Alabama News-Digest*, Jan. 25, 1940. A special supplement of this issue of the Birmingham, Ala., CIO weekly contains a complete history of the UMW in Alabama. See also Spero and Harris, *Black Worker*, pp. 357-62.

15. C. P. Anson, "A History of the Labor Movement in West Virginia" (Ph.D. diss., University of North Carolina, 1940), pp. 98-100, 116-117, 122-23; Spero and Harris, *Black Worker*, pp. 367-70.

16. U.S. Senate, 76th Cong. 1st sess., *Report of the Committee on Education and Labor: Violation of Free Speech and the Rights of Labor*, no. 6, pt. 2, "Private Police Systems, Harlan County, Ky." (Washington, D.C., 1939), p. 1920.

17. See W. D. Lane, *Civil War in West Virginia* (New York, 1921); A. F. Hinrichs, *The United Mine Workers of America and the Non-union Coal Fields* (New York, 1923).

18. For an account of the revolts and dual movements of the miners in this period, see Parker, *Coal Industry*, pp. 77-81.

19. Waldo E. Fisher, "Bituminous Coal," in H. A. Millis, et al., *How Collective Bargaining Works* (New York, 1942), pp. 268-69.

20. H. R. Cayton and G. S. Mitchell, *Black Workers and the New Unions* (Chapel Hill, N.C., 1939), pp. 321-23, 358-61; Jonathan Daniels, *A Southerner Discovers the South* (New York, 1938), pp. 281ff.

21. Fisher, "Bituminous Coal," pp. 270-75.

22. The veins in which the coal is located in Alabama are generally thin, and the coal contains a high percentage of impurities. Both increase the cost of recovery.

23. See, e.g., Spero and Harris, *Black Worker*, p. 375.

24. Cayton and Mitchell, *Black Workers*, pp. 344-48; G. S. Mitchell, "The Negro in Southern Trade Unionism," *Southern Economic Journal*, 2 (Sept. 1936), 30. Quotations from Norgren, "Negro Coal Mine Worker," based upon material collected by the present writer.

25. Norgren, "Negro Coal Mine Worker."

26. Data from Hotchkiss, *Mechanization*, p. 210; U.S. Department of the Interior, Bureau of Mines, Bituminous Coal Division, *Weekly Coal Report*, July 11, 1942, table 8. The machines under discussion here are primarily mobile loaders, which entirely eliminate hand loaders, but the figures also include "scrapers" and "duckbills," for which the displacement rate is not so heavy. Conveyers and pit-car loaders are not included in these data. These last two types do not eliminate hand loaders, but affect mainly certain maintenance jobs and speed up operations. They do not affect Negroes disproportionately. For a description of the various machines, see Hotchkiss, *Mechanization*, pp. 113-42.

27. W. H. Young, et al., "Mechanical Mining," *Coal Age*, 47, no. 2 (Feb. 1942), 66-68.

28. S. H. Slichter, *Union Policies and Industrial Management* (Washington, D.C., 1941), p. 271.

29. See tables 13.1 and 13.2.

30. Slichter, *Union Policies*, pp. 271-72.

31. E.g., the agreement between the Alabama Coal Operators Association, and UMW, District 20, for 1937-39, makes no mention of the subject of seniority.

32. The 1941 Appalachian agreement reads in part: "Seniority affecting return to employment of idle employees on a basis of length of service and qualification for the respective positions brought about by different mining methods or installation of mechanical equipment is recognized. Men displaced by new mining methods or installation of new mechanical equipment so long as they remain unemployed shall constitute a panel from which new employees shall be selected" (*UMWJ*, July 15, 1941).

33. Slichter, *Union Policies*, pp. 362-63; Fisher, "Bituminous Coal," pp. 276-77.

14

Race and the United Mine Workers' Union in Tennessee: Selected Letters of William R. Riley, 1892-1895

RONALD L. LEWIS

Historians know very little about early labor organizers who laid the foundations of many modern unions. This invisibility is particularly true for that small number of dedicated black activists who sacrificed their own economic interests, safety, and sometimes dignity, for the labor union cause. Certainly this was the case of William R. Riley who emerges momentarily from the dark corners of the past only to disappear again without a trace. Among the few known general facts about Riley is a record of his association with the Knights of Labor in the coal fields of his native southeastern Kentucky. Moving to Jellico, Tennessee, probably during the 1880's, Riley continued his efforts to unionize the coal miners of the region. Apparently he was successful, for by 1892 the membership had elected him Secretary-Treasurer of United Mine Workers of America, District 19, a large territory which included much of Tennessee and parts of Kentucky. In addition to mining, Riley also preached the gospel, and appears to have received a better than average education than was typical for a man of his race and social class in that day. While he was not a nationally recognized labor leader, Riley's experiences were typical for the black union organizer of the 1890's, and his observations mirror race relations at the grass roots level of the labor movement during that crucial era in American history when the structure of industrial society was undergoing dramatic changes.

The relationship between blacks and the American labor movement has always been tempestuous. During the antebellum era, local craft organizations almost universally excluded Negroes, and all too frequently artisans prevented them from working at their crafts in order to maintain those jobs for whites only. Attempts to reconcile differences of opinion between black and white labor spokesmen generally failed during the late 19th century. The National Labor Union, established in 1869, revealed a deliberate ambivalence about organizing blacks, and absolutely opposed the active black commitment to Republican politics. Consequently, black labor leaders, such as Isaac Myers of Baltimore, organized their own Colored National Labor Union the following year. Similarly, during the 1880's, racism in the Farmers' Alliance spawned the parallel structure known as the Colored Farmers' Alliance. Although the two groups worked together, any basis for further cooperation was swept aside when the Populists gained power and ushered in a full-fledged system of segregation in the South.[1]

By the end of the 19th century, this legacy of racism became institutionalized in the constitutions and by-laws of the various trade brotherhoods. The governing documents of many of these unions contained provisions which explicitly barred black members. Racial exclusion had so hardened into accepted practice that the American Federation of Labor abandoned in 1895 any further attempts to pressure unions which discriminated against blacks for fear that the unions would shun the Federation and thereby insure its demise.[2] The Federation apparently thought it wiser to organize the brotherhoods than to change their attitudes. The very low percentage of black workers in the skilled trades to this day reflects how thoroughly racial exclusion is entrenched in the craft unions.

One of the major currents of the late 19th century was a rising class consciousness among white workers which manifested itself in an impetus toward labor solidarity previously unknown on such a scale in America. Given the nature of the black experience since emancipation, however, along with the traditionally poor race relations between black and white workers, it is not surprising to find that a strong counter-current had developed independently among black Americans. In 1896 the United States Supreme Court legalized segregation in Plessey vs. Ferguson, and reinforced the growing conviction among blacks that little reliance could be placed on working in coalitions with whites. Survival required a shift in strategy from inter-racial cooperation to a new emphasis on self-help and racial solidarity. The times seemed to dictate such an approach, and leaders such as Booker T. Washington gained national prominence for enunciating how this strategy might be successfully implemented. Most, if not all blacks, probably agreed with Washington's assertion that the true friends of black workers were the capitalists who supplied them with jobs, rather than the unions which excluded them. Whereas white unionists saw control over services as an opportunity to improve wages and conditions, Washington and his followers viewed the unions with suspicion since they intruded between the worker and his employer. If unions continued to exclude them, Washington advised white labor leaders that blacks would be justified in becoming strikebreakers.[3]

The response of white union men toward this approach was predictably hostile, but actually they were confronting a dilemma of their own creation. A change in the power relationship between labor and capital required labor unity. Yet racism had effectively excluded a large segment of the work force and given black workers little reason to entrust their fate to white-dominated unions. In order to neutralize the inherent tension in their position, white unionists followed the circular reasoning that since blacks often were not union members they must be anti-union, and therefore, enemies of the labor movement.

Between 1892 and 1895, the related issues of white racism and black anti-unionism flared into an open and heated debate in the *United Mine Workers' Journal,* the official organ of the United Mine Workers of America. In this debate, several blacks actively participated. William R. Riley was among them, and his letters express the grievances of black coal miners generally. The basic problem lay with the locals rather than the national organization, which had always prohibited discrimination on the basis of race.[4] Since power in the UMW flowed upward from the grass roots, national officials could exert only limited pressures on the daily affairs of individual locals and districts. Consequently, it was nearly impossible to control the racial prejudices of the membership. Riley's letters touch on the main issues as they affected individual black workers. They were disturbed by white miners' demands that blacks support the union during strikes and by paying dues, and yet ignored the needs of blacks when work was plentiful and ostracized them as a matter of course. Blacks could not work with whites without the cry of "social rights" being raised, and the unions refused to support the black miners' rights to higher paying jobs, or positions of responsibility. Even elected black union officials, such as Riley, encountered discrimination from fellow officers who hesitated to break racial taboos by associating too closely with him in public.

The letters of William R. Riley reveal the contradictory demands placed upon black union organizers. Although his primary loyalty was to the broader principles of labor unity, he nonetheless was forced to confront white racism at one pole, and black racial solidarity at the other. Still, Riley seemed to maintain his commitment to labor principles, for he fearlessly struck out at white miners who discriminated against black "brothers," and released a special venom against anti-union blacks. These miners Riley castigated as "niggers and dogs," a "pullback" to the race.

Riley's letters indicate how profoundly black union organizers differed from conservative bourgeois blacks regarding the power struggle between capital and labor and the relationship of blacks to that effort. Riley's letters portray a black man caught between progressive ideals and reactionary social realities.

Jellico, Tenn., Feb. 27, 1892

I thought I would write these few lines to let the many readers of your valuable paper see and know the way the colored miners are treated in this part of the country.

Before I left here to go to the Columbus convention[5] I was called to Newcomb, Tenn., to see after some trouble there. When I got to Newcomb I found that a colored checkweighman[6] had been elected and the white miners at that mine declared that no negro should weigh their coal. They made several excuses, such as that the man was not competent, the next excuse was that he had kicked against the former checkweighman, the third was that he was not legally elected. After hearing their excuses I offered to take the colored man off that had been elected, if they would agree to support a colored man that was competent and had not kicked against the former checkweighman. Then the Master Workman[7] of that place told me in plain words that the body of white miners had agreed to not support a colored man. After he openly told [of] the determination of the whites, the colored miners said that the white miners had promised to divide the checkweighman's office with them, the whites had promised if there was one half colored they should have the place half of the time, if there was one third they should have it one third of the time, etc., but instead of standing to their promise the whites have filled the office for more than five years, and yet they declare that the negro shall not weigh their coal. At Altamont, Laurel Co., Ky., the company put a colored man in the mine acting as assistant bank boss and the whites declare that they won't work under any negro and the drivers won't pull the coal that is dug under a negro boss. And now I would like to know how under heaven do the white miners expect for the colored people to ever feel free and welcome in the order of Knights of Labor or United Mine Workers of America,[8] when their so-called brothers don't want them to get not one step higher than the pick and shovel. And yet, whenever there is anything in the way of trouble expected, or when anything is wanting in the way of finance these very same men will come up to the colored man and say, "Brother J. we must all stick together, for we are all miners, and your interest is mine and mine is yours; we must band together." This talk you see reminds one of the story of the spider and the fly, the majority of the white miners only need a colored brother in time of trouble.

And how can you ever expect the colored people of the South to become an organized body as long as such work is carried on, which is an open violation of the laws of the order. And yet this matter is given little or no attention. When this subject was brought up by me in the convention at Columbus, that the officers should see that this color line law was fully carried out, that any place or places that made any difference in persons because of their color, and that their character should be taken away from them, they tabled the question and left it so. Now, I think something should be done about this matter. The colored people need to be organized in the South. But how can this be done by the people whom they regard as their enemies? I cannot tell. I hope some steps will be taken at once to right these matters.   Wm. R. Riley,[9] Sec.-Treas., Dist. 10.

Jellico, Tenn., August 13, 1892

With your permission I want to talk with the boys in a rambling way. In the first place, I want to let your readers know that the miners of Jellico region are buying flour, beef steak and chicken, and the merchants of Jellico were saying this evening that they had not seen so many $20 bills in Jellico for years as were handled by the miners of certain mines. What I mean by all this is, work is good, and there is no more eating dry bread at some of our houses for a little while, and while our work is good our men are not wasting any time with picks and shovels, and no race prejudices are heard of now as there was last winter. Of course, I don't mean to say by this that we have all good men here, for this is not the case, but the good men have got the majority on their side and they make the minority follow in line.

And now a few words to Brother R. L. Davis. In speaking about the men at No. 3 mine, Brother Davis seems to be a little behind the times. Did you not know that the worst enemies we have to contend with are among our own race?[10] Did you not know that they will seek more undue advantages over you than anyone else? What? A nigger? He is the worst animal living against his race, and when I say nigger I mean nigger and not colored people. Now, let me say, that they have surely made a man of me. I used to try to fight it out with them and I soon found out that my money would not last at that foolishness because they would take a good beating just to get a chance to have me arrested to swear against me and loud swearing some of them would do; they came near swearing me baldheaded before I learned any sense. But now, I can laugh at their folly when they try to make war against me and say all colored and white men will consider the source it came from. And again; I think a man that this class of men don't talk about are not worthy of an office in the labor ranks. I am by this class like I am by my church people. When I go to a place to preach and this class of people run to me, talking about some old sister or brother over yonder, the first thing pops into my mind is, "Over yonder is the light of Christianity in this place, and here sets the hounds of —— howling on their tracks, barking at their good name, barking at their future prosperity and barking at their religious examples that they set before them from time to time." But when I hear of some good sister or brother that everybody likes and praises, an old Scripture passage presents itself to me: "Woe unto the person whom the world speaks well of." Now, I do love to hear of officers of our organization being spoken hard of, and I do like to hear of them having a hard, hard time. It will make them read the laws more carefully and fill them out to the letter. It causes the man to try to post himself to meet any emergency that may cross his path; and, let me say, do away with the man that everybody is well pleased with. So Brother D., continue to press forward, make all the colored and white friends that you possibly can, and don't worry over the niggers and dogs.[11] "Brother Willing Hands,"[12] you must not speak a word of praise about me, I am not used to my race praising me, it might give the brain fever for ever. William R. Riley[13]

Jellico, Tenn., Sept. 5, 1892

You must really excuse my delay in sending in my report of our convention which convened on August 17, 18, and 19 last, for we have been so busy over the Coal Creek trouble[14] that everything else has been neglected. However, our convention was very largely attended with delegates from all over the district and business was carried on very smoothly until the election of officers commenced, when Brother W. C. Webb[15] was placed before the convention for re-election for the office of president. He positively refused to allow his name to come up before the convention, then it was that our convention came to a standstill for nearly a day, trying to persuade Brother Webb to accept of the position as president again, but he would not accept. After trying for a day to get Brother Webb to accept the office, then Brothers G. H. Simmons, J. W. Cox and S. P. Herron were placed before the convention for president. S. P. Herron was elected president. A. Vaughn of Coal Creek was elected vice president, but owing to the misconduct of A. V. the office was declared vacant before the convention adjourned and Brother John R. Rhodes of Coal Creek was elected vice-president in A. Vaughn's place. Our next officer to be elected was secretary-treasurer. Brothers Mullan, William Rhodes and myself were placed before the convention and there were only four votes cast in the convention that I did not get on the first ballot, after which a motion to make my election unanimous was offered, which resulted in three of my four opponents who voted for me. Now I need not tell the readers that one vote that I did not get was not a white vote, because any white man would have been too intelligent to not vote with the whole convention. But this was a so-called colored man belonging to an assembly that all of the white men had drawn out of, so his colored brother told, and the white men say the reason they did draw out was because the mine workers of that labor assembly had not paid one cent of dues for twelve months and the other leading officers, who are colored men, are holding from two to four rooms in the mines working three to six men, double-shifting their places, driving the night mule themselves for extra cars, depriving a driver of the work where he could make his $1.75 per day, and the white men say that they would not live in an assembly where their brothers carried on such work.

Now, what I want the colored people to know, is simply this, that the negro is the worse enemy to one another that they have on top of dirt; there is a class of them that are so begrudging and jealous of their own race that they will do anything regardless of principle or anything else to keep one another rising one step above them. And this very class does more kicking about the white man not letting them have a show[16] than a Kentucky mule; and I want to ask my people, how under heavens can you ever expect the white man to place any confidence in them when they don't have any in one another. If whites say that the negro is not worthy of any office or don't deserve any, are they not paying you off with your own money? Have you not set this example for them to go by? Have you not said by your own ways and actions that your own race is not entitled to anything? I think you do. Now, let me say to the colored people who are trying to be men second to no man, continue to battle on for the right, seek wisdom and be wise, act honest men and by so doing both white and colored men will love to respect you, and God himself will bless you and our children, which are very apt to be the second edition of their parents, will come on after you and take up your work where you left off and push it on. Yes, my people, wake up and ask yourselves these questions: How am I to live in ignorance? How long am I to be a pullback to my race? How long am I to be a stumbling block for the cause of labor, justice and humanity? Say as the prodigal did: I will rise and join the labor union and rally for its rights, defend its cause and be known among my own craftsmen as a man among men.

Hoping that the readers will excuse this rambling letter and with best wishes to the *United Mine Workers' Journal*, I am yours fraternally,   Wm. R. Riley,[17]
Sec'y Treas. Dis. 19, U.M.W. of A.

Jellico, Tenn., Sept. 26, 1892

Again Brother Editor, I shall trouble you for a little space in your valuable columns. Times are still very lively in Jellico region, plenty of work every day and everywhere. I visited two picnics this month, given by Local Assembly 1855, Grays, Ky., and Local Assembly 1129, Red Ash, Ky. They had quite a good time at each place, financially and peacefully. Brother S. P. Herron was with me at both places; he seems to enjoy the picnics splendidly, and wished that picnics would last forever so he could look at the pretty mountain girls.

The Coal Creek trouble has been quite a set back to our district. We spent all of last year getting the lower part of the district into the union, and after we had accomplished our work there here comes this trouble and we lose the greater part of our year's work. Our only hope is that the national will help us a little this fall in our field work so as to put us on the fence again.

We have great confidence in our new president and believe with the proper backing he will lead us on to victory. Our executive board is also a cool, level-headed set, whom everyone believes will be an honor to the district.

Now just a few words to Brother "Willing Hands."[18] My brother, you seem to think that I was wrathy at the negroes. Now, I do think that I made a clear distinction in spelling these two words. I never wrote any harm about the negro at all, for I have no fight to make against them. But I wrote, and will continue to write, against the niggers and dogs. We have tried petting, coaxing and soft words with these curs for years, and we have gained nothing from them only hard times. They say that we are only trying to make a living without working, call us d—— sell outs, money seekers, etc. I believe in the saying of St. Paul, "When the child is young feed it on the sincere milk of the breast, but when it gets old feed it on strong meat." Now, we did believe years ago that these curs were young in the labor movement, therefore we were very tender and mild with them, but now we think it is time for them to be grown men, and should be fed on strong meat. We can see that it is nothing but pure niggerish, doggish principle that is in these curs, and soft talk will do no good. My brother, I live in the South among these people and know whereof I speak. Of course there are some as good people in the South as there is the world, and again there are some of the worst curs that ever lived, and Webb, Riley, nor no one else can change them. With all due respect to Brother "Willing Hands" and success to the *United Mine Workers' Journal*, I am fraternally yours,   Wm. R. Riley[19]

Pioneer, Tenn., March 17, 1893

As the evening is so bad and the boys have not got out from work I must beg for a little space in your papers to let the boys know what the pair of Bills[20] are doing in District 19.

Well, Billy Webb and myself started out over the district on the 8th of March, to see if one pair of Bills could win. In our meetings in the Jellico region we left everything wherever we met. We struck the C.S.R.R.[21] on Saturday morning at Junction City, and went to Barren Fork where we had a very good meeting and the whole house voted to a man to do all they could to support the order. This was encouraging. I parted from Billy at Hellenwood and I came to Coal Creek, Tenn., and I went up to Briceville, where I met up with the district vice pesident, standing in a small crowd, but that worthy officer never let on that he saw me. After waiting for him to show up as though he knew me, and then seeing that he was not going to do so, I called him aside and asked him if he thought we could get the men together for a meeting. He said no; he thought not, as the Odd Fellows met that night, but said that if I could get the men on the Creek together, it would be no trouble to get the men at Briceville to organize. He further said that his assembly had a committee [which] were out looking after the colored people up there, and if they could not succeed in organizing them, that they would send for me. With this kind of treatment from one of our officers, I left for Coal Creek. After working there three days I succeeded in reorganizing the colored people of that place, which I think will make a noble order. As these colored men have always shown by their ways and actions they wanted to be organized men, but are treated so bad by their so-called white brothers that they don't feel like they are recognized in the order as knights. They are willing to try the order again, thinking that the white men of Coal Creek will yet recognize the importance of treating them as brother miners.

And now I do hope that Brother J. J. Jones, vice president of District 19, will go to work and make his words true by organizing Briceville.

A few words to the many who are discussing the paper question.[22] Boys, the *United Mine Workers Journal* is good enough for me now as it is, but if you can better it I will still read it, but for God's sake don't make it any smaller.

With best wishes to our paper and its readers, I am fraternally yours,
Wm. R. Riley[23]

Jellico, Tenn. [n.d.]
I thought, as there has been no news in your valuable columns from District 19 for quite a while, I would venture to write a few lines. Work is very good and has been reasonably good ever since the suspension, and the boys seem to be saving their little mites[24] some better than usual. I moved down to my little farm place, near Oswego, Tenn., last month for the purpose of going into the gardening business this spring. Here I found more colored miners than there is anywhere in this region. At one place, really about two-thirds of the miners are colored.

I began to talk labor to the boys, as none of them belong to the order, and some of the white miners that used to be strong labor men, or rather acted so years ago, are here, and I proposed to them that we would go to work and organize the camp, as I knew that I could do so, as the leading men here were my intimate friends and stood together in other places. The result of my efforts was this: These so-called white brothers went around to all of the weakest of the colored men and told them that Riley had left all of his property in Jellico and moved to Oswego to get to be checkweighman, and wanted them organized in order that the district would not go down, etc., etc., etc.

Now I want to give the whole cause of this talk. In the first place these men belong to that class of white people that I always styled as dogs; in the second place they tried to keep all the negroes away from here, but after the Indian Mountain strike in 1893 the colored people got a good footing here.[25] These dogs kept up part of their bluff by saying that no negro should weigh coal here, like they have said at most every other place in the district by either words or actions.

Now then, the black boys of course were not afraid to weigh, but just did not have the time, and when I came here they knew, first, that Riley has always been known in this country to be one of those fellows that is too lazy to run (without a leader) and plenty of time for anything that I wanted to do; and as they cared nothing for the organization, they took this step to kill the whole thing to gain one little point, viz., checkweighman. So you can see what kind of cattle we have through here. Secondly, there is another who would be in the order but they don't want to be sitting in the lodge room with negroes; they want the negroes' money; they want his support in time of trouble, but as for offices they don't want Mr. Negro to have not one.

The negroes of the South are opening their eyes on this as well as other things. They want more recognition. And if the Southern negroes are ever thoroughly organized or anything like it, it must be done by men of their own race. Can you blame them, when their white brother, so-called, will come out of the lodge room with him at 10 p.m., and if, while on his way home he meets a drunken white man and the white man wants the negro to run and the negro is too lazy to run, and won't take a whipping, this drunken white man can just go to some of his brothers and tell his tale, and they will all have their Winchesters and be ready to kill the brother negro before day. Such is the case here in the South and no mistake. As you shall hear from me soon again on the standing of our district in general, I will close, wishing you success, I am yours for the cause of labor.

Wm. R. Riley[26]

1. Although many specialized studies have been completed on the topic of segregation in the late 19th century, general references can be found in C. Vann Woodward, *The Strange Career of Jim Crow* (New York, 1955). A classic study of black labor during this period is Sterling D. Spero and Abram L. Harris, *The Black Worker, 1915-1930* (1931; reprinted ed., New York, 1974). The best single volume relating to blacks and the labor movement is Philip S. Foner, *Organized Labor and the Black Worker, 1619-1973* (New York, 1974).

2. Marc Karson and Ronald Radosh, "The American Federation of Labor and the Negro Worker, 1894-1949," in *The Negro and the American Labor Movement,* ed. Julius Jacobson (Garden City, N.Y., 1968), pp. 155-87.

3. August Meier and Elliott Rudwick, "Attitudes of Negro Leaders toward the American Labor Movement from the Civil War to World War I," in ibid., pp. 27-48. See also Booker T. Washington, "The Negro and the Labor Unions," *Atlantic Monthly,* 101 (June, 1913), 756-57.

4. For a study of one black coal miner from Ohio, Richard L. Davis, who reached national prominence in the UMW and was also the most active black participant in this debate, see Herbert G. Gutman, "The Negro and the United Mine Workers of America: The Career and Letters of Richard L. Davis and Something of Their Meaning, 1890-1900," in *The Negro and the American Labor Movement,* ed. Jacobson, pp. 49-127. In 1890 Davis was a delegate at the founding convention of the UMW and also won election to Ohio's District 6 Executive Board. He declined the nomination for District Vice-President, but won election to the National Executive Board in 1896 and again in 1897. He died prematurely in 1900 at age thirty-five from "lung fever" (ibid., pp. 55-56).

5. Riley referred to the annual convention of UMW, District 6, which met in January 1892 in Columbus, Ohio (*UMWJ,* Jan. 28, 1892).

6. Prior to the use of machine loaders in underground mines, coal was handloaded into cars by individual miners who identified their cars with special chips. A company "weighmaster" then weighed each car and the miners were paid according to the tonnage they produced. The system was laden with abuses, such as understating the tonnage, which worked to the detriment of the miners. Therefore, one of the early changes sought by the UMW was company acceptance of a "check-weighman" who weighed the coal along with the company's employee in order to prevent cheating. The checkweighman was elected and paid by the miners themselves to insure his loyalty. He was, therefore, usually a strong labor man of tested conviction and known influence in the community. How race affected the chances of a black being elected to that post depended on local race relations. Prejudiced whites usually objected to dependency on a black checkweighman.

7. "Master Workman" referred to a local assembly leader of the Knights of Labor, a semi-secret labor organization founded in 1869 on the one big union concept.

8. In January, 1890, several rival miners' organizations met in Columbus, Ohio, and merged into the United Mine Workers of America. During its formative years, the UMW competed with the dying Knights of Labor which had organized a large number of coal miners into its National Trades Assembly 135. Despite the rivalry at official levels, rank-and-file workers themselves often made little distinction between the two groups. Some miners even maintained dual membership. While union officials vigorously denounced "dual unionism," for a few years after the founding of the UMW, many workers and some local officers served both the Knights and the UMW. Riley apparently recognized that he would be addressing himself to "exclusive" as well as "dual"

unionists. Indeed, it is possible that he held dual memberships himself. (Archie Green, *Only a Miner: Studies in Recorded Coal-Mining Songs* [Urbana, Ill., 1972], p. 166).

9. *UMWJ*, Mar. 3, 1892.

10. Mine Number 3 was located at Rendville, Ohio, where Richard L. Davis, the black UMW official was employed. Number 3 employed a sizable black work force. The mines in the Rendville sub-district had all gone out on strike under an agreement that none of them would work until all agreed to return. The other mines resumed full operation, however, when the miners at Number 3 were still out, thus placing them in a vulnerable position (*UMWJ*, July 21, 1892). Apparently, this caused considerable friction among blacks at Number 3, and since Davis was black *and* a union official, he fell under suspicion. Davis wrote that he was considered "dangerous" by some of the black miners at Number 3 who vowed to replace Davis as Checkweighman. While many of these men were "true as steel," Davis believed that most of the black workers were more race conscious than class conscious, and therefore constituted a danger to union recognition in the district. In fact, he wrote, they believed that capital had a "right to its supremacy and that labor should bow submissively to the demands of capital." Moreover, they did not like "being led by white men" (*UMWJ*, Aug. 11, 1892).

11. In response to Riley's letter, Davis wrote that he was delighted to see that there were others besides himself who had "the pluck and the energy" to express their thoughts in print. He hoped that "our people" would reconsider their position. While Riley might have a majority of "good men" in Tennessee, at Number 3 they were in the distinct minority. At the last meeting, for example, one of these black anti-union men took the floor and asserted that if there had been no union, pay and conditions would not have been any different than they were then. Davis admonished them for being "blind in every sense of the word" (*UMWJ*, Sept. 1, 1892). Another black union activist, F. H. Jackson, also of Rendville, Ohio, in a subsequent issue of the *UMWJ*, encouraged Riley and Davis to continue their valuable efforts. He thought Riley's letters were "grand," for he had "written my sentiments all the way through" (*UMWJ*, Sept. 15, 1892).

12. "Brother Willing Hands" was a pseudonym for a black UMW organizer whose given name remains unknown. He generally applauded the letters of Riley, and other black unionists, published in the *UMWJ*.

13. *UMWJ*, Aug. 25, 1892.

14. The Coal Creek "war," "rebellion," or "trouble," took its name from the Creek, along which most of the mines were located in northeastern Tennessee. The village of Coal Creek was renamed Lake City in 1936. The struggle itself occurred between miners, operators, and the State of Tennessee, over the use of convict labor in the coal mines. This practice earned the state revenues and saved the expense of another prison, but cost miners a means of livelihood.

The uprising against the system began in the spring of 1891 when the miners struck the Tennessee Coal and Mining Company and were subsequently replaced by convicts. What followed over the next two years was a series of incidents which followed the same scenario: Miners "armies" captured the mines, sent the convicts to Knoxville or Nashville by train, whereupon the Governor returned them under military escort. By the spring of 1893 the state government determined to bring an end to the orderly but defiant activities of the coal miners. Train loads of troops were sent to the coal fields with artillery and Gatling guns which they used to disperse the miners.

Although the miners lost the battles, they won the war. Public opinion was so aroused that by 1896 the State found it inexpedient to renew the convict lease system. Pete Daniel, "The Tennessee Convict War," in *Tennessee Historical Quarterly*, 34 (Fall 1975), 273-92; Green, *Only a Miner*, pp. 155-91; Philip S. Foner, *History of the Labor Movement in the United States* (New York, 1955), vol. 2, pp. 219-29.

15. William C. Webb was President of UMW District 19 (Jellico, Tenn.) during the Coal Creek troubles, and was a leading spokesman for Tennessee miners. Apparently Webb did not practice racial prejudice in his union activities, and evidence exists that he possessed a strong social conscience: "The miners of the South for several years have been but little better treated in the convict camps than the colored man before the late war. Emancipation must come legally or the people will take the law in their own hands. And why not?" (*UMWJ*, July 30, 1891).

16. "Show" referred to a job, or to an opportunity to earn a living. "Kicking" was a popular term for complaining.

17. *UMWJ*, Sept. 8, 1892.

18. This letter was signed in Brazil, Ind., and appeared in the *UMWJ*, Mar. 24, 1892. A black organizer himself, "Willing Hands" experienced similar difficulties with white racial hostility when conducting union work in Kentucky.

19. *UMWJ*, Sept. 29, 1892.

20. Referred to William C. Webb and William R. Riley himself.

21. The Chattanooga Southern Railroad ran between Chattanooga, Tenn., and Gadsden, Ala. The line was later renamed the Tennessee, Alabama & Georgia Railway Company. The reasons for the strike are unknown.

22. The "paper question" referred to a mild debate among readers of the *UMWJ* over the paper's format.

23. *UMWJ*, Mar. 30, 1893.

24. By "mites" Riley meant small sums of money which the miners had saved from their meager wages.

25. Blacks probably went to work at Indian Mountain in 1893 as strikebreakers and stayed on after the strike ended. This was a common pattern of entry for blacks into employment which previously had been closed to them. The pattern prevailed in many American industries until recognition of the unions as collective bargaining agents was mandated by the federal government during the 1930's.

26. *UMWJ*, Feb. 7, 1895.

15

The Collapse of Biracial Unionism: The Alabama Coal Strike of 1908

RICHARD A. STRAW

In July 1908 the United Mine Workers of America authorized the calling of a strike in Alabama because of the refusal of many large coal companies there to renew a wage agreement that had expired the year before. This strike was one in a series that befell Alabama between 1894 and 1920, and it was as devastating in its destruction of life and property as it was in its effects on the UMW in District 20.

The UMW first entered Alabama in 1893, only three years after the union was founded in Columbus, Ohio. When it was organized, unlike most other labor unions, the UMW erected no barriers against Negro membership; in fact, it actively sought to organize them mainly because of the northern operators' reliance upon blacks as strikebreakers and because of the competitive advantage their cheap labor gave to southern operators. A major objective of the UMW was to "unite in one organization, regardless of creed, color or nationality, all workmen employed in and around coal mines,"[1] and for a number of years the union employed one national and several district Negro organizers to facilitate the unionization of black miners. The official UMW's position towards black miners is significant not only because of its variance with the vast majority of labor organizations at the time (including the AFL of which it was the largest union) but also because the UMW formulated its firm stand on the necessity of biracial unionism during a time when blacks were experiencing the rapid deterioration of their political, economic, and social status on a national level. The union's radical racial policy originated because of the UMW's role as an industrial rather than a craft union and because of the "evangelical egalitarianism" which characterized its leadership at the time. "Anti-Negro diatribes," which were commonly seen in journals between 1890-1910, "were rare in the UMW publications despite the difficulty in organizing Negro miners fresh from rural areas and despite the use of Negro strikebreakers."[2]

Although there was considerable anti-union sentiment expressed by blacks in this century's first decade, Alabama's black miners exhibited a strong fidelity to unionism during the 1908 strike. "The failure of the UMW to gain a permanent foothold in Alabama was not due to the operators' use of an industrial army reserve which was frequently used to defeat the union's purpose in northern Appalachia, but rather to southern social prejudice."[3]

The period between 1890 and 1908 was a boom time for Alabama's coal

country. Total coal production in 1908 was three times what it had been in 1890.
In 1890 there was approximately 8,000 coal miners with 3,600 being Negroes.
At the turn of the century the number of black miners had increased to 9,700 out
of a total of just under 18,000.[4] During this period operators were hiring
hundreds of unskilled black workers, realizing that if they kept the standard of
living as low as possible, they could sell their coal for less than the unionized
northern fields, thus enabling them to break into the lucrative Great Lakes
market. The union pressed its struggle to organize all the miners in Alabama
into one interracial union. By 1902 the UMW claimed that 65% of the miners in
Alabama were organized, and one half of this number were Negroes. In 1904 the
UMW called a strike because many large companies called for the open shop.
The strike lasted for two years and the UMW invested a million dollars in the
losing cause. Many of the operators who had not demanded the open shop in
1904 refused to renew their contracts in 1908; another crisis was upon the
shoulders of the struggling miners of Alabama. During the two month strike of
1908, the UMW spent another $100,000 in its effort to construct an interracial
industrial union in Alabama.[5] By 1908 the leaders and rank and file of the
UMW had achieved their goal of a strong biracial union, but it could not stand in
the face of the racist and anti-union attitudes of the "New South."

In early June 1908 the 11th Annual Convention of the UMW in District 20
was called to order with fifty-eight delegates attending. The usual business of
the convention was completed rapidly. J. F. Sorsby, a black miner, was elected
district vice-president, and three members of the eight-man District Executive
Board were Negroes.[6] The 1908 convention faced the usual task of arranging a
wage scale to present to the operators, but this year the job was even more
difficult. Most of the large commercial companies that had closed for repairs
had announced their intention of re-opening with non-union labor unless the
UMW dropped its wage demand by ten cents per ton. The final conference
between miners and operators on July 2, 1908, resulted in a basic disagreement.
The operators insisted on a ten cent cut in wages which would have reduced the
wage per ton to 17½ cents. The UMW could not accept this. The operators
argued that they could not compete with the non-union mines without reducing
the miners' wages by at least ten cents.[7] These commercial companies, which
employed around four thousand miners, threatened to sever all relations with the
union unless the UMW reconsidered its position. The miners, after reconven-
ing, offered a base scale of fifty-five cents per ton, but the operators refused.[8]

On July 6, 1908, because of the unwillingness of the commercial operators
to offer the union miners a wage of 55 cents per ton the International Executive
Board of the UMW authorized a strike in Alabama.[9] The operators indicated
early that there was little hindrance of the mining process due to the strike, but
the union claimed that operations at sixteen non-union mines were disrupted
and that the union ranks had been increased by several thousand. The Birmingham *News* reported on Monday July 6 that many UMW locals, badly
demoralized since the strike in 1904, took steps toward reorganization. The
UMW also made every effort to gain the support of all the miners in the state,
those employed by both the "captive" furnace mines and the commercial mines.

As the strike entered its second day the miners were confident that the

UMW would offer financial aid to the thousands of men whom they anticipated would be unemployed as the strike spread. Those men who encouraged miners in all the coal mines of Alabama to lay down their picks were undoubtedly pleased when W. R. Fairley, Alabama's representative to the UMW International Executive Board, stated, "the national organization will take care of the men. We will be in a position to supply the needs of the striking miners and to wage the fight successfully."[10]

Throughout July and August the operators made numerous attempts to run their mines with the use of scab labor. To be sure, striking miners opposed the principle of the open-shop and responded to the illicit operation of the mines with either violence or the threat of violence. Throughout the district acts of violence were committed, either by striking miners or law enforcement officials, which resulted in both personal and property damage.

In what appeared to be an almost eager display of anticipation of violence between union and non-union miners, Sheriff John Higdon of Jefferson County began swearing in special deputies on the very first day of the strike. Being a special deputy during an industrial conflict was either a highly profitable job or one that offered unusual excitement because Higdon reported that his office had been deluged with letters from men all over the U.S. wanting to be sworn in as special deputies. The office reported, however, that long lines of local men had showed up to apply for the positions.[11]

There was a great deal of violence during the strike with most of it being directed at scab miners and trains carrying scabs, and the union officials engaged in a constant rhetorical battle with the sheriff over who was to blame. H. H. O'Neal, president of UMW local at Republic, Alabama, called on Sheriff Higdon and assured him of UMW support in preserving order. O'Neal told the sheriff that any union miners detected in a violation of the law would be quickly turned over to the authorities.[12] Fairley stated in a newspaper interview that the UMW would not tolerate any violence from its members since he was aware the public would use this against the union.[13] The operators were not convinced, and acting according to certain lessons they had learned from the violent strike of 1904, they began hiring their own special guards to protect their mining camps.[14]

On July 15, Fairley issued a statement in which he severely criticized the actions of the more than 100 special deputies that Sheriff Higdon had sworn in to "preserve law and order." Fairley characterized the strike situation as a "reign of terror," and charged deputies and guards with arresting men without warrants. "They are breaking up meetings and taking our men by force to the company's office at Sayreton to force them to go to work." Fairley was convinced that "there had been no violation of the law by miners since the strike began" and that the violence on the part of the deputies and guards was perpetrated in order to instigate violence among the striking miners.[15]

As the strike passed into its second week the violence intensified, as did the steadfastness of the opposing parties. The union claimed it received large accessions to its ranks, while the operators stated that the furnace companies had lost only a few men and that there had been little interruption of their business. After one week of making a "supreme effort to organize the state" seven thousand miners were idle, many were homeless and all were under the watchful glare of over one hundred heavily armed guards who patrolled the mining camps and surrounding territory. The UMW hastily constructed commissaries where food was doled out to hungry women and children while mass meetings and demonstrations were held daily by the striking coal diggers. At the Bessie mines, Joe Jerrill, president of the UMW local there, stated that only a few men remained working and these were watched by forty heavily armed guards. He claimed that the mines had "assumed a military appearance with nightly patrols and around the clock guarding."[16] By the beginning of the second week it was clear that more than a ten cent wage increase was at stake. The union was struggling for its very existence in Alabama, and the operators were fighting to crush it.

The amount of violence in the Birmingham area increased substantially around July 13. The furnace and coal operators, after a meeting Wednesday morning, July 15, issued a statement deploring the serious turn the strike situation had taken. The key to the violence lay in another statement issued by the operators. They claimed they were bringing large numbers of men into the district to replace the striking miners. They said that "labor agents had been unusually active in neighboring fields, and the companies would continue to pour outside labor into the district until output was again normal."[17] Unfortunately the evidence does not indicate whether these strikebreakers were black or white.

Although it is difficult to get any clear estimate of the number of black strikers, there seems to be a rather clear indication that the vast majority of those strikers arrested were black, and that the law enforcement officials, as well as the newspaper editors, viewed the existence of large numbers of "idle" Negroes as a serious and direct threat to the security of the law-abiding white population. On the morning of July 15 at Sayreton, Alabama, several special deputies arrested thirteen Negroes and a white man who were gathered in a woods near the mine with other striking miners. The deputies alleged that the men were "hooting" others who were going to work. Union officials denied this and claimed that the men were holding a peaceable meeting. During the arrest thirty or forty shots were fired, and two of the arrested Negroes were wounded. Following this incident some of the union officials swore out a warrant for the arrest of Special Deputy C. T. Huggins, charging him with assault with intent to murder. The deputy was arrested but released after bond was posted.[18] This was one of many incidents described in great detail by the two Birmingham newspapers, and it indicates that there was at least some commitment from Higdon to control the actions of his forces. At Sayreton the next night everything was quiet as a result of speeches by Fairley and Higdon. The striking miners, apparently wanting to know the law so they could uphold it, listened in earnest to Sheriff Higdon's speech. In an obvious attempt to bolster the union's confidence in him, Higdon announced he had warrants for the arrest of fifteen special deputies—signed by union men—claiming that his only mission was to protect all against property and personal destruction.[19] But even with this show of faith by the sheriff, it seems clear that, considering their experiences, the striking miners were not consoled by his closing words: "Just so long as each of you conducts himself properly you have nothing to fear from the deputies. In fact you should feel that a deputy is just as much your friend as he is someone else's. His sole mission is to see that the law is not violated either by strikers or corporations."[20]

Although the union's bitterness about the violence that characterized the strike was generally directed toward the special deputies. Sheriff Higdon was occasionally the object of scorn. The *Labor Advocate,* the official journal of the Birmingham Trades Council, called him a "little czar" and "anarchist," and it stated that in Jefferson county, "Negro pimps were picked up from the worst dives and given sheriffs badges."[21] Although black miners constituted a significant portion of union strength in Alabama, there was a tremendous amount of concern expressed by the union as to the possible employment of blacks as deputy sheriffs. The exact reasons for this apprehension are unclear, but it appears from the rhetoric that the white population as a whole, including the integrated UMW, was extremely fearful of having large numbers of armed Negroes in their midst. In an official statement issued from UMW headquarters in Birmingham on July 21, Fairley denied that there were large mobs of armed Negro strikers roaming the countryside and intimidating non-union miners. But he also said, "There is nothing said about Negro deputies being appointed by Sheriff Higdon, one of whom shot indiscriminately, endangering the lives of women and children at Pratt City last Friday." He continued, stating that, if Negroes were appointed to positions on the Birmingham police force, there would be a "full sized riot by the white citizens of Birmingham for the indignity heaped on them."[22]

Higdon denied ever having hired any Negro deputies. In a reply to Fairley's charge the sheriff remarked that he did employ several Negroes to care for the horses and that occasionally they would accompany deputies on official business. On July 25 Fairley again verbally attacked the Sheriff for his hiring practices. Having blacks accompany deputies on official business was, according to Fairley, worse than regularly commissioning a Negro. Fairley asserted that, "if the sheriff has armed Negroes running around loose without commissions, the citizens of the community, and especially the striking miners, are living in grave peril. If he is allowing these men to accompany deputies and act as officers, no man can measure the danger to the community."[23] It is puzzling that the biracial UMW would be so concerned that the sheriff employed Negroes. Perhaps Fairley was worried that the armed blacks would attack the white strikers. It is more logical though to assume that he was aware of the great differences of opinion among blacks about the value of labor unions and understood that there was very little racially based solidarity in the black community.

The miners' union had added over eight thousand new members since the beginning of the strike, and with the vast majority of local miners remaining loyal to the union the operators were forced to import scab labor. Since the operators were re-opening and threatening to re-open their mines with imported laborers the possibility of violence was imminent.

Strikers were reported patrolling highways, dynamiting houses, and intimidating non-union miners, and hundreds of union men were jailed, threatened, and mistreated by the special deputies. Throughout July and August almost daily occurrences of hootings, beatings, and small riots were reported. The most serious outbreaks of violence involved the attack by strikers on trains carrying imported labor to the strike area, and the lynching of a Negro striker by a crowd led by two special deputies.[24]

In the early morning hours of July 16, a coachload of strikebreakers, bound for the Adamsville mine of the Birmingham Coal and Iron Company, was attacked at the small junction of Jefferson by perhaps three hundred men. The scabs were dragged from the train and chased down the track with the armed men in pursuit. According to one newspaper's report not a shot was fired by the seven guards on the train, but the windows were riddled with bullets and the special deputies were disarmed with guns at their heads. The next afternoon a far more serious outbreak occurred. Just as a trainload of strikebreakers approached the same junction, perhaps one thousand strikers and sympathizers opened fire on the train. The thirty deputies on board quickly exhausted their ammunition supply and with one of their group fatally wounded the train escaped through a tunnel in a mountain, while "volley after volley blazed forth from Winchester rifles: the hills on each side and the slope above the tunnel literally swarmed with armed men, constantly firing from behind rocks and trees."[25] After what was labeled, "a most exciting battle, which knows few equals in Alabama since the civil war,"[26] Governor Braxton Bragg Comer, an industrialist, and former lessee of convict labor, issued the following public statement: ". . . I am afraid the miners do not comprehend that the peace of the state must be preserved. I trust the difficulties will be settled without any serious results." Comer went on to say that he intended to do everything in his power, "without infringing on the rights of any citizen, to maintain the peace of the state."[27] In what appeared to be the first major public statement that placed the strike in racial terms, Major G. B. Seals of the Alabama National Guard described how an advance guard has discovered "the Negroes ambushed near an old mill." He stated that the blacks were, "just a sample of the opposition," and claimed that "very few white people" had anything to do with it. "The Negroes are armed to the teeth, and seem to be directed by white men, although the Negroes are everywhere in predominance."[28]

Throughout the last days of July and the first weeks of August a "reign of terror" had indeed descended upon the mining region of Alabama. The killing of a non-union miner, the wounding of a non-union and a union miner, the burning of a non-union miner's home, a number of assaults upon non-union men, and the dynamiting of an air shaft, all occurred on Tuesday and Wednesday, July 28 and 29.[29] Early on the night of July 31 a group of black strikers gathered in a wooded area near Mine #1 at Pratt City. This mine was surrounded by a line of deputy sheriffs. Inside this line was a military line and inside this was the camp and mine. Although the majority of the group was dispersed by deputy sheriffs, some were able to slip past the guards and open fire on the camp. After a short skirmish they were repulsed. Later the next week two pitched battles were fought at Lewisburg, and about midnight on August 4 an attempt was made to blow up the stockade which housed the imported miners at that town.

Although several companies of Alabama National Guardsmen had been

stationed in the area, with the approval of the UMW, more drastic law enforcement methods were required according to Frank Evans, special correspondent to
the Birmingham *Age-Herald* and an almost daily commentator on the strike.
Evans wrote, "There is a spirit of unrest manifested here. It is procured by the
assemblies of striking miners who are listening to addresses by leaders imported
from other points." To Evans these "gatherings and harsh utterances by the
speakers caused anxiety and fear on the part of idle men who really desired to be
at work in the mines." Evans was giving vent here to a feeling that characterized
much of Birmingham's citizenry. He argued that the industrial work force in
Alabama was basically satisfied, and that outside-enforced idleness, especially
among the black miners, was the breeding ground of violence. Evans saw only
one solution to this crisis: "not all the soldiers in Alabama nor every deputy
sheriff can stop this disturbance and this devilment, unless they are given the
authority to disperse assemblies of madmen and force them to retirement in their
homes or parts far away from these mines." He asserted time after time that an
early adjustment to the strike was in the hands of the governor. "By signing his
official signature he can establish martial law, and that is the remedy."[30]

This policy was in fact instituted by Governor Comer when he advised
Sheriff Higdon to act according to a statement given the governor by S. D.
Weakley, a former chief justice of the Alabama Supreme Court. Weakley wrote
the governor that "any meeting calculated to excite alarm is an unlawful
assembly and can be dispersed."[31] Comer ordered Higdon to allow no assemblies near mines, to permit no marching along public highways and to instruct
his men to attend meetings and arrest incendiary speakers.

Comer's apparent concern for protecting life and property was not emulated
by some other citizens of Alabama. On Monday evening August 3 the house of
Findlay Fuller, a black non-union miner, was dynamited and completely destroyed. When Major Noble of the National Guard arrived at the house he
questioned Fuller and determined that he had blown up his own house! Although Fuller was arrested and placed in jail he was soon out. His bail was paid
by his employer. After allowing their bloodhounds to search the area, the sheriff
arrested another Negro, Will Millin, a union miner, for the dynamiting. Millin,
however, claimed he was "sitting up with a sick friend" when the explosion
occurred. Millin was taken to the jail at Brighton Tuesday night August 4 just as
a mass meeting of the white citizens of the town was breaking up in the same
building, a meeting at which the outrage of the night before was severely
condemned and a vigilance committee organized to keep down lawlessness.
Upon returning to the jail in the morning the sheriff discovered Millin gone.
Millin was found hanging from a nearby tree, his neck broken. After a short
investigation two special deputies, R. B. and Lou Tyler, were arrested and
charged with murder.[32] In those first two weeks of August there seemed to be no
end to the horrible violence that had gripped the strike area.

Easy targets for retaliation were trains carrying scabs. On August 8 one
conductor, one deputy sheriff, and one non-union miner were killed, two
soldiers, four deputies, two non-union miners, and three officials of the Tennessee Coal, Iron and Railroad Company were wounded, as a result of an attack on a
special three car Louisville and Nashville train, in Bibb County. The train was

carrying a large number of strikebreakers as well as a company of National Guardsmen and thirty deputy sheriffs. The train was traveling fast, and when it was just about a mile out of the village of Blocton, the engineer noticed a pile of cross ties on the tracks. As he slowed, approximately one hundred men opened fire on the train from behind the rocks twenty or thirty yards from the track. The arrests came swiftly. Early Monday morning thirteen blacks and fourteen Slavs were arrested for the murders. According to a reporter, "at one time things took on a squally look," but apparently a strong desire to reenact the tragedy of Brighton was suppressed.[33]

While the union pressed for recognition as the representative of Alabama's coal miners, the businessmen and public officials of Alabama were unable to understand the importance of this one fundamental element of industrialization. Arbitration of their grievances and recognition of the union were for a variety of reasons choices not open as possible ends to the conflict. Apparently force and intimidation were the only means to achieve industrial harmony according to the operators and politicians. Frank Evans advised the governor that the "anarchy and lawlessness must be stopped by force, full force." Although the Alabama militia was present in considerable numbers (there were over 1,000 in the strike zone by the middle of August), they were received warmly by the strikers. It was the deputy sheriffs, unskilled and undisciplined, that the miners despised. The Reverend W. A. Lewis opened an outdoor barbecue given the white union miners by the Alabama Farmers Union by telling the miners that the soldiers were the miners' friends and that the only "enemies the miners had were 'Higdon's dirty deputies.' " A large force of deputy sheriffs and soldiers were maintaining surveillance of the picnic, and when Lewis made his remarks about the deputies, chief deputy Lucien Brown arrested the minister. G. F. Howle, editor of the Birmingham *Register*, was also arrested after telling of the lynching at Brighton, where no reward was offered to the public for information leading to the arrest and conviction of those guilty. He then referred to the recent slaying of a Negro prisoner as he was escaping from the courthouse. He exclaimed that the man was shot in the back while still handcuffed. "The men who did this shooting are still in the employ of the sheriff." Howle's arrest immediately followed.[34]

The harassment of both union and non-union miners continued through the last days of August, and by the end of that month it was obvious that the UMW could not sustain itself in the face of hostile government officials and public opinion. Frank Evans again offered a solution to the strike on August 4, 1908. The solution was to "rid the district of men who inflame passions." He analyzed the strike as being one where 4,000 union miners, fortified and encouraged by the UMW, were keeping 20,000 men who desired to work from doing so. But Evans was not totally anti-union. He felt that there were many miners who were loyal to the miners' cause because of the protection it afforded their families, but he was fearful of the effect the idleness was having on those of a "lower class." It must be remembered, he argued, "that the state of Alabama, through its penitentiary system, graduates from the coal mines every year large numbers of skilled miners—ex-convicts, white and black, who though they may have paid the penalty of their crimes, are still criminally intent."[35] Evans was convinced that this element was being aroused unnecessarily against the operators by the union organizers. These men were idled by the strike and their idleness bred a viciousness and madness that, according to Evans, paralyzed business and promoted social disorder. Evans' solution was a familiar one in southern history: expel the outsider since it is he, and not the social order or class structure, that is at fault.

This same sentiment was echoed by the leaders of the business establishment in Birmingham. At several meetings during the second week of August it was unanimously decided by local businessmen and merchants that the "leaders of the ignorant men must be made aware of their responsibility." Robert Jemison, a leader of Birmingham's business community thought that the leaders of the strike who were "trying to keep men from working when they want to work should be ordered out of the state." The businessmen had an obvious financial interest in seeing the strike come to an end, and they were in agreement with Evans that force was the only solution. The sentiment among the businessmen was that if the governor was not going to declare martial law then it was the duty of the citizens to organize themselves to fight against the union leaders and the "revolution" that was gripping Alabama.[36]

The governor was persuaded by this and other displays of public sentiment. Comer had remained basically non-committal up to the middle of August, stating that he was only concerned with the protection of lives and the preservation of order. But on August 10, he issued an official proclamation that clearly indicated his intention to protect the rights of non-union miners in Alabama. He declared that the "whole powers of the state will be exerted for the protection of everybody who desires to work, even if it should be necessary to use all the military forces in the state for that purpose." Comer, too, was convinced that the work force in Alabama was merely attempting to go about the "peaceful prosecution of their labors" and that the UMW leaders imported into Alabama were responsible for all of the industrial discord in that state.[37] Ironically, on that same date, John P. White, the international vice president of the UMW, arrived in Birmingham from Indianapolis to direct the strike situation.

White's strategy in directing the strike was to boost the morale of the miners, to attempt to keep other miners out of the area, and to seek arbitration as a solution to the strike. White knew that the only way the UMW could win recognition from the operators was to deny them a source of outside labor, and he placed an official circular in the *United Mine Workers Journal* in which he appealed to the members of organized labor everywhere to "stay away from Alabama until the present industrial struggle is over."[38] White also injected into the situation a degree of confidence that is essential to the success of any struggle. He explained to the miners of Alabama that if they could deny labor to the operators, they would be forced to recognize the union and provide a decent wage scale. White argued that "at no time in the history of Alabama mining has a strike ever manifested its effectiveness so completely than at present." He estimated that by the middle of August 1908 "nearly 18,000 men" were members of the UMW in District 20 and were "standing loyally by the cause."[39]

White also knew that if he could get the operators to the conference table to talk about their differences this would in fact be a rather strong concession by the operators to the principle of recognition. Responding to a petition which requested that the miners and operators arbitrate their differences, White and Fairley stated that they were "willing to submit to arbitration."[40]

But the representatives of Alabama's coal operators, the newly formed Alabama Coal Operators' Association, would have nothing to do with what they called a "Blood Stained Organization." In a statement issued in response to the petition asking for arbitration, the ACOA stated that the "United Mine Workers have but one demand—that we recognize the union and again bow to the tyranny of its leaders." The operators were adamant in their basic position that they would "never again permit the UMW leaders to control" their operations and they refused to have any "dealings with the United Mine Workers of America."[41]

The union was persistent in its efforts to secure a negotiated settlement to the strike. T. L. Lewis, president of the UMW, telegraphed G. B. McCormick, president of the ACOA, on August 24, asking for a conference with a view of ending the strike. Remaining true to their promise, the ACOA promptly denied the request. In his response to the union McCormick stated the commitment of the ACOA to the principles of the open-shop and strongly condemned the murders and violence allegedly committed by union miners.[42]

By the end of August, even though the union seemed to be holding its own with regard to preventing production at mines and the employment of scabs, the end of the strike was imminent. While the operators were being pushed harder and harder to fill orders for coal, the violence continued and the public outrage grew accordingly. By August 28 when Governor Comer summoned Lewis, White, J. R. Kennamer, president of District 20, and W. D. Ryan, national secretary-treasurer of the UMW, to a conference in Birmingham, he had decided to end the strike. Comer simply issued the union officers an ultimatum. The governor stated that if the strike was not ended very soon he would be forced to call a special session of the Alabama legislature to enact such laws that would enable him to deal with the strike. What the governor had in mind specifically was an amendment to the vagrancy law that would allow him to arrest every union miner out of work.[43] The union could not stand up under the pressure, so on Sunday August 30 an executive order was signed by Lewis, White, and Ryan which officially brought the strike to an end.[44]

The quick conclusion of the strike was related almost exclusively to the adroit use of racial prejudice of the operators to incur the wrath of public opinion against the UMW. By the middle of August the union was under severe attack from all sectors of Alabama society for promoting what was termed "social equality." The issue came to dominate much of the discussion surrounding the strike and it was an important part of the outrage and hysteria that prompted Comer to issue his ultimatum on August 28. The union came under attack from the operators frequently for its efforts "to force social equality between blacks and whites" in Alabama. Comer reported to the UMW officials at their August 28th conference that "members of the legislature in every sector of Alabama" were very much "outraged at the attempts to establish social equality between white and black miners."[45]

Although the union was committed to a policy of not barring membership to individuals because of race or creed, it was quick to deny the charge of promoting social equality. G. C. McCormick of the ACOA received a telegram on the 25th of August from Lewis which stated that the union was not in favor of social equality. The UMW president declared that the miners' union was merely in favor of equal wages for equal work in the mines.[46]

Further defense of the union's position came in an editorial in the *Labor Advocate*. The editors give an insight into the private, as well as the official, attitude of the union toward the organization of black miners. The UMW organized blacks in Alabama for purposes of self-defense, since the union knew that if it did not, the operators would use them as strikebreakers and to keep down the wages of white miners. Therefore, the white miners were "forced to take blacks into the organization for self-protection." Arguing that the union in no way fostered social equality, the *Advocate* stated that the white miners "associate with blacks in the mines because the operators force them to do so . . . and outside of the mines upon all matters pertaining to their work and organization, and nothing more." The union's position was emphasized by the statement that "there is not at present and never was and can never be social equality between the whites and blacks in this state."[47] The miners knew that they differed very little in their basic prejudices from the operators and government officials, but they also knew that the operators would use the issue of social equality as one more weapon against an already unpopular union in their fight to destroy it.

As the violence increased and more men were idled by the strike, the populace became more concerned with the racial implications of the industrial struggle. Idleness among striking Negro miners was of great concern. Frank Evans, the columnist for the *Age-Herald*, grew steadily more distressed over the numbers of idle blacks who congregated in the small mining towns around Birmingham. "Idleness," he wrote, "always begets crime and leads to unhappiness and misery." He went on to associate this idleness with a "criminal assault by Negroes upon white women in two of the strike districts."[48]

The importance of the biracial nature of the UMW, and the fear that it engendered in the hearts of white Alabamians, surfaced dramatically on August 8. Evans attended a miners assembly of about five hundred persons, both white and black, at Dora, Alabama, and was there struck with the "racial danger" inherent in the strike. He wrote:

It was left for a Negro preacher from Empire to take the stand and give utterance to remarks that cannot prove conducive to a readjustment of conditions and resumption of peace and order. It is a lamentable condition that incites and permits ignorant Negro leaders to address assemblies of white women and children as social equals advising as to moral and social questions and alluding to those delicate matters of social status which can only be discussed properly with fair women in the private home and by husband and father. It was a third of a century ago that the people of Alabama by rigid force and even the shedding of blood stopped the advance of a threatening peril which endangered our social fabric. It was the inculcation in the minds of blacks of the idea of social equality. The terrible poison then was sought to be applied for political purposes by the carpetbaggers from the North, and for a time the cloud seemed ominous, but the Caucasian blood of this state was aroused to resentment and to the defense of the home fireside. When today this correspondent saw the comingling of white and black at Dora, where he beheld the sympathetic arms of a Negro extended toward and embrace a white speaker to impart to him a secret of his bosom, in the very presence of gentle white women and innocent little children I thought to myself: has it again come to this?[49]

Indeed it had in the minds of most of the observers and participants in Birmingham during August 1908. "This is a white man's country, and there will be no nigger domination here,"[50] the sheriff of one Alabama county said to a meeting of miners. The union was convinced that statements such as this proved that "insatiate capital" was using the blacks to "make slaves of the whites."[51]

The citizens of Birmingham were formulating opinions about the union officials which were based on a set of very old attitudes about southern race relations. In contrast to the situation in Springfield, Illinois, during the summer of 1908, where a violent riot had occurred, the cry in the South was not to kill Negroes, but to run out of the territory the white men who were upsetting the racial harmony that supposedly existed in Alabama. One Birmingham businessman wrote about Vice President White: "Why should we permit him to come into our county and organize the Negroes against the white people of the district, and destroy the good feeling that has existed. Do we want a 'Springfield riot' in our midst, started by this carpetbagger? It is time to show these insolent violators of the peace and dignity of our state that Alabama is no place for them."[52]

There was a great fear among whites in Alabama that the promotion of social equality by the UMW would eventually lead to even greater discord than was present during the strike. Evans wrote that "no reasonable man, white or black, can doubt for a moment that the Negro is a valuable asset of these southern states. As a race they are useful, productive, and when exempt from the false teachings and domineering influences of bad white men they are always in a happy condition, so long as the social line is strictly drawn between whites and blacks." But in the eyes of Evans and the operators the union leaders were attempting "every day to obliterate this line."[53]

Evans took advantage of a speech given by Booker T. Washington in the northeast again to blast the racial policies of the UMW. Evans criticized Washington for addressing a northern audience when "this is the place where the voice of Booker T. Washington should be applied before his race in vigorous manner." He again emphasized that idleness, imposed by the strike, had made "bombthrowers, midnight assassins, cutthroats, and murderers out of members of Booker T. Washington's race."[54]

One of the most scathing attacks upon the union and its leaders came from a citizen of southern Alabama who wrote a letter to the Birmingham *Age-Herald* while visiting that city. J. V. Allen exclaimed that if "Fairley and his black co-conspirators would have invaded southern Alabama and perpetrated the same damnable deeds he has inflicted on the people of Jefferson County, nothing further would be needed but the coroner." He too used the race issue to arouse sentiments against the union when he claimed that the UMW officials were "guilty of efforts to overthrow" the area's social structure and "break down barriers sacred to the whole South."[55]

More vitriolic assessments of Fairley and the union came from two other citizens of Alabama. Walter Moore and Guy Johnson proclaimed that social equality had been established and sacred traditions trampled in the dust by the union's effort. They argued that "under Fairley's leadership it seemed the limit had been reached. Foreign agitators (it is unclear here whether they referred to northern organizers or to Fairley, who was born in Great Britain) not content are now organizing white women and black women into unions called Women's Auxiliaries." They ask rhetorically, "just how much damage to life, property and morals does this agitator Fairley and his associates have a right to inflict on this community before the deadline is reached." It was apparent to these two defenders of southern tradition that the citizens of Birmingham were "short on law or manhood, if not both."[56]

One of the most interesting statements of this virulently anti-union sentiment came in a newspaper column entitled "What the Women Think of It" written by Dolly Dalrymple. The attitudes expressed and the personal biography seem so pat and contrived as to raise questions about its authenticity. To her it seemed "absolutely inconceivable that any man, or association of men, should deliberately set about to upset the primary social laws of our beloved South." She shuddered and was saddened by the fact that anyone could suggest that such a thing as "social equality be tolerated or even countenanced." In a conversation with an operator Dalrymple claimed she commented upon the situation, and stated she could not believe the horrors perpetrated by the union. Whereupon she was told by the operator that "in one camp on a small tract of land there were several hundred men, women and children, white and black and that this camp was one of several, where equally bad conditions" existed.[57]

How bad these conditions were depended upon your viewpoint, and your attitude about the union. In perhaps his most prejudicial act of the whole strike, Governor Comer, on August 26, 1908, issued orders to the military authorities to cut down the tents of the striking miners and "now allow the establishment of more tented camps by coal miners." According to press releases this action was taken by the governor for "the preservation of public health." But Comer did not hesitate to reveal his real motives in a meeting with Kennamer the night before he issued the orders. Kennamer "located the governor at seven o'clock that night" and asked him if he intended to issue orders to cut down the miners' tents. Comer replied that he had. Kennamer then requested a conference on the matter before the governor's order was implemented, but Comer would not agree, stating, "You know what it means to have eight or nine thousand niggars idle in the state of Alabama, and I am not going to stand for it."[58] In an attempt to thwart the governor's severe action, President Lewis told the governor that the union would "transport out of the state every Negro who was on strike and make it a white man's strike." But Comer would not budge from his decision, and declared that he would not even permit "white men to live in tents or in camps in Alabama" under the UMW's jurisdiction.[59]

The UMW responded to these attacks in various ways, but none proved fruitful. The skillful use of racial prejudice by the operators completely alienated the union and its members from Birmingham society, and made any kind of victory impossible. A master of understatement, Fairley declared in Indianapolis on August 28, that some prejudice against the miners' officers had been aroused in Alabama. He felt the miners' cause had been seriously damaged by the charges of social equality leveled at the union, but he explained that the union had been organizing black miners who had been brought into the district to replace strikers only as a measure of union self-preservation. But he knew that even this had prejudiced the miners' cause in the minds of the people of Alabama.[60]

By the end of August the operators and the Birmingham press had successfully shifted the emphasis of the strike. The union was no longer dealing with an industrial question, but with a racial problem. Union Vice President White recalled that "one evening a committee of Birmingham citizens waited for me and informed me that I had better call the strike off." He told them he "had no power to declare the strike off," and if he had he "would not do it." The committee argued that "no matter how much merit there may be in the miners' cause you cannot change the opinion of the people in this country that you are violating one of the principles the South holds near and dear." Then threatening White, the citizens declared that before they would "allow this to be done" they would "make Springfield, Illinois look like six cents."[61]

"That old race antagonism" so clearly defined by this committee of citizens was "the one great feature of this strike and one of the main things that caused its dissolution." According to White, the situation in Birmingham was so tense that "a small boy could have started a riot in the streets that would have caused countless numbers of innocent people to lose their lives." White felt that the use of the racial issue was resorted to by the operators only "when they saw that the UMW had completely tied up the industrial situation in that country." They then "went to the old closet and brought out the ghastly spectre of racial hatred and held it before the people of Alabama."[62]

So effectively was the "ghastly spectre" used that as a result of the strike the UMW's strength in Alabama was reduced from approximately 18,000 to 700. President Kennamer of District 20 reported at the UMW Convention in 1909 that out of the 20,000 or so miners in Alabama who were sympathetic to the union's cause, only about 700 paid dues to the organization. He explained that the reason why they did not have more members was "because they are discharged whenever the operators find they are paying dues." Of the coal miners in Alabama a year after the strike, approximately 65 to 70% of them were Negroes, and in his address to the convention Kennamer praised the black miners for their loyalty and bravery, proclaiming that "there are no better strikers in the history of the UMW" than the black miners of Alabama.[63]

Three weeks after the strike began Fairley addressed a mass meeting of miners in Birmingham at which time he dwelt long on the importance to the miners of the outcome of the present strike. "The destiny of labor in the South," he said, "depends upon whether victory or defeat shall crown us at the close of our fight."[64] Fairley was uncannily accurate in his prediction. The UMW did not attempt any widespread organization in Alabama for a decade. The fears and hatreds displayed in this strike and others in the late 19th and early 20th century South were major factors in checking the growth of unionism in the region.

1. Article 2, Constitution of the International Union, United Mine Workers of America (Indianapolis, Ind., 1924, printing 3).

2. Herbert G. Gutman, "The Negro and the UMW," in *The Negro in the American Labor Movement*, ed. Julius Jacobson (Garden City, N.Y., 1968), p. 83.

3. Sterling D. Spero and Abram L. Harris, *The Black Worker, 1915-1930* (New York, 1931; reprint ed., 1974), p. 357.

4. Gutman, "Negro and the UMW," p. 70.

5. Spero and Harris, *Black Worker*, p. 357; Gutman, "Negro and the UMW," p. 111.

6. *Birmingham Labor Advocate*, June 12, 1908.

7. *Birmingham News*, July 2, 1908.

8. *Birmingham Labor Advocate*, July 10, 1908.

9. *Birmingham News*, July 6, 1908.

10. Ibid., July 7, 1908.

11. Ibid., July 9, 1908.

12. Ibid., July 11, 1908.

13. Ibid., July 10, 1908.

14. *Birmingham Age-Herald*, July 8, 1908.

15. *Birmingham News*, July 13, 1908; July 15, 1908.

16. Ibid., July 14, 1908.

17. Ibid., July 15, 1908.

18. *Birmingham Age-Herald*, July 16, 1908.

19. *Birmingham News*, July 16, 1908.

20. Ibid.

21. *Birmingham Labor Advocate*, July 17, 1908.

22. *Birmingham News*, July 21, 1908.

23. Ibid., July 25, 1908.

24. Both the *Birmingham News* and *Age-Herald* carried daily stories of the shootings, bombings and beatings that occurred in the mining regions during July and August 1908.

25. Ibid., July 16, 1908; *Birmingham Age-Herald*, July 18, 1908.

26. *Birmingham Age-Herald*, July 18, 1908.

27. Ibid.

28. Ibid., July 19, 1908.

29. Ibid., July 30, 1908.

30. Ibid., Aug. 3, 1908.

31. Ibid., Aug. 8, 1908.

32. Ibid., Aug. 6, 1908.

33. Ibid., Aug. 9, 1908, Aug. 10, 1908; *Birmingham News*, Aug. 10, 1908.

34. *Birmingham Age-Herald*, Aug. 21, 1908, Aug. 23, 1908.

35. Ibid., Aug. 4, 1908.

36. Ibid., Aug. 10, 1908.

37. B. B. Comer, "A Proclamation," *Birmingham Age-Herald*, Aug. 11, 1908.

38. *UMWJ*, Aug. 15, 1908, p. 1.

39. Ibid., Aug. 20, 1908, p. 1.

40. *Birmingham Age-Herald*, Aug. 19, 1908. There is some question as to the number of signatures that appeared on the petition calling for an arbitrated settlement of the strike. Fairley and White claimed that it held 20,000 while the Alabama Coal Operators' Association said it had only 600 signatures on it.

41. "Statement of the Alabama Coal Operators Association," *Birmingham Age-Herald*, Aug. 19, 1908.

42. *Birmingham Age-Herald*, Aug. 25, 1908.

43. Ibid., Aug. 29, 1908; United Mine Workers of America, *Proceedings of the Consecutive Constitutional Conventions of the UMWA* (Washington, D.C., 1909), p. 865.

44. *Birmingham Age-Herald*, Aug. 31, 1908.

45. Ibid., Aug. 25, 1908; Aug. 29, 1908.

46. Ibid., Aug. 26, 1908.

47. *Birmingham Labor Advocate*, Aug. 28, 1908.

48. *Birmingham Age-Herald*, Aug. 7, 1908.

49. Ibid., Aug. 8, 1908.

50. *UMWJ* (Aug. 15, 1908).

51. Ibid.

52. G. H. Estes to Editor, *Birmingham Age-Herald*, Aug. 21, 1908.

53. *Birmingham Age-Herald*, Aug. 22, 1908.

54. Ibid., Aug. 25, 1908.

55. J. V. Allen to Editor, *Birmingham Age-Herald*, Aug. 26, 1908.

56. Walter Moore and G. R. Johnson to Editor, *Birmingham Age-Herald*, Aug. 24, 1908.

57. *Birmingham Age-Herald*, Aug. 30, 1908.

58. *UMW Proceedings*, vol. 2, p. 865.

59. Ibid., p. 866. Comer's firm stand on the tent issue can be attributed to his anti-unionism certainly, but he was also being consistent about health, which was a grave concern at this time in Alabama.

60. *Birmingham Age-Herald*, Aug. 28, 1908.

61. *UMW Proceedings*, vol. 2, p. 873.

62. Ibid., pp. 871-872.

63. Ibid., p. 863.

64. *Birmingham Age-Herald*, July 30, 1908.

PART SIX

Blacks and Local Politics

Leon F. Williams and Jack Guillebeaux address the modern period of black mountain politics. According to Williams, white Appalachian xenophobia and the zealous guardianship of freedom from outside threats nourished the image of a calm climate in the region prior to the industrialization of the hills. The ensuing gap between blacks and whites rendered blacks in the region invisible to national movements for social justice and outside the programmatic objectives (as administered by locals) of governmental efforts such as the Appalachian Regional Commission (ARC). Guillebeaux was one of the main organizers of the Black Appalachian Commission (BAC). This activist group monitored the resource allocations of the Appalachian Regional Commission. With a group of indigenous blacks, often meeting in adult education seminars at the Highlander Center, he led a movement to act on the title of his essay: "Not Just Whites in Appalachia."

16

The Vanishing Appalachian: How to "Whiten" the Problem

LEON F. WILLIAMS

THE MODERN EXODUS

Nine years have passed since a social work professor confided, with candor, to a class of eager young West Virginia University social work students that, "Appalachia may one day become one of the few regions in America without a black population."

This comment was made in 1964 and the passing years have been witness to the inexorable trek of blacks out of Appalachia to the ghettos and marginal neighborhoods of urban America, pushed by the indifference and unresponsiveness of the Appalachian region . . . a modern day exodus, unheralded and unmarked.

Few, it seems, mourn the passing of so many Appalachian black citizens and also, just as few are willing to respect the role of the black in Appalachian history. The experience of black Appalachia is firmly rooted in the selfsame excesses of modern industrial development, with its penchant for racial and class exploitation, that have affected poor white Appalachians.

A NEED TO CORRECT HISTORICAL OVERSIGHTS

Despite the prevailing literature, Appalachia is not simply a region populated by poor whites. Calling on the author's own experience as a black Appalachian, together with bits and pieces of a history more legend than documented fact, we find, theoretically, that this region was settled to a substantial degree by slaves and indentured white servants fleeing from exploitation and angry with established practices in Colonial America. The hills, in their exquisite isolation, became havens for the disenchanted black and white, as well as the scattered Native Americans, who needed to escape burdensome drudgery and slavery.

Up until the beginning of this Century, these hills nurtured a culture fired by resentment and suspicious of authority. Concepts such as individualism, self-sufficiency, close family and kinship ties, often used to describe the mountain culture, were practical defenses against a hostile world which would use men as beasts of burden.

Most significant is the fact that the Appalachian black settlers enjoyed similar freedoms within the hills to those enjoyed by their white counterparts. Black/white animosities, which were becoming more intense in the slave holding states, were negligible in the mountains, owing more to the mutual enmity directed toward a common external foe to the North, South, and East.

Intermarriage was common practice in the mountains between blacks, whites and Native Americans; untroubled by the "black codes" of the antebellum South in which "race mixing" became a capital crime. Mike Ross, of the Fairmont (West Virginia) Clinic of the United Mine Workers, in his numerous speeches depicting the life style of the coal miners, often observes that only in Appalachia could mixed marriages be tolerated in communities of less than 1,000 inhabitants.

By mountain standards, the thing not to be violated was a man's right to privacy, pride and self-respect . . . his right to be "let alone," "left in peace" to pursue his own and his family's ends. It was not an idyllic life, clinging as one must to the somewhat precarious and barren hills, but, indeed, it was not a life of servitude, "toddying" to the interests of those who would exploit them . . . a man was his "own man." "Much of Appalachia, from just before World War I to the mid-1930s, became the arena for class warfare. Older miners, now working or pensioned, were raised in conditions of continuous civil conflict, bloodshed, starvation, terrorism, family degradation, upper class fear and hatred . . . unseen elsewhere in our own times."[1]

Those who are students of the "class struggle" also accept its inherent racism. The existence and persistence of highly individualistic and proud black and white mountain "natives" must have posed a considerable threat to the industrial powers who needed manpower to exploit the resources of Appalachia, especially if the interests of these two forces should combine to repulse the alien force. Race hatred, skillfully employed in other U.S. regions to disenfranchise the Indian nations, while preserving the demeaning role of the Southern black, seems on reflection, a natural device to further the aims of industrial philosophy that utilized inter-class dissension and rivalry to weaken "class consciousness" . . . the "divide and conquer" principle.

During the "bloody years" (1920-1930) another group of blacks were brought in from the deep South and pressed into service as strike breakers, incurring the wrath of the white miners and setting a new tone for black/white relationships. As company towns continued to spring up, black miners found themselves ghettoized into coal towns with names like "Harlem," "Osaka," "Rhoda," "Stonega"; mountain "Harlems" with black life styles all their own. Other blacks found themselves under siege in more "open" communities and experienced the effects of rampant "Jim Crowism," with segregated public facilities, schools, recreation facilities, etc.

In essence, the poor white Appalachian, struggling against dominance by the big powers was given a scapegoat . . . the black "scabs," and the expanding black population, in competition for dwindling resources, in particular, jobs. The gap between the two groups widened as animosity and the habit of peaceful co-existence was soon overcome.

WHITENING THE PROBLEM

Statistics extolling the black exodus from the South during the decades beginning, especially, with 1950, while accurate, failed to note that a significant portion of that black migration was from the Appalachians sections of the nation. The decline in agriculture and the coal fields hit blacks hardest, as they were the first fired and were not privy to the skill training needed or had not the resources to take advantage of the new mining and agricultural technology.

When Appalachia was discovered in the 1960s, already the population of blacks had dwindled to an "inconsequential" number. Here . . . [in] a region that stretches from Mississippi to New York, were millions of *white* [sic] Americans locked in a cycle of poverty and despair which rivaled the plight of underdeveloped nations."[2]

As the quote indicates, Appalachia was envisioned as white. Congress passed the Appalachian Regional Development Act in 1965 and the Appalachian Regional Commission was created. This opened the floodgates for almost a billion dollars in aid to the region—not a penny of which was earmarked for the black Appalachian; he did not exist.

Jack Guillebeaux, Executive Director of the Black Appalachian Commission, writes: "Although more than 1,300,000 Appalachians are black, one out of every fourteen, they somehow remain invisible during the discovery of 'white Appalachia.' When the region was being studied and new programs planned, the black Appalachian was overlooked, although he was worse off economically than the white Appalachian and his troubles were compounded by racial discrimination. Aside from a lot of publicity, not much has been done for whites a decade after the discovery of Appalachia. And less has been done for black people."[3]

There is a dearth of statistics on the plight of blacks in Appalachia, especially in the Central and Southern regions. But it seems doubtful that their plight is hardly better than the pessimistic statistics for blacks generally. Herbert Hill, in the *University of Colorado Law Review,* estimates that at the present rate of income increase, equality (economic parity) with whites will be achieved (by blacks) by the year 2275, a period of over *three centuries.*[4]

Black Appalachians, if there is a general problem characteristic, suffer most from discrimination, malnutrition and those related problems produced by mechanization in agriculture. Yet, the major thrust for reforms in the region is directed toward the mining industry and concomitant problems such as black lung, miner's pensions, widow's benefits . . . hardly the type of "universals" which take into account the problems faced by all Appalachians.

Racism in hiring, discrimination in public welfare, poor nutrition, bad housing, and discrimination in education, coupled with labor, hiring and safety issues in the mining industry, would more nearly address the plight of Appalachia, both black and white. For instance: "thirty-nine percent of the black people in West Virginia are below the poverty level. This is approximately twice as high as the percentage of whites (21.6) in poverty."[5] Yet, these statistics are hardly ever used to describe the Appalachian problem.

Further, West Virginia, the most pivotal Appalachian state with its 67,342 black citizens, has not managed to draw attention to their plight which finds that one quarter of the black homes in the state lack some or all plumbing facilities. This is over 50 percent more than white homes in the same condition.[6]

The exodus of the young, talented black population from the Region continues unabated, despite the fact that the flight to the cities seems to have abated somewhat for blacks nationally. It remains to be seen whether the consequences of this flight will be beneficial to the black Appalachian, since the consequences of migration are still being debated. In many ways the flight has been a detrimental one to the Region since outmigration drains it of its youth and talent; talent needed to rebuild the Region.

Historically, other regions have gained by having Appalachian blacks, owing to their particular zeal and creative individualism. Booker T. Washington, born at Malden, West Virginia, comes to mind, as well as Charley Pride, entertainer, Carl T. Rowan, journalist, Dick Allen of the Chicago White Sox, Robert Horton of the Detroit Tigers, and many others. Black Appalachians can be found in the forefront of their professions nationally, as civic leaders, social welfare professionals, educators and, under proper conditions, the finest products of Appalachia.

Unfortunately, Appalachia has been painted with the broad stroke of a white brush which has obliterated and distorted the contributions of its second largest population group. It is time that Appalachia confronted this oversight and examined the nature of the black Appalachian experience. A close look at the system will reveal, among other things, rampant "institutional" forms of racism. Few blacks in the region can find reasonable employment, and are often denied employment through discrimination in union and job practices. Even the United Mine Workers Union, the most non-discriminating American union movement, cannot boast of blacks in key union positions. Education, though under a non-discriminatory mandate, finds a dearth of black teachers and the racial tensions between black students and the white schools, throughout the region, is becoming much more the rule than the exception. The black student is systematically denied access to higher education, except in so far as he has an athletic talent to parlay into grants-in-aid. If he has his wits about him, he seeks a school outside the region which satisfies his desire to socialize with other blacks. Should he remain in the region, he may attend college for four years without seeing a black faculty member.

Many solutions have been proposed to solve the problem of the "invisible" black population but no solution will meet with success unless it secures the cooperation of white Appalachians of influence who are willing to risk reaffirming the place of blacks in Appalachian history, who are not passive toward racism and the struggle for social justice, and who value the "total" Appalachian experience rather than the myopic, pathological conception of Appalachia as a scattered, whites-only ghetto whose basic needs can be met with increased black lung benefits.

CONCLUSIONS

At a time when the South has awakened to the counterproductiveness of racial discrimination, Appalachia as a region and West Virginia, within its heartland, seems more than ever committed to the divisive principle of "separate but equal" for blacks and whites in education, in housing, in social and political access. To date there appears to be only one organization committed to the plight of black Appalachians, the Black Appalachian Commission (BAC). Founded in 1969 under the auspices of the Council of Southern Mountains, the BAC has established an agenda for Appalachian blacks which includes: priority setting and resource allocation of federal and non-federal programs which are aimed at Appalachia, to insure that black needs are articulated; mobilizing and focusing the resources of the black community on issues related to it. The organization is based in Atlanta, Georgia, but plans to move to either West Virginia or Kentucky soon.

Most states within or bordering the Region have State Human Rights Commissions concerned about discrimination but they are hamstrung by public apathy and indifference. The problem of racial discrimination in the Appalachian Region is not exclusively one of legislative enterprise but one of heart, soul, and feeling. Beginning with each individual in each hamlet or city, the Appalachian must commit himself to an open society, free of class and racial discrimination—a people-centered effort to restore to the Region its own unique history of effective integration and full participation.

The author is pessimistic, feeling that the ravages of exploitative industrialism have left a deep scar on the relations between blacks and whites, but a beginning can be made through citizen pressure on groups and institutions such as:

1. Higher Education, which should establish affirmative action programs to increase the participation of black and poor white Appalachians at that level. These institutions must be encouraged to train better teachers, social workers, nurses, etc. who are free of racial stereotypes and would become the core of an effective leadership group committed to combating racial discrimination.
2. Since it is likely that blacks in the Region will never have the numbers nor the indignation to force change in an apathetic system, white action groups must take the lead in combating the myths and stereotypes of racism. Racism is a white problem and discrimination in public accommodations affect the business and social atmosphere of a community to the extent that all of the community suffers, businesses will not relocate into it, talented people will not settle there, and the youth of that community will not remain. The exodus from the South in the 1950s was just not one of economics but one of an atmosphere in which young people could no longer stomach a regressive society. Appalachia is rapidly gaining this image.
3. Appalachian political institutions are among the few in America in which no blacks are represented . . . black candidates should be found and encouraged to run for office and engage in partisan political activity based on coalitions of black and white interest groups.
4. Public education has been described as the most racist institution in America and only a concerted effort on the part of Appalachians will succeed in getting the bigots out of the classroom; of providing relevant educational experiences in black history and the black experience at that level for black as well as white students. This is the least optimistic proposal as it seems racial tensions are increasing in our primary and secondary schools at a time when, perhaps, we have the least knowledgeable and racially astute core of educators to handle such incidences.
5. No single effort or movement designed to change the Appalachian situation should be conceived of without input from the black community; not a "token" to meet federal or state guidelines, but because it is right and in the interest of justice. This means that

white organizers must make a conscious effort to insure the participation of all interested in their efforts, not conveniently discounting blacks because there is no "highly" visible population nearby.

If Appalachia is to evade the consequences of a "redneck" or "cracker" image, steps must be taken to redress the plight of its black citizens. By "whitening" the problem, Appalachia has insured the entrenchment of race hatred and stamped itself as a closed society, unchanging and unchangeable, and with it goes the once proud heritage of a people who refused to participate in a system which would pit them against their neighbors over something as inconsequential as skin color.

1. Mike Ross, "Mike Ross Talks about the Life Style of the Coal Miner," *UMWJ,* July 1, 1970 (reprint).

2. See chapter 17, this book.

3. Jack Guillebeaux, "Appalachian Blacks Are Getting Themselves Together," *Raleigh* (N.C.) *News and Observer,* Aug. 6, 1972.

4. Herbert Hill, *University of Colorado Law Review,* as quoted in West Virginia Human Rights Commission, *The Combined Annual Report* (Charleston, W. Va., Dec. 1972), p. 16.

5. Ibid.; U. S. Bureau of the Census, *Census Report, 1970* (Washington, D.C., 1971).

6. *Census Report, 1970,* p. 37.

17

Not Just Whites in Appalachia

JACK GUILLEBEAUX

During the early 1960s, America discovered Appalachia. Here tucked away among the stunningly beautiful mountains and valleys of a region that stretches from Mississippi to New York were millions of white Americans locked in a cycle of poverty and despair which rivaled the plight of the underdeveloped nations.

Congress passed the Appalachian Regional Development Act in 1965, and the Appalachian Regional Commission was created. In came the poverty fighters, the big money, the special programs and studies. Almost a billion dollars has been poured into the region since the inception of the Commission.

But it was not until the annual meeting of the Council of Southern Mountains in 1969 that the black Appalachian was recognized. At this meeting pressure was put on the council to choose its board members from among the poor and to fight the battles of strip mining and control of the region's natural resources. Three new commissions were established—the Commission on Youth, the Poor People's Self Help Commission and the Black Appalachian Commission (BAC). The latter was the first recognition of the fact that the plight of black people is an integral part of the definition of Appalachia and its problems.

Although more than 1,400,000 Appalachians are black, one out of every 14, they somehow remained invisible during the discovery of "white Appalachia." When the region was being studied and new programs planned, the black Appalachian was overlooked, although he was worse off economically than the white Appalachian and his troubles were compounded by racial discrimination.

Aside from a lot of publicity, not much has been done for whites a decade after the discovery of Appalachia. And less has been done for black people. But the poor and their leaders have finally realized that it is they themselves who must break the "cycle of poverty." And they are beginning to move.

Activity began slowly for the Black Appalachian Commission. For almost a year it had no money to call its members together. Finally, with the financial assistance of three organizations, a meeting of approximately 70 black leaders was called to broaden the base of BAC and discuss priorities for the group. After much discussion and planning and with the substantial support of yet another organization, BAC received funds, some of which were channeled through CSM, to begin a study of blacks in the region and to mobilize them.

In July, 1971, the efforts and sacrifices of many months came to fruition.

More than 200 black people answered the call for the first Black Appalachian Conference at Black Mountain, N.C. Resource persons representing more than 25 national and regional organizations and agencies attended the conference. To their surprise, they learned that many resources existed in the "audience"; here were people who had the experience and expertise needed to develop the black community. Beyond the sharing of much information, many acquaintances were made and plans were set for the continuation of a black regional program. Perhaps the most important thing that began was the very real functioning of a regional community.

The groundwork was laid for black Appalachians to begin the process of freeing themselves from poverty and oppression as a community. Part of the excitement of this event was reflected by the fact that many conferees, after a full weekend of meetings, stayed on to compare notes, make plans, and share fellowship with the brothers and sisters they had so recently met.

At this time BAC is still in the early stages of development. Meet some of the people who helped in its organization and now serve on its board of directors.

Carl Johnson, chairman of the board of directors, lives in Hillcrest Apartments in Asheville, N.C. Almost five years ago Carl organized the tenants in the public housing project in which he lives to protest the neglect and deterioration of the community. Changes and improvements were sought through a rent strike. After many weeks of ridicule, persecution, and extreme pressure from the press, the Housing Authority and the power structure of the city, Carl and the strikers won their battle. As a result of the strike, the housing administrator was fired and major improvements were made on the apartments. Recognition and representation was given to the tenants' organization in the decision-making process. The power relationship between blacks and the city administration was altered positively, and Carl was recognized as a powerful and important leader in Asheville.

Because Carl is a man of limitless energy, he is into many things, is known in national circles, and is the man who probably has given most to the development of the Black Appalachian Commission.

Don Pitts of Beckley, W. Va., is a struggling young lawyer who has committed himself to tackling cases with high social value—police brutality and civil rights violations—but low profit. But don't feel sorry for Don; he seems content with his modest home, the modest office on which he did the carpentry work, and the more than modest challenge he has set for himself. His services are sought even by whites who turn to him as the only lawyer who will fight the system. Don also has an eye for politics, and is now in a race for a seat on the house of delegates of the West Virginia State Legislature. The threats and intimidations that Don and his family have faced are a part of his struggles to relieve the oppression of the poor in West Virginia.

Joe Grant of Spartanburg, S.C., is a student at Wofford College. Like many black college students, Joe's education is coming to him at a sacrifice. That is not an obstacle, however. Neither are all the ramifications of living in public housing, for Joe Grant is an activist. He is interested in politics and has worked in many political campaigns and voter registration projects. He was active in a third party effort in South Carolina. Joe is interested in the history and implications of third party politics as they relate to the black community. If you talk to Joe you get the feeling you are talking with a person who has somewhere to go and knows how to get there.

Mrs. Mary Brown of Abingdon, Va., recently spent a few days in the hospital. The pressure of weeks and weeks of fighting her CAP director, board, and what seemed to her like the whole world, got to be too much. Mary is recognized throughout her community as an established leader who is trying to make the CAP serve the poor. After the battle in the program that eventually caused Mary to be publicly cursed and slandered, we find Mary back in the arena and her director gone. If you know Mary Brown, you can't feel too sorry for her because she is a born fighter who does not pity herself even though her struggles are constant and difficult. Fortunately for Mary her strong interest in her community is equaled by that of her husband Oscar Brown. If you are around Abingdon and hear someone say "look ahead and vote for Ned," you probably will be talking to a supporter of Oscar (Ned) Brown who is running for a post on the town council. The years of struggle have developed in him leadership qualities which he now shares with BAC.

Wilber Miller of Roosevelt City, Ala., has an easy-going manner which disguises a man of strong conviction, acutely aware of the black struggle and totally dedicated to his goal of helping to build Roosevelt City. Black folks in Roosevelt City who have decided to build an alternative to Birmingham have traveled a road paved with problems. Building Roosevelt City requires perseverance and a knowledge of laws and resources to get around barriers set by the power structure and to deal with the politics of the black and white communities. Wilber Miller now shares his abilities with other black leaders from across Appalachia as they attempt to build BAC as an alternative to powerlessness on the regional and national levels.

Similar qualities and strengths come from BAC's other board members: **John Price** of Kingsport, Tenn.; **Jeff Long** of Carrollton, Ga.; **Mrs. Helen Taylor** of Starkville, Miss.; **Mrs. Gwendolyn Shaw** of Asheville, N.C.; **Jesse Pennington** of West Point, Miss.; **Mrs. Viola Cleveland** of Middlesboro, Ky.; **Mrs. Barbara Jones** of Fairmont, W. Va.; **Mrs. Jean Smith** of Roanoke, Va.; **Mrs. Wylla Dean Harbin** of Harlan, Ky.; **Mrs. Alice Nixon** of Pittsburgh, Pennsylvania.

Where is BAC at this point and where is it trying to go?

BAC addresses itself to the nitty-gritty talk of mobilizing the resources of the Black Appalachian community. BAC will attempt to (1) become the tool that will increase communication between black leaders; (2) encourage and enable people to get together; (3) identify and channel resources to leaders and groups in the field; (4) attempt to become the organization through which black people throughout the region will speak to the problems and issues that affect them.

A little more than a year ago BAC confronted the Appalachian Regional Commission with its failure to meaningfully involve blacks in its programs. At that time ARC had no affirmative-action civil rights program. A recent ARC communication states: "The Commission adopted an equal opportunity grievance procedure for internal operations as well as an affirmative action policy for local development districts." But the communication credited this to President Nixon's stand on civil rights and equal employment, rather than to the Black Appalachian Commission's visit to the commission.

Obviously, black Appalachians must be able to watch and challenge federal programs and institutions that discriminate against blacks. And BAC must be a tool at the grass roots level for unifying blacks in the region.

Black Appalachians who are at the bottom of the socio-economic ladder in Appalachia have limited power as long as their struggles are isolated in Asheville, N.C., Hazard, Ky., Starkville, Miss., and Steubenville, Ohio. But the vision that was born in 1969 has become a reality. Today black Appalachians are combining their resources and acting as one community to challenge their oppressors, continue the fight for justice in their villages and towns and carry the battle to the nation's capitol.

PART SEVEN

Personal Anecdotal Accounts of Black Life

Part 7 seeks to link the scholarly and analytical tracts to the "word" as expressed in the recollections of blacks in the mountains. Reginald Millner conducted an oral history project which produced a narrative of his Virginia family which was drawn to West Virginia after the Civil War. As depicted by the son, the miner becomes the persona of black miners in the central highlands of West Virginia, where blacks concentrated to realize some of the gains of political enfranchisement.

A picture of the class distinctions among blacks in the mountains emerges from Pearl Cornett's foray into his own life. He was one of the thousands of black migrants from eastern Kentucky to Cincinnati and Cleveland, Ohio, but he returned. He recalls his atypical city experience as a college-educated black teacher and plant worker; he found "success" outside the hills, following the Appalachian hard-work ethic, and returned nostalgically to Hazard, Kentucky, after retirement. Pearl's story resembles that of the white return migrant and sharply differs from that of most emigrating blacks.

We have no way of gauging how many black "victims" of the coal and steel industry Dobbie Sanders represents as, in his eighty-fifth year, he talks with college students about life in the mills and mines of the Birmingham area. Militant in tone, the quick-paced passage combines the anger of a bitter man with factually sound information. Most likely the resulting picture, both positive and negative, typifies life for black Appalachians.

18

Conversations with the "Ole Man": The Life and Times of a Black Appalachian Coal Miner

REGINALD MILLNER

Lives of great men all remind us
  We can make our lives sublime,
And, departing, leave behind us
  Footprints on the sands of time;

Footprints, that perhaps another,
  Sailing o'er life's solemn main,
A forlorn and shipwrecked brother,
  Seeing, shall take heart again.
Henry Wadsworth Longfellow,
  "A Psalm of Life"

In 1951 when I was born, my father James Efferson Millner was 45 years old. Though over half of his life had already been lived, he was still quite an energetic man.

As I grew older I observed how the years began to take their toll on my father's health. Black lung, arthritis, diabetes, and being "just plain tired" were constantly deteriorating his health. However, he was never without kind words of advice and interesting experiences to share, or just general conversation. He loved to talk and I learned to listen.

This article, a small tribute to the man and his struggles, transcribed from taped interviews, is intended to give insight into the life of a Black Appalachian coal miner. I hope this interview conveys to you, the reader, a fair share of the information I most fortunately have received since the day I was born.

One day after this article was completed, on June 11, 1978, James Efferson Millner paid his final dues. He died in Princeton where he lived with his family for the past 28 years.

JAMES E. MILLNER

Well, as far back as I know and from what I have been told, it began with Matt and Henry Millner, my great-uncle and grandfather respectively. In 1869 when the Millner brothers came into Henry County, Virginia, there was great speculation as to where they came from or if they were on the run. It has been said that they were the slave descendants of the Patrick Henry plantation. Nonetheless, the brothers Millner settled, married, and began sharecropping on separate 40-acre farms in Henry County near Martinsville, Virginia.

My father, Henry II, born January 28, 1882, was the third son of Henry I, who was the younger of the original two Millner brothers. Henry I had nine children by his wife Sally Hairston Millner and three children out of wedlock. Henry as well as Matt recognized and supported all of their children as a matter of principal, a quality that was passed down through the Millner lineage.

Henry's sons were Moses, Matt, Henry my father, Efferson, and Tom, who is the only remaining member and who now lives in Martinsville, Virginia. The daughters were Anne, Judy, Amanda, and Eve. Henry II married Letcher Hairston in 1904 and she gave birth to a son, James Efferson Millner, on October 25, 1905, in Martinsville, Virginia.

Letcher Hairston was a strange blend of Spanish-Indian and African, as was Henry, except the Indian was more dominant in Letcher, especially in her temperament. I remember like yesterday an incident that happened with my mother when I was about seven years old. I came home from school and told her about my teacher whipping me, which I probably deserved. But my mother obviously didn't see it that way. She walked five miles to the school carrying my baby brother Joe in her arms, with me and my other brother Howard tagging along, whipped my teacher, and walked back home, all in time to prepare dinner for Poppa when he came home from the mines that evening.

She was a strong woman and Poppa was a very determined man. Sharecropping never agreed with my father. So he tried his hand on the railroad for a while before leaving Henry County in 1908 for the coalfields of southern West Virginia.

Eckman in McDowell County was where we first lived before moving to Flora—now called McComas—in Mercer County. I remember they had a saloon there where they made their own whiskey in the back. Mora was a boom town then where at one time over 10,000 people got their mail at the post office. Well, we finally settled in Berwind, also in McDowell County. Because of the terrible working conditions of those times—strikes and layoff—one was almost always looking for another job, and we, like most mining families, moved from one coal camp to another.

Poppa hadn't been working long at Berwind—braking—when 11 coal cars piled up on him December 24, 1911. The accident occurred as a result of a trapper not being in position on his job. A trapper is a man who opens and closes metal doors across the track in the mines which section off various compartments inside the mine. My father, who was the brakeman riding the front car, and the motorman on the last car had expected the door to open. They rammed into the door, cutting one of Poppa's legs completely off and crippling his other leg. The motorman was not injured.

We didn't live too far from the mine entrance on that Christmas Eve morning 1911, and I can vividly remember hearing Poppa scream at the top of his lungs as they brought him out of the mine on a stretcher. My mother was screaming while some women were holding her back and screaming too. The doctor walked alongside the stretcher injecting Poppa with a needle while a nurse soaked up blood and added bandages. The doctor stayed with Poppa all that day and late into the evening until the train came to carry him to the hospital in Welch.

Poppa stayed in and out of hospitals for a couple of years. When Momma died suddenly in July 6, 1913, of "overheating," Poppa had to be carried to the funeral in a chair. He couldn't walk for three years, during which time the Pocahontas Coal Company gave us a home to live in and $90 a month. Pus still oozed out of Poppa's crippled leg and he had to dress it twice a day, until one morning in 1922 when a piece of coal popped out of it. For 11 years the doctors had failed to detect the lump of coal in my father's leg.

After the accident, Poppa first got a job picking slate at the Sagamore tipple near McComas because the tipple boss there was also the foreman at the job where Poppa got hurt. The tipple boss said he had always felt responsible for the accident. Poppa had one wooden leg and the other was stiff. He walked on a crutch and a cane and carried two pearl-handled thirty-eights in his back pockets. He was always present and outspoken at all local union meetings, sold moonshine liquor, but didn't drink, and did whatever else was necessary to provide for his family.

In 1915 Poppa was remarried to a cousin of my mother's. "Cousin Sara," as we called her, was very antagonistic toward her three stepsons and eventually I had to leave in order to avoid the conflict between us. I first "shanied around"[1] with some other young miners in the McComas area. It was cheaper and easier to live that way rather than alone.

At the age of 17 I started working at the Grand Creek Mine in McComas loading coal and later as a brakeman. In those days a coal loader's job was about as rough work a man could do. This particular job required men working in pairs to first hand drill about ten or 12 holes in the facing of a wall of coal. The hand drill used was very similar to a large wooden hand drill. The two men would then set the holes with a half to a stick of dynamite, go about a hundred feet away to a seemingly safe area, and fire the charge. After waiting about ten or 15 minutes for the smoke to clear, the pair would then move in cautiously to first set the timber posts used for roof support and then with the use of a pick and a shovel load the large lumps of coal into coal cars.

Because of the low ceilings of from three to five feet in most mines, the work was always done with a bent back or while on the knees. On top of this, a coal loader was then paid according to the amount of coal he loaded. Man, it was really rough work. These conditions didn't change until the early 1950s when machine operations replaced the hand loading and hourly wages were also set.

One observation I want to make here is that the coal companies have always tried to further punish the old miner, who struggled so long and hard under such adverse conditions to give the miners of today the rights they deserve. One can easily view this through the inequality in the U.M.W. separate pension funds. Also, the fact that time and time again old miners are unduly denied their black lung benefits, because coal companies have destroyed records and company doctors won't acknowledge that a claimant has contracted the dread disease.

In many cases—a few close friends of mine have suffered the same fate—an old miner will die as a result of pneumoconiosis (black lung) before he has had a chance to use the money awarded him, and often before his claim has even been processed. The miner's family would then receive the benefits, but as usual his struggle as a miner has carried him to his grave.

After working about two years, I left the Crane Creek Mine and got a job at the Sagamore Mine across the road, also in McComas. This was a much better job. I went on as a brakeman in the mines and later I worked at the cleaning tipple which was cleaner and safer work than on the inside.

There were few Black motormen in the mines at that time, so braking was about as good of a job as one would expect to get. I was a damn good brakeman. A good motorman would like to work with brakemen like me. I could cut loose eight or ten cars at a time, let them shoot into a section of the mines on their own momentum, run ahead of the string of empties, as they were called, and brake, and set them so they could be loaded. Then I had to catch my motorman on up the main line and repeat the maneuver. Otherwise, the motorman would have to push the cars off on to their individual sections, and my job would only have been to get off, cut them loose, and get the brakes. Therefore, a good brakeman like me, could save quite a bit of time and money for a coal company.

The coalfields were virtually a melting pot of various cultures. There were Spanish, Hungarians, Italians, Blacks, and native whites working and inter-mingling in and around the McComas area during the 1900s and 1920s. In my opinion there was more interrelating between the four immigrant groups and Blacks than between the native whites and any other single group. This is probably because there was more trust between the non-English-speaking people and the Blacks as opposed to between the whites and the non-English-speaking people. As a result of the mutual trust as well as the language barrier, Blacks were oftentimes chosen representatives of the immigrant community. There was a large concentration of Italian miners in these southern coalfields. As a result the Italian "Black Hand" was an active force in the area.

One of my most outstanding memories is of the time I was about 11 years old when we lived in Piedmont in McDowell County and I was on my way to the company store for Poppa. It was winter and there was snow on the ground. A man ran down the hill from a house above the company store, but before he reached the bottom another man came out of the same house, pulled a gun, and fired three shots into the fleeing man's chest as he turned trying to pull his revolver from his pocket to defend himself. The man on the porch put his pistol back into his coat pocket and walked back across the hill. The other man lay dead in the blood-red snow at the bottom of the hill. I immediately learned the rule of the three monkeys: see no evil, speak no evil, hear no evil. The police questioned me several times about the killing but no one was ever identified.

There was a Black detective from Welch, in McDowell County, named Joe Possums, who was famous for having gone all the way to Italy to bring back two members of the notorious "Black Hands." Possums successfully apprehended the two men, contacted Italian authorities and had the men extradited back to McDowell County where they were tried and convicted of murder and sentenced to Moundsville.

Poppa was a good friend of Joe Possums. He once hired Possums to look for me when I ran away from home to avoid a beating from Poppa, because of something my stepmother had told him. I had gone across Northfork Mountain to Northfork Hollow and first lived with a couple of "shaney guys" from Georgia. I told them I didn't have a home. They had planned to take me home to Georgia on the next trip and leave me on their farm. They treated me very good—bought me magazines and clothes—but I soon left them for another family.

My new family consisted of a man and a woman who didn't have any children. They too were good to me, and it was about three or four months after I had run away that I was finally discovered. I was setting on the porch reading a magazine when a woman who was an old friend of Poppa's came by. When I saw her, I jumped up and ran and hid in the toilet, but the woman followed me to the door and ordered me to come on out. I remember her words. "James, your Poppa is about to go crazy looking for you, come out of there, boy!" Poppa had hired Joe Possums, who had searched down home in Virginia and all around the area for any sign of me. Possums was unsuccessful and only charged Poppa 50 dollars for the three-month search.

Poppa was also a good friend of the Black Sheriff Calhoun of McDowell County. During the 1920s the Black county of McDowell, once called "the free state of McDowell County," was in its heyday. Not only were there Black law officers and public officials but also doctors and judges. Poppa had known most of these men from the 1900s before his accident. He had spent time drinking and socializing in the company of these men. Of course later Poppa never drank alcohol, though he sold it as well as made wine every spring, which he usually gave away as gifts.

In 1925 I moved to Raleigh County, primarily because Alec Tabb, a friend from McComas, had wanted me to play ball with them. I started braking at the East Gulf mine and started playing second and third base for the East Gulf Red Sox. Whites and Blacks played in two separate and unequal leagues. The Black league definitely had the superior ball players. And the McComas Monarchs definitely had an overall superior ball team. When we beat the Bluefield Smart Sets in 1928 for the championship, I played catcher and second base. Roosevelt Carter, from Crystal, West Virginia, was also in the McComas area, pitched that game. He was one hellava pitcher. He could put more stuff on a ball than you could come up with names for.

Roosevelt once stood in as a pitcher for the Smart Sets against the well-known Satchel Paige and the Homestead Grays of the old Negro League. Roosevelt won that game, and each team split a doubleheader that day. Roosevelt had a well-deserved reputation as a pitcher, as did Alec Tabb who was famous for his fast ball. I used to catch for Alec, and, man, was he fast! I was also always a hell of a hitter. I hit quite a few home runs for the Monarchs but started striking out from overswinging when I was hitting most of my home runs. My batting was better when I just tried to get a good hit.

Some of the other outstanding teams in the coalfields were the Elkhorn Red Sox, who finally beat us for the championship. The Raleigh Clippers were also one of the best teams around, and the Bishop State Liners were plenty good—they were the best around for years.

However, in 1928 I was married for the first time to Lucille Graves, after which I returned to Martinsville, Virginia, to work pushing bricks in a wheelbarrow at a brickyard. I fell off a scaffold, broke three ribs, and ended up back in the West Virginia coalfields.

My youngest brother Joe died suddenly in 1929. It was said that he was poisoned by a second cousin over a mutual girl friend they had. Poppa had three children by his second marriage. They are Melinda, Francis, and Lee, all of whom Howard and I loved very much and helped in any way we could. However, they were never as close as Howard, Joe, and I, and now there was only Howard and I.

In 1929 when the bottom fell out of the stock market, I was braking at the Sycamore Mine of Pocahontas Fuel Company and had just received a raise. Of course I was laid off immediately like most men, and I went to hoboing. I hopped a train going to Portsmouth, Ohio, and rode as far as the outskirts of Columbus. There were men hoboing all along the tracks and hobo camps were everywhere. Sometimes I would see whole families hoboing. Conditions were unbelievable.

There was no work to be found in Ohio, so another fellow and I caught a drag of empties back into West Virginia. I came through Vulcan and Iaeger, where I bathed and shaved in the Tug River. After sleeping all night on a pile of crossties, a fellow hobo gave me some cornbread and piece of fatback. It was one of the best meals I ever ate. Man, I was hungry!

A train once stopped in a tunnel near Cedar Bluffs and as a result of me being too close to the engine I nearly suffocated. I was green when I first started hoboing but I became very good at hopping trains. I had some good teachers. There, amongst those wandering hobos, were some of the most intelligent men you ever wanted to meet. Many had traveled across country several times, had an abundance of knowledge and compassion, and gave it up readily. It's strange but I felt very close to those men who I never would see again, at least in this life.

After barely escaping with my life several times and avoiding railroad "dicks"[2] all the time, I finally came home to my wife Lucille who was working for some big shots in Bluefield, Virginia. She occupied one small room above a garage belonging to the people she worked for. I began to get one or two days of work a week in the mines. One Christmas Eve I worked and drew $5.00 in scrip. I borrowed $5.00 from a friend and put on my only pair of bibbed overalls. We bought a quart of homebrew. It was Prohibition and times were hard, but we had one hell of a Christmas.

After Roosevelt came to office things began to pick up. Roosevelt also gave us, the miners, the rights to organize under N.R.A. [National Recovery Administration, 1933-1935] and we grew strong. Poppa was always involved in the Mine Workers Union, but I became active in about '30 or '31. I was first chosen as recording secretary for the United Mine Workers Local 6031, Sycamore. I gave that position up after two terms to serve as check weighman for the same local.

This was the heyday of the U.M.W. and we became strong under John L. Lewis's leadership. In the strike of '36 we provided for the striking miner by taking all the funds from the Union Treasury and buying the necessary goods, which miners would then sign for and repay back into the fund when work continued. Only as a result these Union stores, known as "jot 'em down stores," a lot of people were able to make it until the strike was over. I served six terms as a check weighman and several terms as a committee man, and I've seen the company do some awful things to some people.

I remember while I was acting recording secretary for Sycamore 6031 when the local president came to me to borrow some union funds. I declined, but the man was in bad shape and his family had no food. I gave him $15 out of my own pocket and had him sign a paper that the funds came directly from me and not the union fund. The Pocahontas Fuel Company had pressured the man into this situation by not allowing him credit at the company store and by working him in the worst areas in the mines.

I could get credit at the company store only after I became a check weighman and they knew I was making good money. Some men would draw checks with a yellow snake on the envelopes which meant that funds, sometimes a man's entire wages, were taken out for debts owed at the company store. Grown men would stand there and cry after receiving a check that had been so tagged. In some cases coal companies would even pay men in scrip that could only be cashed at the high priced company stores.

It was virtually slavery!

However, it was under Roosevelt and N.R.A. which gave miners the right to collective bargaining that enabled the U.M.W. to grow strong. Lewis had been head of the U.M.W. in the 1920s but didn't have the tools until N.R.A. in the '30s gave him clout to come back and build the strongest union in the nation.

In 1939 my father, like all the old and crippled miners, was cut off by the coal company. In the same year, while I was check weighman, Derrick Stamper, a few more local union officials, and I were investigated by the F.B.I. for communist activities. Of course none of us were guilty of anything more than reading the *Daily Worker,* the communist paper. The same thing occurs today and probably more frequently.

In 1943 I left West Virginia after failing the draft intentionally for the third and last time, because of high blood pressure. A couple of fellows, my brother Howard, and I all went for induction at the same time. We drank moonshine and took aspirins, and rubbed lye soap under our armpits, in order to raise our blood pressure. It worked for all of us except Howard, who was inducted and luckily survived the service and the War.

I first landed a job reserved for whites only, at the shipyard in Wilmington, Delaware. My identity was never discovered to be "coloured." Later I got a job in Philadelphia at the Buds Machine Plant. It was here that I became most aware of the communist movement in the United States. I attended meetings and carried a membership card for a while, and again I was investigated for communist activities. One morning I came downstairs from my apartment onto Opal Street where I lived in Philly. There was a young blond-headed man with a light colored overcoat on the doorstep. He asked for me by name and when I identified myself he flashed his F.B.I. identification and told me he would like to ask me some questions. We talked briefly about my communist activities and he left. I found it all quite amusing.

I remember when Henry Wallace was nominated for President of the United

States on the Progressive ticket at Shide Park in Philadelphia, Pennsylvania, in 1948. A crowd of 18,000 people rose to their feet as a man rode in, standing up in the back of a convertible Cadillac. We thought it was Henry Wallace but we were not a bit surprised to see Paul Robeson, with both hands clinched and raised in the victory salute—coming in standing in the back of a Cadillac.

Paul Robeson could move people like no one else. His acting, his singing, his words, and particularly his deeds were always outstanding. Black union men like Richard L. Davis, who also became the victim of institutionalized attacks directed against those seriously involved in the struggle for the betterment of the masses.

The communists, like the unions, have always been quick to use Blacks for organizational purposes but have deserted them, like rats leaving a sinking ship, when they came under fire. This is the greatest hypocrisy of the struggle. Along with Paul Robeson was singer Frank Sinatra, who was a communist sympathizer. But look at where the two men are today!

Another example is John L. Lewis, who sold us out by making no provision for protecting the workers he already had when mechanism came in. As a result, mostly Blacks were laid off while whites were trained to operate the machines. Again Blacks felt the brunt of the change caused by another curve in the road to industrialization. I know a lot of old miners at least felt let down by John L. Lewis after we all worked so hard and sacrificed so much to get the union where we did.

Lucille, my first wife, and I never really made it very well together. At first our marriage was fine, but she started to get on the bottle pretty heavy as time went on. We spent most of our 20-year marriage separated. We finally got our divorce finalized in 1943 and I never saw her again. In 1955 they found her body chopped up in a bag at a Cleveland garbage dump. She was a very beautiful woman and I loved her very much but we probably married too young. Luckily, we never had any children.

I was remarried in 1944 to Lucy Hodge and we started a family. Now, we first lived in Wilmington, Delaware, and then in Philadelphia, Pennsylvania. I never liked the atmosphere of the overcrowded city, so we returned to West Virginia in 1950. I worked in a punch mine for a while and then I worked on the building of the West Virginia Turnpike. We worked 12 hours a day for $1.50 an hour, and many violations in construction were overlooked in the hasty work that was half-done on that turnpike. I injured my back while working and received compensation for a while. When my compensation ran out we were in the mid-'50s depression. I had sold moonshine in the '30s, so I returned to my old craft in order to support my family, while working part-time washing cars.

In 1959 on Thanksgiving Eve, I was arrested by Federal revenuers while bringing 48 gallons of moonshine out of Virginia across Pocahontas Mountain. It was an obvious setup. I received three years probation because I had a family. I returned to Philly to work construction with my brother Howard, who maintained a little position in his local union. After a year and half in Philly, I returned to West Virginia and landed a bullshit political job as a custodian at the State Road office building in Princeton. I also became very involved in the N.A.A.C.P. and the Community Action Program; the Civil Rights Movement was still pretty big then.

We integrated schools and school activities, the Y.M.-Y.W.C.A. in Bluefield, City Park, and park facilities in Princeton and demanded equal hiring and
firing practice throughout the area. We also sued the State and city police for
civil rights violations, as well as the well-known Shotts of Bluefield, West
Virginia, for monopolizing the media. We won most of it, and that is only a
fraction of the fight we've fought here in Mercer County area.

My greatest personal satisfaction came in winning a $20,000 black lung
settlement after fighting the coal companies I worked for, the lawyers I hired, the
doctors, and the courts—but after five long years I won.

One factor I have to recognize here is the fact that on the final appeal in my
black lung case I was delighted to see a Black judge hearing my case. I was
proud to see the man in that position. I was also sure that his ears would be more
sympathetic in my cause than his previous colleagues'. My delight proved right.
Twenty thousand dollars is a meager amount to receive at the cost of one's
health, but if I had to do it all over again I think I would do it the same way,
except for a few minor changes viewed through wiser eyes.

You see, it was basically the principals my father laid down before me that
guided me to where I am today. I had no recourse or desire to do anything except
to step in those footprints—that my father left imprinted "in the sands of
time"—and to always continue in the struggle.

1. "Shanied around" refers to a shantey, a small one- or two-room shack usually owned by a
coal company or simply abandoned, but used by various working miners as they migrated from coal
camp to coal camp.

2. Railroad "dicks" is a term used by hobos for the railroad detective, who posed a daily
hazard for the hobo.

19

The Mountain Negro of Hazard, Kentucky

PEARL CORNETT

The reason we left Kentucky, we thought that there wasn't [enough] income coming to the family to educate our children and do the things we felt parents should be able to do. This was back in the early fifties; teachers' salaries were low and the biggest industry in these mountains was coal. Many of the coal camps were closing and men were leaving the mines and going to northern cities to get work. At that time my salary was about $225 a month. This was for ten months of the year. I was principal at Dunham High School in Letcher County, Kentucky, [which] was all black.

Then you heard a great talk about integrating the schools in Kentucky. [As a black] I feared integration in that they might integrate the students and not the teachers, and I thought black teachers would be cast aside and white teachers would be retained. Now in Kentucky I can definitely say that this was an ungrounded fear because they did use the black teachers.

[My mother] didn't like the idea of me leaving. None of my people, the older ones, felt that I should go. I didn't tell them I thought that I would be unemployed if the schools were integrated. My real reasons, I just didn't reveal to anyone. My wife and I, we just felt that we'd have a better chance to make a go of it and this, I guess, meant income, because we didn't feel that we were making the money we should make. I taught with many women who was married to coal miners and the coal miners that did have work made good money. So, socially there was a difference: they had income from their husbands and their own income, and when you take $225 against what they had, why it just sort of gives you a feeling of insecurity among the people that I worked with. Those were some of the reasons that I left.

I was born and reared right here near Town Mountain. My mother was a highly motivated person. Although she had very little education she expected a great deal out of her children. She expected education to solve all of our problems. Even our father who had about a second-grade education, his idea was, "Educate my children." That's all they talked about in the home. There were eight of us and we lived in a common ordinary home here in the mountains, but it seems like they always dreamed that if they could just educate their children that would be fulfillment for all the insecurities, and all the things they longed for in their lives. Even after our dad died when I was thirteen, [Mother] never let us get to the point where we felt that we couldn't do what had to be done. Her idea was: you don't feel sorry for yourself, you just get out and work for what you want. She had many character-building mottos. Any time I said, "I can't" do something, she'd say:

I can't is a coward,
A poor, pale, puny imp.
No meal in his bag
And he walks with a limp.

She would just make you see what "I can't" was.

She sang a great deal in her work. Sometimes I'd kid her: "Mama, do you ever get tired of singing?" She'd say, "Alas for those who do not sing and die and carry all their music with them." She was a wonderful, wonderful person that would inspire you without you really knowing what she was doing.

[When I finished the eighth grade] rumors were that a high school [for blacks] was going to start and my aunt taught the ninth grade one year to give us a start so we wouldn't have to go away from home. The next year they did start a county school for blacks in Vicco, that's thirteen miles away, and a city school for whites here in Hazard. It had to be done on a segregated basis because of [the] Day law. Some man by the name of Day around 19 and 8 had a law written into the Kentucky constitution about educating blacks and whites in the same building. Anyone who taught mixed classes would be fined a hundred dollars a day, and any student who sat in mixed classes would be fined fifty dollars a day. That was the Day law. So we had to catch a taxi at our own expense and pay our way to Vicco to get to the county school. I went to school there [for the tenth grade] and then for the second year [of high school I went to Cincinnati].

I found out after I got there that I was nothing like ready to be a junior in high school [so I repeated the tenth grade in Cincinnati]. I think that was one of the best things that [could have] happened, [because] I did get a good education from one of the very best high schools in the country. There I was very backwards, although I had always thought at home here that I was very bright and wide awake. I'd never been out of these hills before and [was suddenly] turned loose in a large five-story school building, a block long each way, where classes changed on bells. I remember having my schedule so messed up I'd always end up with the same two classes in the afternoon because I was using my lunch period for a class period. The first evening when school was out I kept going all the way around this building looking for a way out. There was no exits on the basement floor to the street; you had to come up a flight of steps to get out. I don't know how many times I circled trying to get out of the building.

I was just about the most homesick person that you'd want to see. I remember I went to a movie one night and Kentucky was the setting. You could hear the whippoorwill just as plain; Will Rogers was setting there rocking; and Stepin Fetchit was playing "The sun shines bright in my old Kentucky home." I couldn't hold it back, I just boohooed. I wanted to get home so badly. After I stayed there enough to get oriented I began to enjoy it. I would come home every summer and I'd really look forward to going back and would be afraid that for some reason I wouldn't get to go back to finish high school.

[I graduated from Woodward in '35 and] this was those hard years, Depression years, so there wasn't much work to get. I came back home and this was when I realized that I'd have to go on to college. I went to Kentucky State College in Frankfort in '35, finished college there, and then came back home to start teaching for $89.10 a month. [By] '47 I was [teaching], driving a school bus [and] I coached football for about $200 a month. After I made principal I got $225 a month.

I [had] a friend that I'd gone to college with that lived in Ohio, who was urging me, "Come to Cleveland, come to Cleveland. You can make it big." I left this principal's job. My superintendent hated to see me go. He said, "This is the way you fellows do: you run away when things are booming outside and then when things get tough you'll be back looking for jobs."

We stayed in [Cleveland's] inner city for less than a year [and] I told Eloise, "Honey, we've got to find us a place outside of Cleveland, or we've got to go back home, one, because this is no place to bring up children." Having studied some of these social problems that [cities] have, I guess that made me more familiar with what I'd see going on. I know there's many people that live in the ghettos who have outstanding families and I think there are many, many losers who have lost their families that live in ghettos and I just didn't want to have to take that chance. If we had had to live in the inner city I guess I would have been back home quicker because the inner city is definitely a poor place to bring up kids.

We bought thirty-five acres of land [in] a small rural suburb of Cleveland [that had] good farm land, all level and tillable. I don't know how we were lucky enough to [buy] that because many blacks had been looking for a place like that. I guess that whole spirit that I was telling you about my mother had something to do with it: whatever you want you just go after. Wanting a place out, I just begin to look. When I'd see a place advertised I'd go out and check on it. I know a lot of black people would have somebody else call and they'd start getting the runaround early. We found this place, the owner was wanting to get away from Cleveland in the worst sort of way. I bought it with a friend of mine that worked at the same plant I worked at. We had a two-family house on this farm, with up and down, so he and I went in together and bought it.

I guess we'd been there three or four months and been making the payments [when our] real estate dealer come out one day. He said, "Boys, I haven't been telling you fellows this, but they've been raising a lot of Cain about you. They are wanting to get you out of the community in the worst kind of way. Some of the influential people out here have forced the Westside Federal to foreclose, but don't worry, I've been doing some work."

There was a Negro group that was taking over a savings and loan charter. He knew the ones in charge and he told them about us. This fellow that was head of Supreme Savings and Loan came out and looked at our place. We were working, sweating away, when he came. He liked what he saw. He said, "Boys, don't worry about your farm, I'm going to buy this mortgage." We never had any more trouble after that. The first few Sundays we was out there the cars would come by just bumper to bumper, filled with whites staring, looking at us, to see what's going on. That was the movement, I guess, to get us out.

The kids enjoyed everything they had there. They had good standing in the school, in the community, in the church. We worked with people and served on committees; just really lived a real involved life.

I worked for General Motors, mostly, as an arc welder. A big corporation like that is very impersonal. *Who* is General Motors? You never heard of him. It's some foreman standing over you that's trying to push out of you all the production he can for somebody that's going to get a big vacation out of it, or a big bonus. You do have the feeling that you're sweating for somebody else's glory. The attitude towards work a lot of times on these jobs is to do as little as possible. In your small towns you'd have people who're more interested in giving a fair day's work for a fair day's pay. In the city a lot of times they like workers from the Appalachian region for the fact that they'd put in a fuller day than the average city worker. They'd been used to hard work: mining, farming, or whatever. In the city fellows were used to an easier pace and you'd come up with some hard work, he just sort of shirked it and shunned it.

At one time I guess we had this feeling that we would not come back, but I could never completely cut the ties with the mountains because my people were here. When we both began to feel this way we just decided to come home and we haven't regretted it.

Looking back how would you compare the quality of life in Cleveland and Hazard?

This doesn't have near as much to offer socially and culturally that a place like Cleveland has [where] there are all kinds of stage plays, ice follies, and athletics going on. All year long there is something to attend or something to go to that's really exciting and worthwhile. There's no comparison along those lines. You might say, "Why would you leave a place like that to come back?" and many people don't. In my case, those things just don't hold the fascination for me that they held at one time. Having seen it, why it's not hard to walk away from. It all depends upon what you're looking for. If it's peace and quiet you probably want to get away from the crowds and the pushing. Anything you went to, there was a large crowd.

Maybe the things that I really set value on were things of childhood, the things my mother said, her simple ways of looking at life and some of her mottos, things that seemed to apply more in a city like this than they would in a place like Cleveland. I guess if I'd been born and reared in a place like Cleveland I'd probably never come to a place like Hazard to live, but having been born and reared here it was pretty easy to come back to.

In a small town everybody knows you, everybody speaks. [I'll] be in the garden working and I'll see a hand [wave], sometimes a white hand, sometimes a black, it doesn't matter. Same thing if I go down to the bank, I can stop and chat with the teller quite a while. This means a lot. I'll go to a Little League baseball game, well, you're sitting up there with the mayor and he knows you. When you go to a Little League baseball game in Cleveland I'd know a few of the parents, but I wouldn't know any mayors. There's not the rush and the dog-eat-dog atmosphere in a small town that you have in the city. Seems like everybody takes things seriously. It's just the old traditional way that they go about religion, even. Of course, I don't get along with that so much. The church in Cleveland was far more active, the outreach was much greater than it is here. When you think about ministers from Yale Divinity School compared to some of the ministers we have here, there's quite a difference. All in all, I think a small town compensates in other ways for some of the things that you give up in a city like Cleveland. Many of [our friends in Cleveland] couldn't understand why we wanted to come back. They thought, "Oh, you're glad to be in a place like this and not in the mountains of Kentucky," but they didn't realize how I felt about it.

20

"If I Could Go Back . . .":
An Interview with Dobbie Sanders

GROESBECK PARHAM AND GWEN ROBINSON

Fairfield, Alabama, is a company town, one of 17 residential areas near Birmingham built by the United States Steel Corporation. Nearly everyone who lives here works—or has worked—in US Steel's local mills or mines.

Dobbie Sanders is one of those former employees. Now 85 years old, Dobbie spent more than a quarter century working for US Steel, and the years have reshaped his body. His eyes are blurry; his feet, covered with callouses; his fingers, thick and rough—one with a tip missing.

Sanders lives in a small house on the corner of Fairfield's Sixty-first Street and Avenue E. Each day, he walks slowly about his yard, dressed in a pair of greasy overalls. A passerby may see him squatting on the ground repairing a broken lawn mower, or leaning underneath the hood of a car, or fixing some electrical gadget. Sometimes, he sits for hours looking through one of the trunks in his yard, searching for objects that take him through his past: his baby sister's dress from their family farm, a pair of his brother's old gloves, records of outdated wage rates at US Steel, flyers from the International Labor Defense and various unions, his retirement papers, old insurance policies.

The objects that still fill Dobbie's life are many and various, revealing his journey from a Mississippi farm to Alabama's steel factories, from Birmingham to Chicago and back again. Like many black sharecroppers, he left the farm for higher wages and independence near the turn of the century. He found the company bosses instead. He went north looking for a means to advance himself, and enrolled in a school of electronics. He could make good money in the North, he says, but he felt he had to come home. And in Fairfield, he couldn't find a job that met his new skills. He stayed, though, and persevered.

Today he sits on a yellow quilt, beneath a thin aluminum boat propped up by a single oar, and reads again the papers of his youth.

"Yessir," he says as he rises from his quilt. "I'm a Mississippi man."

Born in Bigbee Valley, Mississippi, near the Alabama line, Dobbie grew up with nine brothers and three sisters. They all began working at an early age. "My whole family sharecropped on the land of P. Q. Poindexter, a big white millionaire down in Bigbee Valley," he recalls. "I worked from the time I first remembered myself. My father died when I was one year-two months old, but Mama told me he was a ditch digger. He dug ditches around the big farm to drain off the water.

"Mama raised us all. She was a mama and daddy too. She did a good job cause we didn't have nothing. We did all the work and got nothing in return. Poindexter would credit us the tools, hogs, mules, cotton, corn seed and a pair of brogan shoes and jean pants. At the end of the season when it came time to add up, we would always owe him more money than we had to pay him, no matter how big the crop. We would always end up in the hole. We grew and raised everything, but he took it all. Course we had enough food cause we raised it. But that's all we had.

"Every morning when the bell was rung, we had to get up and go out to the barn. Mr. Poindexter had hired a black man as the bell ringer; he was a wage-earner. When we got out to the barn to get our tools and stuff, it would still be dark. We would take our plows out to the field, and when the sun started rising, we were supposed to be sitting on our plows ready to work. The sun was the sign. And we would work and work and work until it got dark.

"Mr. Poindexter had hired a white overseer who rode through the fields on a horse telling us what to do. He never beat us; but Mama used to tell us how, when she was coming up, that the white overseers would beat the people with a whip. Sometimes we'd be out in the middle of the field working, and mama would just bust out and start cryin and hollerin. She'd say, 'If Bill was here, I wouldn't have to be doin all this hard work.' Bill was my daddy. I was small then, and didn't understand why she was crying. But after I got up some size I understood.

"Lots of times people thought about leaving the farm, but if you tried to, the owner would take away everything you had. Your tools, mules, horses, cows, hogs, clothes, food, everything. But things were so bad that people still left.

"My oldest brother left home in 1919 and came to work in Fairfield at the US Steel Wire Mill. On May 8, 1922, I left. Mama had died, and I just wanted to wear good clothes like some of the rest of the boys. Hell, if you worked all the time and somebody took all you made, you'd leave too.

"After I left, I went and worked in the Delta at a levee camp as a wheeler, helping to pile dirt on the river bank to make a dam. I was paid about $1.75 a day. I stayed there a little while and then left. I hoboed, caught rides, and walked my way to North Carollton. That's near Yellow Dog, Mississippi. I worked there for awhile laying 'y' shaped tracks at the end of railroad line until they laid me off. Then I hoboed on trains and walked until I got to Sulls, Alabama, working my way on up to Fairfield.

"In Sulls, I worked in the mines with my brother, Jim. I only worked for a month and had to quit cause I was too tall for the mines. My head kept hitting up against the roof. I told my brother I was going up to Fairfield to get a job in US Steel's Wire Mill and stay with another one of our brothers, William. Jim said OK, but told me, 'Make sure you work enough to feed yourself.'

"And I did. When I got to Fairfield I stayed with William and his wife in Annisburg, next to Englewood.[1] I started working in September, 1922. William's wife would go down to the company store and get food, and the company would deduct it from my paycheck every two weeks."

When he first entered industry, Dobbie Sanders followed a path beaten by thousands of black Southern workers before him. Even before the Civil War, blacks played a crucial role in southern industry, and especially the iron business. As far back as 1812, 220 slavés were owned by the Oxford Iron Works of Virginia. In the Tennessee Cumberland River region, one iron company owned 365 slaves in the 1840s, and 20 other establishments in that area worked more than 1,800 slaves. In 1861, the Tredegar Iron Co. of Richmond employed the third largest iron-working force in the United States, and half of the 900 men were slaves. Altogether, an estimated 10,000 slaves worked in the South's iron industry.

Before the Civil War, Selma had been the major site of Alabama's iron works, but in 1865 the city fell and its plants were destroyed. Other coal and iron plants were soon constructed throughout the state and began to grow and merge. In 1871, Birmingham was founded as the ideal location for an industrial steel complex which required easy access to coal, iron, water and transportation. Eventually the Tennessee Coal & Iron Co. (TCI) became the uncontested leader in Alabama's steel business, and in 1892, it moved its headquarters to "The Magic City," a name Birmingham soon earned for its phenomenal growth. Fifteen years later, J. P. Morgan absorbed TCI into his US Steel empire.

In 1910, 13,417 blacks were employed in US blast furnace operations and steel rolling mills, the vast majority in the lowest paying, dirtiest, most tedious jobs. At this time, almost three-quarters of all common laborers in the steel and iron industry were black, though they were only 8.2 percent of the skilled workforce and 10.7 percent of the unskilled workers. Of those few skilled black workers, almost 40 percent were employed in Alabama—635 men.

Like Sanders, many of these workers had recently come from nearby farms in search of freedom from their hard times. Most didn't find it.

"When I started working at US Steel's Wire Mill, the company owned the houses, food and clothing stores, hospitals, schools, churches, everything. And they deducted everything out of your pay check—food, clothes, rent. Sometimes we'd work the whole pay period and time come to get paid, and we'd draw nothing but a blank slip of paper. That mill was rough. When I started working there in 1922, we were doing 10-hour shifts at $2.45 a day, as many days as the man told us to come in. Later, they went on the 8-hour day at $3.10 a day, but we still had to work 10-hour shifts. We had no vacation, no holidays, no sick leave, no pension, no insurance, no nothing. It was rough.

"I went ahead and got married in 1927. Most of the women in town did clean-up work. A lot of them worked in the basements of Loveman's and Pizitz' Department Stores shining shoes and scrubbing floors. No dark-skinned women drove the freight elevators even."

Dobbie Sanders had come to Fairfield frustrated with working long hours and getting nothing for it. Now he found himself in the same situation.

"One day back in '27 or '28, I just got tired of the whole thing and quit work. I enrolled in the L. L. Cooke School of Electronics in Chicago. L. Cooke was the Chief Engineer of Chicago. Even though I had only finished the third grade, I was a good reader. I used to read all of my brother's books. I'm a self-educated man.

"When I was in electronics school, I learned how to make and fix door bells, wire up burglar alarms, wire houses and everything else. I'll even wire you so anybody touches you, you'll ring. I wired up that old dog pen out there just so it would touch the old dog up lightly when he tried to step over the fence. It'll touch you up lightly too if you try to git in."

Sanders points with pride to a thick, dusty electronics textbook printed in 1927 by L.L. Cooke Electronics School, Chicago, Illinois. Many sentences in the book have been underlined, with numbers from 1 to 10 marked beside them.

"You see, at the *end* of each chapter there are ten questions. The *answers* are in the chapter. I put the numbers of the questions next to the answers. Then I underlined the answers. I made everything in that book, and I read and studied every page of it. That's why I can fix so many things.

"I can fix everything except a broken heart, can't fix that.

"After I left Chicago, I went on to Detroit. I was making good money there, too, just fixing things. But I came on back to Fairfield. You know how it is bout home. You know everybody and everybody knows you. Plus, when I was away I was living with other people. You know how it is.

"So when I got back here, the head of the school in Chicago called the people at US Steel, and told them what I could do. But they said they wasn't hiring no colored electricians. They still made me do electrical work sometimes, but they just didn't pay me for it.

"US Steel is one of the dirtiest companies in the world. And if the working people of this country would ever get together, they could run the whole thing. That's why I like that worker/farmer form of government."

While working in Fairfield, Dobbie Sanders became involved in a number of groups fighting for black and working people's rights. One was the International Labor Defense (ILD), organized by the Communist Party in 1925 to fight extra-legal organizations such as the Ku Klux Klan. ILD members had become active in highly publicized campaigns to free Tom Mooney, Warren Billings, Nicola Sacco and Bartolomeo Vanzetti. In 1931, the ILD came south as the main organizers of the Scottsboro Boys' defense in Birmingham. Over the next few years, the ILD was able to turn national attention to the South and to the trial of nine young blacks facing the death penalty on charges of raping two white women. Blacks and a few whites throughout the south supported the ILD and the Scottsboro Boys, contributed money from church offerings and attended rallies. At one Birmingham meeting, 900 blacks and 300 whites turned out.

"Yes, the ILD was in here with the Scottsboro Boys, and I was right along with them. I used to pass out leaflets for them down at the plant. I would stick em in my lunch bucket and tie em round my waist and ankles. On the way inside the gate, I would open up my bucket, untie the strings and let the wind blow the leaflets all over the yard. I'd just keep steppin like nothin ever happened. There's always a way, you know."

But he is reluctant to talk much about the organization's programs. He laughs, "You go ahead and talk some. I done already gone too far. Why, I been 75 miles barefoot, and on cold ground, too. But I'll just say this: it was all about obtaining a higher standard of living."

Sanders was also a member of the United Steelworkers of America, which began organizing in Alabama in the late 1930s and joined the state's long tradition of integrated unions. That tradition started with the United Mine Workers before the turn of the century. By 1902, the UMW had organized about

65 percent of all miners in the state, a majority of them black. Racism and social segregation were continual problems for the union, but even in 1899 a few blacks were able to hold the presidency of locals that included white members. A series of long strikes took place in the first decades of the century, one from 1904 to 1906, which weakened the union immensely. But the UMW kept returning—in the teens, in the 20s, and again in the 30s.

Throughout this period, attempts were made to organize the steel industry, but that feat was not accomplished until the birth of the Congress of Industrial Organizations (CIO) in 1936. Under the leadership of UMW president John L. Lewis, one of the top priorities of the CIO was the organization of the steel industry. The CIO established the Steel Workers Organizing Committee (SWOC) for that purpose, which later grew into the United Steel Workers of America (USWA).

Dobbie Sanders joined USWA in its early years. "Before the union came in here in the 1930s," he explains, "it was rough. We didn't have any say in anything. I was one of those who helped get people signed up. We had to slip and sign our cards and pay our dues. When the Steelworkers ran into trouble, they'd just call in the Mine Workers. Them boys would come in here from Walker County with snuff running down their chins, both black and white. And they didn't take no stuff. If it wasn't for Ebb Cox and the Mine Workers, we never would have got a union."

Cox was one of the Steelworkers' most determined leaders, encouraging workers to join the union wherever he could—in churches, in the bars and on the streets of Fairfield. Tall and light-skinned, with no formal education, he became one of the staff. He was the object of much anti-union and anti-black violence in Mississippi and Georgia as well as Alabama, but he continued his relentless fight for the union. He was eventually elected the first black member of the Alabama CIO Executive Board.

Dobbie Sanders was also a union leader in Fairfield. "I put food in a lot of women's and babies' mouths by writing out Step One-and-a-Half in the promotion line in the wire mill. Step One was on the broom. Step One-and-a-Half was classified as the "helper," even though you'd actually be doing the work (of the person on the Step Two job). This was so the company could get away with paying Step One-and-a-Half wages even though you'd be doing Step Two work.

"After the union had come in, I wrote a provision that said that after so many hours on the job, a man had to be given a chance to bid for the job, and be paid the right wages. I took it to my supervisor, and he couldn't do nothing but accept it. Hell, before this thing was written up, they'd keep a man in Step One-and-a-Half for a hundred years. Yessir, that mill was rough.

"And we had a lot of people working against us too. Not just the company, police and sandtoters (informers), but most of the preachers. Man, them preachers is a mess. Most of em ain't no good. Brainwashing, that's what they all about. They should have been race leaders, but instead they are race hold-backers. And the people who support them are crazy, too. Does it make any sense to pay somebody to hold you in the dark? These preachers go around here charging people to keep them looking back. Goin around here tellin people bout heaven. How you gon git to heaven after you die, and you can't even get to 19th

Street in downtown Birmingham when you are alive. When you die you can't even go to the undertaker, they have to come and get you. So how you gon go to heaven?"

Dobbie stayed at the mill for more than 25 years, doing the same work at the end that he had when he started. "I retired on March 31, 1959," he remembers with the precision that he has for only a few significant facts of his life.

Since then he has lived at the corner of Sixty-first Street and Avenue E in Fairfield, surrounded by the memories of his life. "I tell you," he says softly, looking up from his boxes, "if I could go back through the whole thing again, I'd git me one of them easy shooting guns, the kind with a silencer on it. And I'd be a killer."

Appreciation for this interview is extended to the Southern Investigative Research Project of SRC and to numerous individuals: Dr. Glover P. Parham, Emory O. Jackson, Demetrius Newton, Asbury Howard, and above all to Dobbie Sanders, Hosea Hudson, and the black steelworkers in the Birmingham district who created this story.

1. Annisburg and Englewood were the first areas built for black families working for US Steel. Although now a part of greater Fairfield, the areas were originally separated from the white neighborhoods by a row of bushes that Dobbie Sanders calls "The Iron Curtain."

PART EIGHT

Selected Demographic Aspects

Part 8 reviews major research studies, including census references, and presents an analysis guided, in part, by a conscious attempt to follow the work of Belcher ("Population Growth and Characteristics") and Brown and Hillery ("The Great Migration, 1940-1960") in Ford's classic *The Southern Appalachian Region*. William H. Turner draws on these studies to illustrate the social and economic trends and present status of the black population in Appalachia.

21

The Demography of Black
Appalachia: Past and Present

WILLIAM H. TURNER

This essay reviews changes in some of the demographic, social, and economic characteristics of the black population in central and southern Appalachia only. There is no consensus on the exact boundaries of the region. First, any historical overview of blacks in the region is subject to artificial geographic constraints, since current definitions have been standardized around boundaries drawn in the early 1960s by the Appalachian Regional Commission. The political exigencies which the ARC lines reflect encompass areas of New York State, Mississippi, Alabama, and Pennsylvania. My definition of Appalachia and my focus are less broad than those of the ARC because I exclude Maryland, Mississippi, New York, Ohio, and Pennsylvania. The data reported below (excepting the occupational portion of the analysis—specifically my treatment of coal-mining counties) define Appalachia as ARC counties in Alabama, Georgia, Kentucky, North Carolina, South Carolina, Tennessee, Virginia, and West Virginia. I devote attention to some other counties because blacks in the "most truly Appalachian areas" emigrated there from areas that the ARC regards as Appalachia.[1] In particular, many blacks who now live in eastern Kentucky and West Virginia arrived from Alabama and (to a lesser extent) from Mississippi in pursuit of coal-related employment.

Most of the data presented in this report are from the Bureau of the Census; the dicennial censuses and the Current Population surveys have been used as primary sources. In addition, figures are presented from previously published material; for the sake of continuity and comparability, statistics have been disaggregated from tabulations that appeared in other sources for inclusion here.[2]

HISTORICAL TRENDS, 1820-1980

1820-1900. Limited information is available on the black population in Appalachia prior to the first census in 1790. Table 21.1 shows the figures for the period 1820-1980. Harry Caudill makes some vague references to black slaves in Kentucky in the 1830s.[3] James Taylor wrote an abolitionist document in 1862 in which he mentioned that 165,336 blacks in eight Appalachian subregions had been tallied in the 1850 census.[4] If we accept this count as valid, blacks were 15

TABLE 21.1   Population of the Appalachian Region, 1820-1980

Year	All Races (thousands)	Blacks (thousands)	Blacks (%)	Change in Black Population (%)
1980	10,997.6	987.8	8.98	12
1970	9,192.2	880.4	9.5	-6
1960	8,860.7	935.7	10.5	0.08
1950	8,783.9	927.7	10.5	2
1940	8,175.8	909.3	11.1	4
1930	7,269.2	876.2	12.0	8
1920	6,457.4	806.6	12.4	13
1910	5,220.7	703.9	13.4	5
1900	4,766.5	672.0	14.0	5
1890	3,830.7	572.0	14.9	18
1880	3,167.7	469.9	14.8	24
1870	2,302.8	354.4	15.3	4
1860	2,086.6	338.6	16.2	-1
1850	1,739.0	297.8	19.5	29
1840	1,355.1	241.6	17.8	13
1830	1,088.8	209.7	19.2	45
1820	754.4	114.4	15.1	--

Source: U.S. Bureau of the Census, reports of U.S. population from the Fourth Decennial census (1820) through the Twentieth.

percent of the population in Appalachia 160 years ago (table 21.1 excludes some areas included by Taylor).

Three decades earlier, in 1790, when the first federal census was taken, one person in five in the United States was black. The general pattern of black population concentration during this period indicates that most blacks could be found in Alabama—where they numbered one in three at the time of the Civil War (see table 21.2). Interestingly, Kentucky counties had a larger number of blacks in 1820 than other slaveholding Appalachian states, but the plantation system of agriculture evolved farther south, and the proportion of blacks in the state's Appalachian region did not exceed 16 percent after the decade of the 1870s.

Alabama, Georgia, North and South Carolina, and Tennessee compose the southern portion of Appalachia. In 1900 (see table 21.2), of the 672,000 blacks in Appalachia, 4 in 10 (40.8 percent) lived in Alabama. Most of these, of course, lived in Talladega, Madison, and Chambers counties. By the turn of the twentieth century, the area of Birmingham (Jefferson County) marked the spot of blacks' concentration in the Appalachian portion of the state. South Carolina's five Appalachian counties ranged between one-quarter and one-third black until 1900. Because of the emigration of Europeans to the backcountry of the South, the natural increase of blacks and their out-migration from the region made for considerable increases in the number of whites and a generally stable ratio of blacks through 1900, especially in Tennessee. Even so, the black population in Appalachian Alabama tripled between 1820 and 1830, increased by one-third in the next decade, and increased two and one-half times between 1840 and the end of the nineteenth century. Beginning in 1900, the proportion of blacks in southern Appalachia continued to decline relative to the white population.

Tennessee, Kentucky, Virginia, and West Virginia, despite relatively large percentages of blacks migrating to the coal-mining counties in about 1890, had few blacks compared to the southern region between 1820 and 1900. In Kentucky, for example, the black population of Appalachia would be considerably lessened if Clark, Garrard, Lincoln, Madison, Montgomery, and Pulaski counties were dropped from the analysis.[5] Virginia, with thirty-two Appalachian counties, held 40 percent of the *total* black population of the United States in 1790. Botetourt County's black population was 60 percent of the total by 1900. Overall, in this region, Tennessee had the largest number of blacks; beginning in about 1860, the number of blacks there exceeded the count in Virginia and West Virginia combined.

If we disaggregate the percentage of blacks in Appalachian counties of the southern states reported in the census between 1860 and 1900,[6] we see that blacks in all of Appalachia increased throughout the 1880s. Appalachian Kentucky lost population between 1850 and 1880, but the Appalachian counties of Virginia, Alabama, Tennessee, and North and South Carolina showed small to moderate increases in black populations. By 1900, though, especially in West Virginia, populations of blacks had increased threefold. In the 1870 census, blacks in West Virginia lived mainly in Kanawha, Greenbrier, and Monroe counties. Between 1870 and 1890—only twenty years later—blacks in these three counties alone increased from 5,540 to 18,900. By 1900, McDowell County (which includes Gary, Welch, Keystone, and Elkhorn) boasted the state's largest and most progressive black population. Twenty years earlier, in 1880, McDowell County had had a total of three blacks!

1900-1950. Belcher notes that it is generally impossible to make valid statements about the origins of white settlers in Appalachia. Several standard works on the area, however, suggest that blacks in the mountains in the early 1800s were either escaped slaves or bondsmen brought to the region to work mountain farms.[7] After Reconstruction, though, it became much easier to document the presence of blacks, as the employment of workers in the mines and in related occupations increased 500 percent between 1890 and 1900. For a number of reasons, including operator-union jockeying and the improvement in blacks' economic position, West Virginia, Kentucky, southwestern Virginia, and Tennessee became havens for blacks leaving Alabama for Kentucky, Tennessee, and West Virginia and, to a lesser extent, leaving the Carolina Piedmont for the central highlands.

In the Appalachian portion of Alabama, large numbers of blacks migrated as rural sharecropping peasants to the mines and mills around Birmingham; by 1900, they constituted 46 percent of all miners in the area. Blacks, as noted above, made up a very small proportion of West Virginia's population until the late 1880s. Although there were only 1,122 blacks in all of Fayette County, West Virginia, in 1880, by 1886 there were 1,000 black miners, and by 1890 blacks totaled 3,054. Spero and Harris note that most of these blacks had come from the agricultural sections of Virginia and North Carolina.[8] It appears that the black populations in all Appalachian counties (except those in West Virginia) decreased relative to white populations in the first three decades of this century.

TABLE 21.2 Population Trends in Eight Appalachian States, 1820–1980
(Appalachian Counties Only; Population in Thousands)

	1820	1830	1840	1850	1860	1870	1880	1890	1900	1910	1920	1930	1940	1950	1960	1970	1980
ALABAMA																	
All races	66.4	177.7	286.0	343.9	441.0	390.2	577.0	770.8	931.0	1,129.3	1,343.2	1,515.1	1,698.6	1,859.1	1,981.0	2,038.2	2,425.3
Blacks	21.3	61.4	86.0	109.3	135.6	130.6	167.8	281.1	274.8	322.0	364.0	384.7	419.4	441.8	466.2	431.6	484.4
Blacks (%)	32	35	30	32	31	33	29	28	30	29	27	25	25	24	24	21	20
Change in black population (%)	–	65	28	22	19	-4	28	30	26	17	13	6	9	5	5	-7	12
GEORGIA																	
All races	25.1	54.6	87.2	149.8	187.0	245.5	330.6	386.6	438.6	486.5	537.6	497.8	557.6	609.0	644.0	813.8	1,102.2
Blacks	4.1	9.0	14.9	23.4	31.6	41.8	59.9	67.7	77.1	82.5	79.7	65.0	63.3	59.2	62.1	64.8	70.4
Blacks (%)	16	17	17	16	17	17	18	17	17	17	15	13	11	10	9	8	6
Change in black population (%)	–	54	40	36	26	–	43	13	14	7	-3	-18	-3	-6	-5	4	9
KENTUCKY																	
All races	164.6	183.3	190.2	234.8	270.4	340.6	452.1	534.6	655.2	736.7	854.9	973.1	1,102.4	1,072.7	925.5	867.5	1,075.3
Blacks	28.9	38.3	35.4	38.2	33.6	37.9	42.1	42.8	37.0	37.5	39.9	38.0	36.0	27.6	22.4	18.4	17.7
Blacks (%)	18	21	19	16	12	11	9	8	6	5	5	4	3	3	2	2	2
Change in black population (%)	–	24	-8	7	-14	11	11	2	-14	1	6	-5	-5	-23	-19	-29	-4
NORTH CAROLINA																	
All races	83.7	110.7	127.6	158.0	187.0	194.4	290.3	307.3	437.9	500.4	581.1	614.7	702.4	768.3	939.1	1,039.0	1,211.7
Blacks	11.8	17.0	18.5	23.1	27.1	29.1	38.7	51.3	51.7	57.5	61.4	86.3	80.8	89.1	91.9	94.1	111.5
Blacks (%)	14	15	14	15	15	15	15	14	11	11	11	14	11	12	10	9	9
Change in black population (%)	–	13	1	20	15	7	25	25	1	10	6	29	-7	9	3	3	19

	1820	1830	1840	1850	1860	1870	1880	1890	1900	1910	1920	1930	1940	1950	1960	1970	1980
SOUTH CAROLINA																	
All races	28.7	47.4	53.2	60.6	67.8	69.2	108.3	134.5	183.1	230.5	269.2	332.8	370.0	432.7	484.9	550.5	658.1
Blacks	6.8	13.0	13.8	18.4	19.8	20.4	36.5	44.3	58.7	67.9	70.6	77.0	79.0	81.1	87.5	92.7	110.1
Blacks (%)	24	27	26	30	29	29	34	33	32	29	26	23	23	19	18	17	16
Change in black population (%)	-	48	5	25	7	38	78	21	33	15	4	9	3	3	8	6	19
TENNESSEE																	
All races	180.7	251.0	286.9	356.4	402.3	456.9	571.7	679.6	829.5	920.1	1,011.1	1,175.6	1,355.7	1,527.8	1,624.3	1,737.5	2,071.1
Blacks	20.8	36.4	36.7	43.1	50.6	50.2	65.6	78.7	82.1	84.6	77.6	89.2	93.2	97.3	102.8	101.9	118.5
Blacks (%)	12	15	13	12	13	11	11	11	10	9	7	7	7	6	6	6	6
Change in black population (%)	-	46	1	15	15	1	31	20	4	3	-8	15	4	4	5	1	16
VIRGINIA																	
All races	68.5	88.1	99.5	133.2	154.5	163.9	219.3	254.6	332.4	373.9	396.9	430.9	487.2	508.8	455.3	391.4	504.4
Blacks	10.2	14.8	14.8	18.8	19.2	27.2	33.5	36.5	46.7	37.3	27.1	21.2	20.0	16.8	13.5	12.2	10.4
Blacks (%)	15	17	15	14	12	17	15	14	14	10	7	5	4	3	3	3	2
Change in black population (%)	-	31	15	21	2	29	23	8	28	-20	-27	-21	-1	-16	-20	-10	-15
WEST VIRGINIA																	
All races	136.7	176.0	224.5	302.3	376.6	442.1	618.4	762.7	958.8	1,221.1	1,463.7	1,729.2	1,901.9	2,005.5	1,806.4	1,744.3	1,949.6
Blacks	10.5	19.8	21.5	23.5	21.1	17.1	25.8	32.6	43.9	64.1	86.3	114.8	117.7	114.8	89.3	67.3	65.0
Blacks (%)	8	11	9	7	6	3	3	3	5	5	6	7	6	6	5	4	3
Change in black population (%)	-	47	8	8	-11	-21	33	21	26	32	26	25	-1	-2	-25	-25	-8

Source: U.S. Bureau of the Census, reports for years indicated.

TABLE 21.3   Population of Eight Appalachian States, 1980, and
Change in Population since 1960

	Blacks, 1980 (thousands)	Change since 1960 (%)	All Races, 1980 (thousands)	Change since 1960 (%)
Alabama	484.4	3.9	2,425.3	22.4
Georgia	70.0	13.3	1,102.1	71.1
Kentucky	17.7	-26.5	1,075.3	16.1
North Carolina	111.5	21.3	1,211.7	29.0
South Carolina	110.1	25.8	658.1	35.7
Tennessee	118.5	15.2	2,071.1	27.5
Virginia	10.4	-22.9	504.4	10.7
West Virginia	65.0	-27.2	1,949.6	7.9

Source: Population figures for 1980 were derived from U.S. Bureau of the
Census, 1980 Census of the Population and Housing, PHC 80 for the states
listed (Washington, D.C., 1980); percentages were derived from the 1980
figures and the 1960 tabulation of total and black Appalachian counties
for individual states as designated by the ARC.

In coal-mining counties, though, the rate of black population growth varied with the expansion of the coal industry.

Between 1900 and 1930, mining employment increased by 800 percent in West Virginia and Kentucky, and in some counties (such as Harlan in Kentucky) the number of blacks increased tenfold. Harlan County listed 564 black citizens in 1910 and 5,898 at the time of the Great Depression in 1930. As mining activity increased in eastern Kentucky and West Virginia, the number of black miners decreased in Alabama.[9] In the region as a whole, however, the percentage of blacks has declined steadily since 1870, when blacks represented 15 percent of the total population. By 1930, there were 876,200 blacks in Appalachia—with 43 percent in Alabama (a quarter of that state's total population)—and 38,000 blacks in Appalachian Kentucky, a mere 4 percent of the state and regional total of blacks. Therefore, while certain coal-mining counties in West Virginia and Kentucky contained percentages of blacks above the national average in 1930, the urban areas of the region were replacing such "boom towns" as centers of black population in Appalachia. Of course, Birmingham, Alabama, Chattanooga and Knoxville, Tennessee, and Charleston, West Virginia (by 1930), contained twice as many blacks as the remaining 345 counties in Appalachia combined.

The decade of the 1940s was the beginning of the great migration of whites from Appalachia. For blacks the exodus began ten years earlier. Georgia had a net loss of blacks in the decade of the 1930s, as did Virginia and Kentucky. Except for Floyd and Harlan counties, every county in Kentucky's Appalachian region lost population between 1930 and 1940. Between 1940 and 1950, the number of blacks increased slightly in Alabama (+ 5 percent), South Carolina (+ 3 percent), and Tennessee (+ 4 percent). Close inspection of county data shows the increases concentrated in Jefferson, Spartanburg, and Knox and Hamilton counties, respectively. In the remaining states, black out-migration in the 1940s decade was considerable: 7 percent fewer blacks lived in North Carolina in 1950, and fully one-fourth of Appalachian blacks in Kentucky left the region between World War II and 1950. In Kentucky, West Virginia, and southwestern Virginia, the number of blacks employed in mining had a great impact on their heavy out-migration between 1940 and 1950. The number of

TABLE 21.4 Distribution of Black Population within and beyond
Appalachian Counties in Eight States, 1980

	Total (No.)	Inside Appalachian Counties		Outside Appalachian Counties (%)
		No.	%	
Alabama	995,623	484,450	48.6	51.4
Georgia	1,465,457	70,420	4.8	95.2
Kentucky	259,490	17,710	6.8	93.2
North Carolina	1,316,050	115,570	8.7	91.3
South Carolina	948,146	110,126	11.6	88.4
Tennessee	725,949	118,520	16.3	83.7
Virginia	1,008,311	10,470	10.3	89.7
West Virginia	65,051	65,051	100.0	100.0

Source: Gloria Jackson and Ester Piovia, Appalachia and Its Black
Population: Selected Social and Economic Characteristics (New York,
1972), table 12.

blacks in Harlan County, Kentucky, decreased by 25 percent between 1940 and 1950, whereas it grew by 27 percent the previous decade. A similar pattern obtained in West Virginia's coal fields a decade later (1960).

1960-1980. In 1980, approximately 1.3 million blacks lived in all of Appalachia (I use all predesignated counties; see table 21.3). The counties included in this analysis held roughly 987,600 blacks (9 percent of a total population of just under 11 million persons). If we disaggregate from the total picture, we see that most Appalachian blacks lived in several standard metropolitan statistical areas (SMSAs). In Alabama, these included Anniston, Gadsden, Huntsville, Talladega, Dadeville, and Tuscaloosa. Of course, there is the anomaly of Jefferson County, Alabama (Birmingham), which houses fully two of every five blacks encompassed by the Appalachian boundaries used here. In Appalachian Georgia, the largest concentrations of blacks are in those counties which are contiguous to Fulton (Atlanta), including urbanized areas of Marietta and Rome. Kentucky counts Boyd (Ashland), Madison (Richmond), and Pike (Pikeville) counties as standard metropolitan statistical areas. The blacks of Madison County at 3,185, however, were triple the number in Boyd; Pike County had fewer than 400 blacks in 1980. In general, blacks have not counted for more than 10 percent of eastern Kentucky's population since 1880, although certain counties in the coal fields there reached that range in the 1940s. North Carolina's 1980 data show that blacks there are concentrated in Buncombe County (Asheville) and Forsyth (Winston-Salem) and, to a lesser extent, in Burke (Morganton), Caldwell (Lenoir), and Rutherford (Rutherfordton) counties. The blacks in South Carolina's five Appalachian counties live within the 100-mile circle that embraces Greenville and Spartanburg. Of the approximately 110,000 blacks in these contiguous counties (16 percent of the total), eight in ten live in these two SMSAs. Tennessee, with perhaps the most industrially diversified set of Appalachian counties, listed ten SMSAs among its fifty-one counties. Of the state's 118,500 blacks, 70.7 percent lived in the metropolitan areas of Chattanooga and Knoxville. Virginia's Appalachian counties are small for the most part, with but a single SMSA in the entire region

TABLE 21.5 Population of Eight Appalachian States, by Age, 1970

	Under 5 Years		5-14 Years		15-24 Years		25-44 Years		45-64 Years		65 Yrs. & Over	
	All Races	Blacks	All Races	Blacks	All Races	Blacks	All Races	Blacks	All Races	Blacks	All Races	Blacks
Alabama	9	11	20	25	17	18	24	18	20	18	10	9
Georgia	9	11	20	25	18	20	25	20	20	17	9	7
Kentucky	9	10	21	21	17	19	21	18	21	19	11	13
North Carolina	8	11	19	22	18	19	25	21	20	19	10	9
South Carolina	9	11	20	25	18	19	25	22	21	16	8	7
Tennessee	8	11	19	22	17	19	25	20	22	19	10	10
Virginia	8	10	19	20	17	18	23	20	22	21	10	11
West Virginia	8	9	19	22	17	18	22	16	22	16	11	13

Source: Jackson and Piǫvia, Appalachia and Its Black Population, tables 4 and 5.

(Tazewell County). This county, along with Pulaski and Botetourt, held 40 percent of all blacks. West Virginia's black population trends follow the pattern in Kentucky and Virginia. McDowell (Gary and Welch) and Jefferson (Charlestown) counties have the highest ratios of blacks in the state—although it must be noted that these are not among the more populous counties in the state. Cabell County is one of the state's most populous counties (101,627 in 1980), although blacks represent less than 5 percent of the total. Metropolitan Charleston (Kanawha County) had the largest black population in West Virginia in 1980 (13,776, or 6.4 percent, of 215,953 persons).

The southern Appalachian counties analyzed here (Alabama, Georgia, North and South Carolina, and Tennessee) have black populations that are presently stable—as in the case of Alabama—or are growing, as indicated by the steady increases in the number and ratio of black persons in South Carolina. Black populations in each of these states tend to localize in SMSAs; even when Birmingham, Chattanooga, and Knoxville are factored out, this statement remains true in the moderate sized cities of southern Appalachia such as Asheville, Winston-Salem, and Spartanburg/Greenville in the Carolinas. Black populations in eastern Kentucky, southwestern Virginia, and the coal fields of West Virginia are rapidly dwindling.

Table 21.4 shows that nearly half of all Alabama blacks live in the state's thirty-five Appalachian counties. In the remaining states, such as Virginia, the Appalachian blacks are a very small numerical minority of the state's population. They number between 9 percent and 21 percent of all blacks in the state. Ethnographic studies could usefully investigate whether urban black Appalachians (the "majority of the minority") have fewer problems with cultural identity and self-concept and whether they suffer to a lesser extent from economic deprivation relative to other groups that form a very small, isolated minority—both the regional white population and non-Appalachian blacks in the state. According to Bellows, Appalachia's black population declined as a whole during the decade from 1960 to 1970, with all states except Maryland showing a decrease relative to total population; in every Appalachian state, the black population "either decreased faster or increased slower than the total population."[10]

TABLE 21.6   Population under Fourteen and over
Sixty-five Years of Age in Eight Appalachian
States (percent), 1970

| | Under 14 | | Over 65 | |
	All Races	Blacks	All Races	Blacks
Alabama	29	36	10	9
Georgia	29	36	9	7
Kentucky	30	31	11	13
North Carolina	27	33	10	9
South Carolina	29	36	8	7
Tennessee	27	33	10	10
Virginia	27	30	10	11
West Virginia	27	31	11	13

Source: Jackson and Piovia, Appalachia and Its Black
Population, table 6.

The 1970 census and analyses of it made by various researchers illuminate
selected social indicators of the black Appalachian population.

AGE DISTRIBUTION, FERTILITY
RATES, AND OUT-MIGRATION

In 1970, there were relatively few children under five years old, black or white,
living in Appalachia. Blacks' out-migration from the area, and the decline in
fertility, are apparent from the fact that the bottom level of the age pyramid is
narrower than the five-to-fourteen-year-old group. Bellows, De Jong, and
Belcher dispute the significance of 1960 data on black fertility in Appalachia.
Each agrees, however, that whites in Appalachia had higher fertility ratios than
blacks in 1960.[11] Blacks in urban areas of Appalachia have fertility rates lower
than those in rural areas, causing the group picture of fertility to differ significantly from that which usually obtains for blacks nationally.

An obvious inference to be drawn from table 21.5 is that blacks had a
higher out-migration rate than whites in the sixties. The declining fertility ratio
of Appalachian blacks results from their out-migration. There are fewer persons
in the twenty-five- to forty-four-year range (the normal child-bearing cohort)
than would be expected. Brown's data demonstrate a clear connection between
out-migration of young adults and the decline in regional fertility ratios.
Interestingly, though, blacks in Appalachia have proportionately *more* children
than whites in the zero to fourteen-year age group and *fewer* young adults (ages
twenty-five to forty-four).[12] The older groups of blacks were evidently more
fertile when they were twenty-five to forty-five (the absolute decline), perhaps
meaning that significant numbers of young adult blacks leave and send children
back to relatives.[13]

Table 21.6 reflects the finding that the black Appalachian population has
suffered greatly from migration for a long period of time. Unlike the white
regional population, it has not benefited from the migration turnaround of the
1970s. The black population of Appalachia is old, having a median age of forty-
six years, compared with a median age of thirty-two years for the white regional

TABLE 21.7   Black Families with Children under Eighteen Years of Age and with a Female Head of Household in Seven Appalachian States, 1970

	Kentucky	Georgia	North Carolina	South Carolina	Tennessee	Virginia	West Virginia	Appalachian Total Population	Total in Cities
All black families	4,084	13,337	20,547	29,743	22,871	3,034	14,556	108,794	4,943
Families with children under eighteen	1,889	7,564	10,984	17,136	11,969	1,485	7,057	58,459	14,746
Families with children under eighteen and female head of household	561	2,030	3,395	4,219	4,141	328	2,113	16,915	7,627
All families with children under eighteen (%)									
Black population[a]	46.7	56.7	53.5	57.6	52.3	46.9	48.5	53.7	35.2
Total population	56.6	58.3	56.1	57.5	55.8	55.9	54.4	56.0	55.6
All families with children under eighteen and female head of household (%)									
Black population[b]	29.7	26.8	30.9	24.6	34.6	22.1	29.9	28.9	51.7
Total population	11.6	9.5	10.7	11.4	10.9	9.6	10.9	10.7	12.6

aU.S. totals: national, 59.0%; urban, 59.7%; rural nonfarm, 56.0%; rural farm, 51.7%.
bU.S. totals: national, 30.9%; urban, 32.9%; rural nonfarm, 20.4%; rural farm, 14.2%.
Source: David Bellows, "Appalachian Blacks: A Demographic Analysis" (master's thesis, Rutgers University, 1974).

population. This fact is of course illuminated by the low fertility statistics for the black regional population. The structural conditions thus exist for low ratios of children to women (a larger part of the population is sixty-five or older), and the ratio of the sexes is of course highly skewed.

In Alabama, Georgia, and South Carolina, the under-fourteen cohort in the black population differs significantly in size from its counterpart in the white population. The difference in this cohort is not as large in the remaining states under study. Barnum revealed that Kentucky (like Virginia and West Virginia) had higher proportions of blacks migrating from the coal fields.[14] The fact that youth in the area remains proportionally on a par with southern urbanized black Appalachian youth supports the thesis that a traditional informal extended-family adoption pattern persists. Studies of the elderly group may be the most fruitful avenue to the understanding of value patterns among Appalachian blacks. The urbanized Appalachian black would give clues to the self-concept hypothesis advanced by Philliber and Obermiller.[15] Correspondingly, studies are needed on distortion in the working-age population as it affects the economic position of blacks in the region. No doubt the distortion works to their detriment (in a collective political sense) and explains in part why these blacks are significantly worse off in terms of interconnected indicators of the quality of life.

Table 21.7 takes the analysis from children to "families." It shows that blacks in Appalachia, except in Virginia, have fewer children under eighteen than all blacks, but a higher percentage of them live in female-headed families. The percentage of all black Appalachian children growing up in female-headed families is nearly three times as great as the corresponding figure for whites. Urban black children are twice as likely to live in such families as rural black children, although the figure for rural black children is significantly higher than it is for their rural and rural nonfarm peers. The pattern is the same for blacks nationally—showing that Appalachian black women (urban and rural) are unmarried, are having children, and tend toward the extended family, raising children left behind by other grown female kin.

School enrollment figures for Appalachia's black children are in line with their proportion of the total population. As table 21.8 shows, there is no regularity in the pattern of school enrollment among counties in the region.

Though blacks were 33 percent of the total population in Jefferson County, Alabama, they were 40 percent of the public school enrollment in 1970. In several other places, blacks accounted for higher percentages of school enrollment than they did of the total population. With fewer young adult blacks present to participate in the social and political process of maintaining schools, it is worth considering how black students fare in the educational systems of Appalachia.

The record of West Virginia is noteworthy with respect to historically accessible institutions of higher education. Despite a Presbyterian aversion to human bondage and slave labor, West Virginia, like other states, adopted in 1872 a constitutional provision that "white and colored persons shall not be taught in the same school." When there were roughly 25,000 blacks in the state, Storer College was established through private means in Harpers Ferry, surely a

TABLE 21.8   Public School Enrollment in Selected Appalachian Counties, 1970

	No. of Public School Students	No. of Black Public School Students	% of Black Public School Students
Alabama (Jefferson Co.)	135,378	54,332	40
Georgia (Carroll Co.)	9,852	2,450	25
Kentucky (Harlan Co.)	10,629	889	8
North Carolina (Forsyth Co.)	49,831	13,798	28
South Carolina (Spartanburg Co.)	38,820	10,189	26
Tennessee (Hamilton Co.)	57,481	14,542	25
Virginia (Pulaski Co.)	6,812	542	8
West Virginia (McDowell Co.)	14,952	3,440	23

Source: Jackson and Piovia, Appalachia and Its Black Population, table 13.

fitting location. Following the passage of Morrill II, West Virginia's legislature established the Colored Institute, absorbing Storer's money in the process. This secondary school, together with Bluefield Colored Institute, was created to "train" blacks entering the state. As the population of blacks doubled between 1890 and 1910 (in 1910 it was 64,000; it is only 65,000 today), college-level institutions became available to blacks. In 1927, at the time when industrial education for Negroes was becoming an established institutional goal, West Virginia State College was considered a first-rate institution with a well-trained teaching staff. The black population of the state had declined by the mid-fifties, however, and white students in Bluefield and West Virginia State now out-number blacks by a ratio of 8:2.

A longitudinal study of achievement, major area of study, and career mobility of black Appalachian collegians would undoubtedly be revealing about black colleges in the region. Surely the fact that blacks leave is well established; but we know very little about the effect on the region when black natives do not return after college. A longitudinal study should, of course, center in Alabama, where seven historically black colleges exist. North Carolina's Winston-Salem State University, together with other institutions of higher education, draws black students from the Appalachian region of the state. There are two histor-ically black junior colleges in Rock Hill, South Carolina, and South Carolina State College has a long record of graduates from the Spartanburg-Greenville region. Knoxville and Morristown in East Tennessee, along with Lynchburg's Virginia College, make for a total of fifteen historically black colleges within the Appalachian boundaries of my study. If we include the same kind of colleges within states in this particular group, the total comes to fifty-six: thirteen in Alabama; ten in Georgia; one in Kentucky; eleven and eight in North and South Carolina, respectively; seven in Tennessee; and six in Virginia. Beyond this group, Ohio (two), Pennsylvania (two), Mississippi (eleven), and Maryland (four) combine to bring the total to seventy-five historically black colleges in ARC-designated counties. Of course, West Virginia's historically black colleges are now predominantly white.[16]

Adult black Appalachians are twice as likely not to have more than five years of schooling than the general population (table 21.9), especially in Alabama and the Carolinas, where most black Appalachians live. If we exclude the urban regions of Appalachia, fully half of the blacks more than twenty-five

TABLE 21.9   Education and Illiteracy in Eight Appalachian
States (percent), 1960

	Population Twenty-five and Over with Less than Five Years' Education		Illiterate Population, Fourteen and Over
	All Races	Blacks	Blacks
United States Total	8.3	23.5	2.4
Alabama	16.3	36.0	4.2
Georgia	17.6	39.7	4.5
Kentucky	13.8	23.8	3.3
North Carolina	16.5	32.0	4.0
South Carolina	20.3	41.2	5.5
Tennessee	14.8	27.8	3.5
Virginia	13.1	29.4	3.4
West Virginia	11.0	23.5	2.7

Source: Jackson and Piovia, Appalachia and Its Black Population, table 15.

years old have less than five years of education. This educational deficiency is greater than the national black norm and certainly has grave consequences as it perpetuates the cycle of poverty. Lack of education in the urban setting affects the employability of individuals; "technologically obsolete" people find themselves unable to support families or to pursue any other culture (way of life) than that of poverty. The educational deficit of course adds to the powerlessness, political lethargy, present-orientation, and other manifestations of social-psychological modes of adaptation analyzed by Billings.[17]

INCOME AND GENERAL EMPLOYMENT PATTERN

Gary Fowler compares the general context of poverty in Appalachia with the case of blacks there and concludes that "blacks are significantly worse off in terms of income."[18] The coal industry, the primary factor which pulled black migrants to eastern Kentucky, West Virginia, and Virginia, is a dying source of income for blacks.

The vast majority of blacks in the three states depended on mining as *the* major source of income between 1930 and 1970. Blacks, in each case, accounted for at least 10 percent of all miners in these states a half century ago. By 1970, the retirement of black miners and the out-migration of young ones, given the shift to machine-intensive operation, meant that fewer blacks were employed in the industry overall. In fact, there are more white women employed in coal mining than black men, even though women have been in the industry less than two decades.

In Appalachia's bituminous coal-mining region (eastern Kentucky, southwest Virginia, and eastern Tennessee) are located eighty-five of the counties in the region that are economically worst off. In Kentucky and Virginia, the proportion of blacks employed in mining is smaller than the percentage of the total population so employed. As for selected other industries (agriculture, construction, manufacturing, and private households), Appalachian blacks typically hold low-status, low-income jobs.

Table 21.10 shows that, in the four decades between 1930 and 1970, the

TABLE 21.10 Employment in the Bituminous Coal Industry, by Race, 1930–1970

	1930			1940			1950			1960			1970		
	All races (no.)	Blacks (no.)	Blacks (%)	All races (no.)	Blacks (no.)	Blacks (%)	All races (no.)	Blacks (no.)	Blacks (%)	All races (no.)	Blacks (no.)	Blacks (%)	All races (no.)	Blacks (no.)	Blacks (%)
Alabama	23,956	12,742	53	23,022	9,605	42	19,920	6,721	34	7,728	1,970	26	4,515	826	18
Kentucky	54,307	7,364	14	54,676	5,474	10	63,566	2,958	5	30,456	923	3	21,480	445	2
Tennessee	8,735	578	7	9,534	168	2	9,265	90	1	3,916	39	1	1,630	8	0.5
Virginia	12,629	1,511	12	20,086	1,190	6	24,790	894	4	15,799	560	4	12,403	104	0.9
West Virginia	97,505	22,098	23	106,935	18,356	17	125,931	15,313	12	53,111	3,544	7	40,513	1,685	4

Source: Donald T. Barnum, The Negro in the Bituminous Coal Mining Industry, (Philadelphia, 1970), and David Walls, Dwight Billings, Mary Payne, and Joe F. Childers, Jr., A Baseline Assessment of Coal Industry Structure in the Ohio River Basin Energy Study Region, (Lexington, Ky., 1979).

TABLE 21.11 Employment of Blacks in Selected Industries in Six
Appalachian States, 1970

	Georgia	Kentucky	North Carolina	South Carolina	Tennessee	Virginia
Total employed	22,783	4,527	32,968	42,254	34,075	3,834
Agriculture	653	294	663	1,079	497	128
Mining	111	204	40	81	93	70
Construction	1,333	531	1,463	2,941	1,541	263
Manufacturing	9,529	827	12,432	16,333	9,566	1,987
Private households	9,515	790	3,597	5,479	4,234	534

Source: Bellows, "Appalachian Blacks."

TABLE 21.12 Occupational Distribution of Blacks and of All Races in Selected
Metropolitan Areas (percent), 1967

Standard Metropolitan Statistical Area	Officials, Managers, and Professionals	Technical	Sales and Clerical	Craftsmen	Operatives, Laborers, and Service	Total
Birmingham, Ala. (Jefferson Co.)						
All races	15	4	27	17	40	100
Blacks	2	3	5	6	84	100
Charleston, W.Va. (Kanawah Co.)						
All races	19	5	21	21	34	100
Blacks	5	1	11	7	76	100
Chattanooga, Tenn. (Hamilton Co.)						
All races	11	3	18	18	50	100
Blacks	1	--a	3	7	90	100
Greenville, S.C. (Greenville/Pickens Co.)						
All races	10	2	15	14	59	100
Blacks	2	--a	2	8	89	100
Knoxville, Tenn. (Knox Co.)						
All races	18	5	19	14	40	100
Blacks	4	6	6	7	78	100
Winston-Salem, N.C. (Forsyth Co.)						
All races	14	4	18	12	54	100
Blacks	1	1	5	2	91	100

aLess than 0.5%.
Source: Jackson and Piovia, Appalachia and Its Black Population, table 18.

number of black mine laborers drastically decreased. Blacks in Tennessee and Virginia account for less than 1 percent of the total mining labor force, according to 1970 figures. While the number of black miners in West Virginia is twice the figure for Alabama, the southernmost fields have a higher percentage of blacks working in the industry.

As table 21.11 indicates, nearly one in six Appalachian blacks works in private households. When the data are further disaggregated to show how blacks are distributed within occupational categories—see table 21.12—the greater proportion are unskilled workers in service jobs in both the manufacturing and the construction sectors.

Jackson and Piovia found that black Appalachians in urban areas were

TABLE 21.13 Employment of the Black Appalachian Labor Force Aged Sixteen and Over, by Sex, 1970

	Georgia	Kentucky	North Carolina	South Carolina	Tennessee	Virginia	West Virginia	Appalachian Total Population[a]	Appalachian City Population
Males									
Employed	12,060	2,399	16,957	22,417	17,325	2,291	7,530	85,573	33,571
Unemployed	473	360	776	751	1,087	135	639	4,266	1,568
Females									
Employed	10,721	2,146	15,759	19,837	16,750	1,543	7,163	74,377	31,596
Unemployed	615	113	1,219	1,293	1,188	128	590	5,175	2,279
Males unemployed (%)[b]									
Blacks	3.8	13.1	4.4	3.2	5.9	5.6	6.3	4.9	4.4
All races	2.3	6.9	2.3	2.0	4.2	3.8	5.2	4.0	3.0
Females unemployed (%)[c]									
Blacks	5.4	5.0	7.2	6.1	6.6	7.7	7.6	6.5	6.7
All races	4.1	5.6	5.4	4.3	6.1	5.3	5.8	5.4	4.7

[a]Includes Maryland as less than 0.5 of 1% of total black Appalachian work force.
[b]U.S. totals: national, 6.3%; urban, 6.5%; rural nonfarm, 5.7%; rural farm, 4.2%.
[c]U.S. totals: national, 7.7%; urban, 7.4%; rural nonfarm, 9.7%; rural farm, 9.5%.
Source: Bellows, "Appalachian Blacks."

considerably disadvantaged, according to the pattern of their occupational distribution. In Birmingham, for example (table 21.12), black workers are disproportionately represented in common labor and service occupations. "In Chattanooga and Greenville (SC), less than one half of one percent of the black workers and only 1 to 5 percent of black workers are in professional and managerial positions."[19] In Charleston, West Virginia, blacks represented 3 percent of the total work force but 30 percent of all service workers.

Blacks in rural Appalachia, as noted above, live in economically depressed areas characterized by substantial unemployment. The supply of labor exceeds the demand for workers, who remain unemployed for relatively longer periods of time than the national average. The facts of persistent and substantial unemployment are shown by Bellows's data in tables 21.13 and 21.14. Blacks, especially women, suffer a higher rate of unemployment in Appalachia and less stability when they are employed. The experience of the common laborer or service worker is representative. Bellows draws a dismal picture: "Taking roughly eight percent unemployed, together with the roughly fifteen percent underemployed, we have nearly a quarter of the black Appalachian workforce employed less than full time." The income statistics and poverty of nearly a third of Appalachian black families speak for themselves; 12 percent of the total population have incomes below federal poverty levels. As a whole, per capita income in the region was roughly 78 percent of the national average in 1965.[20]

Perhaps the condition of blacks in coal towns is most apparent from the fact that 42 percent of the black families in Appalachian Kentucky live in poverty (table 21.15), with a third of these fully 75 percent below the poverty level. (Households with poverty status had an annual cash income below $3,000 in 1970). This figure applies to the standard index based on a family of four. Median income of all black Appalachian households (about $5,000 in 1970) is extremely low when compared to that of white regional households ($7,100). Median income for black households with male heads is roughly 90 percent of that for white households with male heads. Black female-headed households have a median income that is 89 percent of that for their white counterparts. Of course, the overall disparity of median income among black households results in part from the proportionately larger number of black female heads of household.

Appalachian states vary in their number of low-income households. Still, as the percentage of low-income households rises, blacks are more likely to constitute 10 percent of the total population. In areas that blacks had vacated by 1970, a higher percentage of marginally employed or unemployed whites remained. Remaining blacks were likely to be poorer than the average person. The reader should be careful to note that the data in table 21.16 *do not* apply to the percentage of blacks living in low-income households. The percentage figure noted in the row for black population applies only to the percentage of blacks in the population of the county. We can see from table 21.16, however, that the percentage of the black population is higher in those counties where the percentage of low-income households is highest, for example, Jefferson County in Alabama, Harlan County in Kentucky, Forsyth County in North Carolina, Hamilton County in Tennessee, and McDowell County in West Virginia.

We can draw inferences about the percentage of low-income black house-

TABLE 21.14 Weeks Worked in 1969 by Appalachian Black Males and
Appalachian Total Male Population Aged Sixteen and Over

	Kentucky	Georgia	North Carolina	South Carolina	Tennessee	Virginia	West Virginia	Appalachian Total Population[a]	Appalachian City Population
All who worked (thousands)									
Blacks	3.0	13.7	23.6	24.2	19.9	2.6	11.3	100.1	38.8
All races	193.5	218.4	280.1	180.4	453.9	117.1	425.1	1,925.0	406.1
50-52 weeks (%)									
Blacks[b]	56.8	59.2	59.6	68.3	61.7	62.9	61.5	62.0	63.5
All races	56.8	72.1	67.3	73.1	67.3	68.2	65.9	67.3	71.0
27-49 weeks (%)									
Blacks[c]	17.5	26.1	25.0	20.3	23.2	20.1	20.0	22.6	22.0
All races	28.4	18.7	21.5	16.6	21.0	22.3	21.6	21.2	18.0
Less than 27 weeks (%)									
Blacks[d]	25.7	14.7	15.4	11.4	15.0	17.0	18.5	15.3	14.5
All races	14.8	9.2	11.2	10.3	11.7	9.5	12.5	11.5	11.0

aIncludes Maryland as 0.5 of 1% of total work force.
bU.S. totals: national, 58.2%; urban, 59.5%; rural nonfarm, 52.8%; rural farm, 48.1%.
cU.S. totals: national, 27.1%; urban, 26.8%; rural nonfarm, 27.9%; rural farm, 32.1%.
dU.S. totals: national, 14.7%; urban, 13.6%; rural nonfarm, 19.3%; rural farm, 19.6%.
Source: Bellows, "Appalachian Blacks."

TABLE 21.15 Families with Income below the Poverty Level and Families Receiving Income from Social Security and Welfare, 1970

	Kentucky	Georgia	North Carolina	South Carolina	Tennessee	Virginia	West Virginia	Appalachian Total Population[a]	Appalachian City Population
All families with income (thousands)									
Blacks	3.3	13.0	20.4	23.5	22.5	2.5	19.6	100.7	42.3
All races	170.3	197.2	249.1	158.0	404.8	106.7	398.6	1,735.4	369.7
Below poverty level (%)									
Blacks[b]	41.8	31.2	30.4	32.3	35.5	27.0	31.9	32.5	32.3
All races	44.4	16.2	18.0	14.1	22.0	24.4	20.5	21.8	13.9
Below 75% of poverty level (%)									
Blacks[c]	29.7	20.6	20.7	20.8	25.1	21.7	22.2	22.2	22.3
All races	32.1	10.3	11.8	9.0	14.9	16.3	14.0	14.7	9.2
With Social Security income									
Blacks[d]	37.7	20.4	25.4	19.0	24.5	35.6	40.7	25.9	23.9
All races	37.9	20.7	24.4	19.7	24.7	32.2	30.0	26.7	22.0
With income from welfare									
Blacks[e]	20.9	15.2	12.4	7.6	16.7	8.7	13.5	13.0	13.8
All races	15.8	7.3	4.7	3.3	6.2	4.4	6.5	6.7	4.5
With income 75% of poverty level with income from welfare (%)									
Blacks[a]	70.4	73.9	60.0	36.6	66.6	40.2	60.9	58.5	62.0
All races[b]	49.2	70.9	40.0	36.5	41.4	27.3	46.3	45.1	49.2

aIncludes Maryland as less than 0.5 of 1% of total.
bU.S. totals: national, 29.8%; urban, 25.9%; rural nonfarm, 49.2%; rural farm, 49.0%.
cU.S. totals: national, 21.0%; urban, 17.9%; rural nonfarm, 36.1%; rural farm, 36.5%.
dU.S. totals: national, 18.4%; urban, 17.1%; rural nonfarm, 24.7%; rural farm, 27.0%.
eU.S. totals: national, 17.6%; urban, 17.2%; rural nonfarm, 19.9%; rural farm, 18.2%.
Source: Bellows, "Appalachian Blacks."

TABLE 21.16   Distribution of Low-Income Households
and Black Population for Selected
Appalachian Counties, 1970

State and County	% of Low-Income Households	Black Population No.	%
Alabama			
Jefferson	22	206,461	32
Tuscaloosa	28	28,964	25
Madison	17	28,517	15
Talledega	29	20,045	31
Calhoun	23	17,342	17
Kentucky			
Madison	28	2,746	6
Harlan	38	2,335	6
Clark	24	1,965	8
Pike	40	1,305	2
Montgomery	31	1,133	7
Georgia			
Floyd	18	9,697	13
Carroll	24	7,531	17
Hall	22	6,015	10
Polk	23	4,636	16
Bartow	22	4,376	13
North Carolina			
Forsyth	15	47,825	22
Buncombe	20	15,825	11
Rutherford	23	5,412	11
Burke	16	4,809	8
Caldwell	16	3,688	7
South Carolina			
Greenville	16	39,829	17
Spartanburg	20	36,482	21
Anderson	21	19,046	18
Cherokee	26	7,098	19
Pickens	17	5,537	9
Oconee	25	4,051	10
Tennessee			
Hamilton	19	47,416	19
Knox	23	23,084	9
Sullivan	19	3,235	3
Washington	25	3,081	4
Blount	23	2,737	4
Virginia			
Pulaski	24	1,804	6
Botetort	24	1,527	8
Tazwell	27	1,337	3
Covington	15	1,212	12
Bristol	25	1,079	7
West Virginia			
Kanawah	18	14,347	6
McDowell	34	9,373	18
Raleigh	32	8,078	12
Mercer	31	5,460	9
Fayette	32	5,198	11

Source: Jackson and Piovia, Appalachia and Its Black
Population, table 20.

holds from the data in table 21.17, which shows that blacks in coal-mining states are more likely to receive social security income than those in other Appalachian regions. Overall, the proportion of blacks receiving income from social security is only 11 percent greater than the proportion of all Appalachian families.

The fact that inadequate housing is a severe problem in Appalachia was addressed by a recent ARC report.[21] In the four counties listed in table 21.18, the housing prospects of blacks are diminished not only because blacks do not have the income to qualify for bank loans but also because acres suitable for housing are held off the market by corporate owners of the area's vast coal reserves. Only in Pride Terrace, in Harlan County, Kentucky, have blacks risen above substandard and inadequate housing conditions.[22] In metropolitan areas of Appalachia, Jackson and Piovia showed that "the proportion of overcrowded rental units occupied by blacks in Forsyth County North Carolina and Jefferson County Alabama was 21 and 30 percent, respectively—double the white rate."[23] A regionwide average of 32 percent of blacks lived in units that lacked plumbing. Such units represented roughly one-tenth of all occupied units.

CONCLUSIONS AND THOUGHTS FOR FURTHER RESEARCH

Blacks came to north and central Appalachia a century ago. Industry in eastern Kentucky, southwest Virginia, and portions of West Virginia is now technologically outmoded and is undergoing extensive machine-intensive modernization. The central region moved from the single-based economy some years earlier and shows noticeable in-migration to meet the labor demands of a diversified marketplace. Birmingham, which dominates the southern region, is largely recognized as a modern industrial and trade center. In spite of a decade of reawakening that has been noted by Tom Gish ("There is a sense of well-being in the area that was not here before—it is not the same sense of desperation") and by ARC Commissioner Al Smith ("I've got more hope for the region than I had . . . twenty years ago"), blacks in Appalachia are in a relatively depressed socioeconomic position.[24]

The rate of total population growth in the region equaled the national average from 1970 to 1973, but such has not been the case for blacks. Black depopulation in Appalachia has continued through the 1970s, except in selected SMSAs in the southern region. The incidence of black poverty in Appalachia was higher than that for blacks nationally, and black median income is generally about half the median income for whites in Appalachia. The only plain distinction between Appalachian blacks and their white neighbors is the fact that blacks have a higher percentage of very poor families on welfare. Their misery and neglect have been reported in terms of virtually every indicator of social health: (1) higher out-migration; (2) higher dependency ratios; (3) higher percentages of female-headed households; and (4) higher incidence of poverty resulting from lowered educational levels, unemployment, and low-paying jobs. The only group of persons worse off economically than black Appalachians are rural blacks in the United States. Rural Appalachian blacks are likely among America's poorest people.

TABLE 21.17 Poverty Status and Social Security and Welfare of Appalachian Black Families with Income, 1970

	Georgia	Kentucky	North Carolina	South Carolina	Tennessee	Virginia	West Virginia	Appalachian Total[a]	Appalachian Urban Total
All families	13,017	3,310	20,414	23,569	22,508	2,571	19,656	100,736	42,381
Below the poverty level	4,058	1,385	6,193	7,606	7,981	695	4,673	32,757	13,695
Below 75% of the poverty level	2,676	983	4,231	4,898	5,644	557	3,257	22,348	9,450
With Social Security income	2,657	1,247	5,183	4,476	5,518	915	5,959	26,089	10,123
With income from welfare	1,978	692	2,533	1,793	3,758	224	1,984	13,071	5,863

[a]Includes Maryland as 0.5 of 1% of total number of black families in Appalachia.
Source: Bellows, "Appalachian Blacks."

TABLE 21.18 Housing Characteristics for Selected Appalachian Counties
beyond Standard Metropolitan Statistical Areas, 1970

	Clark Co., Kentucky	Harlan Co., Kentucky	Pulaski Co., Virginia	McDowell Co., West Virginia
Owner-occupied housing (%)				
All races	61	59	73	61
Blacks	51	56	73	60
Median value ($)				
All races	15,400	5,000	10,500	5,000
Blacks	6,000	5,000	6,000	5,000
Renter-occupied housing (%)				
All races	39	41	27	39
Blacks	49	44	27	40
Monthly rent ($)				
All races	63	30	55	30
Blacks	39	30	30	30
All housing				
Percent lacking plumbing				
All races[a]	18	41	24	41
Blacks	16	42	53	52
Median number of rooms				
All races	5.2	4.7	4.9	4.6
Blacks	4.9	4.3	4.8	4.4
Percent overcrowded[b]				
All races	8	16	11	18
Blacks	13	21	22	22

Note: Counties were selected on the basis of the size of their black populations
and the percentage of households with incomes under $3,000.

[a]Includes all year-round housing units, whether occupied or not.
[b]Housing with more than one person per room.
Source: Jackson and Piovia, Appalachia and Its Black Population, table 23.

If Appalachian blacks must move to urban areas to improve their lot in the
future, the data nevertheless show that out-migration from Appalachian regions
is lower than from rural sections. Four in ten black Appalachians in the southern
region live in nonmetropolitan counties, and the proportion is higher in Kentucky, West Virginia, and Virginia. In these areas, the rate of black unemployment is highest of all the subregions in which alternatives to mining
employment are severely limited. Migration from these areas is likely to
stabilize within two decades, leaving a group destined for retirement. Floyd and
Fleming counties in Kentucky, and Scott, Lee, and Wise in Virginia, may have
no blacks in a few decades.

Bellows reasons on the basis of the "relatively high percentage" of blacks
in construction and manufacturing that the future may offer blacks enhanced
economic opportunity and stabilized incomes,[25] especially in the urban regions
of the southern highlands. Blacks in construction and manufacturing show a
higher degree of satisfaction than nonmetropolitan blacks.

The blacks of the coal-mining region offer the most unique case for
sociological research. Investigation is needed to determine the relative influence of poverty *and* racial discrimination on their status, but this group appears
to be a permanent fixture in the region's economic structure, representing the
permanently entrapped black poor (the black underclass of Appalachia).[26] In
addition to revealing pockets of black poverty, studies of structural factors over
time would show the systematic connections between blacks' lack of mobility

and institutional racism (unions, institutional practices in education, and local customs).

Research into the aspirations of black rural and coal-town Appalachians would provide information of great value in testing hypotheses about the effects of long-term poverty and modes of adaptation. Of special note here is the key function of extended-type black Appalachian families and the informal adoption or foster care of young children and the elderly.[27] Finally, the data that I have considered suggest the advisability of studying the cultural ethos of blacks isolated in coal towns as it reflects their occupational obsolescence and persistent poverty. Localized participant-observation research could tell us much about (1) individual expression, (2) verbal communication, (3) intergroup and intragroup relations, and (4) the vast spectrum of value complexes. While the facts of the picture are dismal generally, they warrant intensified study if we are to penetrate beyond the pessimism and despair. There is no better time to begin research on a condition that has always been bad and has never been studied.

1. Belcher's work and that of Brown and Hillery are used mainly for their reputations as classic base-line studies of the Appalachian population. Their data cannot be compared with the data in this study because the definition of the region differs. For example, Belcher does not include all West Virginia counties as I do here; he omits seventeen of the counties used commonly in the ARC state analysis of Kentucky, and for him, Alabama has five rather than thirty-five counties in the Appalachian region. See John C. Belcher, "Population Growth and Characteristics," and James A. Brown and Gregory A. Hillery, Jr., "The Great Migration, 1940-1960," in *The Southern Appalachian Region: A Survey*, ed. Thomas R. Ford, Lexington, Ky., 1967.

2. For a fuller discussion of the methodological reasons for the differences between this and the ARC definitions of the region, see David Bellows, "Appalachian Blacks: A Demographic Analysis" (master's thesis, Rutgers University, 1974).

3. Harry Caudill, *Night Comes to the Cumberlands* (Boston, 1963), p. 21.

4. Of note in Taylor's work is the fact that he offers a county-by-county analysis which conforms (roughly) to the definition used here of Appalachia. See James W. Taylor, *Alleghenia: A Geographic and Statistical Memoir* (St. Paul, Minn., 1862). By adding Alabama to Taylor's count, we arrive at a total number of blacks roughly equal to that shown in table 21.1 here.

5. These counties ring Appalachia and were, in fact, part of the slaveholding portion of Kentucky.

6. The percentages were reported by E. Franklin Frazier, *The Negro in the United States* (New York, 1957), on the basis of U.S. Bureau of the Census, *Negro Population Report of the United States, 1790-1915* (Washington, D.C., 1918). This report considers (Appalachian) New York, Pennsylvania, and Ohio to be in the North, while all other Appalachian states are placed in the South. See also U.S. Bureau of the Census, *A Century of Population Growth: From the First Census to the Twelfth, 1790-1900* (Washington, D.C., 1909).

7. See, for example, William Lynwood Montell's *The Saga of Coe Ridge: A Study in Oral History* (Knoxville, Tenn., 1970).

8. Sterling D. Spero and Abram L. Harris, *The Black Worker, 1915-1930* (1931; reprint ed., New York, 1974).

9. Herbert Northrup, *Organized Labor and the Negro* (New York, 1944).

10. Bellows, "Appalachian Blacks," p. 42. This work, the most recent areawide analysis, is based on three studies: (1) Michael Burland, *The Status of Black People in Appalachia: A Statistical Report* (New York, 1971); (2) Eli March and A. King, "Blacks in Appalachia, Population Trends: 1960-1970," *Current Statistical Report*, no. 4 (Washington, D.C., 1970); and (3) Gloria Jackson and Ester Piovia, *Appalachia and Its Black Population: Selected Social and Economic Characteristics* (New York, 1972).

11. Bellows, "Appalachian Blacks," p. 23; Gordon F. De Jong, *Appalachia Fertility Decline: A Demographic and Sociological Analysis* (Lexington, Ky., 1968); Belcher, "Population Growth and Characteristics."

12. Brown and Hillery, "The Great Migration."

13. Robert B. Hill, *Informal Adoption among Black Families* (Washington, D.C., 1977).

14. Donald T. Barnum, *The Negro in the Bituminous Coal Mining Industry* (Philadelphia, 1970).

15. William W. Philliber and Phillip J. Obermiller, "Black Appalachian Migrants: The Issue of Dual Minority Status," paper presented at the Fifth Annual Appalachian Studies Conferences, Virginia Polytechnic Institute and State University, Blacksburg, Va., March 26-28, 1982.

16. See William P. Jackameit, "A Short History of Negro Public Higher Education in West Virginia," *West Virginia History*, 37, no. 4 (July, 1976); Henry Bullock, *A History of Negro Education in the South* (Cambridge, Mass., 1976).

17. Dwight Billings, "Culture and Poverty in Appalachia: A Theoretical Discussion and Empirical Analysis," *Social Forces,* 53 (December 1974).

18. Gary L. Fowler, "Locating Southern Migrants in Northern Cities," paper presented at the Symposium on Southern White Rural Poverty and Urban Migration, Central States Anthropological Society Meeting, Chicago, 1973.

19. Jackson and Piovia, *Appalachia and Its Black Population.*

20. Bellows, "Appalachian Blacks," p. 54.

21. Ben A. Franklin reviewed the study under the title "Opinions Differ on Success of Appalachian Commission," reported in the Lexington, Ky., *Sunday Herald-Leader,* Sept. 27, 1981.

22. The saga of a black Appalachian housing cooperative is recounted in an interview with the group's organizer, Mrs. Mattye Knight. See Shelia Poole, "From Sanctified Hill to Pride Terrace," *Louisville Defender,* Feb. 18, 1982, p. C25.

23. Jackson and Piovia, *Appalachia and Its Black Population,* p. 46.

24. John Stephenson and David Walls, *Appalachia in the 60s: Decade of Reawakening* (Lexington, Ky., 1978).

25. Bellows, "Appalachian Blacks."

26. Douglas G. Glasgow, *The Black Underclass* (Washington, D.C., 1980).

27. Hill, *Informal Adoption.*

Selected Bibliography

EDWARD J. CABBELL AND WILLIAM H. TURNER

Edward J. Cabbell's master's thesis, "References and Resources on Black Appalachians" (Appalachian State University, 1982), comes closer than any other document to being a comprehensive bibliography on Black Appalachia. The present listing consists of works judged to be relevant to further study of topics covered in this anthology. Single asterisks (*) denote resource works recognized as "major." Some of these works are shelved by libraries as handbooks and/or as guides to selected subjects, and are noted here as much because materials pertaining to black life in Appalachia are scarce as because they afford important glimpses of Black Appalachian history, culture, and so on. The works do supply sufficient information, however, to give the researcher some starting points. Two asterisks (**) indicate more general studies. Entries without asterisks focus directly on Black Appalachia.

PART ONE. BASIC APPROACHES

Armheim, Carolyn, Sr., Mary N. Garrett, and Louise Stevenson. *Black Appalachian Resource Book*. Cincinnati: Appalachian Community Development Association, 1981.

Boggs, Beth, Marilyn Eheman, Cherly Henkel, Linda Hoover, Barbara Kitchen, and Beverly Lewis. *The Black Appalachian Reader*. Cincinnati: Appalachian Community Development Association, 1981.

Clark, Cedrix X. "White Researcher in Black Society." *Journal of Social Issues*, 20, no. 7 (1973), 88.

Durant, Thomas J., and Clark S. Knowlton. "Rural Ethnic Minorities: Adaptive Responses to Inequality." In *Rural U.S.A.: Persistence and Change*. Edited by Thomas R. Ford. Ames: Iowa State University Press, 1978.**

A Guide to Appalachian Studies. Special issue of *Appalachian Journal*, 5 (Autumn 1977).*

Kentucky Commission on Human Rights. *Kentucky's Black Heritage*. Frankfort: Commonwealth of Kentucky, 1971.**

Porter, Julia D. "The Case of Appalachians." *Educational Comment*, 7, no. 20 (1979).

Reddick, L. D. "Black History as a Corporate Colony." *Social Policy*, 3, no. 1 (May-June 1976), pp. 50-55.**

Sawyer, Ethel. "Methodological Problems in Studying So-Called 'Deviant' Communities." In *The Death of White Sociology*. Edited by Joyce Ladner. New York: Vintage Books, 1973.**

Turner, William H. "Black Appalachians." In *Encyclopedia of Southern Culture*. Jackson: University Press of Mississippi. Edited by William Ferris, forthcoming.

PART TWO. HISTORICAL PERSPECTIVES

Cabbell, Edward J. "Mountain Heritage: The Legend of John Henry." *Mountain Life and Work,* 11, no. 7 (November 1978).

Caruso, John Anthony. *The Appalachian Frontier.* New York: Bobbs-Merrill, 1959.**

Cressey, Paul F. "Social Disorganization and Reorganization in Harlan County, Kentucky." *American Sociological Review,* 14 (1949), 204-21.**

Logan, Rayford, and J. Fred Rippy. "The Negro and the Spanish Pioneers in the New World." *Journal of Negro History,* 6 (April 1921), 69-78.**

New York Public Library. *Dictionary Catalog of the Schomberg Collection of Negro Literature and History.* Boston: G. K. Hall, 1962.*

Pinchback, Richard B. *The Virginia Negro Artisan and Tradesman.* University of Virginia, Phelps-Stokes Fellowship Papers, no. 7. Richmond: William Byrd Press, 1920.

Porter, Kenneth W. *The Negro on the American Frontier.* New York: Arno Press, 1971.**

Spencer, Samuel R. *Booker T. Washington and the Negro's Place in American Life.* Boston: Little, Brown, 1953.**

Taylor, James W. *Alleghenia: A Geographic and Statistical Memoir.* St. Paul, Minn.: James Davenport, 1862.

PART THREE. COMMUNITY STUDIES

Allen, Fayetta. "Blacks in Appalachia." *Black Scholar,* 5 (June 1974), 64.

Berea College, Hutchins Library, Weatherford-Hammond Appalachian Collection. *A Fifty-Year Gathering of County Histories . . . Adair to Yancy: 423 Mountain County and Local Histories from Eight States "Home Counties" to Berea Students.* Berea, Ky.: Berea College, 1977.

Caudill, Harry M. *Night Comes to the Cumberland.* Boston: Atlantic-Little, Brown, 1963.

Feld, Rose C. "What I found in Lynch, Kentucky." *New Age Illustrated,* March 1926.**

French, Jac. "Segregation Patterns in a Coal Camp." Master's thesis, West Virginia University, 1953.**

French, Lawrence. "The Isolated Appalachian Black Community." Paper presented at the annual meetings of the Rural Sociological Society, San Francisco, August 27–30, 1975.

Reeves, David. "Black Appalachians in the City." *Mountain Life and Work,* 52 (August 1976), 18-26.

United States Department of the Interior. Bureau of Mines. *Houses for Mining Towns.* Bulletin no. 87. Washington, D.C.: Government Printing Office, 1914.**

PART FOUR. RACE RELATIONS

Minard, Ralph D. "Race Relations in the Pocahontas Coal Field." *Journal of Social Issues,* 8 (1952), 58-64.

Montell, William Lynwood. *The Saga of Coe Ridge: A Study in Oral History.* Knoxville: University of Tennessee Press, 1970.

Smith, Douglas C. "Race Relations and Institutional Responses in West Virginia: A History." *West Virginia History,* 39, no. 1 (October 1977), 550-568.

Turner, William H. "Race: The Ignored Dimensions of the Colonial Analogy as Applied to Powerlessness and Exploitation in Appalachia." *Western Journal of Black Studies,* 7, no. 1 (Spring 1983), 10-20.

United States. Coal Commission. Living Conditions Section. *Records of the Division of Investigation of Labor Facts*. Washington, D.C.: U. S. Government Printing Office, 1923.*

PART FIVE. BLACK COAL MINERS

Barnum, Donald T. *The Negro in the Bituminous Coal Mining Industry*. Philadelphia: University of Pennsylvania Press, 1970.

Brainerd, Alfred. "Colored Mining Labor." *AIME Transactions*, 14 (1885/86), 78-80.

Chappel, Louis W. *John Henry: A Folk-Lore Study*. Jena: Frommannsche, 1933.

"Handling the Negro Miner in the South." *Coal Age*, 5 (1914), 875.

Harris, A. L. "The Negro in the Coal Mining Industry." *Opportunity*, Fall 1926.

Hawley, Langston T., "Negro Employment in the Birmingham Metropolitan Area." In *Selected Studies of Negro Employment in the South*. Report no. 6. National Planning Association Committee of the South. Washington, D.C.: National Planning Association, 1955.

Mell, P. H. "The Coal and Iron Interests of Alabama." *Coal*, 1 (1982), 389-91.

Nyden, Paul. *Black Coal Miners in the United States*. New York: American Institute for Marxist Studies, 1974.

Spero, S. D., and Abram L. Harris. *The Black Worker, 1915-1930*. 1931. Reprint ed., New York: Atheneum, 1974.

Surface, George T. "The Negro Mine Laborer: Central Appalachian Coal Fields." *Annals of the American Academy of Science*, 33 (1909), 338-52.

Walker, William S. "Occupational Aspirations of Negro Family Members in a Coal Mining Community." Master's thesis, New York University, 1950.

Williams, John R. "Immigrant and Negro Labor in the Coal Mines." In *The Negro in American History*. Vol. 2. Edited by William Benton. New York: Encyclopaedia Britannica Education Corporation, 1969.

PART SIX. BLACKS AND LOCAL POLITICS

Brier, Stephen. "Interracial Organizing in the West Virginia Coal Industry: The Participation of Black Mine Workers in the Knights of Labor and the UMWA, 1880-1894." In *Essays in Southern Labor History*. Edited by Gary Fink and Merle E. Reed. Westport, Conn.: Greenwood Press, 1978.

Fisher, Stephen L. "Dissertations Relating to the Study of Appalachian Politics." *Appalachian Notes*, 5, no. 4 (3d quarter, 1975), 255-260.*

Turner, William H. "Highlander in the Center of the Civil Rights Movement." Paper presented at the Sixth Annual Appalachian Studies Conference, Pipestem State Park, Pipestem, W. Va., March 17-19, 1983.

Walton, Haynes. *The Study and Analysis of Black Politics: A Bibliography*. New York: Scarecrow Press, 1973.**

PART SEVEN. PERSONAL ANECDOTAL
ACCOUNTS OF BLACK LIFE

Broadnax, Eliza (interviewed by Randy Lawrence). "Making a Way out of Nothing." *Goldenseal*, 5, no. 4 (Oct.-Dec., 1979), 231.

Caudill, Harry M. "The Mountain, the Miner, and the Lord." *Appalachian Heritage*, 9 (Summer 1974), 28-39.

Epstein, Dena J. *Sinful Tunes and Spirituals: Black Folk Music to the Civil War.* Urbana: University of Illinois Press, 1972.**

Farley, Yvonne S. "Homecoming." *Black Culture in the Mountain State.* Special issue of *Goldenseal,* 5, no. 4 (Oct.-Dec. 1979), 241-47.

Nyden, Paul J. "Clint Thomas and the Negro Baseball League," *Goldenseal,* 5, no. 4 (Oct.-Dec., 1979), 248-56.

Witt, Matt. *In Our Blood.* New Market, Tenn.: Highlander Education and Research Center, 1979.

PART EIGHT. SELECTED DEMOGRAPHIC ASPECTS

Belcher, John C. "Population Growth and Characteristics." In *The Southern Appalachian Region: A Survey.* Edited by Thomas R. Ford. Lexington: University of Kentucky Press, 1962.*

Bellows, David. "Appalachian Blacks: A Demographic Analysis." Master's thesis, Rutgers University, 1974.

Brown, James S., and George A. Hillery, Jr. "The Great Migration: 1940-1960." In *The Southern Appalachian Region: A Survey.* Edited by Thomas R. Ford. Lexington: University of Kentucky Press, 1967.

Bruland, Michael. *The Status of Black People in Appalachia: A Statistical Report.* New York: NAACP Legal Defense and Education Fund, 1971.

Campbell, Rex, D. Johnson, and G. Strangler. "Return Migration of Black People to the South." *Rural Sociology,* 51 (1977), 802.

Fowler, Gary L. "Population Sketches of Black Appalachia." Department of Geography, University of Illinois, Chicago Circle Campus, January 6, 1982. Typescript.

Hillery, George A., Jr. "Population Growth in Kentucky: 1820-1960." Bulletin 705. Lexington: University of Kentucky Agricultural Experiment Station, February 1966.**

Jackson, Gloria, and Ester Piovia. *Appalachia and Its Black Population: Selected Social and Economic Characteristics.* New York: National Urban League, 1972.

Johnson, Daniel M. "Black Return Migration to a Southern Metropolis: Birmingham, Alabama." Ph.D., Department of Sociology, University of Missouri, Columbia, 1973.

March, Eli, A. King, and M. Lem. "Blacks in Appalachia, Population Trends: 1900-1970." *Current Statistical Report,* no. 4. Washington, D.C.: Appalachian Regional Commission, 1971.

Philliber, William W., and Phillip J. Obermiller. "Black Appalachian Migrants: The Issue of Dual Minority Status." Paper presented at the Fifth Annual Appalachian Studies Conference, Virginia Polytechnic Institute and State University, Blacksburg, Va., March 26-28, 1982.

OTHER

Moore, Carolyn B. *Out-migration in Appalachia: An Annotated Bibliography,* III. Council of Planning Librarians Exchange Bibliography, no. 1024.**

Ross, Charlotte T., ed. *Bibliography of Southern Appalachia.* Boone, N.C.: Appalachian Consortium, 1976.*

Resource Guide

Compiled by
EDWARD J. CABBELL

CULTURAL ORGANIZATIONS

Afro-American Center for the Performing Arts. 848 Bland St., Bluefield, WV 24701. A community-based dance and drama group that draws upon various themes and materials within Appalachia.

Appalachian South Folklife Center. P.O. Box C, Pipestem, WV 25979. A non-profit educational organization dedicated to a mountain heritage of freedom, self-respect, and independence with human dignity to the end that people of all races, faiths, and nationalities may better understand one another and to work and live together for peace, brotherhood, and plenty for all.

Beck Cultural Center. 1927 Dandridge Avenue, Knoxville, TN 37915. A museum that collects, assembles, preserves, and displays cultural materials of blacks in Tennessee.

Black Appalachian Advisory Council. P.O. Box 1186, Princeton, WV 24740. Under the umbrella of the Appalachian Studies Conference, this organization seeks to promote an awareness and understanding of the black experience in Appalachia through academic research and study of blacks in Appalachia.

Black Culture Center and Interracial Education Program. Berea College, CPO 134, Berea, KY 40404. Cultural and educational programs at Berea College are designed to develop an interracial sense of history and cultural pride at the first interracial college in the South.

Carpetbag Theatre. 3018 E. Fifth Ave., Knoxville, TN 37914. A community-based professional theatre company with minority writers, artists, dancers and musicians. Its ensemble company has received acclaim for its original productions.

Council on Black Appalachians. c/o Council of the Southern Mountains, P.O. Box 1188, Clintwood, VA 24228. A reorganized group (1983) of the Black Appalachians Commission established under the umbrella of the Council of the Southern Mountains in 1969. The group became inactive in 1975. The present organization is designed to address the social, political, and economic plight of black Appalachians.

Eastern Kentucky Social Club. c/o Office of the Dean, College of Arts and Sciences, Kentucky State University, Frankfort, KY 40601. The umbrella organization for social, benevolent, and educational issues. Members include blacks with roots in Eastern Kentucky. Chapters exist in Cleveland, Chicago, New York City, Dayton, Cincinnati, Detroit, Louisville, Lexington, and Hartford, Conn. The club holds an annual reunion and publishes *Sojourner*.

Highlander Research and Education Center. Route 3, Box 370, New Market, TN 37820.

A gathering place for dozens of groups throughout Appalachia and the South who want a place where they can talk freely without fear of reprisals, and work with others to gain greater self-determination. Sponsors a "We Shall Overcome" fund (grants of $500 maximum) to projects that seek to preserve and develop black culture.

John Henry Folk Festival. P.O. Box 135, Princeton, WV 24740. An Appalachian intercultural heritage festival that emphasizes cultural exchanges in the music of the southern highlands from a black perspective.

John Henry Memorial Foundation, Inc. P.O. Box 135, Princeton, WV 24740. A non-profit group established to research the heritage, culture, and life history of blacks in Appalachia as well as the John Henry folk legend. The group has produced an annual John Henry Folk Festival since 1973 and John Henry Records and Black Diamonds magazine since 1978.

SERVICE ORGANIZATIONS

Buffalo Soldiers. P.O. Box 590, Institute, WV 25112. A community-based, non-profit service organization designed to help youth and elderly develop a sense of Afro and Appalachian history and pride.

Greater Cumberland Corporation. P.O. Box 115, Drawer G, Cumberland, KY. 40823. A non-profit housing organization that sponsors low- and moderate-income housing in Cumberland, Kentucky.

Neighborhood Improvement Association, Inc. P.O. Box 1186, Princeton, WV 24740. A community-based, non-profit organization designed to achieve decent, safe, and sanitary housing for low- to moderate-income households in the predominantly African-American neighborhoods in Princeton, West Virginia.

FILMS AND FILMSTRIPS

Banjo Man: The Life and Music of Uncle Homer Walker. New York: Texture Films, 1976. 26 min., b&w, 16mm. A film that reveals the life and music of a 78-year-old, black clawhammer banjo player who lives in the mountains of southwestern Virginia. Taj Mahal narrates this film.

Blacks in Eastern Kentucky. Produced by University of Kentucky Appalachian Center, Lexington, Kentucky, 1981. 50 mins., color, 16 mm. An interview format looking into the various themes in the history and current status of black communities in Appalachia, with John B. Stephenson, Director of UK Appalachian Center and William H. Turner, Assistant Professor of Sociology at UK.

Born for Hard Luck. Delaplane, Virginia: Tom Davenport Films, 1976. 29 min., b&w, 16 mm. A portrait of Arthur "Peg Leg Sam" Jackson, a traveling patent-medicine show musician. Captioned.

Clinchco: The Story of a Coalmining Town. Whitesburg, Kentucky: Appalshop, 1982. 30 min., filmstrip. The story of a former coal camp in southwestern Virginia with a substantial black population. Also available in video.

Legend of John Henry, The. Santa Monica, California: Pyramid Films, 1974. 11 min., color, 16mm. An animated tale of the John Henry folk legend. Roberta Flack sings and narrates this folk tale. [See also below.]

'Sho Is Good to See You Again. Produced by William H. Turner, in cooperation with Appalshop, Whitesburg, Kentucky, 1981. 32 min., color, 16mm. A lively documentation of the 13th Annual Reunion of the Eastern Kentucky Social Club.

Includes interviews with migrants and footage of black communities/people in
Harlan and Letcher counties of Eastern Kentucky.

RECORDS INTRODUCING TRADITIONAL
BLACK APPALACHIAN MUSICIANS

Baker, Etta, guitarist [115 Brackett St., Morgantown, NC 28655]. *Music from the Hills
of Caldwell County*. Physical Records (Stereo 12-001), 1975. Traditional guitar and
banjo tunes by blacks in Caldwell County. Also includes numbers by Vora Phillips,
Theopolis Phillips, Fred Reid, and Babe Reid.

————. *Instrumental Music of the Southern Appalachians*. Tradition Records (TLP
1007), 1956. Nine tunes by Etta Baker, Boone Reid, and Lacey Phillips are included
in this collection of twenty banjo, fiddle, guitar, dulcimer, and harmonica tunes
recorded in the mountains of North Carolina and Virginia.

Gilmore, Earl, vocals, piano [Box 313, Clinchco, VA 24226]. *From the Depths of My
Soul*. June Appal Recordings (JA 022), 1977. A gospel musician with a blues
influence in his music.

Martin, Bogan and Armstrong, guitar, fiddle, mandolin, bass, vocals [c/o Wm. Howard
Armstrong, 430 East Warren, Apt. 307, Detroit, MI 48201]. *Barnyard Dance*.
Rounder Records (2003), 1972. Core members of the Four Keys String Band (which
originated in Huntington, West Virginia, in 1931) play popular songs of the '20s and
'30s, the blues, and old timey fiddle tunes.

————. *Martin, Bogan & Armstrong*. Flying Fish (003), 1974. Early black string
band performance.

————. *That Old Gang of Mine*. Flying Fish (FF-056), 1978. After 50 years, this
black string band still reveals distinctive individual as well as ensemble talents.

Rucker, James "Sparky," guitar, vocals [2226 Brooks Road, Knoxville, TN 37403].
Bound to Sing the Blues. Tradition Records (SR-372), 1974. Strong renditions of
blues, spirituals, freedom songs, and bottleneck guitar style by a young black
Appalachian musician.

————. *Cold and Lonesome on a Train*. June Appal Recordings (JA 017), 1977.
Sparky shouts, howls, moans, murmurs, admonishes, and demands attention on
this album of traditional and original songs.

————. *Heroes and Hard Times*. Green Linnet (SIF 1032), 1981. Black American
ballads and other story songs are presented in this album of inspiration and
education.

PRESENTATIONS OF THE LEGEND OF JOHN HENRY

Bradford, Roark. *John Henry*. New York: Literary Guild, 1931. A novel based on the folk
elements of the John Henry legend.

Chappell, Louis W. *John Henry: A Folk Lore Study*. Jena, Germany: Frommannsche
Verlag, Walter Bidermann, 1933; reprint, Kennikat Press, 1968. Scholarly research
that establishes a factual-historical basis for the John Henry legend.

Dorson, Richard M. "The Career of 'John Henry'," *Western Folklore*, 24, no. 3 (July
1965), 155-64. A folklorist traces the development of the John Henry legend.

Green, Archie. "John Henry Depicted." *John Edwards Memorial Foundation Quarterly*,
14 (1978), 126-43. A folklorist traces John Henry's appearance in graphic forms.
Includes a checklist of John Henry depictions.

————. "Fred Becker's John Henry." *John Edwards Memorial Foundation Quar-*

terly, 15 (1979), 30-37. Nine graphics on John Henry produced by WPA Federal
Arts Project artist Fred Becker between 1935 and 1939.

_____. "John Henry Revisited." *John Edwards Memorial Foundation Quarterly,* 19
(1983), 12-31. The folklorist discusses Brett Williams's discography/bibliography,
John Henry: A Bio-Bibliography (Greenwood Press, 1983). Includes a checklist of
books and journals, sheet music, LPs, animated films, sculpture, fine art, folk art,
and miscellaneous John Henry depictions.

Johnson, Guy B. *John Henry: Tracking Down a Negro Legend.* Chapel Hill: University
of North Carolina Press, 1929. An attempt to describe in some detail the legend of
John Henry.

Keats, Ezra Jack. *John Henry: An American Legend.* New York: Pantheon Books, 1965.
A book for children based on the legend.

Killins, John Oliver. *A Man Ain't Nothing But A Man.* Boston: Little, Brown and
Company, 1975. A short story of the legendary John Henry.

Miller, Jeffrey. *John Henry.* Clintwood, Virginia: Council of the Southern Mountains,
1973. A small pamphlet that reveals the significance of John Henry as a laborer as
well as a folk hero.

Williams, Brett. *John Henry: A Bio-Bibliography.* Westport, Connecticut: Greenwood
Press, 1983. The ambiguous John Henry legend is made much more conclusive by
this comprehensive discography/bibliography. An excellent checklist of John Henry materials.

FICTIONAL LITERATURE

Alther, Lisa. *Original Sins.* New York: Knopf, 1981. Race relations in the mountains are
among the plethora of themes in this novel.

Bowen, Robert. *Tall in the Sight of God.* Winston-Salem, N.C.: John F. Blair, 1958.
Autobiographical fiction about a Negro family from Wilkes County, N.C.

Cather, Willa. *Sapphira and the Slave Girl.* New York: Knopf, 1940. Character sketches
of Sapphira Dodderidge Colbert and her maid. Colbert is a Virginian who marries a
man who runs a mill in a Blue Ridge frontier town.

Caudill, Rebecca. *A Certain Small Shepherd.* New York: Holt, Rinehart, and Winston,
1965. [CMS Bookstore] A miracle occurs on a Christmas night when a handi-
capped child finally learns to talk. A black family is involved in the climax of the
story.

Curry, Jane. *Daybreakers.* New York: Harcourt, 1970. In West Virginia three children
(two black and one white) discover a fantasy world outside their ugly milltown.

Demby, William. *Beetlecreek.* New York: Rinehart, 1950. [CSM Bookstore] A story
illustrating the inevitable sufferings of both blacks and whites in a back country
southern town when they violate the race relations system.

Ehle, John. *Move Over, Mountain.* New York: Morrow, 1957. Jordan Cummings, a North
Carolina truck driver, and wife Annie, face problems of being black and poor.

_____. *The Journey of August King.* New York: Harper and Row, 1971. A western
North Carolina farmer, circa 1850, risks life, property, and reputation to save an
escaping slave girl.

Forbush, Elizabeth. *Savage Sundown.* Los Angeles: Pinnacle Books, 1980. A novel
based on an actual 1912 racial incident in northeastern Georgia that results in
banishment of blacks from the area.

Ford, Jesse Hill. *The Liberation of Lord Bryon Jones.* New York: Atlantic Monthly Press,
1965. A novel of violence and racial tension set in the foothills of Tennessee.

Grubb, Davis. *Shadow of My Brother.* New York: Holt, 1966. A novel of racial violence
set in the southern mountains.

Hamilton, Virginia. *M.C. Higgins, the Great.* New York: Macmillan, 1974. [CSM Bookstore] M.C. Higgins is a thirteen-year-old black boy who in the space of two days finds himself confronted with his feelings about the hill country, the world beyond, and his family.

Harben, William Nathaniel. *Mam' Linda: A Novel.* New York: Harper, 1907. A novel about a black woman in Appalachia.

Holley, Juliette Ann. *Jamie Lemme See.* Radford, Virginia: Commonwealth Press, 1975. [CSM Bookstore] The world as seen through the eyes of a young black boy in the coal fields of West Virginia.

McMeekin, Isabel. *Journey Cake.* New York: Messner, 1942. Juba, a free colored woman in the Yadkin Valley of North Carolina, takes her dead mistress's children over the mountains to Kentucky to join their father.

————. *Juba's New Moon.* New York: Messner, 1944. Another story of the invincible Juba and the youngsters she guards in the wilds of Kentucky.

Perry, Octavia. *My Head's High from Proudness.* Winston-Salem, N.C.: John F. Blair, 1963. An account of a Negro man's search for pride and independence in the mountains of North Carolina and Virginia.

Reece, Byron. *The Hawk and the Sun.* New York: Simon and Simon, 1957. A young school teacher takes a stand on the race problem and sets off a chain reaction leading to her dismissal. The setting for this novel about segregation is a Burke County, N.C., town.

Streeter, James. *Home Is over the Mountains.* Westport, Conn.: Garrard, 1972. The true story of the journey of five black children in Tennessee.

Upchurch, Boyd. *The Slave Stealer.* New York: Weybright and Talley, 1968. An itinerant peddler in the southern mountains before the Civil War aids runaway slaves and helps a young and beautiful girl to escape.

Yerby, Frank. *A Woman Called Fancy.* New York: Dial, 1951. [CSM Bookstore] A novel by a black author about a nineteen-year-old white girl who flees to Augusta, Georgia, from the Carolina hills when her parents agree to sell her into marriage to a sixty-five-year-old man to pay her father's drinking debts.

THESES AND DISSERTATIONS

Allen, Gerald E. "The Negro Coal Miner in the Pittsburgh District." Masters, University of Pittsburgh, 1927.

Anastasia, Joseph. "The Attitudes of White High School Seniors Towards Negroes and the Causes of Racial Unrest: A Survey Report." Masters, West Virginia University, 1969.

Bailey, E. Brasher. "The Negro in East Tennessee." Masters, New York University, 1947.

Barnett, Arthur. "The Social and Economic Status of Pupils in the Senior High Schools for Negroes in the State of West Virginia." Masters, Ohio State University, 1933.

Bland, Marion F. "Superstitions about Food and Health among Negro Girls in Elementary and Secondary Schools in Marion County, West Virginia." Masters, West Virginia University, 1950.

Brown, Mary V. "A History of the Negroes of Monongalia County." Masters, West Virginia University, 1959.

Brunell, John P., Jr. "The Guineas of West Virginia." Masters, Ohio State University, 1952.

Carter, R.G. "A Study of the Progress of Negro Education in Saint Clair County, Alabama." Masters, Alabama State College, 1953.

Caruthers, Eugene. "An Investigation of the Exceptional Child in the Negro Secondary School of East Tennessee." Masters, East Tennessee State College, 1957.

Chambers, Vaughn D. "Differences between Negro and Caucasian Students at John Sevier Junior High School." Masters, East Tennessee University, 1968.

Clay, Earl Charles. "The Negro in Greenbrier County, West Virginia: A Social, Economic, and Educational Study." Masters, Virginia State College, 1946.

Conway, Eugenia Cecilia. "The Afro-American Traditions of the Folk Banjo." Ph.D., University of North Carolina, Chapel Hill, 1980.

Coulter, Roy D. "The Negroes of Chattanooga, Tennessee." Bachelors, Vanderbilt University, 1934.

Cunningham, Addie J. "What Progress in Health Has Been Made among the Negro Youths of the Elementary School Age for the Past Ten Years in Talladega County, Alabama." Masters, Alabama State College, 1952.

Diamond, Michael Jay. "The Negro and Organized Labor as Voting Blocs in Tennessee, 1960-1964." Masters, University of Tennessee, 1965.

Dixon, Hertha. "A Survey of Library Facilities in the Negro Schools of Tuscaloosa County, Alabama." Masters, Alabama State College, 1952.

Drain, John R. "The History of West Virginia State College from 1892-1950." Masters, West Virginia University, 1951.

Fife, Robert O. "Alexander Campbell and the Christian Church in the Slavery Controversy." Ph.D., Indiana University, 1960.

Foster, Clementine R. "A Critical Study of Negro Education in Cleveland County, North Carolina, from 1944-1954." Masters, North Carolina College, 1958.

French, Jack. "Segregation Patterns in a Coal Camp." Masters, West Virginia University, 1953.

Fuller, R. V. "A Study of the Physical Education Problems as found in Negro Schools in East Tennessee." Masters, Tennessee Agricultural and Industrial University, 1956.

Givhan, Mercer A. "Factors Contributing to the Educational Development of the Negro schools in the Jefferson County (Alabama) School System, 1945-1951." Masters, Alabama State College, 1952.

Glass, Daniel. "A Study of the Causes of Drop-Outs and Irregular Attendance among Boys in the Four Negro Schools of Talladega County, Alabama." Masters, Tuskegee Institute, 1953.

Head, Holman. "The Development of the Labor Movement in Alabama Prior to 1900." Masters, University of Alabama, 1955.

Heath, Emily P. "A Study of the Relationship Existing between Amount of Education Completed by White and Negro Heads of Household in Floyd County." Masters, University of Georgia, 1948.

Heller, Steven A. "A Study of Teacher Attitudes regarding School Desegregation in Five Selected Tennessee School Systems." Ed.D., University of Tennessee, 1971.

Hill, Ralph L. "A View of the Hill: A Study of Experiences and Attitudes in the Hill District of Pittsburgh, Pennsylvania, from 1900-1973." Ph.D., University of Pittsburgh, 1973.

Holley, Marie E. "A Study of Absenteeism in Tazewell County One-Room Negro Elementary Schools." Masters, Ohio State University, 1954.

Horton, Frazier Robert. "Negro Life in Watauga County." Bachelors, Agricultural and Technical College of North Carolina, 1942.

Ingram, Milton J. "A History of Negro Education in Wilkes County, North Carolina." Masters, North Carolina Agricultural and Technical College, 1954.

Ivey, Saundra K. "Oral, Printed and Popular Culture Traditions Related to the Melungeons of Hancock County, Tennessee." Ph.D., Indiana University, 1970.

Jackson, Minnie L. "A History of the Development of Schools for Negroes in Walker

County, Georgia." Masters, Tennessee Agricultural and Industrial State University, 1958.

Johnson, Paul M. "Integration in West Virginia since 1954." Masters, West Virginia University, 1960.

Jones, Abraham. "The Status of Negro Teachers in Blount, Cullman, DeKalb, and Marshall Counties, Alabama, 1953-1954." Alabama State College, 1954.

King, Louis Eugene. "Negro Life in a Rural Community." Ph.D., Columbia University, 1951.

Laing, James T. "The Negro Miner in West Virginia." Ph.D., Ohio State University, 1933.

Levy, Charles. "School Desegregation in Warren County, Virginia, during 1958-1960: A Study in the Mobilization of Restraints." Masters, University of Chicago, 1961.

London, Martha. "An Analysis of the Types of Retardation in the Elementary Department of Five Negro Union Schools in Rural Cleveland County." Masters, North Carolina Agricultural and Technical College, 1954.

Mannis, Martha. "A Study Designed for the Attitudes of the Negro Teachers of Bedford County, Virginia, toward In Service Teacher Education." Masters, North Carolina Agricultural and Technical College, 1954.

Martin, Arlee. "History of the Development of Negro Public Schools in Bradley County, Tennessee, 1931-1951." Masters, Tennessee Agricultural and Industrial University, 1952.

Maynor, Theodore. "A Historical Analysis of Student Drop-Outs in the Negro Schools for Bibb County, Alabama." Masters, Alabama State College, 1954.

Miller, John. "A Socio-Economic Survey of the Negro Population of Ashe County, North Carolina, with Suggestions for Utilization of This Data by the Negro School." Masters, North Carolina Agricultural and Technical College, Greensboro, 1953.

Mitchell, Cleophus. "A Study of the Changes in the Educational Levels of Negro Teachers in Jefferson County, Alabama, 1930-50." Master's, Fisk University, 1952.

Monico, Francis W. "The Negroes and the *Martinsburg Gazette*, 1799-1833." Master's, West Virginia University, 1959.

Montell, William Lynwood. "A Folk History of the Coe Ridge Negro Colony." Ph.D., Indiana University, 1964.

Moore, George. "Slavery as a Factor in the Formation of West Virginia." Master's, West Virginia University, 1947.

Musser, Carl Wilson. "Economic and Social Aspects of Negro Slavery in Whythe County, Virginia, 1790-1860." Master's, Columbia College, George Washington University, 1958.

Pitts, Willie M. "A Survey of the Bluefield State College Library, Bluefield, West Virginia." Master's, Atlanta University, 1958.

Posey, Thomas. "The Labor Movement in West Virginia, 1900-1948." Ph.D., University of Wisconsin at Madison, 1949.

Rakestraw, Isaac K. "Negro Education in Cocke County." Master's, University of Tennessee, 1956.

Redd, Callie G. "An Examination of the Negro Character in Selected Fiction by White East Tennessee Writers." Master's, East Tennessee State University, 1972.

Reece, Cortez D. "A Study of Selected Folk Songs Collected Mainly in Southern West Virginia." Ph.D., University of Southern California, 1955.

Roethler, Michael D. "Negro Slavery among the Cherokee Indians." Ph.D., Fordham University, 1964.

Sheeler, John Reuben. "The Negro in West Virginia before 1900." Ph.D., West Virginia University, 1954.

Smith, Douglas C. "The West Virginia Human Rights Commission: A History of Its Formative Period." Master's, West Virginia University, 1972.

————. "The West Virginia Human Rights Commission during the Gavett-McKinney Era, 1961-1966." Ph.D., West Virginia University, 1975.

Smith, Elizabeth V. "An Accounting Study of the Educational Progress of Knoxville Negro Pupils over a Sixteen-Year Period." Master's, University of Tennessee, 1959.

Starr, Donald H. "The Educational Progress of the Negro Schools in Cherokee County, Alabama, from 1930-50." Master's, Alabama State College, 1952.

Stealey, John Edmund. "The Salt Industry of the Great Kanawha Valley of Virginia: A Study in Antebellum Internal Commerce." Ph.D., West Virginia University, 1970.

Stone, Barbara. "Survey of Student Opinion toward Desegregation at the University of Tennessee." Master's, University of Tennessee, 1957.

Talbott, Forrest. "Some Legislative and Legal Aspects of the Negro in Question in West Virginia during the Civil War and Reconstruction." Master's, University of Minnesota, 1924.

Traubert, Anna. "Abolition of Negro Slavery in West Virginia, 1861-1866." Master's, Columbia University, 1932.

Tribble, Gloria Dean. "An Evaluation of Basal Readers Currently Being Used by Students of Appalachian, American Indian, Negro, Oriental or Spanish-American Background in the State of Ohio." Ph.D., University of Akron, 1973.

Truesdell, Fred L. "The Development of Negro Education in Rutherford County, North Carolina." Master's, North Carolina Agricultural and Technical College, 1954.

Walker, William S. "Occupational Aspirations of Negro Family Members in a Coal Mining Community." Master's, New York University, 1950.

Whitman, Robert H. "Development of the Health Program for Negroes in Franklin County, Tennessee from 1940-1953." Master's, Tennessee Agricultural and Industrial University, 1953.

Williams, Ellis R. "Contacts of Negroes and Whites in Morgantown." Master's, West Virginia University, 1952.

Sources and Contributors

Kenneth R. Bailey, "A Judicious Mixture" (chapter 10), originally appeared in *West Virginia History* in January 1973. Bailey is vice-president for administration at West Virginia Institute of Technology. His publications include numerous articles on labor in West Virginia, and a book, *Mountaineers Are Free: A History of the West Virginia National Guard.*

Edward J. Cabbell, "Black Invisibility and Racism in Appalachia" (chapter 1), appeared in *Appalachian Journal,* 8 (Autumn 1980). Cabbell holds the master's degree in Appalachian Studies from Appalachian State University, Boone, North Carolina. He is founder and director of the John Henry Memorial Foundation, lives in Princeton, West Virginia, and, in addition to community organization work, teaches at Concord College, Athens, West Virginia.

David A. Corbin, "Class over Caste" (chapter 9), has been reprinted from Corbin's book *Life, Work, and Rebellion in the Coal Fields: The Southern West Virginia Miners, 1880-1922* (Urbana: University of Illinois Press, 1981). Corbin recently received a fellowship from the National Endowment for the Humanities to complete his history of West Virginia mining.

Pearl Cornett, "The Mountain Negro of Hazard, Kentucky" (chapter 19), first appeared as "The Cruel Choice" in *Our Appalachia: An Oral History,* edited by Bill Weinberg and Laurel Shackleford (New York: Hill and Wang, 1977). Cornett grew up in Town Mountain, Kentucky, near Hazard. He became a schoolteacher and served in the army in World War II. He died in Town Mountain in 1976.

W.E.B. Du Bois, "The Black Worker" (chapter 12), is from his *Black Reconstruction in America, 1860-1880* (1935; reprint, New York: Russell & Russell, 1956). Copyright 1935, 1962 by W.E.B. DuBois. Reprinted with the permission of Russell & Russell Publishers. William Edward Burghart DuBois was a founder of the NAACP, editor of *Crisis* magazine, and a prolific writer and scholar of the Afro-American experience. He died in Egypt in 1965.

Jack Guillebeaux, "Not Just Whites in Appalachia" (chapter 17), appeared in *South Today,* 3, no. 10 (June 1972). Guillebeaux at the time of this writing was executive director of the Black Appalachian Council. He has served in various capacities in his native Black Mountain, North Carolina, and in Georgia in human service-related organizations. Currently, he is Deputy Director of the Federation of Child Care Centers of Alabama, Montgomery.

James C. Klotter, "The Black South and White Appalachia" (chapter 6), is reprinted from *Journal of American History,* 66 (March 1980). Klotter is executive director of the

Kentucky Historical Society and editor of the society's journal, *The Register.* He is an acknowledged authority on southern history.

James T. Laing, "The Negro Miner in West Virginia" (chapter 7), appeared first in *Social Forces,* 14 (March 1936). Laing concentrated in the sociology of race relations. He held positions in the department of sociology at Kent State University, and upon retirement returned to his native West Virginia.

Ronald L. Lewis, "Race and the United Mine Workers' Union in Tennessee" (chapter 14), is reprinted from *Tennessee Historical Quarterly,* Fall 1977. Lewis is professor of history at the University of Delaware. He is author of *Coal, Iron, and Slaves* and, with Philip S. Foner, is editor of *The Black Worker: A Documentary History from Colonial Times to the Present.* His latest book is *The Darkest Abode: The Black Coal Miner in America, 1760-1960.*

Reginald Millner, "Conversations with the 'Ole Man' " (chapter 18), appeared in *Goldenseal,* 5, no. 1 (January-March 1979). Millner is a writer/journalist specializing in Black Appalachian studies, and a counselor for the Community Action Program of Indianapolis.

Herbert R. Northrup, "The Coal Mines" (chapter 13), is from his *Organized Labor and the Negro* (New York: Harper and Brothers, 1944; reproduced and reissued by Kraus Reprint Co., 1971; © Herbert R. Northrup). Northrup, a professor at the University of Pennsylvania, Wharton School of Economics, Industrial Research Unit, has published widely on black employment in southern industries, the economics of labor relations, and the impact of government manpower programs.

Nell Irvin Painter, who penned the foreword, is professor of southern history at the University of North Carolina, Chapel Hill. Her publications include *Exodusters: Black Migration to Kansas after Reconstruction* and *The Narrative of Hosea Hudson: His Life as a Negro Communist in the South.* Her *Disquieting Portents* will be published in 1985.

Groesbeck Parham and **Gwen Robinson,** "If I Could Go Back . . ." (chapter 20), is reprinted from *Southern Exposure,* 4, nos. 1 and 2 (1976). Parham is a native of Fairfield, Alabama, and lives in the Birmingham area. She has gathered many oral interviews and has written on Birmingham's black labor history. Robinson has taught history in Dartmouth's Black Studies Program and is currently directing a research project in Chicago on minorities in the construction industry.

Russell D. Parker, "The Black Community in a Company Town" (chapter 8), first appeared in *Tennessee Historical Quarterly,* 37 (1978). Parker specializes in U.S. antebellum social history, and is professor of history at Maryville College, Maryville, Tennessee.

Theda Perdue, "Red and Black in the Southern Appalachians" (chapter 3), is adapted from her book *Slavery and the Evolution of Cherokee Society, 1540-1866* (Knoxville: University of Tennessee Press, 1979). Perdue is associate professor of history at Clemson University. Among her publications are *Nations Remembered: An Oral History of the Five Civilized Tribes, 1865-1907* and *Cherokee Editor: The Writings of Elias Boudinot.* Her *Native Carolinians* will be published in 1985.

John H. Stanfield, "The Sociohistorical Roots of White/Black Inequality in Urban Appalachia" (chapter 11), was written especially for this volume. Stanfield, a specialist in the sociology of black institutional life in the U.S., was on the faculty of the University of Tennessee at the time this article was written. Currently he is on the faculty of sociology, with a joint appointment in Black Studies, at Yale University.

Richard A. Straw, "The Collapse of Biracial Unionism" (chapter 15), is reprinted from *Alabama Historical Quarterly,* Summer 1975. Straw, assistant professor of history at Radford University, specializes in Appalachian history with major emphases in coal mining and folk culture in preindustrial Appalachia.

William H. Turner, "Between Berea (1904) and Birmingham (1908)" (chapter 2), appeared in a slightly revised version in the Fall 1983 issue of *Phylon: The Journal of Race and Culture.* "The Demography of Black Appalachia: Past and Present" (chapter 21) was written especially for this volume. Turner is completing a Ford Foundation/ National Science Council-sponsored research project on blacks in Appalachian Kentucky. He currently serves as dean of the College of Arts and Sciences at Kentucky State University.

Booker T. Washington, "Boyhood Days" (chapter 5), is from his autobiography, *Up from Slavery,* first published in 1901 and reprinted many times. Washington, a Malden, West Virginia, native, was the prime architect of black politics in the late nineteenth and early twentieth centuries in the United States. His position and that of W. E. B. Du Bois on the race question stand as the major extremes in the sociology of black/white relations in the U.S. Washington founded Tuskegee Institute in Alabama.

Leon F. Williams, "The Vanishing Appalachian" (chapter 16), originally appeared in *Social Work in Appalachia,* 5, no. 2 (1973). Williams was serving on the faculty of West Virginia University at the time his article appeared. He is currently a professor in the College of Social Work at Boston College.

Carter G. Woodson, "Freedom and Slavery in Appalachian America" (chapter 4), first appeared in *Journal of Negro History,* 1 (April 1916). Woodson is the "Father of Afro-American Studies," having founded the Association for the Study of Negro Life and Culture. He studied at Berea College in Kentucky and received the doctorate in history at the University of Chicago. His *The Miseducation of the American Negro* coincided with his inauguration of Black History Week.